THE KING'S
THREE FACES

BRENDAN McCONVILLE

The King's Three Faces

THE RISE & FALL OF ROYAL AMERICA, 1688–1776

. . . .
. . .
. .
.

Published for the
Omohundro Institute of Early American History and Culture,
Williamsburg, Virginia, by the
University of North Carolina Press,
Chapel Hill

The Omohundro Institute of Early American History and Culture
is sponsored jointly by the College of William and Mary and the Colonial
Williamsburg Foundation. On November 15, 1996, the Institute adopted the
present name in honor of a bequest from Malvern H. Omohundro, Jr.

Set in Minion type by Tseng Information Systems, Inc.
Manufactured in the United States of America

Library of Congress Cataloging-in-Publication Data
McConville, Brendan, 1962–
The king's three faces : the rise and fall of royal America, 1688–1776 / Brendan McConville.
p. cm.
Includes bibliographical references and index.
ISBN 978-0-8078-3065-9 (cloth : alk. paper)
ISBN 978-0-8078-5866-0 (pbk. : alk. paper)
1. United States—Politics and government—To 1775. 2. United States—Politics and government—
1775–1783. 3. Monarchy—Great Britain—Public opinion—History—18th century. 4. Public opinion—
United States—History—18th century. 5. Political culture—United States—History—18th century.
6. Great Britain—Foreign public opinion, American—History—18th century.
I. Omohundro Institute of Early American History & Culture. II. Title.
E195.M33 2006
973.2—dc22
2006005196

The paper in this book meets the guidelines for permanence and
durability of the Committee on Production Guidelines for Book Longevity
of the Council on Library Resources.

This volume received indirect support from an unrestricted book
publications grant awarded to the Institute by the L. J. Skaggs and
Mary C. Skaggs Foundation of Oakland, California.

Parts of this book are drawn, in different form and with permission, from the following articles by
Brendan McConville: "Pope's Day Revisited, 'Popular' Culture Reconsidered," *Explorations in Early
American Culture*, IV (2000), 258–280; "Confessions of an American Ranter," *Pennsylvania History*,
LXII (1995), 238–248; "The Rise of Rough Music: Reflections on an Ancient New Custom in
Eighteenth-Century New Jersey," in William Pencak, Matthew Dennis, and Simon P. Newman, eds.,
Riot and Revelry in Early America (University Park, Pa., 2001), 87–106.

10 09 08 07 06   5 4 3 2 1
11 10 09 08 07   5 4 3 2 1

Behold the Man who had it in his Power

To make a Kingdom tremble and adore

Intoxicate with Folly, see his Head

Plac'd where the meanest of his Subjects tread

Like Lucifer the giddy Tyrant fell

He lifts his Heel to Heaven but points his Head to Hell.

Verse placed below an inverted print of George III,

seen by John Adams in Baltimore in 1777

ACKNOWLEDGMENTS

Book projects take a number of years to research and write, and all who engage in these projects owe debts of thanks. Certainly, this project is no different. Librarians and archivists at the Library of Congress, the National Archives, the Library Company of Philadelphia, the Historical Society of Pennsylvania, the New-York Historical Society, the New York Public Library, the New Jersey Historical Society, the Rhode Island Historical Society, the Massachusetts Historical Society, the Maryland Historical Society, the Historical Society of Delaware, the American Antiquarian Society, the libraries of the State University of New York — Binghamton, the Houghton and Widener Libraries at Harvard University, Mugar Memorial Library of Boston University, the Isaac Royall House (where I was very generously assisted by Fred Schlicher), the Boston Public Library, the Winterthur Museum and Library, and the John Carter Brown Library offered assistance and repeatedly demonstrated the virtue of patience.

Some institutions offered invaluable financial assistance in the completion of this project. The McNeil Center for Early American Studies provided me with a year to do research in the archives of the Philadelphia area. The director of the McNeil Center, Dan Richter, not only offered invaluable advice and support but also read the entire manuscript in an earlier stage, this while directing a center that grows more lively (and larger) with each passing year. The John Carter Brown Library and SUNY — Binghamton also generously supported this project, allowing me to have additional leave time for research and writing.

The McNeil Center, the John Carter Brown Library, the Omohundro Institute of Early American History and Culture's Annual Conference, the Maryland Seminar in American History, the Brown University History Department, and the British Association for American Studies Conference, Glasgow, Scotland, allowed me to present pieces of this book. In each case, I benefited mightily from the comments and criticisms of the participants.

John Murrin and Rhys Isaac acted as readers for the Omohundro Institute of Early American History and Culture and offered their usual telling insights into the manuscript. Fredrika Teute has been helpful and encouraging while offering her own well-thought criticisms. Kathy Burdette has endured my efforts to rework Institute editing policies and caught more than one abuse of the English language. Together, the readers and the editor have made *The King's Three Faces* a good bit better than it was when they first received it, and I am grateful for their assistance.

While institutions help make books, they are, happily, written for people. While teaching at SUNY — Binghamton, I enjoyed the help and assistance of a number of my colleagues and students as I worked on this project. Mel Dubofsky, Dave Hacker, Bonnie Effros, Sarah Elbert, Pepi Levene, Nancy Henry, Greg Geddes, Karen Kaminski, Heather Schwartz, Dianne Cappiello, Joe Torre, Tunis Cooper, Lance Sussman, and Michelle Harris all encouraged (or enabled, depending on your view) this project. At Boston University, my graduate students Erik Cooper and Andrea Mosterman have assisted me and otherwise helped maintain my enthusiasm for early American history.

My friends in and out of the profession have endured more talk about the eighteenth century than any reasonable group of people should be expected to. Dallett Hemphill, Simon Newman, Cynthia Van Zandt, Tim Harris, Tim Shannon, Phil Benedict, Susan Branson, Ed Grey, Sam Korsak, Tom Slaughter, Robert Johnston, Rachel Wheeler, John Smolenski, Bill Pencak, and Evan Haefeli have all at various times listened to me go on at length about colonial America's monarchical character. They have done so with good humor, and four people, Dallett Hemphill, Evan Haefeli, Karin Wulf, and Phil Benedict, read most or all of early versions of the manuscript and offered excellent advice to improve it.

Three friends, Brad Thompson, Jay Samons, and Brian Keegan have endured the ups and downs of this book, and my life, for a long time. Their advice has been honest, and their opinions well thought and original. The first has assailed me about the value of political philosophy and Canada for twenty years now, broadening my intellectual horizons with the former and providing me a huge target of humor by the latter. The second has developed in me a deeper understanding of myself and the society we live in and withstood with patience my futile efforts to achieve a drag-free float on the West Branch of the Delaware. The third has for over three decades stood by me in all circumstances, as I have wandered from place to place, and through life's triumphs and tragedies. In all cases, they have acted the part of friend in a model manner.

Finally, I want to thank my wife and mother for their love and support. My mother has encouraged me to be my own person from earliest childhood and to call things as I see them regardless of whether that is the accepted view. My wife, Kristen, married an Irish bachelor when he was completing a book about kings and colonists, thus demonstrating uncommon devotion — and optimism.

Although, like all authors, I hope to reach the broadest audience, this tiny one, closest to home and heart, is the most important to me.

Brendan McConville
Boston University
December 12, 2005

CONTENTS

ILLUSTRATIONS

ABBREVIATIONS

AAS

American Antiquarian Society, Worcester, Mass.

AHR

American Historical Review

APS

American Philosophical Society, Philadelphia

HSP

Historical Society of Pennsylvania, Philadelphia

MHS

Massachusetts Historical Society, Boston

NJA

Archives of the State of New Jersey, 1st Ser., I–XLII (Trenton, N.J., 1880–1949)

NJHS

New Jersey Historical Society, Newark

NYHS

New-York Historical Society

WMQ

William and Mary Quarterly

THE KING'S
THREE FACES

PRINCES AND POPES IN
THE AMERICAN PROVINCES

· · · ·
· ·
·

On November 5, 1764, diarist John Rowe recorded that "a sorrowful accident" had happened in Boston's North End. A giant "carriage" constructed by the neighborhood's residents, carrying effigies of the pope and other figures, had "run over a Boy's head" during a raucous procession, "and he died instantly." In response to the tragedy, the authorities dismantled the effigies and sought to destroy a similar cart in the South End—the "North and South end Popes," as they were known. However, when the magistrates "went to the So. End [they] could not Conquer upon which the South End people brought out their pope and went in Triumph to the Northward" to seek victory in the traditional battle between the neighborhoods that occurred on Boston Common every November 5. "At the Mill Bridge," Rowe continued, "a Battle begun," the North End people "having repaired their pope." Neighborhood pride was on the line—the North End had always prevailed in these battles—but on this day, a repaired pope would not do, and "the South End people got the Battle. . . . Brought away the North End pope and burnt Both of them at the Gallows," with "several thousand people following them" to see the spectacle on Boston Neck. So ended the annual celebration of the foiling of Guy Fawkes's 1605 plot against James I and the English nation.[1]

Certain images predominate in popular imagination when we think of colonial America. Somber Puritans, heads bowed in prayer when not hunting witches at Salem; broad-hatted Quakers, preaching peace in the City of Brotherly Love; yeoman farmers chopping wood and tending crops; dignified Indian chiefs negotiating with the ever-increasing number of white settlers; Virginia tobacco planters living in Georgian mansions on the Northern Neck, served by African slaves; and deerskin-clad frontiersmen opening new lands and fighting against the various Indian nations—all these come to mind. Scholars have refined these images and added new ones to their more specific conversations: visions of midwives and

1. John Rowe diary, Nov. 5, 1764, MS, MHS.

PLATE 1. *"Boston Affairs" (detail). By Pierre Eugène Du Simitière.*
This drawing of a Pope's Day cart in a New England town, done in the 1760s,
shows the traditional effigies of the devil and those who would do his bidding being
dragged by young people. The Library Company of Philadelphia

wenches, merchant entrepreneurs, aggressive artisans, confidence men, enlightened intellectuals, and evangelical preachers seeking to save souls from eternal
hellfire. But mobile papist archetypes crushing innocent children, followed by
nighttime battles on Boston Common? This all seems to be foreign, un-American,
at best the manifestation of lower-class rowdiness in a busy colonial port, at worst
a display of religious bigotry.

Yet it was none of these things. Boston's North and South End gangs were remembering Pope's Day, one of a number of annual royal rites at the core of political life in an imperial America that existed before 1776. In that lost world, public
holidays did not celebrate exceptionalism and democracy but rather expressed
intense pride in Britain's kings and rejoiced in the empire's victories in the con-
tinuous struggle against Catholicism. The political culture's central focus was a
physically distant but emotionally available Protestant British monarch who had
the provincial population's impassioned loyalty.

This all-encompassing royal America has been gradually wiped from our national memory. Royalism, it has seemed to the general public and most American scholars, had never really taken deep root in colonial society. The provinces'
social diversity and truncated (by European standards) social structures sup-

posedly inhibited faith in king and country and paved the way for a republican America. But was this really the case?

To answer this question takes a seemingly impossible leap of faith, for it requires us to forget the American Revolution. We are still, despite the best efforts of historical writers, so conditioned by the overwhelming power of the democratic reality created in the last two hundred–plus years that we can only imagine American history as some variant on that omnipresent worldview. The Revolution thus has remained, like the Civil War, the Great Depression, and World War II, a scholarly vortex that sucks all that came before it into its deterministic bowels. Despite decades of proclaimed hostility to "whiggish" and teleological history, most historians still treat the years between 1688 and 1776 as a long prologue to the revolutionary crisis or American society's broader modernization. There are at least three identifiable strains in this historiography: one with the imperative to explain the emergence of American national character and democratic government; another that examines the roots of American capitalism; and, more recently, a host of studies seeking the origins of America's racial attitudes.[2]

2. Jon Butler pushes the origins of an American self back to the 1710s and postulates all developments from that point as contributing to the creation of an American identity. Butler directly and forcefully juxtaposes his views against those of Gordon S. Wood, Richard L. Bushman, John M. Murrin, and T. H. Breen, those advocates of what he calls the Europeanization model of the colonial period. See Jon Butler, *Becoming America: The Revolution before 1776* (Cambridge, Mass., 2000), 3–4. Those "Europeanizers," particularly Wood (*The Radicalism of the American Revolution* [New York, 1991] 1–92) and Bushman (*King and People in Provincial Massachusetts* [Chapel Hill, N.C., 1985]), are, in fact, writing in the same broad tradition as Butler. Bushman and Wood are sophisticated restatements of the whig tradition in that they see a gradual republicanization of provincial politics, political discourse, and social relationships in the eighteenth century. The overlapping templates of monarchy and republicanism, as Wood has called them, coexisted until the imperatives imparted by republicanism and modernizing social tendencies eroded through colonial societies' monarchical veneer. Bushman, while cognizant of the importance of the relationship of king and people to Bay Colonists, emphasizes the ways in which the king was a diminished figure and the society nascently republicanized. Even as ardent a student of the empire as Jack P. Greene clings to an emergent neoliberal perception of the colonists engaged continually in a "pursuit of happiness." See also Winthrop D. Jordan, "Familial Politics: Thomas Paine and the Killing of the King, 1776," *Journal of American History* (hereafter cited as *JAH*), LX (1973), 294–308; Darrett B. Rutman, "George III: The Myth of a Tyrannical King," in Nicholas Cords and Patrick Gerster, eds., *Myth and the American Experience* (New York, 1973); Michael Kammen, "The American Revolution as a Crise de Conscience: The Case of New York," in Richard M. Jellison, ed., *Society, Free-*

The historians who subscribe to these approaches believe that major changes develop over time and that looking for their early manifestations will tell us much about them. This approach has persistent emotional appeal: it is forward looking, modernizing, and in the American context, democratizing. One thing leads to another; things that look alike tend to be related. Thus the provincial world has been filled with protorepublicans, readers of Country pamphlets, rising assemblies, plain-folk Protestants, budding contract theorists, protocapitalists, protoproletariat, protoliberals, modernizers — in short, future Americans.[3]

Although several influential scholars writing within these whig traditions have invoked the term *monarchy*, it was the adherents of two smaller schools of historical thought who tried consciously to avoid early American history's teleological pitfalls: the imperial historians and the students of provincial anglicization.[4] The original imperial historians viewed the empire from London and thus

---

dom, and Conscience (New York, 1976); William D. Liddle, "'A Patriot King, or None': Lord Bolingbroke and the American Renunciation of George III," *JAH*, LV (1979), 951–970; Peter Shaw, *American Patriots and the Rituals of Revolution* (Cambridge, Mass., 1981); Jerrilyn Greene Marston, *King and Congress: The Transfer of Political Legitimacy, 1774–1776* (Princeton, N.J., 1987), 13–63; Benjamin Lewis Price, *Nursing Fathers: American Colonists' Conception of English Protestant Kingship, 1688–1776* (Lanham, Md., 1999). None really engages the question of why the colonists would behave the way they did.

3. The most sophisticated statement in this strain is Wood's *Radicalism of the American Revolution*. Wood maintains that

> despite the colonists' sense that they were only thinking as any good Englishmen would, they did draw from that British culture its most republican and whiggish strains. . . . Many colonists had little reason to feel part of His Majesty's realm or to respect royalty. Many white foreign immigrants had no natural allegiance to a British king, and they often settled far from established authority in the colonies. . . . But even those English colonists who were proud of being Englishmen were not very good monarchists (110).

Such statements, designed to establish the republicanized or republicanizing character of provincial life, are unsupported or, in the case of these particular quotes, supported by a statement from an English general in the midst of the imperial crisis. The initial statement in this vein was put forth by Bernard Bailyn, who declared that "if American politics through the eighteenth century was latently revolutionary in this sense — if in these ways the patterns of ideas that would give transcendent meaning to the events of the 1760s and 1770s was already present decades earlier — the ultimate dangers had nevertheless been averted" until the imperial crisis made them all too real (Bailyn, *The Origins of American Politics* [New York, 1968], 160).

4. Some scholars have tried to engage the monarchical reality that leaps from the

understood the American colonies as one component of a larger polity. They focused on the empire's governing structures, its institutions, and its personnel. This school largely died out in the 1930s, but interest in empire has revived in recent years. These new studies have focused on aspects of imperial politics and ideology in the home islands.[5] Anglicization's early advocates were the first to

---

period's surviving intellectual artifacts in order to better understand the emerging American reality they understand as the central fact of eighteenth-century history. An example of the immense power of that approach over our thinking is Alan Tully's very fine study, *Forming American Politics: Ideals, Interests, and Institutions in Colonial New York and Pennsylvania* (Baltimore, 1994), 1–8. Tully is fully aware of the imperial position of the colonies in his study and of the distorting influence of the republican synthesis on studies of the pre-1776 period, yet spends much of his study determining how the political culture of these colonies became American.

5. The best known of these imperial studies are David Armitage, *The Ideological Origins of the British Empire* (Cambridge, 2000); Eliga H. Gould, *The Persistence of Empire: British Political Culture in the Age of the American Revolution* (Chapel Hill, N.C., 2000); Kathleen Wilson, *The Sense of the People: Politics, Culture, and Imperialism in England, 1715–1785* (New York, 1995); Stephen Conway, *The British Isles and the War of American Independence* (Oxford, 2000); Linda Colley, *Britons: Forging the Nation, 1707–1837* (New Haven, Conn., 1992); David Hancock, *Citizens of the World: London Merchants and the Integration of the British Atlantic Community, 1735–1785* (Cambridge, 1995); Jack P. Greene, *Peripheries and Center: Constitutional Development in the Extended Polities of the British Empire and the United States, 1607–1788* (New York, 1990); Alison Gilbert Olson and Richard Maxwell Brown, eds., *Anglo-American Political Relations, 1675–1775* (New Brunswick, N.J., 1970); Fred Anderson, *Crucible of War: The Seven Years' War and the Fate of Empire in British North America, 1754–1766* (New York, 2000); Eric Hinderaker, *Elusive Empires: Constructing Colonialism in the Ohio Valley, 1673–1800* (New York, 1997); Richard White, *The Middle Ground: Indians, Empires, and Republics in the Great Lakes Region, 1650–1815* (New York, 1991); David S. Shields, *Oracles of Empire: Poetry, Politics, and Commerce in British America, 1690–1750* (Chicago, 1990); and Andrew Jackson O'Shaughnessy, *An Empire Divided: The American Revolution and the British Caribbean* (Philadelphia, 2000). Also useful is Benedict Anderson, *Imagined Communities: Reflections on the Origin and Spread of Nationalism* (New York, 1983).

These new studies were built on the foundation laid by the old imperial school. The most famous of those scholars is Charles Andrews, but in this study I have found Charles Howard McIlwain's *American Revolution: A Constitutional Interpretation* (Ithaca, N.Y., 1923) to be the most useful. It is a remarkably insightful study; Greene has built on some of these insights in his work, expanding them in new and useful ways. Lawrence Henry Gipson, *The British Empire before the American Revolution*, 15 vols. (New York, 1939–1970),

question colonial America's democratization and looked at how provincial institutions, particularly the bench and bar, were remodeled along English lines in the eighteenth century. A second wave of studies in this vein has examined provincial Americans' accelerating consumption of British goods. Overall, these studies suggest that nascent Americanization has been read back into a very different period.[6]

Like most scholars of my generation, I accepted the whiggish schools' central premises while being aware of these imperial-centered approaches. A democratization or republicanization of politics marked by rising assemblies, economic expansion and liberalization, and new egalitarian evangelical Protestant religious movements were the dominant trends in provincial life that explained change. Monarchical allegiance was superficial, social stratification became a problem, and patriarchy as a social and political principle was eroding. Belief that some form of modernization drove change in colonial America still dominated the historiography of the period, and I endorsed its logic.

I thus began *The King's Three Faces* with no agenda other than that of simply examining how provincials' thinking about monarchy changed in the short century between the Glorious Revolution of 1688 and the American Revolution. In time, I came to see provincial political culture and the first British empire in a very different way than it had been presented to me. To accept the received wisdom about the period, I came to think, silenced most of its voices and misrepresented those we do hear. Progress toward a republic and a liberal capitalist society, toward the America we know, had been read back through the Revolu-

-----

was the last of that school, although his active career overlapped with Greene's. A number of articles have also examined imperial issues. The best is T. H. Breen, "Ideology and Nationalism on the Eve of the American Revolution: Revisions Once More in Need of Revising," *JAH*, LXXXIV (1997), 13–39.

6. John M. Murrin, "Anglicizing an American Colony: The Transformation of Provincial Massachusetts" (Ph.D. diss., Yale University, 1966). Particularly suggestive is Murrin's essay, "The Myths of Colonial Democracy and Royal Decline in Eighteenth-Century America: A Review Essay," *Cithara*, V, no. 1 (November 1965), 52–69; T. H. Breen, "An Empire of Goods: The Anglicization of Colonial America, 1690–1776," *Journal of British Studies*, XXV (1986), 467–499; and Breen, *The Marketplace of Revolution: How Consumer Politics Shaped American Independence* (Oxford, 2004). Both Murrin and Breen have offered partial views on how the anglicization of the society can be reconciled to the Revolution and the libertarian society that eventually emerged. Murrin highlights the power struggles between gentry factions (the Otis family and the Hutchinsons) whereas Breen suggests how the consumption of goods created shared experience and identity. I have built on aspects of their insights within the text.

tion's distorting lenses into a different time with its own political-cultural-social dynamic.

In the royal America that existed between the Glorious Revolution and 1776, that which we call political culture, the milieu in which politics takes place, was decidedly monarchical and imperial, Protestant and virulently anti-Catholic, almost to the moment of American independence. The anglicization of colonial governments and legal procedures was linked to the establishment of a calendar of officially orchestrated annual celebrations of Britain's Protestant rulers, their families, and the historic triumph of Protestantism over Catholicism. These rites expressed an ecumenical Protestant political culture whose values and symbols bound a transatlantic empire.

Writers who lived in this society internalized and reinforced its values. Almost everything printed between 1689 and 1775 expressed an intense admiration for the monarchy and situated their rulers both within a dynastic British history that ran back to the Anglo-Saxons and in terms of the ongoing struggle between pan-European Protestantism and Catholicism, absolutism, and popery. Shaped by what they saw, heard, and read, an ever-growing number of provincials identified themselves as Britons and referenced versions of British and English history as their own. A flood of goods from the home islands encouraged these provincial Britons to affect English manners and consumption patterns. The Hanoverian dynasty that ruled Britain after 1714 became the purveyors of good taste even as merchants and hawkers commodified their names and likenesses. For seven decades, without hesitation or hypocrisy, provincials proclaimed their love of Britain's Protestant monarchs and loathing for the kings' enemies, particularly papists of all stripes.

It makes little sense to examine such a society through modern notions that separate secular from sacred life. Religious devotion and denominational allegiances were loaded with political implications. Politics were intertwined with religion and religious identity on all levels of society, as all British Americans knew. By addressing religious developments apart from the political culture they occurred in, we have unintentionally distorted early American politics.

Obviously, other scholars have noticed aspects of this monarchical America that emerge from reading eighteenth-century sources, but the sum total seemed to me quite distinctive. Devotion to the monarchy, the imperialization of political life, patriarchy as political and social expectation, a British historical understanding and perception of time, intense fear of Catholics, and a growing, mobile yeoman population that perceived its relationship to the king as a personal one: these factors explain much of what occurred in public life in America between 1688 and 1774.

Accepting the reality of this royal America, with its jumble of monarchical rites and royally focused affectations, brings into sharp relief a historically unrecognizable British Empire and a pattern of change distinctive from the whiggish teleologies that dominate our understanding of the period. In some respects, the empire's political culture looked the exact opposite of what has been commonly assumed. In the home islands, the Glorious Revolution's constitutional settlement located sovereignty in the King-in-Parliament and more or less settled the balance of power in the government. Effectively, this situated authority in the House of Commons and the imperial bureaucracy. People tried to forget the seventeenth century's violent problems, when English society was rendered by civil war and revolution that saw one Stuart king executed and another forced into exile with his heirs. The occasional Stuart conspiracy unsettled the national peace after 1689, but these were sporadic, ill planned, and tainted by the deposed house's French and Catholic connections. Political patronage, the Church of England's control of religious and social life in countless communities, fear of Europe's Catholic powers, and a fixed and controlled land tenure system maintained allegiance to the post-1688 order. It had to be so, as many eighteenth-century Englishmen felt tepid at best toward their German-born Hanoverian kings, royal rites declined markedly in England, Jacobitism remained current in some circles, and republicanism took hold among coffeehouse radicals.

Provincials, their worldview shaped by political spectacles and a print media that celebrated Britain's Protestant princes, came to understand the Glorious Revolution's legacy and the Hanoverian dynasty very differently. They saw the national settlement as establishing the Protestant succession and a Protestant political culture built around a cult of benevolent monarchy. Parliament had no symbolic role in imperial political rituals, its history was poorly understood, and it was diminished in political discussions. For colonists, the monarch apart from Parliament became the primary and common imperial link, the empire's living embodiment.

This dramatic reorientation of the colonies' political culture after the Glorious Revolution was not tempered by the establishment of the social conventions or political structures that helped stabilize the social orders in the home islands. State patronage remained extremely limited in the colonies, and the creation of new institutions was slow in relationship to population growth. The courts, the primary point of contact between the empire's authority and the mass of yeomen, were understood as a royal prerogative, and court procedures referenced all authority to the monarch. Provincial religious diversity stood in stark contrast to the church establishment of England itself. Freehold land tenure was far more common in the colonies, and farmers violently resisted efforts to establish tenancy as normal in parts of the countryside. However, these attributes did not make the colonists protorepublicans. Married as they were to royal political spectacles and a slavishly loyal print culture, the result was a polity sewn together by passions rather than patronage in the American provinces. British North Americans championed their British king with emotional intensity in print, during public political rites, and in private conversation.

These divergent understandings of the king and the British constitution ultimately undid both the colonies' internal peace and the empire itself. As the political and social context changed after 1740, this (for lack of a better term) institutionally unconditioned royalism became latently subversive to the provincial order and ultimately to the entire empire. Explosive population growth, an expanding print culture, new ethnic and racial tensions, and warfare with the French and Native Americans encouraged some provincials to manipulate the language and rites of empire. Political factions fighting over property rights, paper money, and institutional power appropriated imperial holidays for partisan ends. England's ambiguous, brutal seventeenth-century history was used to justify all types of behaviors. Rioting yeomen struggling for ownership of untold millions of acres in North America invoked a benevolent king to legitimate their violent actions, and rebelling slaves repeatedly claimed that the distant monarch intended to free them. Native Americans invoked Britain's kings against their American subjects as more settlers moved into the interior. In incident after incident, colonists revealed that they loved the king, but they did not share a universal understanding of his nature, political patriarchy, the British constitution, or even whether they lived under an imperial, British, English, or customary constitution. This book's title describes these subjective understandings of king and constitution that proved so crucial to unhinging the empire.

This fragmentation helped tear the Anglo-American world apart because it expressed conceptual divergences from metropolitan norms. The failure to successfully extend the British state's financial structures to America after the Seven Years' War grew as much from provincial society's royalization as it did from any other ideological factor. Affection for and faith in imagined kings and constitutions, coupled to unique understandings of British history, informed the colonists' actions in the imperial crisis as much as Country thought or natural-rights ideology did. Royal rites shaped the pattern of resistance in the streets as mobs confronted royal officials. The belief that the Glorious Revolution's settlement might manifest itself in their charters or in natural law informed colonial defiance of metropolitan norms. Only in 1774–1775 did that royal America finally collapse amid a potent but decentralized terror against those loyal to the empire. An iconoclasm against royal emblems followed, punctuated by a series of symbolic regicides in the summer of 1776. In the terror's aftermath, the long struggle to make a workable republican society began.

Seen this way, colonial history becomes more than a preparation for the Revolution or the seed ground for the hyperdemocratic America we now live in. Rather, profoundly different assumptions shaped that world. By rejecting teleology, we let the colonists' lives speak to our own, not as agents of an emergent modernity but rather as human beings who inherited and adopted certain beliefs that they then used to confront change. By conceptualizing the period in this fashion, I am not claiming that provincials did not read republican- or Country-influenced tracts, that commerce did not expand dramatically, that election days and assemblies were not important, that religious revivals did not take place, or that no social oppression existed. But these changes occurred within the period's predominate political culture. Royalism was a primary force of change before 1776.

The King's Three Faces is divided into three sections. These are loosely chronological, but it is not a standard narrative of the provincial period, moving through "events" or fixating on personalities like Jonathan Edwards, John Peter Zenger, or George Whitefield. Rather, its focus is on the effects of royalization on the provinces. The first section, "The British Peace," examines colonial political culture between the Glorious Revolution and the 1740s. In this period, the cult of Protestant monarchy and British national identity became firmly rooted by means of annual royal rites and a growing, regulated print culture that focused on a uniquely Protestant historical time line as the root of the British nation. The new identity of provincial Briton was accepted by Protestant populations increasingly proud to be part of a transatlantic empire that could defend them from their Catholic enemies in New France and Spanish Florida. Under the influence of representations of a benevolent monarchy, provincials established emotional links to king and country.

The second section, "Three Faces," explores the relationship between the British peace's gradual breakdown in the 1730s and 1740s and the fragmentation in understanding of the monarchy and the imperial order. The emotional ties to the monarchy and empire that had developed in the first half of the eighteenth century were not linked to the state's institutional development. The empire's patronage structures remained immature, and the provincial land tenure system remained chaotic. This disjuncture encouraged some of the best-known conflicts in the colonial period as men struggled for honor and place. As population growth continued apace, the problem became acute, encouraging violent challenges to the provincial order and studied plans to reform the structure of the empire.

The third section, "A Funeral Fit for a King," examines the collapse of empire.

The need for reform was understood by a host of Anglo-American intellectuals throughout the eighteenth century, but their speculations on the character of the needed changes did not bring forth a new empire. The failure to reform left the empire vulnerable to challenges from within, like the Stamp Act protests. The imperial crisis can in part be understood as a conflict over monarchs and imagined constitutions conducted through the royal political culture's language and rituals.

The King's Three Faces is the story of the rise and collapse of royal America between the Glorious Revolution and the American Revolution as told through that period's own political culture rather than through the future's political demands. Even those historians that accept the reality of a monarchical society have imagined provincial Americans as little republicans waiting to burst from their monarchist shells. What it was to be an American subject, in love with king and country, has been lost to us. But, for the people of that time, it was a consuming attachment, one that separated their lost world from our own.

PART ONE
THE BRITISH PEACE

. . . .
. . .
. .
.

1

TYRANNY'S KISS

DISORDER AND ORDER IN THE
AMERICAN COLONIES

. . . .
. . .
. .
.

Between 1660 and 1702, the English colonies in North America suffered through a series of violent upheavals. The European population's expansion at the Native Americans' expense sparked a series of wars. Conflicts over property rights and legal processes led to more violence, and political-religious tensions in the home islands encouraged additional disorder. The relationship of these different developments to one another remains now, after three centuries, as uncertain as it was for those who lived through them.

A common causal thread, though, ran through those troubled times. The disorder grew from the Crown's disjointed efforts to absorb the settler societies in North America into a greater English empire between 1660 and 1689. By the time these efforts began in earnest in the 1670s, however, colonial subcultures were already distinctive enough for their members to view metropolitan English norms as alien and thus threatening. The Stuart kings were doubly suspect because of their embrace of the Catholic religion and their family's repeated efforts to rule without Parliament. In the political-cultural conflict that developed between colonists and kings, seemingly minor things like kissing a book as part of an oath could be understood as a tyrannical act designed by a popish ruler to covertly bring on arbitrary government.

Ironically, it was the overthrow of the Catholic James II in the Glorious Revolution that ultimately forced local colonial elites to accommodate an emerging imperial political culture, albeit one centered on a cult of Protestant monarchy. The events of 1688–1690 in the British Isles had aspects of an armed coup, a foreign invasion, a religious war, a dynastic struggle, and a political revolution. James's people, almost entirely Protestants, mistrusted their Catholic ruler, the Church of England denounced him, military commanders, lords, and others deserted him, and James ultimately fled to France after suffering the cruelest fate of all: his overthrow was led by his Protestant daughter, Mary, and her Dutch husband, William (James's nephew as well as his son-in-law!), backed by William's Dutch army. William and Mary, as one colonial put it, had saved Englishmen everywhere from "Popery, Slavery and Arbitrary Power."[1]

James's overthrow and the establishment of Protestant monarchy by parliamentary act created new problems. William and Mary, aided by much of the English political nation, had successfully usurped the throne, but they produced no heirs. Mary's Protestant sister, Anne, ascended to the throne in 1702 after William's death, but she, too, failed to produce an heir. A crisis ensued in 1714 and 1715 when the nearest royal Protestant relation to the queen, a German prince, George, elector of the minor state of Hanover in western Germany, ascended to the throne. With the support of Parliament, George established the Hanoverian dynasty as the monarchs of Great Britain in the face of armed resistance by the Jacobites, those who still supported the right of the Catholic heirs of the exiled Stuart king, James II, to the throne. The Hanoverian succession turned out to be a crucial event in the life of the extended British nation. The first three Hanoverian kings, George I, George II, and George III, would rule for more than one hundred years.

Provincials, like others in Britain's emerging Atlantic empire, were forced to adapt to the new circumstances created by the continuing dynastic struggles in Britain after 1688. Colonists rethought the conceptual basis of monarchical authority and explained the incongruities of imperial institutions. These politically creole societies, based on the foundation established in the seventeenth century but oriented firmly toward the empire, took decades to fully stabilize after the seventeenth-century turmoil sparked by the Stuart kings' efforts to extend imperial control.

· · ·

In Thomas Hobbes's Study: Theories of Monarchy

"Take away," wrote Thomas Hobbes, living a troubled exile in Paris in the 1650s, "in any kind of State, the Obedience, (and consequently the Concord of the People,) and they shall not onely not flourish, but in short time be dissolved." So it had been in England, so it had been for all time, according to the philosopher. Those who attempted merely to reform the state were like the foolish daughters of Peleus (in the fable)" who, "desiring to renew the youth of their decrepit Father, did by the Counsell of Medea, cut him in pieces, and boyle him, together

1. [Increase Mather], *A Brief Relation of the State of New England* . . . (London, 1689), 13, rpt. in W. H. Whitmore, ed., *The Andros Tracts*, II (Boston, 1869), 161.

with strange herbs, but made not of him a new man." This desire for change was "like the breach of the first of Gods Commandements: For there God sayes, Non habebis Deos alienos; Thou shalt not have the Gods of other Nations; and in another place concerning Kings, that they are Gods."[2]

England, as Hobbes knew only too well, had repeatedly breached that commandment. The political nation continued to follow the recipe of Peleus's daughters for disaster in the sixteenth and seventeenth centuries. Defeat in the Hundred Years' War, followed by dynastic instability in the reign of Richard II, led to a series of revolts against the House of Lancaster. The Tudor Henry VIII's inability to produce a healthy male heir, his break with Rome, the English Reformation's contested nature, the sixteenth-century population expansion, and religious differences among Henry's children led to wide swings in political behavior and religious policy. The Scottish Stuart dynasty inherited the throne peacefully in 1603 when Elizabeth I died without heir, but their inability to respond to the realm's problems in a constructive manner led to renewed turmoil. Constitutional ambiguity about the monarch's prerogative and parliamentary authority over finance intersected with serious theological divisions among English Protestants. Civil wars, regicide, a commonwealth, a kind of military protectorate, the Restoration, and finally the Glorious Revolution followed as the political nation struggled for stability.[3]

Centuries of similar problems in the hundreds of independent polities that composed western Europe had led to the creation of a body of political theory to explain and resolve dynastic conflicts. Monarchs ruled the vast majority of these European polities, and thus much of the political writing from the period concerned monarchs, the origins of their sovereignty, and their relationship to the body politic. Loosely, at least three types of legitimate monarchical sovereignty existed in early modern Europe: divine appointment, hereditary right, and election. All remained current in Anglo-American political discussion through to the American Revolution.[4]

Divine-right monarchs claimed God's direct appointment as the source of their dominion. Whereas most late medieval and early modern monarchs maintained that divine sanction legitimated their authority, some saw such anointment as a source of unrestricted power. "Law," as one early-eighteenth-century writer described divine-right absolutism, "could not alter what God had settled."

2. Thomas Hobbes, *Leviathan*, ed. Richard Tuck (Cambridge, 1991), 233–234.

3. J. H. Burns, *Lordship, Kingship, and Empire: The Idea of Monarchy, 1400–1525* (Oxford, 1992), 40; W. M. Spellman, *Monarchies 1000–2000* (London, 2001), 147–187.

4. W. M. Spellman, *European Political Thought, 1600–1700* (New York, 1998), 8.

The Almighty had given these rulers unconditional authority to act as his vice-gerents on earth. Kings were to be obeyed; "blind obedience to the prince" was at absolutism's core. "His power," wrote Hobbes, "cannot, without his consent, be Transferred to another: He cannot Forfeit it: He cannot be accused by them. . . . He is sole Legislator; and Supreme Judge of Controversies."[5]

In this system, church and state drew their sovereignty from the same source, with the state given control of men's bodies and churches their souls. As God ruled heaven, so His anointed delegate on earth, the king, was father to his subjects, with absolute authority. In such realms, "the will of the prince became law." Divine-right rulers passed on their thrones by indefeasible hereditary right, and subjects were required to passively obey their edicts.[6]

The history of excesses committed by Catholic divine-right rulers frightened English Protestants, but some thinkers realized divine-right rule's strengths. It unified the cosmic with the secular in a coherent fashion, reinforced patriarchal rule, and was consistent with the hereditary principles that guided the transfer of property and power from one generation to the next. Moreover, seventeenth-century Englishmen's Protestantism encouraged them to believe that the political order in their own freer society somehow occurred through divine appointment. Language and symbols associated with divine-right theory remained current in Anglo-American political thought until the American Revolution and indeed had an intellectual career in Britain's American colonies.

European society depended on the traditions that kept property and power in the hands of certain families, and thrones were no exception to this. Among those who claimed their crowns by hereditary right were divine-right absolutists, but other types of monarchs based their authority on hereditary claims. Rulers of this sort saw those rights initially established with either some kind of providential divine appointment or conquest (William the Conqueror, Henry VII, William and Mary) or both. "Dominion," Hobbes declared, "is acquired two wayes; By Generation, and by Conquest. The right of Dominion by Generation, is that, which the Parent hath over his Children; and is called PATERNALL." Such monarchs could thus trace their authority to some human event. They understood the

---

5. Gilbert Burnet, *Bishop Burnet's History of His Own Time*, I (London, 1724), 458; Isaac Addington, *An Answer to a Letter from a Gentleman of New Yorke* (Boston, 1698), 2; Hobbes, *Leviathan*, ed. Tuck, 139. Hobbes believed that any sovereignty, whether royal or legislative, had to be absolute. Yet, in practice, he believed in absolute monarchy of a particular type.

6. Addington, *Answer to a Letter*, 2; John Neville Figgis, *The Divine Right of Kings*, 2d ed. (Cambridge, 1914), 5–6.

transferring of the Crown from one generation to the next as further legitimating their dynastic positions. It was for this reason that Henry VIII went through six wives and a religion. Custom and the unwritten English constitution restrained these rulers, but in a vague fashion.[7]

Election of a monarch or a dynasty existed alongside these two better-known forms of monarchical sovereignty as a source of legitimacy. Such elections became critical to Anglo-American political discussions between 1688 and 1776 because William and Mary and then the Hanoverian line owed their places on the throne in part to parliamentary approval given for reasons of religion.

This form of monarchy had medieval origins. Its theoretical basis was refined in the fifteenth century by the Frenchman Jean de Terrevermille and others who questioned whether public offices could and should be held by inheritance. Although they carefully sidestepped whether the monarchy was such a public office, they also clearly indicated that some form of monarchical election would serve realms best. Elective monarchy's advocates argued for the right of corporate or legislative bodies to select individuals and families to respective thrones. There were, Algernon Sydney wrote, different types of elected monarchy, as some kingdoms "have in their elections principally regarded one family as long as it lasted; others considered nothing but the fitness of the person." As late as the imperial crisis, Pennsylvanian John Dickinson celebrated the right of nations to "change their king, or race of kings" and thus preserve "their antient form of government." The Holy Roman Empire, various German principalities, and Poland provided the English nation with vivid examples of elective monarchy in practice. Hobbes bitterly criticized what he called divided sovereignty inherent in such balanced government, but many others believed that election provided some kind of equilibrium between the estates of society and government critical to constitutional health.[8]

7. Hobbes, *Leviathan*, ed. Tuck, 139.

8. Burns, *Lordship, Kingship, and Empire*, 42–45; Algernon Sydney, "Discourses concerning GOVERNMENT," in William Scott, ed., *The Essence of Algernon Sidney's Work on Government* (London, 1797), 75–76. Sydney added, "Some have permitted the crown to be hereditary, as to its ordinary course; but restrained the power, and instituted officers to inspect the proceedings of kings, and to take care, that the laws were not violated." For John Dickinson's comments, see Dickinson, *Letters from a Farmer in Pennsylvania, to the Inhabitants of the British Colonies* (Philadelphia, 1768), 16. The colonial press discussed elected monarchy at length. Colonial writers were particularly interested in the Holy Roman Empire, Hanover, and Poland. For an example, see *American Weekly Mercury* (Philadelphia), Mar. 26–Apr. 2, 1741.

Eighteenth-century intellectuals realized the strength of such an arrangement while also understanding how election damaged monarchical legitimacy. By detaching or weakening the tie between monarchical authority and divine sanction or dynastic history, election threatened to unbalance constitutions and undermine the monarch beyond the electors' intent. These dangers lurked throughout the eighteenth century; the seventeenth-century instabilities in England and the persistent threat posed by the exiled Stuarts assured it would be so. Those loyal to the regime formed after the Glorious Revolution particularly fretted about their dynasties' legitimacy and the role of selection in establishing it.

The theories of monarchy were not just about rulers but about the state and the society's social-religious character. Seventeenth- and eighteenth-century British writers maintained that Catholicism encouraged absolutism, apparently unaware that absolutism, like Protestantism and republicanism, grew up in part in reaction to papal supremacy. "M. P.," a London commentator writing in 1689, declared that a people who first "submitted the freest part of them to the slavery of Popery," that is, their souls, were "easily brought to the Yoke of [political] oppression" by absolutist rulers who claimed God's authority to sanction their actions. Such rulers formed "standing, illegal, and oppressive" armies that then enslaved their populations. Armies allowed the rulers to overrun legislative bodies as well as local customs, thus imposing on the people "the double Tyranny of Popery and Arbitrary Power."[9]

British Protestants saw Louis XIV's persecution of Protestants in France that culminated in their expulsion with the Revocation of the Edict of Nantes in 1685 as a telling lesson about such Catholic, divine-right rulers. "The instance alone of the French King," wrote one English pamphleteer in a familiar lament over the Revocation, "is enough to be named instead of all, because he hath owned and published to the whole World, his part in that Design, and by comparing the Violences, Banishments, and Murders done upon the Protestants at the same time by other Popish Princes," one could see the spiritual cost of divine-right absolutism. These persecutions became a starting point for discussion after discussion of political orders and theories of monarchy in the Anglo-American world.[10]

There was also a sociology of monarchical election. Many mainstream English writers believed that elected monarchs worked best within social systems

9. Figgis, *Divine Right of Kings*, 44, 90, 100, 179; M. P., *Popery and Tyranny; or, The Present State of France, in Relation to Its Government, Trade, Manners of the People, and Nature of the Countrey* (London, 1689), 2.

10. *A Memorial from the English Protestants, for Their Highnesses, the Prince and Princess of Orange* ([London, 1688?]), 6.

in which property was broadly distributed and Protestantism secured. Such systems did not promise constitutional monarchy as we would understand it but offered instead a kind of limited monarch, with "the power of preserving the limitations" of royal power placed somewhere.[11]

Certainly, most seventeenth-century rulers, whatever the foundations of their authority, believed in what we now call state building. That entailed centralization of administrative control over semiautonomous locales as well as the assertion of authority over spiritual belief and economic behavior in a given realm. State building proceeded along two trajectories: the extension of tax structures responsible to monarchy and the spread of political and religious spectacles designed to reinforce monarchical authority into areas distant from the seat of power. Britain's American colonies were far from excluded from state building, and the particular applications there explain much about British America in the eighteenth century.

The political reality in Europe's many polities was, of course, infinitely more complex than theories of monarchy or state would allow. Yet both reality and theory rested on one simple assumption: that hierarchy and monarchy were normal. All those living then believed society should be shaped somehow like a pyramid. They struggled with the shape of their pyramids and suitable types of rulers throughout the seventeenth and eighteenth centuries. Through it all, most European thinkers saw a monarch of one sort or another as crucial to their happiness and safety. The future's radical egalitarianism lay hundreds of years away, and ideals associated with that future—representative government, republicanism, democracy, and the redistribution of property—horrified the common as well as the great. Even advocates saw republics as inherently unstable, and although the period's great writers are associated with the republican tradition, in fact, most writers on both sides of the Atlantic advocated some form of kingship. Monarchy was accepted, and the medieval idea of the king's two bodies, one corporeal and finite, the other legal and infinite, remained current in the British nation, jumping the Atlantic along with the monarch's subjects.[12]

11. [James Wilson], *Considerations on the Nature and the Extent of the Legislative Authority of the British Parliament* (Philadelphia, 1774), 11.

12. Ernst H. Kantorowicz, *The King's Two Bodies: A Study in Medieval Political Theology* (1957; rpt. Princeton, N.J., 1997), is the classic study of this concept in English legal and political theory. The present book's title is derived from Kantorowicz. The literature on royalty, nobility, and the state in Europe is vast and growing. Among that literature is Hillay Zmora, *Monarchy, Aristocracy, and the State in Europe, 1300–1800* (London, 2001); Sergio Bertelli, *The King's Body: Sacred Rituals of Power in Medieval and Early Modern*

Hobbes's observations about kings and kingship, about sovereignty and the state, the thoughts that became *Leviathan*, expressed an anguish both personal and metaphysical. Alone with his thoughts in his exile, he knew, better perhaps than even we do, that the English-speaking world had lost something with the Reformation and with the civil wars of the 1640s that culminated in regicide—something that would not easily be regained. God and man, heaven and earth had come undone. Indeed, the writings that compose resistance theory, Country thought, and republicanism going back to the sixteenth-century Jesuits are one extended lament over the failure of the human and the supernatural to stay in harmony. The idea that these writers celebrate freedom in any way we understand it is nothing more than a comforting illusion.

Looking back through the distorting scope of two centuries of democracy, it is difficult for us to realize just how disturbing the seventeenth-century developments were for Anglo-Americans. The unity between the supernatural and the human world had ruptured; the English nation repeatedly threw down kings despite divine sanction for their authority. Charles I lost his head; his son James was hurled into the political underworld of exile by his own daughter Mary and son-in-law William.

Many who went to America sought to reunify the worlds of God and man. Others wanted to avoid England and Europe's upheavals and make their fortune. But none could avoid the conflicts that engulfed the home islands. God's wrath was on the land, and the colonists in America did not escape the turmoil.

. . .

Subcultures

By the mid-1670s, anyone could see the differences between Massachusetts Bay and England. In 1675, a visiting mariner commented on the contrasts. Massachusetts's laws were different, he noted. "Soe arbitrary" was their government "that it occassions a murmuring amongst all sorts of people." The central problem, he argued, was "government remaining in the hands of a few persons who allthough yearly chosen yet it is done in such a manner as the people have not any voice." No doubt the captain exaggerated his concern for the people, but his description rings true. Custom and the Old Testament had shaped a new political and legal culture on the model of "the laws of the Jews . . . rather than those

---

Europe, trans. R. Burr Litchfield (University Park, Pa., 2001); Charles Tilly, ed., *The Formation of National States in Western Europe* (Princeton, N.J., 1975); Michael S. Kimmel, *Absolutism and Its Discontents: State and Society in Seventeenth-Century France and England* (New Brunswick, N.J., 1988).

of their Mother Country," as one writer put it in the eighteenth century. Writer after writer commented on what they found on the Atlantic's west shores in the seventeenth century. Biracial societies, a babel of European Protestants in New Amsterdam, Quakers planning various religious utopias, and New England's Old Testament–shaped societies all differed from what existed in England.[13]

Scholars have thought of these outposts and communities in regional terms. Generally, historians acknowledge three continental regions: New England, the middle colonies, and the Chesapeake, with some including the islands in the British West Indies as a fourth and the backcountry as a fifth. Contemporaries described these areas as distinct throughout the seventeenth and eighteenth centuries. Unique cultural practices brought from the different regions of England, the British Isles, and northern Europe were fused to particular geographies and regional social structures in North America to create what we would call subcultures.

These subcultures took form in the true period of imperial salutary neglect between 1630 and 1660. In a few decades, tiny settlements became little worlds grown from seventeenth-century merchant transport ships. Some were microsocieties unto themselves, others outposts of growing Atlantic merchant networks established by the Dutch, Swedish, or English trading companies. Visitors noted that even the English-settled colonies seemed alien. Dress, religion,

---

13. "Capt. Wyborne's Account of Massachusetts, 1675," Frederick Lewis Gay Transcripts, II, 36, MHS, Boston. For general discussion of the colonial legal order, see Peter Charles Hoffer, *Law and People in Colonial America* (Baltimore, 1992), 16–24; George Lee Haskins, *Law and Authority in Early Massachusetts* (New York, 1960); G. B. Warden, "Law Reform in England and New England, 1620 to 1660," *WMQ*, 3d Ser., XXXV (1978), 668–690; David Konig, *Law and Society in Puritan Massachusetts, Essex County, 1629–1692* (Chapel Hill, N.C., 1979); David Grayson Allen, *In English Ways: The Movement of Societies and the Transferal of English Local Law and Custom to Massachusetts Bay in the Seventeenth Century* (Chapel Hill, N.C., 1982), 45–54, 70–81; Cornelia Hughes Dayton, *Women before the Bar: Gender, Law, and Society in Connecticut, 1639–1789* (Chapel Hill, N.C., 1995), 15–156; John M. Murrin, "Anglicizing an American Colony: The Transformation of Provincial Massachusetts" (Ph.D. diss., Yale University, 1966); Murrin, "Magistrates, Sinners, and a Precarious Liberty: Trial by Jury in Seventeenth-Century New England," and Gail Sussman Marcus, "'Due Execution of the Generall Rules of Righteousnesse': Criminal Procedure in New Haven Town and Colony, 1638–1658," both in David D. Hall, John M. Murrin, et al., eds., *Saints and Revolutionaries: Essays on Early American History* (New York, 1984), 99–137, 152–206; Bruce H. Mann, *Neighbors and Strangers: Law and Community in Early Connecticut* (Chapel Hill, N.C., 1987). See also Wesley Frank Craven, *The Colonies in Transition, 1660–1713* (New York, 1968).

food, architecture, race relations, economies, and governmental institutions all seemed different from London and England's southern counties.

In the seventeenth century, the midatlantic was probably the most distinctive of these regions culturally and politically. In 1664, when an English fleet under Richard Nicolls captured New Amsterdam, Dutch-speaking settlers dominated the area from Albany to the Delaware River. The ethnic diversity of these settlements startled English observers. In 1678, Governor Sir Edmund Andros described New Amsterdam's merchant community as "of Dutch Extraction and some few of all Nations." New Amsterdam housed Dutch, French, German, and Polish Protestants, a noticeable Jewish community, settlers from various parts of the British Isles, and east and west African slaves. In the 1660s, the upriver Dutch settlements in and around Albany included Dutchmen, Flemish, Germans, a Nordic population, a few African slaves, and a sprinkling of settlers from the British Isles, with a large population of Native Americans nearby. New Englanders of various Dissenting sects had settled on Long Island, and Native Americans continued to live near Manhattan itself in the same period. In its diversity, the New Amsterdam colony mimicked, in an exaggerated way, the Netherlands' cosmopolitan centers.[14]

A tendency among the European Protestant populations toward Batavianization, the acceptance of Dutch norms, had developed in New Netherlands by 1660. Enough of these Batavian norms survived the English conquest of 1664 to create a distinctive, ethnically disparate subculture in the midatlantic that endured into the eighteenth century.[15] In 1695, an observer would describe New York as

14. "Answer of Gov. Andros to Enquiries about New York," in E. B. O'Callaghan, ed., *The Documentary History of the State of New-York*, 4 vols. (Albany, 1850), II, 91; John Miller, *New York Considered and Improved, 1695*, ed. Victor Hugo Paltsits (1903; New York, 1970), 37n–39n, 53–55; Joyce D. Goodfriend, *Before the Melting Pot: Society and Culture in Colonial New York City, 1664–1730* (Princeton, N.J., 1992); Stefan Bielinski, "The People of Colonial Albany, 1650–1800: The Profile of a Community," in William Pencak and Conrad Edick Wright, eds., *Authority and Resistance in Early New York* (New York, 1988), 5.

15. On Dutch legal customs, see David E. Narrett, "Dutch Customs of Inheritance, Women, and the Law in Colonial New York City," in Pencak and Wright, eds., *Authority and Resistance in Early New York*, 27–55. For Batavianizing tendencies and their political implications, see John M. Murrin, "English Rights as Ethnic Aggression: The English Conquest, the Charter of Liberties of 1683, and Leisler's Rebellion in New York," in Pencak and Wright, eds., *Authority and Resistance in Early New York*, 56–94. See also Robert C. Ritchie, *The Duke's Province: A Study of New York Politics and Society, 1664–1691* (Chapel Hill, N.C., 1977); Julius Goebel, Jr., and T. Raymond Naughton, *Law Enforcement in Colonial New York: A Study in Criminal Procedure (1664–1776)* (New York, 1944); Lawrence H.

"peopled by severall nations," adding, "there are manifold and different opinions of Religion." As late as 1705, Lord Cornbury would complain that New York's communities remained Dutch and that only English ministers and schools would "make this colony an English colony."[16]

To the north and the east of these polyglot settlements, Puritan migrations in the period 1620–1640 and subsequent theological differences created six New England colonies. Many of the migrants came from southeast England, a region with its own distinctive way of life, some of which was replicated in the new societies. That said, these immigrants, particularly those who arrived in 1630 with John Winthrop and the ministerial elite, established the New England Way not only in religion but in all aspects of life. Although we have been conditioned to define New Englanders by religious belief, a deeper picture edges into our mind's eye as we imagine congregations dressed in dark colors, seated by social rank, age, and gender, listening to preachers assure them of their spiritual unworthiness. Clothing, cooking, household and public architecture, dress, gender norms, and naming practices all helped define the region in New England as elsewhere in colonial America. As one eighteenth-century writer stated of seventeenth-

---

Leder, *Robert Livingston, 1654–1728, and the Politics of Colonial New York* (Chapel Hill, N.C., 1961). For the continuing political implications of this tendency in the eighteenth century, see Adrian Howe, "The Bayard Treason Trial: Dramatizing Anglo-Dutch Politics in Early Eighteenth-Century New York City," *WMQ*, 3d Ser., XLVII (1990), 57–89; Randall Balmer, *A Perfect Babel of Confusion: Dutch Religion and English Culture in the Middle Colonies* (New York, 1989); Beverly McAnear, "Politics in Provincial New York, 1689–1761" (Ph.D. diss., Stanford University, 1935); Patricia U. Bonomi, *A Factious People: Politics and Society in Colonial New York* (New York, 1971); Brendan McConville, "Conflict and Change on a Cultural Frontier: The Rise of Magdalena Valleau, Land Rioter," *Explorations in Early American Culture / Pennsylvania History*, LX (1998), 122–140; Cynthia A. Kierner, *Traders and Gentlefolk: The Livingstons of New York, 1675–1790* (Ithaca, N.Y., 1992); Linda Briggs Biemer, *Women and Property in Colonial New York: The Transition from Dutch to English Law, 1643–1727* (Ann Arbor, 1983); Donna Merwick, *Possessing Albany, 1630–1710: The Dutch and English Experiences* (Cambridge, 1990); Brendan McConville, *These Daring Disturbers of the Public Peace: The Struggle for Property and Power in Early New Jersey* (Ithaca, N.Y., 1999), 11–27; John E. Pomfret, *The Province of West New Jersey, 1609–1702: A History of the Origins of an American Colony* (Princeton, N.J., 1956); J. M. Sosin, *English America and the Restoration Monarchy of Charles II: Transatlantic Politics, Commerce, and Kinship* (Lincoln, Neb., 1980).

16. Miller, *New York Considered and Improved*, ed. Paltsits, 67; Lord Cornbury to the Society for the Propagation of the Gospel in Foreign Parts (hereafter cited as SPG), Oct. 22, 1705, New York, SPG microfilm, reel 13.

century New England, "the manners of the People" were quite distinct from those in London and other areas of England. As late as the 1760s, William Livingston claimed that his New England contemporaries still maintained with "a kind of precision and rigidness" the manners of seventeenth-century English Puritans.[17]

Although the individual New England colonies have rightly been understood as parts of a greater whole, significant theological and political differences existed therein. The New Haven Colony, established in the late 1630s on Long Island Sound's north shore, based its legal code closely on the Old Testament, severely limited trial by jury, used a freehold land tenure system common in Kent, and, in the early years, dressed women head to toe, complete with a chadorlike veil. Rhode Island's experiment in toleration led the colonists to embrace most Dissenting Protestant sects, whereas Massachusetts and New Haven marginalized or excluded all but nonseparating Congregationalists. The Connecticut Colony, centered around Hartford, established a more open form of Congregationalism in regard to church admission and tolerated Presbyterianism. Plymouth Colony's churches separated completely from the Church of England. All the colonies limited the political franchise to white male Christian propertyholders. There is some evidence to suggest that the differences between the New England colonies reflected differences in regional origins in England, though more arcane theological questions also clearly divided them.[18]

17. *The Letters and Papers of Cadwallader Colden*, IX, *Additional Letters and Papers, 1749–1775, and Some of Colden's Writings*, NYHS, *Collections*, LXVIII (New York, 1937), 245; William Livingston, *A Letter to the Right Reverend Father in God, John, Lord Bishop of Landaff* (New York, 1768), 9.

18. David Hackett Fischer, *Albion's Seed: Four British Folkways in America* (New York, 1989), is the major statement of the regionalist approach to American origins. It has been heavily criticized in a number of forums, most extensively in the *William and Mary Quarterly*. The argument's basic outline has yet to be debunked in my view for seventeenth-century America. Fischer's drive to find commonality, however, has masked a significant diversity of origins, beliefs, and behaviors in the different regions of America. Those studies that have explored those differences in New England's cultural fabric and institutional structures include John M. Murrin, "The Legal Transformation: The Bench and Bar of Eighteenth-Century Massachusetts," in Stanley N. Katz and John M. Murrin, eds., *Colonial America: Essays in Politics and Social Development*, 3d ed. (New York, 1983), 540–572; Murrin, "Magistrates, Sinners, and a Precarious Liberty"; David Cressy, *Coming Over: Migration and Communication between England and New England in the Seventeenth Century* (Cambridge, 1987); Perry Miller, *Errand into the Wilderness* (Cambridge, Mass., 1956); Isabel M. Calder, *The New Haven Colony* (New Haven, Conn., 1934); Konig,

By the time Charles II regained his father's throne in 1660, the Chesapeake Bay served as the central artery of another regional subculture. In that year, the bulk of what became Virginia's First Families were newcomers to the Chesapeake or had yet to arrive. But a ruling political faction had emerged there around Virginia governor Sir William Berkeley. Although perhaps overly generalized as Cavalier, the colony's elite did have strong ties to the Stuart dynasty and Royalist cause. By the time of Charles II's Restoration, tobacco had already made the Chesapeake a biracial society, as the economies of both Virginia and Maryland were dependent on bonded labor to grow tobacco. Leading planters exported leaf and imported indentured labor from Britain and, increasingly, slaves from Africa to service the crop.

A fundamental demographic reality also distinguished this region from England. Men heavily outnumbered women, to such a degree that gender relations differed significantly. Women before the law received greater leniency than they might have in England. The widow's third (the right to one-third of a deceased husband's estate) created a class of well-off survivors whose control of property and multiple opportunities for remarriage gave them bright prospects indeed by seventeenth-century standards. These privileges would gradually erode as sex

---

Law and Society in Puritan Massachusetts; Virginia DeJohn Anderson, "Migrants and Motives: Religion and the Settlement of New England, 1630–1640," *New England Quarterly*, LVIII (1985), 339–383; Allen, *In English Ways*, 163–204; T. H. Breen, "Persistent Localism: English Social Change and the Shaping of New England Institutions," *WMQ*, 3d Ser., XXXII (1975), 3–28; Richard R. Johnson, *Adjustment to Empire: The New England Colonies, 1675–1715* (New Brunswick, N.J., 1981); Stephen Innes, *Creating the Commonwealth: The Economic Culture of Puritan New England* (New York, 1995); *The Records of the Town of Newark, New Jersey* (Newark, 1864); Kenneth A. Lockridge, *A New England Town: The First Hundred Years, Dedham, Massachusetts, 1636–1736* (New York, 1970). Other articles of importance on the subject include Michael McGiffert, "American Puritan Studies in the 1960's," *WMQ*, 3d Ser., XXVII (1970), 36–67; Murrin, "Review Essay," *History and Theory*, XI (1972), 226–275; books include Sumner Chilton Powell, *Puritan Village: The Formation of a New England Town* (Middletown, Conn., 1963); Richard L. Bushman, *From Puritan to Yankee: Character and the Social Order in Connecticut, 1690–1765* (Cambridge, Mass., 1967); John Demos, *A Little Commonwealth* (New York, 1970); Philip Greven, *Four Generations: Population, Land, and Family in Colonial Andover, Massachusetts* (Ithaca, N.Y., 1970); Michael Zuckerman, *Peaceable Kingdoms: New England Towns in the Eighteenth Century* (New York, 1970); Stephen Boyer and Paul Nissenbaum, *Salem Possessed: The Social Origins of Witchcraft* (Cambridge, Mass., 1974); Robert A. Gross, *The Minutemen and Their World* (New York, 1976); Christopher M. Jedrey, *The World of John Cleveland: Family and Community in Eighteenth-Century New England* (New York, 1979).

ratios moved toward parity, but women's enhanced status remained visible when Charles II took the throne.

As with the other areas, significant religious and cultural differences existed. Maryland engaged in an accidental and unstable experiment in religious diversity that repeatedly led to social violence. Catholics, Quakers, Puritan Dissenters, and members of the Church of England lived in the colony side by side, a situation almost unique in England's fledgling empire. Small groups of Dissenters also entered Virginia from time to time, but they did not become a sustained presence in the colony that proclaimed the Church of England as its spiritual pillar.

The differences in the religious textures of these colonies reflected a fundamental political divergence between them. By 1660, Virginia had long been royalized, and its institutional structure was already more or less fixed. Maryland, in contrast, had been settled by Catholics under the sponsorship of Lord Baltimore and the Calvert family. The Restoration saw the return of its Catholic-dominated proprietary government despite the Protestants' bitter complaints.[19]

These portraits of areas and cultures that had come into being by 1660 will be familiar to anyone with a basic knowledge of colonial America. If we stare at the canvas for any length of time, flaws appear. It would be easy to fixate on the differences within regions. There was much movement, and over time, new settlements and new colonies — East and West Jersey, Pennsylvania, Delaware, North

19. Bernard Bailyn, "Politics and Social Structure in Virginia," in James Morton Smith, ed., *Seventeenth-Century America: Essays in Colonial History* (Chapel Hill, N.C., 1959), 90–115; Edmund S. Morgan, *American Slavery, American Freedom: The Ordeal of Colonial Virginia* (New York, 1975). See esp. 158–169 for Morgan's discussion of economic matriarchy; see also Kathleen M. Brown, *Good Wives, Nasty Wenches, and Anxious Patriarchs: Gender, Race, and Power in Colonial Virginia* (Chapel Hill, N.C., 1996). For Maryland, see Lois Green Carr and David William Jordan, *Maryland's Revolution of Government, 1689–1692* (Ithaca, N.Y., 1974); Carr, Lorena S. Walsh, and Russell R. Menard, *Robert Cole's World* (Chapel Hill, N.C., 1991); Thad W. Tate and David L. Ammerman, eds., *The Chesapeake in the Seventeenth Century: Essays on Anglo-American Society* (Chapel Hill, N.C., 1979); Newton D. Mereness, *Maryland as a Proprietary Province* (Cos Cobb, Conn., 1968); Walsh, "Summing the Parts: Implications for Estimating Chesapeake Output and Income Subregionally," *WMQ*, 3d Ser., LVI (1999), 53–94; Walsh, "Plantation Management in the Chesapeake, 1620–1820," *Journal of Economic History*, XLIX (1989), 393–406; Walsh, "Questions and Sources for Exploring the Standard of Living," *WMQ*, 3d Ser., XLV (1988), 116–123; Walsh and Carr, "The Standard of Living in the Colonial Chesapeake," *WMQ*, 3d Ser., XLV (1988), 135–159 (forum); Carr and Walsh, "The Planter's Wife: The Experience of White Women in Seventeenth-Century Maryland," *WMQ*, 3d Ser., XXXIV (1977), 542–571.

and South Carolina, Georgia — would join those already established on the main-land and in the West Indies.[20]

Still, a loose regional approach to the souls who numbered fewer than two hundred thousand in 1688 is useful for generalizing about their behaviors and their beliefs. Over time, these colonists came to understand that the Stuarts' po-litical projects meant more than arbitrary government. Kingship as practiced by the Stuarts rested within a larger political culture whose values threatened noth-ing less than dissolution of the colonial social orders as they had existed before 1660.

· · ·

Tyranny's Kiss

Tyranny wore a strange disguise in seventeenth-century Boston. On February 15, 1687, Samuel Sewall recorded that "Jos. Maylem carries a Cock at his back, with a Bell in 's hand, in the Main Street. several follow him," Sewall continued, and these blindfolded men "under pretence of striking him or 's cock, with great cart-whips strike passengers, and make great disturbance." A rooster, a bell, and some blindfolds — to us, these seem unusual weapons for a despot. But seventeenth-century New Englanders knew them for what they were. This brutally comic custom signaled the arrival of Shrovetide, a pre-Lenten holiday rich in Catho-lic imagery that the Church of England continued to mark but that had long been banned by Massachusetts's Puritan fathers. To them, the open practice of this Catholic-tainted ritual threatened to rupture the covenant between God and Massachusetts that had existed since 1630.[21]

Joseph Maylem's raucous sprint through Boston's streets caused alarm then, and yet now it is a valuable bridge to that time and place. Maylem was neither simply an idiot with a rooster strapped to his back nor a misplaced Englishman whose behavior was incomprehensible on the Atlantic's western shores. Rather, he ran along the violently unstable fault line between the English core's political culture and those of the North American subcultures.

The Stuart kings' repeated assertions of royal authority between 1660 and 1689 disrupted the delicate balance that had allowed the settler societies to de-velop their unique characteristics and social orders. Charles II and then James II

20. Allen, *In English Ways*, gives ample evidence of differences between villages in seventeenth-century Massachusetts. He roots these in variations in their English places of origin.

21. *The Diary of Samuel Sewall*, I, *1674–1700*, MHS, *Collections*, 5th Ser., V (Boston, 1878), 167.

managed to interfere in the three issues—property rights, institutional power, and godly order—that would allow their opponents to mobilize most colonials against them. The Stuart kings first destabilized and then destroyed the colonial land tenure systems, thus upending those societies' material-legal basis. Further, Charles and then James threatened the colonial elites' status by destroying or crippling institutional structures like the Massachusetts General Court, the New Jersey Assembly, and ultimately the institutional structures of all the northern colonies. Finally, they threatened the religious and ethnic orders already well rooted in the colonies by encouraging the Church of England's growth and, worse yet, toleration. These actions, coupled with the use of Catholic placemen in several colonies, were interpreted as a direct threat to the existing colonial orders and, more broadly, the pan-European Protestant movement.

The southern colonies greeted the Restoration warmly, and most New Englanders responded politely, some even enthusiastically. They saw Charles II as England's deliverer from the Quakers, Fifth Monarchists, and other schismatic sectarians. Bay Colonist John Hull expressed his wish that God might make the restored Stuart "father to the church and fitt him as he did David by long assertion to be as excellent . . . to his English Israel." Such views expressed a common hope on both sides of the English Atlantic.[22]

Other New Englanders were more ambiguous about the Restoration. Writing a century later, Thomas Hutchinson declared in his famous *History of the Colony and Province of Massachusetts*, "I would not be understood that they [the Bay Colony elite] denied the restoration of the former government." But in the margin of his personal copy, he added, "There is sufficient evidence to the contrary." True, it was a remark written long after the fact, but one forged in an unparalleled knowledge of New England's seventeenth-century history and confirmed by the existing primary source base. In particular, the Bay Colony's leaders welcomed two regicide judges, the "Late Kings Murtherers," as they were called, who fled to the colony at the Restoration. New Haven housed a third regicide incognito for almost thirty years. Bay Colony officials stymied the efforts of a royal commission to determine conditions in the colony and put off direct questions from their "Dread Soveraigne." Initially, then, discontent with the Stuarts was expressed in such passive manners.[23]

22. John Hull diary, 1660, MS, 31 of 3, AAS.

23. Mark L. Sargent, "Thomas Hutchinson, Ezra Stiles, and the Legend of the Regicides," *WMQ*, 3d Ser., XLIX (1992), 435; "The Humble Supplication of the Generall Court of the Massachusetts Colony in New England," and Edward Randolph, "Representation of the Affaires of N. England by Mr. Randolph," both in Jack P. Greene, ed., *Great Britain*

The Stuarts' assault on the colonial land tenure systems led to violent confusion that eventually engulfed the entire eastern seaboard. Charles II granted large tracts of lands in the colonies to courtiers who had remained loyal to him during the years of exile after his father's execution. Some of these ran to the tens and hundreds of thousands of acres, indeed even to whole colonies. New Jersey, Virginia's Northern Neck, Maine, the Carolinas, and finally Pennsylvania were all given as gifts or political rewards to those who had pledged their allegiance to the House of Stuart in its darkest hours.

At the same moment, Stuart-appointed authorities in Virginia and New England tried to restrain the demographically expanding white populations from further encroachments on Native American lands. These officials rightly feared that the extension of settlements would lead to widespread violence. The Native Americans themselves quickly came to see that royal authorities might prove a counterbalance to the rapacious demands of local farmers, especially those in New England and northern New York, and these natives began appealing to the king for assistance.[24]

Much of this land so easily granted away had already been converted into farms by yeomen or planters who claimed ownership under colonial charters, earlier royal grants, or direct purchases from the Native Americans. These early settlers were understandably loath to surrender their homes or to begin to pay rent or royal-sanctioned quitrents (dues paid to an acknowledged overlord in lieu of feudal labor) to late-coming Stuart retainers. Widespread fears about the loss of well-established farms allowed local leaders to mobilize yeomen against the Stuarts' intrusions, especially in Maryland, New England, New Jersey, and Virginia, where land issues helped encourage Bacon's Rebellion.[25]

Stuart land policies and reaction to them also shaped the Dutch reconquest

---

and the American Colonies, 1606–1763 (Columbia, S.C., 1970), 62–67, 69; Dixwell Papers, contained within the Wigglesworth Papers, MHS (which contain some account of the regicide John Dixwell's life).

24. Jennifer Pulsipher addresses the issue of royal intrusions into local Native American–settler disputes (forthcoming). For flirtations with royal authority by the New England elite, see Richard S. Dunn, *Puritans and Yankees: The Winthrop Dynasty of New England, 1630–1717* (Princeton, N.J., 1962), 191–356. See also Michael Garibaldi Hall, *Edward Randolph and the American Colonies, 1676–1703* (Chapel Hill, N.C., 1960); Philip S. Haffenden, "The Crown and the Colonial Charters, 1675–1688: Part I," *WMQ*, 3d Ser., XV (1958), 297–311; and the collective body of work on the period by Jack Sosin.

25. Bailyn, "Politics and Social Structure in Virginia," in Smith, ed., *Seventeenth-Century America*, 90–115. The origins of ownership listed in *Revolution in New England Justified, and the People There Vindicated* (Boston, 1691), 18–19, attributed to Edward Raw-

of New York in 1673 during the third Anglo-Dutch war. Samuel Hopkins, an English settler from Elizabethtown, New Jersey, invited a Dutch fleet to attack New York. The townspeople had been in virtual rebellion against the two Stuart courtiers who owned New Jersey, John, Lord Berkeley, and Sir George Carteret, over control of local lands. Hopkins quickly realized that a Dutch reconquest would serve the town's interests. When his ship was intercepted at sea, he contradicted the ship's captain and assured the enemy that "New Yorke was in no condicon to defend itselfe." When the Dutch fleet appeared in New York harbor, the English capitulated. The Elizabethtown settlers and other Jersey yeomen accepted Dutch titles to their land and Batavianized town institutions. New York's population itself had engaged in sporadic violence against the Duke of York's rule since 1664 over troop presence, land policy, and other issues and thus accepted the Dutch return. At the war's end, the Dutch surrendered the colonies, and their troubles, back to Stuart rule.[26]

This central problem of land title only intensified. In the mid-1680s, James II ordered Governor Andros to rescind all nonroyal property rights in New York, New Jersey, and New England. Andros demanded that the settlers repatent their lands and "reserve such acknowledgments" (meaning the quitrents) on any property not held by a direct royal grant, despite the fact that they already paid local taxes.[27] One New Englander bitterly declared that Andros and his assistants had announced "all their lands were the kings, that themselves did represent the king, and that therefore men that would have any legal title to the lands must take patents of them, on such terms as they should see meet to impose."[28] What people, this writer asked, "could endure this?"[29]

Dramatic changes in authority followed this assault on the land tenure system. In May 1686, James II appointed Joseph Dudley royal governor of most of north-

---

son and Samuel Sewall, give the reader some sense of these alternative sources of property and the ways they had become intertwined by the 1680s.

26. *NJA*, I, 126–149, 152–153; *Records of the Town of Newark, New Jersey*, New Jersey Historical Society, *Collections*, VI (Newark, 1864), 49–52; Murrin, "English Rights as Ethnic Aggression," in Pencak and Wright, eds., *Authority and Resistance in Early New York*, 58–60.

27. *A Narrative of the Proceedings of Sir Edmond Androsse and His Complices, Who Acted by an Illegal and Arbitrary Commission from the Late K. James, during His Government in New England* ([Boston], 1691), 7, 9.

28. Beverley W. Bond, Jr., *The Quit-Rent System in the American Colonies* (New Haven, Conn., 1919), 44.

29. [Rawson and Sewall], *Revolution in New England Justified*, 17; Dunn, *Puritans and Yankees*, 248.

ern New England. Ostensibly for reasons of military defense, this consolidation in fact extended imperial control over New England. James decreed local assemblies out of existence and assigned imperially connected individuals known to be hostile to the New England Way, like Edward Randolph, to the new government. Eventually New York, the Jerseys, and Connecticut were joined to this super-colony that became the Dominion of New England. The lack of representative institutions screamed popish absolutism to frightened Protestant populations.[30]

As Stuart officials expanded their authority, troubling alterations were made to New England's legal codes and procedures. Since these practices reflected the population's deeply held spiritual beliefs, any change made to them threatened godly order. In 1684, settlers at Pemaquid, in what became Maine, complained that "the Commander of Pemaquid to apprehend by Forse of armes the kings justis of the pease and thretten other Justis of the Pease with Putting in Irons" when they would not do as they were told by the military. After hearing and ignoring complaints about the Dominion in the Bay Colony and at Hartford, Connecticut, Edward Randolph would famously declare in private conversation that he cared nothing for the laws of New England and that the power of Andros's government was "as arbitrary as the great Turk." These officials even altered marriage practices to conform to English norms; couples about to marry had to post a bond with the governor after 1686. A year later, Andros's administration toyed with recognizing only marriages conducted in the Church of England.[31]

Andros and other imperial officials attempted to anglicize other legal procedures as well. Especially vexing to New Englanders was the question of oaths and oath taking. In the home islands, such oaths, including those taken with hands on the Bible, were a normal method of legally binding members of civil society. But the Puritan oligarchy, guided by their ministerial elite, saw oaths as a threat to godly Calvinist order. The danger, as Samuel Willard so cogently put it, was that "whatsoever is sworn by, is not a meer Medium, but an Object of Worship," and thus the civil ceremony amounted to idolatry. Certainly, "many good and very learned men, have doubted the lawfulness of Kissing or touching the Book in taking a solemn Oath cannot be deny'd." Tyranny's kiss — it created a monumental dilemma of authority and order. If New Englanders accepted these oaths,

30. Greene, ed., *Great Britain and the American Colonies*, 71; David S. Lovejoy, *The Glorious Revolution in America* (New York, 1972), 159.

31. Peter R. Christoph, ed., *The Dongan Papers, 1683–1688*, part 2 (New York, 1996), 359–360; George L. Clark, *A History of Connecticut: Its People and Institutions* (New York, 1914), 171; Thomas Hutchinson, *The History of the Colony and Province of Massachusetts-Bay*, ed. Lawrence Shaw Mayo, I (Cambridge, 1936), 302.

the covenant between New England and God would be broken; moreover, the symbolic system that maintained the Calvinist order of body, soul, and society would be delegitimated. If they resisted, as they ultimately did, they would have to defy king and empire.[32]

Changes in the public representation of power paralleled these changes in the law. The visualization of royal authority in Boston began when officials put up the king's arms in the town's courthouse in the mid-1670s. As Andros began to tighten his grip on New England in 1686, he introduced other totems of imperial authority, normal in England but threatening to New Englanders. Annual imperial holidays were introduced, some of which fell on the Sabbath. Authorities flew flags that included the Cross of Saint George—another idol—and Andros wore his hat during political and religious ceremonies, a taboo among the Puritan elite. Indeed, as Samuel Sewall bitterly observed, at times all these sins melded together. The celebration of the English national holiday, Saint George's Day, on April 23, 1687, led to a military procession where "some officers have red paper Crosses fastened to their Hats." Much to Sewall's disgust, disorder followed the display as the celebrants lit bonfires and set off "fire-works with Huzzas."[33]

The deep-seated belief that these changes amounted to a popish conspiracy against the Protestant American colonies colored the colonists' reaction to them. The intense outburst against Bible kissing and Saint George's flags occurred because cosmic meaning infused the things of civil life. The paranoid fear of Catholics had been part of political life in the English nation since Elizabeth's reign, and events—the massacres of Protestants by Catholics in France, the Spanish Armada's assault in 1588, and the Catholic Guy Fawkes's plot to blow up king and Parliament in 1605, to name a few—normalized anti-Catholicism and antipopery in English political culture. The concerns resurfaced in the 1670s and 1680s with the widespread (and accurate) suspicion that Charles II and his brother James actually were Catholics. It is, given the English nation's political climate, almost inconceivable that the rulers would have been Catholic, but that is exactly what had occurred. Fears of a "Popish Plot" in the late 1670s were followed by the Exclusion Crisis, the effort to remove the Catholic Duke of York from the line of succession to the English throne.[34]

---

32. Samuel Willard, *A Brief Discourse concerning That Ceremony of Laying the Hand on the Bible in Swearing* (London, 1689), 3, 9.

33. Hutchinson, *History of the Colony and Province of Massachusetts-Bay*, ed. Mayo, I, 271; *Diary of Samuel Sewall, I, 1674–1700*, MHS, *Collections*, 5th Ser., V, 167, 173–175.

34. Tim Harris, *Politics under the Later Stuarts: Party Conflict in a Divided Society, 1660–*

These related crises began a reintensification of the anti-Catholic fears throughout the English empire. James II's advancement to the throne and the expulsion of Protestants from France by Louis XIV heightened anti-Catholic feelings in the colonies, particularly in New York and Maryland. In New York, a number of French Protestant refugees fleeing the Revocation swelled an already large non-English-speaking population terrified of a Catholic conspiracy within and attacks by French and Native American Catholics from without. In Maryland, the actual presence of Catholic settlers and governing officials terrified Protestants living in the Annapolis area. "Churches and Chappels," one of them would write, "to our great Regret and Discouragement of our Religion, are erected and converted to the use of Popish Idolatry and Superstition, Jesuits and Seminary Priests, are the Only Incumbents." The Protestant religion, it seemed, was in mortal danger. Other Marylanders believed that leading Catholic councillors had encouraged the Indians to "make haste and kill the Protestants" before they could get assistance from England.[35]

Certainly, the courtiers and royal officials sent to the colonies did nothing to calm these fears and perceptions. The aggressive planting of the still-Catholic-tainted (in Puritan eyes) Church of England in the Boston area drove the town's Congregational leaders to distraction. Upon his arrival in Boston, Governor Andros asserted the right to hold Anglican Church services in the Congregational South Meeting House. Andros and his retainers began remembering the annual saints' days associated with the Catholic past, such as Saint Paul's, and a year later they boldly allowed Joseph Maylem to go tearing through Boston's streets with a chicken tied to his back to mark Shrovetide. A maypole was set up at Charlestown in 1687 on May 1, and Puritan leaders feared that the population might be induced to dance around it as they did in England, thus sinning against God and man. Even in death, the hand of popery as represented by the Church of England grasped at the men of New England. In one case, a Massachusetts man specifi-

1715 (London, 1993), 80–116; J. R. Western, *Monarchy and Revolution: The English State in the 1680s* (London, 1972). *Historical Journal* has carried a number of articles on these themes. See also W. A. Speck, *Reluctant Revolutionaries: Englishmen and the Revolution of 1688* (Oxford, 1988), 1–70.

35. Murrin, "English Rights as Ethnic Aggression," in Pencak and Wright, eds., *Authority and Resistance in Early New York*; J. F., *The Declaration of the Reasons and Motives for the Present Appearing in Arms of Their Majesties Protestant Subjects in the Province of Maryland* (Annapolis, Md., 1689) 3; Carr and Jordan, *Maryland's Revolution of Government*, 47.

cally asked that no member of the Church of England preach at his death, but Andros's Anglican cleric attempted to administer the funeral rites anyway.[36]

The Bay Colony leaders' deepest fear was that toleration might be extended to the Bay Colony, a toleration that would ultimately include Gog and Magog, Quakers and Catholics. As one colonial put it shortly after the events of 1688 and 1689, "The late King James was bound in Conscience to endeavour to Damn the English Nation to Popery and Slavery."[37]

A Briton who looked back saw those days as a time of chaos and fear. Bishop Gilbert Burnet, whose son became an imperial governor, wrote that "this year," meaning 1685, "must ever be remembred, as the most fatal to the Protestant Religion." In February, James II publicly declared himself a Catholic; "in June, Charles the Elector Palatine dying without issue, the Electoral dignity went to the House of Newburgh, a most bigotted Popish family. In October, the King of France recalled and vacated the edict of Nantes." The troubles continued, "and in December, the Duke of Savoy being brought to it, not only by the persuasions, but even by the threatnings of the Court of France, recalled the edict that his father had granted to the Vaudois." "I have" Burnet wrote, "ever reckoned this [year] the fifth great crisis of the Protestant Religion." Within this transatlantic and northern European context, disaster loomed.[38]

Property in danger, popery at the door. Englishmen and colonials viewed their reality through that window. The Stuarts' efforts to centralize colonial government and establish a common institutional architecture for their disjointed empire threatened all that had been built in the colonies in the decades before 1660, or so it seemed to the immediate heirs of the builders.

• • •

Popery Pickled, Protestantism Proclaimed

This first effort to create a royalized America within an imperial framework failed spectacularly as the colonists violently resisted the Crown's efforts. The

36. *Diary of Samuel Sewall*, I, 1674–1700, MHS, *Collections*, 5th Ser., V, 178.

A dispute happened at the grave of one Lilly. He left the ordering of his funeral to his executors. They forbad Mr. Ratcliffe, the episcopal minister, performing the service for burial. Nevertheless he began. Deacon Frairey interrupted him, and a stop was put to his proceeding. Frairey was complained of, and besides being bound to his good behaviour for twelve months, it was thought the process would cost him 100 marks. J. Moodey to Mather, Feb. 8, 1688, in Hutchinson, *History of the Colony and Province of Massachusetts-Bay*, ed. Mayo, I, 303n.

37. Addington, *Answer to a Letter*, 1.

38. Burnet, *History of His Own Time*, I, 655–656.

Indian wars, rioting, and open rebellions against royally appointed governments that swept the eastern seaboard between 1660 and 1688 culminated in a series of rebellions in 1689–1690 that demonstrated colonials' emotional resistance to Stuart authority. The unrest during the Glorious Revolution in Massachusetts, New York, and Maryland reveals the contours of conflict between cosmopolitan culture and royal authority on the one hand and the local oligarchies that dominated the colonies on the other. At stake were the established colonial orders and their relationship to the supernatural.

The Stuart regime's assertion of authority indirectly encouraged disorder before 1688 in Maryland, New Jersey, Virginia, New England, and the Cape Fear region of what became North Carolina. But that unrest lacked the definitive political character of the rebellions that began in 1689, when knowledge of William and Mary's November 1688 landing in England spread to the colonies. The common thread that ran through the resulting unrest was colonials' shared perception that the Stuart monarchy represented a mortal danger to their churches and communities.

News of the Glorious Revolution brought the Stuarts' American experiment in imperial consolidation to a dramatic and violent end. In Boston, rumors of James II's flight to France led to a carefully planned coup. "Several very deserving Gentlemen in Boston, about the middle of April" set a strategy, and on April 18, the conspirators seized the captain of the frigate *Rose*, a number of other royal officials, and ultimately Andros himself. The Bay Colony quickly sent emissaries to the emerging court of William and Mary to explain their actions and plead for a restoration of the charter of 1630.[39]

In New York, the Stuart regime's collapse allowed an unstable situation to develop. With open turmoil throughout the empire, Andros's lieutenant Francis Nicholson departed for England, and the non-English population, "being much against papists," seized the city's fort on May 31, 1689, after someone attempted to fire it. They eventually elected Jacob Leisler, a merchant and a captain in the militia, as their leader. Leisler was prominent among the non-English-speaking population and a militant anti-Catholic. According to one hostile account, Leisler accused all who opposed his seizure of power of being popishly inclined.[40]

The subsequent unrest in New York bordered on civil war. Parties ran through

39. A. B., *An Account of the Late Revolutions in New-England* (Boston, 1689), 9, rpt. in Whitmore, ed., *Andros Tracts*, II, 195–196.

40. Balmer, *A Perfect Babel of Confusion*, 31. See also Jerome R. Reich, *Leisler's Rebellion: A Study of Democracy in New York, 1664–1720* (Chicago, 1953), 55–105; Miller, *New York Considered and Improved*, ed. Paltsits, 68.

the streets of New York "with naked swords in their hands," and the turmoil did not end until Leisler and his son-in-law were executed in May 1691. They had lacked their opponents' contacts in London and were portrayed at the court of William and Mary as usurpers of low character. The upheaval continued to reverberate for decades in New York politics.[41]

Maryland, too, went through a kind of civil war, sparked when the lord proprietor's Catholic governor ordered the population to turn their guns in for repair. In a colony that had been on the verge of religious violence for ten years, it was too much to bear. The subsequent rebellion bore the name of its militantly Protestant leader, John Coode. Coode, unlike Leisler, survived to see the Calverts stripped of their colony for several decades.[42]

By 1690, the first efforts to create an imperial America based on adulation of royalty had failed. The Stuart kings, particularly James II, were unwise rulers who showed little desire to accommodate their subjects in the British Isles or in America. The institutional architecture imagined suitable for the colonists by the Stuarts and their retainers effectively denied any role, voice, or honor for most colonial leaders. The attack on the land tenure systems and religious structures provoked fear throughout the colonies. The Stuarts apparently believed they would create an empire whose institutional structures were all alike, with much enhanced monarchical authority and forced religious toleration.

In actuality, when challenged, the Stuart retainers sent to govern the American marches had neither the might nor the willpower to reaffirm their authority. The pathetic images of Governor Andros and his handful of "Red-coat Centinels" retreating into Boston's fort and of Lieutenant Governor Nicholson fleeing New York stand testimony to this failure. Just as important, the lack of shared religious terrain and political symbols diminished the Stuart officials' ability to engage in what we would call social control before the violence. They were continually open to the charges of being agents of popery. Both Andros and Nicholson went on to further careers in the colonial administration, but the broader Stuart design collapsed.[43]

The colonists imagined that with the success of the rebellions they could continue on in the ways of their fathers. Puritan, Batavian, Cavalier — all thought of the restoration of the world they had known in the seventeenth century, or at least the preservation of key portions of it. But for provincial Americans, em-

---

41. Balmer, *A Perfect Babel of Confusion*, 35; Bonomi, *A Factious People*, 75–76.

42. Lovejoy, *Glorious Revolution in America*, 235–250, 251–270.

43. A. B., *An Account of the Late Revolutions*, 9, rpt. in Whitmore, ed., *Andros Tracts*, II, 197.

pire would mean accommodation and adjustment. Massachusetts would receive a new, royal charter, and everywhere the power of the metropolis was asserted. Eventually, New Jersey, South Carolina, North Carolina, Maryland (temporarily), and Georgia would have their governments royalized. Such royalization meant acceptance of behavior and power arrangements previously understood as ungodly, or un-Dutch, or ungentlemanly.

As long as the colonies remained isolated on the Atlantic's western shore, the dilemma of God's relationship to political man that perplexed the entire empire in the wake of civil war and regicide did not intrude on their existence. The assumption was, except during a few tense moments like the Quaker "invasions" of Boston and Dutch New York in the 1650s and 1660s, that God ordained the established rulers for leadership, and they should thus be obeyed. Institutional structures paralleled; secular and sacred institutions looked alike. They did not fuse at the top as in England, but leaders of church and state in the seventeenth-century colonies were intertwined in such a manner as to normalize the authority of both. This was true in most of New England, in Dutch New York, in Pennsylvania, and in Virginia. Troubled Maryland, with its volatile mix of Catholics, Quakers, and Anglicans, enjoyed far less certainty until the 1690s, as did New Jersey's diverse population. But they were exceptions, not the rule.[44]

The Glorious Revolution's constitutional settlement brought stability to the British Isles but created a new quandary in English America. The relationship of God to political man and his history, coupled to issues of imperial integration, threatened the colonial orders planted in the seventeenth century. When the newly created Board of Trade, designed by imperial authorities to manage colonial affairs, began to push for the royalization of the proprietary and charter colonies in the 1690s, a central question arose and would not go away. What would remain in the colonies from the past?[45]

. . .

From Covenant to Contract

By 1700, New Englanders knew that Protestant empire would place tremendous demands on them. And yet they still clung to the Puritan past. Congregationalism, covenant theology, and the perception of order that had guided New Englanders since 1630 remained current. So there were no surprises when, on March

44. Kai T. Erikson, *Wayward Puritans: A Study in the Sociology of Deviance* (New York, 1966), 107–136; Jane Kamensky, *Governing the Tongue: The Politics of Speech in Early New England* (New York, 1997), 117–125.

45. Greene, ed., *Great Britain and the American Colonies*, 135.

15, 1704, Samuel Willard mounted a Boston pulpit to preach to the governor, the members of the General Court, and the port town's other gentlemen. The day was "set a part for Solemn Fasting and PRAYER," a time of reflection that embodied Calvinist New England's spiritual life. Willard was born to that tradition, educated in it, and embodied it. The central tenet of Puritan theology and society, the federal covenant, provided his theme. "God," he preached, "is said to be for men Federally; when he stands engaged by Covenant to be on a Peoples side." The covenant, he continued, was an external dispensation that "hath its conditions with which the promises of it are connected." When people "near to God by the Covenant which he made with their Fathers" provoked the Lord, He might "set himself against, and to forsake them." Such was the comfort and the danger of Massachusetts's pact with God.[46]

Willard and his listeners understood that events from 1688 to that day in 1704 had brought one question to the fore: could the federal covenant be maintained within the emerging imperial order? Colonists from Virginia to Massachusetts Bay understood the Glorious Revolution as the hand of Providence delivering them from popish enslavement. Yet the revolutionary settlement that came in its wake also created real dilemmas of political values.

In the four decades after 1688, the oligarchic orders that dominated the colonies — the so-called First Families of Virginia, Pennsylvania's Quaker leadership, the midatlantic's Anglo-Dutch-Scottish elite, and especially the New England colonies' Puritan oligarchies — were forced to adapt as Protestant monarchs sought to integrate the empire, albeit in a manner far more acceptable to provincials than James II's efforts had been. They faced a straightforward problem. What would the new imperial order mean to those living on the empire's far fringes? Would institutional structures — political, religious, and legal — be preserved? How would they be reconciled to imperial political culture and control?

Provincials accepted "contract" as an organizing principle to solve these problems and make the empire whole. The Convention Parliament of 1689 had legitimated William and Mary's invasion. The same body's actions had, over time, been explained to the extended nation in part as the election of a new monarchical regime to a vacated throne and the establishment of a new national contract that assured the supremacy of the King-in-Parliament. This lasted throughout the long contest between the deposed Stuarts and the Hanoverians that began in 1714 and cannot really be said to have ended until after the Jacobites' disastrous

46. Samuel Willard, *Israel's True Safety: Offered in a Sermon, before His Excellency, the Honourable Council, and Representatives* . . . (Boston, 1704), 7–8.

defeat at Culloden in Scotland in April 1746. "Contract" thus became a powerful motif in the emerging British Atlantic empire's political life.[47]

A Protestant political culture based on national contract with a limited Protestant monarchy offered the hope of provincial stability after decades of conflict and tension, yet it also created a paradox within the empire. The problem was not contract theory or monarchical election per se. Given the alternative, Protestant provincials readily accepted these as legitimate wellsprings of William and Mary's (and later the Hanoverians') authority.

However, the empire's heterogeneous institutional architecture and the spiritual world's ambiguous relationship to government troubled many. In England, the Glorious Revolution's settlement established that church and state's institutional structures would be paralleled and fused at the top; the Church of England was the state church, and the monarch was its head. The logic of each thus reinforced the other. There was an assumption in the early modern world that that was how it should be, that all institutional structures should look alike within a polity.

But the empire was not this way. In the colonies, the political and church structures did not fuse in the same manner. The king did not head the Dutch Reformed Church, or the Quaker meeting, or the Congregational polities, or the Presbyterian synods. With the issues of monarchical legitimacy and imperial warfare pressing in the years immediately after 1688, the relationship of local institutions to the empire and to the existing value structures was initially glazed over. After the Union of 1707 between England and Scotland, however, the empire's disparate institutional structures along with its wide spectrum of religious beliefs — from Catholic Ireland to ultra-Protestant New England — were clearly problematized. It seemed so unwieldy and incompatible with ordered rule.

Imperial officials continued, in a muted form, the policies of James II and Andros to resolve this paradox. As early as 1695, an observer was calling for a union of New York, the Jerseys, Rhode Island, and Connecticut under the control of one governor, complete with a bishop who would establish the Church of England as the new supercolony's state religion. It was Andros all over again. Although the creation of such a colony may seem fanciful to us today, in fact Richard Coote, Lord Bellomont, was given the governorship of New York and Massachusetts in this period, in part to further imperial consolidations. Intensifying these calls for uniformity was the Church of England's growth in the northern colonies after 1688. The royally sponsored Society for the Propagation of the

47. W. A. Speck, *Stability and Strife: England, 1714–1760* (Cambridge, Mass., 1977), 251.

Gospel began planting chapels in towns and hamlets across the northern colonies, a development that threatened Puritan orthodoxy in Massachusetts, Connecticut, and New Hampshire. Anglican ministers claimed that the established church's presence was essential to the British constitution's functioning. To make matters worse, throughout the 1710s and 1720s, the heirs to the New England Way heard rumors that the charter issued by William and Mary would be revoked and replaced by a church-state structure more in line with that of England.[48]

Thus pressed, colonial writers expanded their musings on God and man to explain the British Atlantic world's institutional diversity and to try to reconcile it with a working imperial order. For these writers, contract had none of the individualistic meanings assigned to it by later generations. Rather, it was used to explain how institutional structures and the church-state relationship could vary so widely in the same extended polity. This line of discussion is most evident in New England's bountiful print culture, created by those seeking to accommodate the New England Way to empire. But this was not just a New England phenomenon. The same struggle to accommodate what was with what was to come occurred in every British province in the Western Hemisphere.

Among the quill-armed champions who stepped forward to take up this challenge, the best known today is Massachusetts cleric John Wise of Ipswich. In two pamphlets, *The Churches Quarrel Espoused; or, A Reply in Satyre, to Certain Proposals Made*, first published in 1713 and then quickly reappearing in 1715, and *A Vindication of the Government of New-England Churches* (1717), he sought to preserve the integrity of Congregational Church structure in a changing empire.

The key to understanding Wise as an intellectual is to see him as a man of his times who dealt with problems as they arose. In the 1680s, when Andros taxed Wise and his fellow Ipswich townsmen in a manner he found unfair, the young minister led the resistance to what he called Catholic, arbitrary power and was jailed for his troubles.

48. Miller, *New York Considered and Improved*, ed. Paltsits, 77–80. Persistent rumors circulated through most of the 1720s that at least Massachusetts and perhaps the two charter colonies would have their charters revoked. This has never been the subject of extensive study, though it was repeatedly mentioned in the Boston newspapers and in a number of pamphlets, including the published sermons written to mark the death of George I. I would like to thank Jack Greene for his insights on this question.

The claim regarding the Anglican Church and the constitution was repeated as late as 1766, when Boston minister Henry Caner declared, in response to policy on newly conquered Quebec, that not extending the Church of England there and everywhere "appears like questioning whether the constitution now in being should, or should not be preserved" (Caner to SPG, Oct. 20, 1766, SPG microfilm, reel 12).

Thirty years later, when the empire and Massachusetts's place in it had changed, he again rose to answer a challenge, this one intellectual and conceptual. He wished to demonstrate his imperial loyalty by publicly championing the contractual Protestant monarchy that appeared after 1688. At the same time, he appropriated contract theory to argue that, in a diverse and far-flung empire like that controlled by Britain, church and state did not need to approximate one another institutionally or fuse in the same way they did in other realms. Rather, Wise sought to protect his beloved Congregational Church polity from threats internal and imperial, from those who advocated Presbyterianism and those who would establish the Church of England. The complexity and paradoxes Wise's task entailed have led to some confusion over his actual goals. But through all his writings runs one consistent thread: New England, he believed, could be in the empire without being of the empire.[49]

Wise used secularized contract theory to defend the Protestant succession and the Hanoverian dynasty. He asserted the origins of civil sovereignty in "the People," the "Will of a Community, yielded up and surrendred to some other Subject," just as the English supporters of Protestant succession did. By "the People," Wise did not mean to assert a modern notion of equality. He still thought of society as rightly divided between the few and the many and thought of a very restricted political nation as "the People." He considered civil government as originating in "Humane Free-Compacts" rather than direct divine intervention, though he carefully tempered this remark with the assertion that good government "is a very Admirable Result of Providence." Such statements have been understood as foreshadowing the American Revolution, but in fact he sought to explain the dynastic struggles of the immediate past that led to the deposing of the House of Stuart. "If a Common Wealth," he asked rhetorically, "be changed into a monarchy, is it Nature that forms, and brings forth the Monarch? Or if a Royal Family be wholly Extinct . . . is it Nature that must go to work . . . to Breed a Monarch before the People can have a King, or a Government sent over them?" Although the Stuart family as a whole was not extinct in 1717, its Protestant branch had died off with Queen Anne three years earlier. "And thus," he continued, "we must leave Kings to Resolve which is their best Title to their Crowns, whether Natural Right, or the Constitution of Government settled by Humane Compacts [monarchical election], under the Direction and Conduct of

49. Historians have seen Wise as being somehow a forebear of the revolutionary future, of a more democratic, individualist, rational society. Although a few writers have questioned this view, it has remained the dominant one. See Gay Transcripts, III, 59, 62–68, esp. 65 (being the court case brought against the Ipswich men, Aug. 23, 1687), MHS.

Reason." Wise's endorsement of contract and his situation of it within a natural rights framework were an implicit endorsement of Parliament's right to place the Hanoverian dynasty on the British throne.[50]

Wise's defense of Protestant monarchy was designed to win acceptance for an institutionally diverse empire. Wise advocated a polity broadly Protestant rather than with an established and uniform church-state structure. In his first extensive writing on the subject, *The Churches Quarrel Espoused; or, A Reply in Satyre, to Certain Proposals Made*, Wise declared he had "no particular Prejudice against any of the Governments of Christian Protestant Churches in the World," even as he insisted, "New-England Churches cannot be mended by Exchange." Parliament "could not have invented an Establishment in Church Order, more for the Service of the Imperial Crown of the British Empire than our present Constitution." The Congregational polity, in other words, was well suited to empire, needing no revisions as imagined either by London or the famous Mathers, Increase and Cotton, whose plans to create a permanent synod he described as "the Spectre or Ghost of Presbyterianism" having "in Intention. . . . Prelacy in it, only the distinct Courts of Bishops, with the Steeples of the Churches Tythes, Surplice, and other Ornaments, do not shew themselves so visible" as in the Church of England.[51]

Wise realized that a more concrete reconciliation of imperial architecture would be needed, and his tactic was to portray New England's religious institutions as essentially compatible with and similar to English civil institutions. He did this by means of selective comparison, a method obviously questionable in its validity but emotionally pleasing to the writer and most likely to many readers as well. "In Honour to the New-England Churches," he declared, "and with veneration for the English Monarchy, . . . there is in the Constitution of our Church Government more of the English Civil Government in it, and it has a better Complexion to suit the true English Spirit, than is in the English Church . . . both as to the Legislative and Executive part of Government." He compared Congregational synod meetings to the House of Commons, "and herein they agree with the English Caution and Wisdom, in the Models of Civil Government of the Empire."[52]

Wise then resituated plausibility — the relationship between church, state, and

50. John Wise, *A Vindication of the Government of New-England Churches, Drawn from Antiquity* . . . (Boston, 1717), 32–34, 44, 71.

51. John Wise, *The Churches Quarrel Espoused; or, A Reply in Satyre, to Certain Proposals Made* . . . (Boston, 1715), 6–7, 38; Peter L. Burger, *Pyramids of Sacrifice: Political Ethics and Social Change* (New York, 1974).

52. Wise, *The Churches Quarrel Espoused*, 42.

God — in terms of the relationship of the imperial order to God's kingdom. "Mixt governments which are . . . of divers kinds . . . yet possibly the fairest in the World is that which has a Regular Monarchy; settled upon a Noble Democracy as its basis." Observers believed, he continued, that the British Empire was such a polity. Most important, "it is a Kingdom, that of all the Kingdoms of the World, is most like to the Kingdom of Jesus Christ, whose Yoke is easie, and Burden light." In other words, the empire's overarching political order was rhetorically parallel with the supernatural world as explained by New England's Congregational ministry.[53]

By establishing the parallel character of the seen and unseen worlds and labeling all a "Noble Democracy," Wise set the stage for the legitimation of New England's unique institutions in the new imperial reality. "A Monarchy has been tryed in the [Christian] Church with a witness, but it has absolutely failed us [popery]." The aristocratic Church of England and the Presbyterians "in a deep Calm threw the Democracy Overboard, and . . . seized Ship and Cargo as their Right and Title; but after some time brought all to Ship-wreck [the Interregnum]." According to the Bible, it was the primitive Christian church's democratic structures that allowed them to "beat out in all the bad Weather of Ten bloody Persecutions. . . . And this is our Constitution, and what can't we be pleased?" New England church structure, he explained, need not parallel England's because the nature of their authority was not the same. Church governance organized like a commonwealth (in the form of Congregational autonomy) was no threat to good monarchical order because church sovereignty was limited to men's souls. Indeed, like England's contractual monarchy, the Congregational polity "has the best" balance. Wise turned to Newton to explain this balance: "A Government so exactly poyzed, that it keeps its Motions Regular like the stupendous Spheres." In such a system, "a Body consisting of very numerous Parts . . . yet the ballance of Power is very exactly and with great advantage preserved."[54]

Wise sought to reconcile the seeming disjunctures between the institutional and constitutional orders of God and man. In so doing, he supported the Protestant succession and tried to make the New England Way seem compatible with the emergent imperial order. He was, in other words, forward looking, but to his future, not ours, and he was hardly the only one thinking this way. "We have now," as one Boston pamphleteer wrote in 1721, "with full Satisfaction found Protection, and Umbrage under the Wings of a Protestant Prince, who holds the Ballance of Europe: And Desires to be in nothing Greater, then in the Happi-

53. Wise, *A Vindication of the Government of New-England Churches*, 50, 51.
54. Ibid., 64, 65, 73, 88–89.

ness of His People." In their minds, such a ruler should be respectful of constitutional balance and willing to act as defender of pan-European Protestant interests. The linking of contractual monarchy to Protestantism offered a means for those raised in the provinces' Protestant subcultures to maintain their traditional values even as they accepted the empire.[55]

In a loose sense, the same negotiation was occurring everywhere in British North America in those now-forgotten years. Some parts of these contracts were formal, others unspoken, but a powerful tendency to create a shared Protestant political identity manifested itself in the American provinces in different forms in the decades immediately after 1688. In New York and New Jersey, a dialogue between the Dutch and their English conquerors began when Richard Nicolls forced Peter Stuyvesant to surrender New Amsterdam in 1664. In 1675, after Dutch forces had briefly recaptured the town, eight New York burghers appeared before English authorities to pledge allegiance to the English Crown while demanding the right to continue Dutch social and religious customs. Their petition was rebuffed, but a pattern of accommodation emerged. The Dutch accepted English overlordship but retained their inheritance practices, property, gender roles, the Reformed religion, and the Dutch language.[56]

Much of what followed in the midatlantic was a continuation of these negotiations. The Duke of York's Charter of Liberties in 1683; Leisler's Rebellion in 1689–1691; the bitter church controversies in New York that led Lord Cornbury to declare of his efforts to establish a minister at Kingston, "They are all Dutch, and don't desire to see an Englishman settle among them"; and the migration of Dutch populations into central New Jersey followed by their involvement in rioting over property rights — all these were part of an ongoing process that established and reestablished the Dutch-speaking population's place in a changing empire.[57]

55. Amicus Patrie, *A Word of Comfort to a Melancholy Country; or, The Bank of Credit Erected in the Massachusetts-Bay* (Boston, 1721), 3.

56. Narrett, "Dutch Customs of Inheritance, Women, and the Law in Colonial New York City," in Pencak and Wright, eds., *Authority and Resistance in Early New York*, 27–55. Narrett describes the surrender on 27 and the petition of the burghers in 1675 on 28. That petition is reproduced in O'Callaghan, ed., *The Documentary History of the State of New-York*, II, 251.

57. Lord Cornbury to SPG, Oct. 22, 1705, New York, SPG microfilm, reel 13. Murrin, "English Rights as Ethnic Aggression," in Pencak and Wright, eds., *Authority and Resistance in Early New York*, 56–94, remains the best short discussion of the period up to Leisler's Rebellion in New York. Very useful, longer treatments are Thomas F. Archdeacon, *New York City, 1664–1710: Conquest and Change* (Ithaca, N.Y., 1976); and Ritchie,

In Virginia, other negotiations occurred. There, an uneasy but working relationship between royal governors, the council, and the House of Burgesses was established over several decades. This led to relative political quiet in the Spotswood and Drysdale administrations between 1710 and 1726. The latter governor was described by the House of Burgesses in an address to George I as having encouraged "with a singular zeal for your majesty's person and family . . . peace and justice in this your majesty's government." In the same period, a series of laws and newly established customs normalized chattel slavery and a strict racial separation.[58]

In South Carolina, the turmoil of the proprietary period and the proprietors' failure to send timely aid to the colonists during the Yamassee War (1715) led the assembly to repeatedly petition for the colony's royalization in order to secure the emerging social order. It was, the assemblymen insisted, only royal authority that could "preserve us from ruin." The colony's exposure to the Spanish to the south, the increasing number of slaves, and the continued Indian threat convinced the settlers that royal protection was the only answer. On that basis, submission for protection, the colony petitioned for a royal government in 1719 and finally achieved political stability early in the 1730s.[59]

Twenty-four years after Samuel Willard mounted his pulpit, another New England minister, Benjamin Colman, preached about the new covenant, the Protestant empire's political compact. It was, he declared, Protestant Britons' right to "chuse him for their Prince and King" who suited the nation and then to "own his right to be over them, and voluntarily subject themselves to him as their ruler." It was this way, "upon the terms and covenant now proposed, which were—that they came peaceably to help him, and that his heart should be knit to them. Thine are we David." The object of this sermon was of course George II, and the covenant that Colman spoke of was between the British nation and their elected Ger-

The Duke's Province. Lovejoy, *The Glorious Revolution in America,* 98–121, 251–270, is also useful. For the Dutch in New Jersey, see McConville, *These Daring Disturbers of the Public Peace,* 58–63, 124–128, 137–163. For a more detailed account of the Dutch in the midatlantic, see Balmer, *A Perfect Babel of Confusion.*

58. For the political relationships, see Percy Scott Flippin, *The Royal Government in Virginia, 1624–1775* (New York, 1966), 108–121, 123. For the issue of slavery, see Anthony S. Parent, Jr., *Foul Means: The Formation of a Slave Society in Virginia, 1660–1740* (Chapel Hill, N.C., 2003).

59. "Petition of the Carolina Assemblymen, March 1717," and "Francis Yonge's Narrative of the Proceedings of the People of South Carolina . . . ," both in Elmer D. Johnson and Kathleen Lewis Sloan, eds., *South Carolina: A Documentary Profile of the Palmetto State* (Columbia, S.C., 1971), 79–83.

man Protestant monarchs. His soothing words reassured the great migration's heirs that God had indeed designed their new imperial world.[60]

The transformation from covenant to contract marked a shift from Providence to history in British North America. The subjects living in these subcultures became, at least officially, moored in secular time rooted in dynastic politics. An overt reorganization of political society, public life, and print culture driven by this reality occurred in every colony. The annual rites of empire that had begun to appear in Wise's time spread rapidly and soon took possession of the imagination of the king's distant subjects. Even those who would resist these changes found themselves accepting the cult of the British Protestant prince.

60. Benjamin Colman, *Fidelity to Christ and to the Protestant Succession in the Illustrious House of Hannover . . .* (Boston, 1727), 5.

2

THE MARCH OF EMPIRE

TIME, RITES, AND THE ROYALIZATION

OF AMERICA

.   .   .   .
  .   .   .
    .   .
      .

In early January 1746, the *American Weekly Mercury* carried a piece entitled "An Essay on the *British* Computations of Time, Coin, Weights, and Measures." The author suggested fixing the visibly flawed Julian calendar by realigning it with the solar year. He called for thirteen months of 28 days, apparently unaware it would provide only 364 days for each year. He advocated naming the new calendar "in perpetual memory of his majesty King *George*, denominated the *Georgian* account," and calling the thirteenth month "*Georgy*, in honour of King George, . . . as well as *July* was denominated from *Julius*, and *August*" from the Caesars. "As to the 366th day in every 4th year," he continued, "might it not be intercalated between the new and old year after *Christmas day*, and be set apart for solemn prayers for the prosperity of our *king* and countries, and be called the *British Lustrum, Olympiad*, or the *national day*."[1]

The author of "An Essay on the *British* Computations of Time" addressed an issue central to the empire's American colonies: the royalization of public life and political time. After 1688, imperial officials established a number of annual rites that celebrated Protestant monarchy and the history that led to it. This political calendar was designed, if the idea of that much coherence is not an overstatement, to establish emotional ties between the most distant colonist and the empire's Protestant rulers, to give the emerging imperial contract human form. The behaviors associated with these rites, like marching in procession, toasting the monarchy, bonfires around which people drank, the illumination of homes, fireworks, and night-time feasting, initially worried some colonials, who feared that such behavior would encourage sin and bring on the wrath of God. Nonetheless, this new political calendar and the behaviors connected to it won wide support

---

1. *American Weekly Mercury* (Philadelphia), Dec. 24, 1745–Jan. 1, 1746.

by the 1730s, as colonials accepted the imperial identity associated with these annual rites. The piety and customary practices that defined life in the seventeenth century were joined to swelling emotions created by imperially related spectacles to shape a new political personality, the provincial Briton. This restructuring—linking inner devotion to the emotions generated by public spectacle—helped define the British peace.

The widespread establishment of these imperial rites should have marked the beginning of a long period of internal stability in Britain's American provinces and the empire as a whole. Colonials willingly expressed their devotion to the Hanoverian dynasty in the annual public celebrations. In short, the British state's ritual structure had been successfully planted in a short period of time.

Dangers lurked, though, in this remarkable political reordering. The royal rites inculcated in colonials an understanding of the monarchy and imperial constitution that diverged from British norms. The Glorious Revolution's settlement came to be understood as assuring the Hanoverian succession and a Protestant political culture. The key imperial tie became the emotional one between the individual and the ruler created in part by the spectacles that celebrated the monarch's life and the defeat of Catholicism in England.

Paradoxically, parliamentary supremacy became firmly established in England in the same period. Royal rites played a far smaller role in the annual calendar, and there was widespread ambivalence about the German-born monarchs. The empire's public political culture became a mirror image of what we have too often assumed, with momentous implications for its future. It was not that a royalized core controlled a latently republicanized or democratic fringe, but rather that the imperial fringe's enthusiasm for Protestant monarchy contrasted sharply with the metropolitan center's apathy toward the monarch. By 1740, this startling imperial paradox had indeed begun to emerge, with momentous implications for the empire. Before it did, though, some fought a rearguard action to preserve what had been.

• • •

Samuel Sewall's Lament

On the evening of June 11, 1696, Samuel Sewall again turned to the ever-expanding diary that would make him Puritan New England's ambassador to modernity. As on so many other days, he stopped to record his struggle against change and history itself. "I strove," he wrote, "with my might that in stead of Tuesday, Thursday, and Satterday in every week, it might be said, Third, fifth and seventh day in every Week." The former custom had pagan origins and thus affronted the God Sewall sought to honor with every action. It was, he knew, a losing battle. He could not "prevail, hardly one in the Council would secund me, and many spake against it very earnestly." The others insisted "twas the speech of the English Nation; mend it in the Fasts; mend it every where or no where; others said persons would scarce know what days were intended; and in England would call us Quakers." Still he fought on, finally appealing to the Bible, declaring, "the Week only, of all parcells of time, was of Divine Institution, erected by God as a monumental pillar for a memorial of the Creation." But it was all to no avail.[2]

The transformation from a covenant to an imperial contract as a guiding political motif was often a subtle one, but it did not go unnoticed by contemporaries. Some rushed to embrace monarchy and imperial norms, whereas others found themselves filled with apprehension as the behaviors associated with empire began to be established. This was true everywhere in British America in one way or another; all somehow lived an unsettling transformation in the years after the Glorious Revolution.

But perhaps no one was more anxious than early Boston's remarkably fretful chronicler, Samuel Sewall. He was obsessive even by the standards of the culture that produced the jeremiad sermon. Yet the coupling of his exacting eye for detail with his belief that every change meant deviation from a Puritan ideal and thus should be recorded are what made him an ideal historical observer. Across the span of his long public life, he watched in growing dismay as the holy commonwealth he knew as a boy became a royal province, as covenant gave way to contract. He understood this change in both cosmic and worldly terms; a growing ungodliness within the population was tied to an assault on the position of Puritan oligarchy that had dominated Massachusetts since 1630.

The belief that the concerns of empire and monarchy would affront God and corrupt the New England Way lay at the center of Sewall's obsession. His complaint with the emerging imperial order revolved around its expression of authority in time, in the annual political calendar that celebrated a monarchy whose appointment was so obviously the product of dynastic struggle. The special covenant between the Puritans and God was being put aside, and an imperial contract that called for the realization of spiritual identity in a temporal Protestant political culture would be its pale substitute. "Tuesday" and "Wednesday" threatened the Puritan commonwealth precisely because they represented the normalization of New England in imperial time and history. Empire placed man before God,

2. *The Diary of Samuel Sewall*, I, *1674–1700*, MHS, *Collections*, 5th Ser., V (Boston, 1878), 428.

situated change within secular reference points, and created a public life centered on political rituals rather than inner spiritual knowledge. For those of Sewall's generation who lived through the beginnings of royalization with an idealized past always calling to them, change and decline became the same thing.

Sewall knew that the imposition of monarchical political culture created a massive dilemma for New England's leadership. Puritans disdained the keeping of yearly holidays; empires depended on them. Puritans honored God; empires celebrated monarchs. To suppress the behaviors associated with empire amounted to defiance of the Protestant monarch and the imperial order. This was not possible; the empire was at war with France, first during King William's War (1689–1697) and then again during Queen Anne's War (1702–1713). There was no alternative in any event, with the deposed male heir of the Stuart family lurking in France.

Sewall recognized the paradox, but, try as he might, he could extract neither himself nor Massachusetts from it. The threat was less obvious than that posed by James II and Andros, but it was the same one. Sewall and others realized that the less coercive, Protestant character of imperial intervention after 1688 had created a more formidable opponent than even the Stuart governor, for the enemy ultimately became themselves. Over time, colonials accepted and then embraced empire and all that came with it.

Although imperialization had begun in 1692 with the new royal charter, Sewall knew that Queen Anne's coronation in 1702 marked the beginning of a sustained cultural assault on the New England Way. Imperial officials quickly enlisted colonials in the battle against their own traditions. The empire's political culture provided manna for those who craved public honor in an oligarchic society that treated it like a rare commodity. At the dawn of Anne's reign, Sewall remembered that, on artillery election day, "Mr. Coleman preaches from Heb. 11. 33. Sermon is well liked of. Had much abode to persuade Mr. Willard to dine with me. Said ministers were disgusted because the Representatives went first at the Proclaiming the Queen; and that by order of our House [the Council of the Massachusetts General Court]."[3]

In the context of that time, such a seemingly trivial matter was critical. Group order in a formal procession carried with it social meaning because such political theater expressed and reaffirmed the established order. By giving the elected representatives priority over the clergy in a ritual designed to proclaim the queen, the council heralded a change in New England that would increasingly trouble

3. *The Diary of Samuel Sewall, II, 1699–1714*, MHS, *Collections*, 5th Ser., VI (Boston, 1929), 57.

Sewall. The procession displayed the representatives as higher in social status than the ministry.

Sewall would soon express a more expansive anxiety over aspects of the cult of monarchy being introduced to New England. His apprehension came to the surface in early February 1703, when he confronted Governor Joseph Dudley over the remembrance of Queen Anne's birthday on the Sabbath. In particular, Sewall challenged the plans to illuminate the public buildings in Boston. This would violate the sanctity of the Lord's Day and encourage behaviors unacceptable to the Puritan leadership. Accompanied by several prominent members of Boston's elite, he acted so that "the profanation of the Sabbath might be prevented." But, instead of the cooperation they expected, these councilmen received the obscuring talk of an imperial bureaucrat determined to assert the monarch's supremacy. "I said," recorded the frustrated Sewall, "twould be most for the Honor of God; and that would be most for the Honor and Safety of Queen Anne." The governor replied evasively, "Twould be hard for him to forbid it, considering how good the Queen was, what successes God had given her. I answered it could not be introduced into the Town-House without his Excellency's Order, for under his Excellency the Government of the Town was (partly) committed to us. Gov.r answer'd not a word." The queen's honor was placed before God, and Sewall could neither accept nor reject this change; to do the latter amounted to treason, whereas the former offended God.[4]

Instead, Sewall became a morbid observer of, and an unwilling participant in, the growing cult of monarchy, often confiding his broken-hearted misgivings to his famous chronicle. In 1710, he recalled another celebration of "the Queen's Birth-Day." He and the other council members treated "the Govr. at the Green Dragon, with Col. Vetch and several others. Mr. Tho. Bridge, Mr. Wadsworth, and Mr. Colman were there . . . After our return to the Council-Chamber . . . I grew weary and uneasy, and even slipped away without drinking [toasting]." These subtle defiances expressed his disdain for the new political culture that ate away at his Puritan soul.[5]

On February 6, 1714, Sewall's worst fears about monarchical political culture's disruptive potential came true. That evening, a magistrate summoned him to deal with a problem at a South End tavern. There were "Disorders at the Tavern. . . . He desired me that I would accompany Mr. Bromfield and Constable Howell thither." Sewall confronted the rowdy celebrants, but, as he angrily recalled, "they refus'd to go away. Said they were there to drink to the Queen's Health, and they

4. Ibid., 72–73.
5. Ibid., 273.

had many other Healths to drink." Since the tavern walkers invoked the queen, their actions were more difficult to suppress. These rowdies, seeing him hesitate, "call'd for more Drink."[6]

Growing insolent, the partyers repeatedly defied their better by means of imperial political culture. They "drank to me, I took notice of the Affront to them. [They] Said must and would stay upon that Solemn occasion. Mr. John Netmaker drank the Queen's Health to me. I told him I drank none; upon that he ceas'd." But the abuse did not end there. "Mr. Brinley," wrote Sewall, "put on his Hat to affront me. I made him take it off. I threaten'd to send some of them to prison; that did not move them. They said they could but pay their Fine. and doing that they might stay. I told them if they had not a care, they would be guilty of a Riot." He took their names and had them arrested the next day, but even then they invoked the monarch against him and those who had assisted him. Two days later, "John Netmaker [one of the revellers] was fin'd 5s for profane cursing; saying to — Colson, the Constable's Assistance, God damn ye; because the said Colson refus'd to Drink the Queen's Health." Royalism's subversive quality was apparent in the passage. Behaviors legitimate in imperial eyes could undermine the order in New England.[7]

The last Stuart queen's death in 1714 brought a sarcastic outburst from Boston's own Pepys. Encountering one of his fellow councillors in what he described as "a very sad countenance," Sewall inquired as to what had occurred. When told the "Sad News!" of the queen's death, the chronicler recorded his relief that the news was not "Boston was burnt again." By the next week, Boston's ruling oligarchy had proclaimed George I king, and Sewall might have looked forward to a return to the Puritan political culture of his youth. The German's claim to the British throne was entirely dependent on his religious faith, as Sewall knew. But this hope was dashed as well, for this German prince needed a British identity more than his native-born predecessor did.[8]

There would be no going back. During a political crisis in February 1715, he "drew up a Proclamation" that used the phrase "King William and Queen Mary of Blessed Memory." Challenged by others for not including the recently deceased Stuart, Queen Anne, along with his beloved Calvinist rulers, he "pleaded when spoken to, They were our Founders." The lieutenant governor, he bitterly

6. Ibid., 421.

7. Ibid.

8. *The Diary of Samuel Sewall*, III, *1674–1729*, MHS, *Collections*, 5th Ser., VII (Boston, 1882), 19.

recorded, "spake hard against it, unless the same was said for Queen Anne, so twas struck out." Even in death, the last Stuart queen kept her grip on the New England soul.[9]

Sewall looked on sympathetically as some clergymen waged a rearguard action against the empire's political culture. In 1715, Sewall recorded with pleasure that "Mr. Wadsworth preaches from PS. 7. 12. Speaks against Health-drinking, Illuminations, Bonfires etc." The new political culture's lifeblood, the public owning of loyalty, offended these ministers, and yet all they could do was launch one sermon after another denouncing the changes.[10]

No minister, no man, no movement could stop the subtle but overwhelming drive to legitimate the monarchy and make real the imperial contract. Year after year, Sewall noted every minor change, every act of defiance directed against the old Puritan oligarchy, every incident where king was placed before God. On April 1, 1719, he "dehorted Sam. Hirst and Grindal Rawson from playing the Idle Tricks because 'twas first of April." Those that did, the ever-grumpy Sewall complained, "were the greatest fools that did so. N.E. Men came hither to avoid anniversary days, the keeping of them, such as the 25th of Decr."[11]

Sewall's disgust never became a transforming force. But that was as much a matter of inner restraint as an acknowledgment of monarchical power. He hated what was happening to his Puritan world, but he realized that the alternatives to the Hanoverian line—regicide and republicanism, absolutism and popery, those riders from the home islands that had tortured the empire in the seventeenth century—were even worse.

So early Boston's most famous diarist began to accept. He, too, found himself marking national anniversaries, but even the fact that it was "Monday, April, the eleventh (Coronation-day of K. William and Qu. Mary)" that he chose to recall ultimately gave him no solace. The long-dead Protestant monarchs were still, after all, only human, and remembering them annually somehow put historical understanding before faith in God.[12]

Sewall did not bear the torturous changes alone. Provincials everywhere shared the journey to empire. The iconography of the first imperial rite to be widely established in the colonies eased the pain caused by this transformation. As difficult as it may seem to believe, hideous effigies of the pope and other

9. Ibid., 38.
10. Ibid., 68.
11. Ibid., 217.
12. Ibid., 249.

Catholics carted and burned on November 5 each year helped seal the imperial contract and make the first British empire real.

• • •

Pope's Day Established

"Yesterday," reported a writer in the *Virginia Gazette*, "being the Anniversary Thanksgiving for the Gunpowder Treason Plot, when King, Lords and Commons were deliver'd from the bloody Designs of the Papists, was kept as usual." This writer knew, as did most of his readers, that the day also marked the anniversary of "the Landing of King William at Torbay, who came to redeem us from standing Armies in Times of Peace, from septennial Parliaments, and other Incroachments of the Prerogative," and that made the day doubly special. Virginians, like Boston's North and South Enders who built the great "popes carts," remembered the importance of November 5 and used that day for political education.[13]

The establishment of Pope's Day as an annual public holiday played a critical part in the negotiation between locale and metropolis over the empire's character. As the writer to the *Virginia Gazette* implied, Pope's Day, the celebration of the foiling of Guy Fawkes's plot to blow up king and Parliament in 1605, provided a yearly reminder to Protestants of the Glorious Revolution's benefits. The celebration's changing nature between the Restoration in 1660 and 1730 could be read as part of the continuing process that reconciled Protestant piety with a secular empire moored in dynastic and historical time. The spectacles altered emotional ties between center and periphery as well as social relationships within the colonies.

Official decrees established Pope's Day as an imperial holiday in the seventeenth century, and, throughout the eighteenth century, it would be legitimated by such declarations. In the 1660s, Charles II ordered November 5 to be remembered as an anniversary holiday throughout England's American provinces. A royal decree to the Massachusetts General Court in May 1665 ordered the Bay Colony's government to keep "the 5th of November" as a day of thanksgiving for "the miraculous preservation of our king and country from the gunpowder treason." In October 1667, the Massachusetts legislature acknowledged November 5 to be a day of public thanksgiving and humiliation, and Pope's Day became an annual holiday in New England.[14]

The London government needed to exert pressure throughout the northern

---

13. *Virginia Gazette* (Williamsburg), Feb. 4–11, 1736.

14. Nathaniel B. Shurtleff, ed., *Records of the Governor and Company of the Massachusetts Bay in New England*, VI (Boston, Mass., 1854), part 2, 211–212, 346.

colonies to establish the holiday because the settlers resisted royal political rites. In a world filled with Samuel Sewalls, how could it be otherwise? For the Dutch in the midatlantic, such holidays represented further anglicization, and the Quakers of West Jersey and Pennsylvania, like New England Puritans, resisted for theological and social reasons. In New England, at least, Sewall and the rest of the Puritan elite continued subtle resistance to the holiday until after 1688.[15]

The Pope's Day celebrations helped reconcile colonists to empire when events after the Glorious Revolution made imperial integration inevitable. Pope's Day gave both impulses—religious and political—play. November 5 focused attention on a historical event (Guy Fawkes's plot) and a historical personality in a manner potentially antagonistic to the northern colonies' religious-political subcultures, based as they were on Calvinist beliefs that included an aversion to annual holidays. At the same time, the holiday celebrated providential intervention that upheld a Protestant ruler and referred, at least early in the eighteenth century, to the Glorious Revolution's triumph over a Catholic, popish ruler. It was this duality that allowed imperial officials to successfully insinuate the rite into the provinces. In so doing, they began the imperialization of public time in British America. Piety was served, political allegiance was owned.

The initial ritual form of November 5 expressed the reconciliation of the colonial past and the cosmopolitan future. Daytime sermons denouncing sin and Catholicism, not unlike the occasional sermons common to Calvinist subcultures in the seventeenth century, became widespread on November 5. It was then celebrated with considerably more mirth in the evening around bonfires, usually on the edge of towns or, as in Boston, on the Common. Warned by decree, crowds gathered and consumed alcohol (often provided by the authorities or leading men) and invariably the pope's effigy would be burned, again usually with official sanction or officially supplied kindling. In 1689, Jacob Leisler reported the burning of just such an effigy during the anniversary's celebration in strife-torn New York City. This act defined the political culture as specifically Protestant.[16]

Colonials derived the practice of creating pope effigies from England. London crowds burned hordes of such effigies on November 5 during the Popish Plot hysteria and Exclusion Crisis of the late 1670s and early 1680s. A detailed account of such a procession in England on November 5, 1673, during one of the initial anti-Catholic, anti-Stuart outbursts was sent by John Pynchon to John Winthrop, Jr. Pynchon reported that "thousands of the City [London] [ap]prentices met in

15. Ibid., 346.

16. Jacob Leisler to Edwin Stede, Nov. 23, 1689, Papers of Jacob Leisler, placed on H-Net by David Voorhees, associate editor.

Paul's churchyard," created a "Pope and his Cardinals in their pontificals," and then "carried them to Smithfield and burnt them with great shouts." Although Winthrop was unlikely to have encouraged New Englanders to emulate them, other travelers brought accounts to North America, and they were amply described in printed material imported from England. Even the regicide John Dixwell, living in hiding in New Haven, received word of the great outburst of antipopery following the uncovering of the purported Popish Plot against Charles II in the late 1670s.[17]

Changes in behavior on Pope's Day after 1688 were related to its overt imperialization. Although early rites seem to have been fixed in their location and focused on the pope and the Providential defense of Protestantism immediately after 1688, by the late 1690s, yearly processions on November 5 became commonplace in the port towns. Processions were, by their nature, territorial and thus political. By parading, those who participated asserted the entire community's antipopish values. The earliest processions in the 1690s still had an iconography centered on the large pope effigy, mounted on a pole or lashed to a cart (carting being a judicial punishment in many areas). This ferocious anti-Catholic symbol remained a part of the processions through the eighteenth century.[18]

However, the processional iconography quickly came to favor the political over the cosmological and theological while still insisting on their fusion. This began in Boston as early as 1702, when the effigy of the Stuart Pretender (the claimant to the throne from the deposed House of Stuart) was added to the cart, a practice that soon spread to other port towns. Anti-Stuart demonstrators in London used the same iconography in 1715–1716 when the Hanoverian succession was in doubt. This iconography might have been in place earlier in London, suggesting transatlantic influences traveling in either or both directions. The effigies' arrangement implied papal control over the House of Stuart as the Pretender was shown to be a puppet of the pope and Satan. The Pretender's image was a potent anti-Catholic symbol for certain, but also a specifically British image, designed to express the unity of an increasingly complex, far-flung empire against a royal house understood to be illegitimate. The processions thus validated the

17. John Pynchon to John Winthrop, Jr., Apr. 24, 1674, in Carl Bridenbaugh, ed., *The Pynchon Papers*, I, Colonial Society of Massachusetts, *Publications*, LX (Boston, 1982), 125–126. For the English precedents, see David Cressy, *Bonfires and Bells: National Memory and the Protestant Calendar in Elizabethan and Stuart England* (Berkeley, Calif., 1990), 147; Francis Prince to James Davids, June 5, 1679, Amsterdam, in Dixwell Papers, box 1, New Haven Colony Historical Society, New Haven, Conn.

18. Esther Forbes, *Paul Revere and the World He Lived In* (Boston, 1942), 230.

Dutch William III and later the German Georges who sat on the British throne by virtue of their Protestant genealogy.[19]

Imperial concerns encouraged the gradual elaboration of processional iconography. The effigies paraded in Boston in the 1740s consisted of the devil, "with a pitchfork in his hand and covered with tar and feathers," his supernatural assistants, the pope, "dressed in gorgeous attire with a large white wig on, over which was an enormous gold-laced hat," and the Stuart Pretender, mounted on a large mobile stage and presented in a manner that suggested Satan's domination over the pope and the Stuarts. Variants on these themes existed. At Newburyport, Massachusetts, the processional cart contained monks and friars to assist the pope, and no doubt other local renditions of the cosmopolitan themes existed across the colonies. At New York, "the Pope, the Pretender and the D——l" were carried through the streets, then "Burnt . . . in the Commons near this City" by a large crowd. Similar celebrations occurred in other northern port towns. Evidence suggests that this base iconography was used as far south as Alexandria, Virginia, and Charleston, South Carolina, although detailed descriptions are only available from later in the century. Certainly, some type of formal parade occurred in Charleston on November 5, 1747. It appears to have been both a celebration of Pope's Day and, more prominently, of the anniversary of William III's landing at Torbay.[20]

At midcentury, provincial concerns over the continued warfare between Britain and Catholic France again altered the iconography and the behavior in the processions, particularly at Boston and New York. In the former port, "Admiral Byng hanging from a gallows" was added to the moving stage, positioned between the devil and the pope; Bing had been court-martialed and shot in England for refusing to fight during a naval conflict against the French in the Seven

19. Nicholas Rogers, *Crowds, Culture, and Politics in Georgian Britain* (Oxford, 1998), 38, 230; Cressy, *Bonfires and Bells*, 141–155.

20. Forbes, *Paul Revere and the World He Lived In*, 95, 230; *New-York Weekly Journal*, Nov. 7, 1748; John Gilmary Shea, "Pope-Day in America," paper read before the United States Catholic Historical Society, Jan. 19, 1888, Library of Congress Broadsides, 5–6. Nan Netherton et al., *Fairfax County, Virginia: A History* (Fairfax, Va., 1978), 110–111, gives a description of a Pope's Day procession in that port town during the imperial crisis that included "effigies of the pope, Lord North, Massachusetts Governor Barnard and Lt. Governor Hutchinson, and the devil." They were "carried through town with fifes and drums and then cast into the flames." Charleston parade: *South-Carolina Gazette* (Charleston), Nov. 10, 1747. The day was also William III's birthday. It strikes me that southern celebrations were perhaps formal out of fear of disorder among slaves, a slave insurrection, or fraternizing between slaves and poor whites.

PLATE 2. *Silver beaker with etching of Pope's Day procession (3 views). By Joseph Leddel. Although the November 5 celebrations of the foiling of Guy Fawkes's 1605 plot to kill James I are most closely identified with the artisans of Boston, the holiday was remembered in many towns and by people at all levels of society. The stylized etching of a procession put on this silver beaker around 1750 in New York City reflected the impact that the imperial rites were having on provincial populations. Museum of the City of New York*

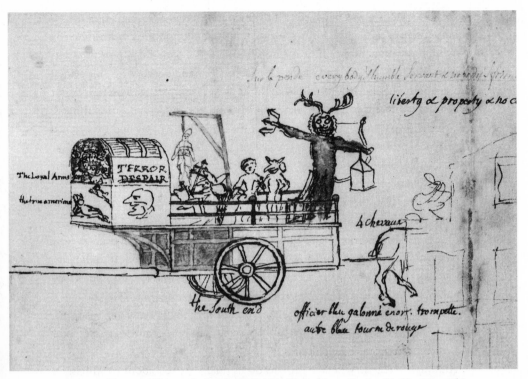

PLATE 3. *"Boston Affairs—the South End" (detail). By Pierre Eugène Du Simitière. This sketch of the cart created by the residents of Boston's South End in 1767 shows that it carried not only the pope, the devil, and their assistants but the "Loyal Arms," almost certainly the arms of the Hanoverian dynasty. The Library Company of Philadelphia*

Years' War. At New York, a Pope's Day procession stopped before a home where a captured French general was imprisoned in 1755. The revelers threatened to tear the house down, only to have the general, familiar with French mobs, send down silver coins to his tormentors, to which the procession responded with cheers.[21]

In the same period, female figures began to be added to the processional carts in New England, particularly in Boston. They acknowledged contemporary concerns over gender relations and morality in a society at war. One of these was certainly "Pope Joan," who embodied the moral corruption of the Catholic, anti-Hanoverian forces arrayed against the first British empire. Joan, an emblem of

21. Forbes, *Paul Revere and the World He Lived In*, 230; Paul A. Gilje, *The Road to Mobocracy: Popular Disorder in New York City, 1763–1834* (Chapel Hill, N.C., 1987), 26; *New-York Gazette; or, the Weekly Post-Boy*, Nov. 10, 1755; Shea, "Pope-Day in America."

Catholic hypocrisy, was believed to be a medieval, cross-dressing woman who became pope and then gave birth during a procession honoring Saint John. By constructing sexual immorality as Catholic and female, the Boston procession-makers sought to expose and mock Papist hypocrisy and perhaps confine sexual expression in their own community to the appropriate channels, a task no doubt increasingly difficult in a port town awash in soldiers, sailors, and prostitutes.[22]

Print allowed those in outlying areas to learn of Pope's Day and experience the ritual vicariously. As early as the seventeenth century, New England almanacs, the mass literature of that time, recorded the "Powder Plot, 1605," on their calendars. In the eighteenth century, the *Virginia Almanac* recorded "Nov. 5 Powder Plot," and the other eighteenth-century almanacs from the region routinely noted the English nation's salvation from popish intrigue in 1605. Often, these publications situated the custom historically and provided instruction on how to perform its rituals. Nathaniel Ames's *An Astronomical Diary; or, An Almanack for the Year of Our Lord Christ 1737* provided instructions of a sort for Pope's Day celebrants. On the calendar's November leaf, Ames wrote, "Ere you pretend / to burn the Pope / Secure the Papists / with a Rope." By procession and print, a politicized understanding of this holiday that fused Protestantism and empire was spread throughout the colonies.[23]

Although the gentry in some towns occasionally fretted about rowdiness in the processions, wiser heads realized the rite's value. Year after year, the Pope's Day celebrations reminded colonial Britons of all ranks of "the Wonderful deliverance the Protestants met with on Nov. 5th." Pope's Day battles were fun, people occasionally got out of control, but there was a deeper purpose to the holiday. It linked emotionally so-called popular beliefs with the culture of power in a Protestant empire, thus defusing social tensions. Pope's Day processions articulated the empire's central values. Although we cannot understand all the motivations that brought people to join in these parades or all the meanings their behaviors imparted to themselves and others, that much, the owning of a Protestant political culture, is clear in the celebrations.[24]

22. Forbes, *Paul Revere and the World He Lived In*, 95; *South End Forever, North End Forever: Extraordinary Verses on Pope-Night; or, A Commemoration of the Fifth of November* . . . ([Boston, 1768]), broadside 36, no. 28, Library of Congress Broadsides.

23. [William Brattle], *An Almanack of the Coelestiall Motions* . . . ([Cambridge, Mass.], 1694), November 5; *The Virginia Almanac for the Year of Our Lord God* . . . *1741* (Williamsburg, Va., 1741), November 5; Nathaniel Ames, *An Astronomical Diary; or, An Almanack for the Year of Our Lord Christ 1737*, November 5 (Boston, 1737).

24. The Diary of John Leach, Nov. 5, 1758, MHS. For a detailed discussion of Pope's

By the 1740s, the Pope's Day rites were part of an imperialized provincial political calendar that had come to include twenty-six official holidays. November 5 celebrations acted as the wedge in establishing this royal political calendar. Because it emphasized Protestantism and God's intervention in preserving the English nation from popish conspiracies, Pope's Day found widespread acceptance in the provinces.

Other celebrations of Protestant monarchy were established in the first three decades of the eighteenth century. Those red-letter days, as they were called, inculcated a devotion to the Hanoverian monarchy among British Americans that seems to have intensified with each passing year.

· · ·

The March of Empire

"Wednesday last," declared the *South-Carolina Gazette* on February 26, 1731/2, "being her Majesty's Birthday, the same was observed here, with all the Demonstrations of Joy suitable to the Occasion." The celebration brought, at least for a day, a halt to the bitter turmoil that had plagued South Carolina for more than a decade and had prompted the royalization of its proprietary government. "The Hon. Col. *Broughton, President,*" it was reported, "and the rest of the honourable Members of the Commons House of Assembly, and the Hon. *John Lloyd,* Esq., their *Speaker,*" joined the royal governor Robert Johnson at the council chambers. Together, they walked in procession to Charleston's fort, "where, under several discharges of the great Guns, the Healths of her *Majesty,* and all the *Royal Family* being drank" before being joined by "a great Number of Gentlemen of the best Distinction in the Province" who were treated to a banquet by the governor. That evening, "Madam *Johnson* made a very elegant Entertainment for the Ladies, at his Excellency's House."[25]

This remembrance of Queen Caroline's birthday reveals the character of royal celebrations, and it offers tantalizing hints as to why provincials embraced them. Such ceremonies pulled together the factious elites, heirs to the turmoil that wracked the colonies in the late seventeenth and early eighteenth centuries, in the common identity of Briton. Those who participated in the rites articulated a sense of imperial order in locales thousands of miles from the throne. By 1740, public spectacles celebrating monarch and empire, involving local elites and military display, occurred at least six times a year in the major population centers,

---

Day, see Brendan McConville, "Pope's Day Revisited, 'Popular' Culture Reconsidered," *Explorations in Early American Culture,* IV (2000), 258–280.

25. *South-Carolina Gazette,* Feb. 26–Mar. 4, 1731/2.

while more modest activities occurred on twenty other days. A never-ending cycle of rites reminded provincials throughout the year of the benefits that flowed from the Hanoverian monarchy and the Protestant imperial order.

These monarchical rites were first marked in the colonies during the unhappy decades of the late seventeenth century. Before 1660, Dutch domination of the midatlantic, the Chesapeake settlements' dispersed physical character, the Puritans' intense hostility to cyclical celebrations, and the political turmoil in the home islands inhibited the royal holidays' establishment. Early attempts by the Stuart kings to institute imperial holidays faltered until late in their era, when James II, anxious to assert his authority in North America, repeatedly ordered that the key anniversaries of his reign be remembered with formal public displays. On April 21, 1685, for instance, the New York authorities ordered "all the foot militia. . . . paraded before the gate of Fort James, on the next Thursday . . . his majesty King James . . . to be proclaimed [his coronation]." That many in the northern colonies were less than eager to embrace this particular monarch can scarcely be doubted, but events changed attitudes.[26]

After James II's flight from the throne in 1688, William and Mary ordered royal celebrations in the provinces to assert their own legitimacy. They used the royal decree; orders carrying the royal seal would arrive in the provinces and command the governing elite to arrange a suitable display of their loyalty on the appropriate days. Initially, the monarchs decreed three annual holidays: the monarch's birthday, coronation day, and Pope's Day. The occasional arrival of imperial governors also warranted ceremonies. Between 1689 and 1720, with the empire at war with France and the colonists keen to assert their loyalty to Great Britain, these celebrations became a normal part of political life in the major port towns.

The monarch's birthday was planted almost as soon as Pope's Day. In 1700, for example, the New York City Council ordered that "the Mayor Provide firewood for Bonfires" on November 4, "being the birth of Our sovereign Lord King William," and for November 5 to celebrate the national deliverance from popery. A document from 1702 recorded that the military officers in New York City treated the king's troops to "madera wyn" on November 4. Evidence suggests coronation day and imperial entrances occurred in the same period, though detailed descriptions do not appear for many colonies.[27]

The celebrations sparked by Queen Anne's ascension in 1702 reveal that Virginians used the same sort of rites. By decree, six militia companies (numbering

26. I. N. Phelps Stokes, *The Iconography of Manhattan Island, 1498–1909*, IV (New York, 1922), 334.

27. Ibid., 426, 432.

around two thousand men), local Native Americans, and the population settled near Williamsburg gathered at the College of William and Mary. Officials announced William's death, the empire's colors were paraded wrapped in black drape, and officials followed them on horses clad in mourning cloth. The governor then proclaimed Anne queen, and the authorities provided entertainment to the assembled crowd over a two-day period.[28]

Over time, the rites of empire became more elaborate. A comparison of imperial entrances in Boston in 1692 and 1730 for native-son governors illustrates the nature of these changes. In 1692, Samuel Sewall reported that "eight Companies and two from Charlestown guard Sir William [Phips, Massachusetts's first imperial governor under the new charter]" when he arrived in the colony. An all-day argument ensued because the welcoming ceremonies threatened to violate custom and the Sabbath. But once the matter was settled, Phips and his councillors walked in this procession "to the Townhouse, where the Commissions were read and Oaths taken." Like the early monarchical birthday celebrations, this entrance was limited in its scope and duration, tempered in this case by the prevalent Puritanism.[29]

By the 1730s, though, royal celebrations had become much more complex. When New England native Jonathan Belcher arrived in Boston to govern the colony in 1730, he found all of Boston "preparing for his . . . Reception . . . the Militia . . . were under Arms . . . to welcome their Captain-General." Throughout the town, the Puritan past's somber aesthetic was put aside; "the Turrets and Balcony's were hung with Carpets, and almost every Vessel was blazon'd with a rich Variety of Colours." As Belcher moved from the harbor toward the town, the castle guns fired a salute to his party. "The Hon. Lieut. Governor and Council, the Judges and Justices, and an almost numberless Multitude of Gentlemen" received their favorite son. Pennants and flags were raised; cheering, bell ringing, and another cannonade followed. Belcher proceeded to the council chambers to hear his commissions read. "The vast Multitude of Spectators," correspondents reported, "express'd, in their united Shouts, an unusual Joy. . . . The . . . Regiment discharged their Duty in triple Vollies." The civil and military authorities then escorted the governor to a dinner, "and the Evening concluded with a Bonfire and Illuminations."[30]

28. Mary Newton Stanard, *Colonial Virginia: Its People and Customs* (Philadelphia, 1917), 139–140.

29. *Diary of Samuel Sewall*, I, *1674–1700*, MHS, *Collections*, 5th Ser., V, 360.

30. *Pennsylvania Gazette* (Philadelphia), Aug. 20–Aug. 27, 1730; Michael C. Batinski, *Jonathan Belcher, Colonial Governor* (Lexington, Ky., 1996), 1–2. See also *Boston Weekly*

A similar elaboration occurred in the midatlantic. A New York newspaper described one imperial entrance thus: "His Excellency our Governour was attended at his House in Fort George by the Council, Assembly, Merchants, and other Principal Gentlemen," Fort George's garrison "being under Arms and the Cannon round the Ramparts firing while His Majesty, the Queen's, the Prince's, the Royal Families, and their Royal Highnesses, the Prince and Princess of Orange's Healths were drunk." That night, while "the whole City was illuminated, his Excellency and Lady gave a splendid Ball."[31]

Developments in the 1730s suggest that provincial Americans embraced the royal holidays. First, the celebrations spread to new areas. By the 1730s, colonials beyond Boston, New York, Newport, Charleston, and other ports had adopted the yearly rites. Second, royal authorities successfully added new holidays—the Queen's Birthday, the Prince of Wales's Birthday, and a number of others associated with royal power—to the four original holidays.

This expansion was in all likelihood related to George II's ascension to the throne and subsequent thirty-plus-year reign. This monarch, his wife, Queen Caroline, and their offspring captured popular imagination in the provinces and provided needed political and symbolic consistency to Protestant Britons throughout the empire. George II's status was further enhanced in British America when provincials learned he had successfully led British and Hanoverian forces against "the French at Dettingen in Germany," as one colonial remembered it. Colonials saw George II as an upholder of British power and the European Protestant interest, and the rites celebrated the Hanoverian monarchy.[32]

As early as the 1710s, populations beyond Boston and New York were celebrating the royal holidays. When James Moore, Jr., took power in South Carolina in 1719, in effect becoming the colony's first royal governor, Charleston's population greeted him with elaborate demonstrations and displays. His arrival highlighted the ability of these rites to establish authority. The proprietary governor, Robert Johnson, tried to resist the transfer of power, but, upon appearing in Charleston on December 21, he found "the militia drawn up in the market-place, with colors flying at the fort, and on-board all the ships in the harbor" as the townspeople prepared an imperial entrance for their new chief magistrate. Johnson soon gave up. In 1739, the *Virginia Gazette* reported on the King's Birthday celebrations. The

News-Letter, Aug. 6–20, 1730; *New-England Weekly Journal* (Boston), Aug. 11, 17, Sept. 7, 1730.

31. Esther Singleton, *Social New York under the Georges, 1714–1776* (New York, 1902), 304.

32. William Tudor, ed., *Deacon Tudor's Diary* (Boston, 1896), 2.

"flag was hoisted on the Capitol [in Williamsburg]; at noon the Cannon at the Governor's House were trebly discharg'd; and at Night, most of the Gentlemens and Other Houses of Note were illuminated." The governor "was pleas'd to give a handsome Entertainment," and throughout the colony the forts and ships fired their cannon. A few years later, the newly arrived settlers of Savannah, Georgia, remembered George II's coronation with "Gun-Firing and drinking healths to the Royal Family . . . under the Flag." The lack of well-developed urban areas in the southern colonies inhibited marching, but meeting under the flag affirmed local loyalties to the extended British nation. Generally, these celebrations were similar to the established pattern in the colonies to the north.[33]

Royal celebrations spread quickly into the southern interior despite the scarcity of towns and cities. This expansion suggests that the population considered them a normal part of life. Even the most isolated population centers felt the importance of reaffirming their place in the empire by public displays of loyalty. John Fontaine, traveling with Virginia's governor Alexander Spotswood in April 1716, recalled, "We set out . . . for Christiana. For this house is the most outward settlement on this side of Virginia. . . . It is an inclosure of five sides, made only with pallisadoes." Despite the settlement's rude character, the garrison thought that an imperial governor's approach demanded an entrance ceremony, and the fort's five cannon "fired to welcome the Governor. . . . After all the ceremony [was] over. . . . we were well entertained." On September 12, 1727, Caesar Rodney, the father of Delaware's Declaration of Independence signer, recalled that his neighbor James Mackey "told me that King George the 2d wast peclaimed [at his coronation] at Philadelphia and New Castel." Although the Delaware countryside might not have had its own ceremonies, farmers there discussed and remembered Philadelphia's imperial rites.[34]

Similar royal celebrations occurred in the British West Indies. In 1741, Barba-

33. Robert M. Weir, *Colonial South Carolina: A History* (New York, 1983); Edward McCrady, *The History of South Carolina under the Royal Government, 1719–1776* (New York, 1899), 34; "Francis Yonge's Narrative of the Proceedings of the People of South Carolina," in Elmer D. Johnson and Kathleen Lewis Sloan, eds., *South Carolina: A Documentary Profile of the Palmetto State* (Columbia, S.C., 1971), 82–83; *Virginia Gazette*, Nov. 3, 1738; E. Merton Coulter, ed., *The Journal of William Stephens, 1741–1743*, I (Athens, Ga., 1959), 92.

34. Edward Porter Alexander, ed., *The Journal of John Fontaine: An Irish Huguenot Son in Spain and Virginia, 1710–1719*, Apr. 14, 1716 (Charlottesville, Va., 1972), 91; Harold B. Hancock, ed., "'Fare Weather and Good Helth': The Journal of Caesar Rodeney, 1727–1729," *Delaware History*, X (1962), 51.

dians celebrated the King's Birthday "with all the usual Demonstrations of Joy." As in the mainland provinces, there was a European-style treating, with "an Ox roasted whole in the Old Church-Yard, in Bridge-Town, which vast Crowds of People from all parts went to see." The participants toasted "the King and Royal Family," and afterward "there was a very splendid Ball at Pilgrims in the Evening . . . all conducted with the utmost Politeness." What is perhaps most striking about this celebration is how much it was like those in Massachusetts and the other mainland colonies. By 1740, loosely standardized royal holidays had been successfully grafted onto British North America.[35]

In the same period, officials added new royal holidays to the political calendar. Provincials began to remember the Queen's Birthday, the Prince of Wales's Birthday, and William III's birthday. Celebrations began to occur with the departures of imperial governors, at the declarations of war and peace, and at other holidays associated with the monarchy. The provincial gentry organized and expanded these celebrations as a means of asserting their own local status by linking it to the imperial order. As early as 1721, New York City's population celebrated the Prince of Wales's Birthday with bonfires and a treat of alcohol provided by the civil authorities. In Boston in March 1732, on "the Anniversary of the Birth of her most gracious Majesty Queen CAROLINE," the city government staged an elaborate celebration. A year earlier, the South Carolina elite had done the same thing, and in 1733 the people of Barbados observed the Queen's Birthday "with the usual Demonstrations of Joy." Virginians celebrated the Prince of Wales's Birthday in 1736 with the firing of guns, a display of the colors, and "other public demonstrations of joy." Across British North America and the British West Indies, the public proclamations of loyalty to the Hanoverians intensified as the eighteenth century progressed.[36]

Although not part of this formal calendar, occasional celebrations also proclaimed the colonists' imperial loyalties. Behavior associated with the annual

35. Samuel Keimer, ed., *Caribbeana: Containing Letters and Dissertations, Together with Poetical Essays, on Various Subjects and Occasions* . . . (London, 1741), 243–244.

36. Stokes, *Iconography of Manhattan Island*, IV, 497; Singleton, *Social New York under the Georges*, 305–306; *New-England Weekly Journal*, Mar. 6, 1732 (also in Henry W. Cunningham, ed., "Diary of the Rev. Samuel Checkley, 1735," Colonial Society of Massachusetts, *Publications*, XII, *Transactions* [Cambridge, 1909], 286); Keimer, ed., *Caribbeana*, 281; Stanard, *Colonial Virginia: Its People and Customs*, 138. For an example of the celebration of the Queen's Birthday in Annapolis, see *Maryland Gazette* (Annapolis), Feb. 25–Mar. 4, 1728/9. For the next year's celebration, see *Maryland Gazette* (Annapolis), Mar. 25–Apr. 1, 1729.

royal holidays was adapted to these events, further strengthening the imperial bonds, at least in theory. In the 1730s, governors' departures began to be processional events. The victories of King George's War and the Seven Years' War brought forth celebrations like that which occurred in New Jersey in July 1763, when William Franklin, "attended by the corporation and principal Gentlemen of this place [Burlington], went in Procession to the Court House, where His Majesty's Proclamation of Peace was read." After this formal ceremony, "they . . . drank the Health's of His Majesty, the Royal Family." By then, these days were joined with twenty-six major and minor imperial holidays and five standard provincial holidays (general fast, Thanksgiving, general election, militia training day and college commencement at Harvard, Yale, the College of New Jersey, and King's College) to form the colonies' formal political calendar.[37]

These celebrations reflected and helped create a peculiar but very real monarchical worldview in all strata of provincial society. Young boys participated in these rites that indoctrinated them in the empire's cult of monarchy. When Governor Henry Ellis arrived in Savannah, Georgia, in February 1757, a children's militia unit paraded and then presented the new governor with a flattering address. "The youngest Militia of this Province," declared the leader, "presume by their Captain, to salute your Honour on your arrival. Although we are of too tender years to comprehend the blessing a good Governor is to a Province, our parents will doubtless experience it in its utmost extent." In New England, Pope's Day brought children into the provinces' anti-Catholic, anti-Stuart, ultra-Protestant culture. In Newburyport, Massachusetts, young boys made small, grotesque popes, mounted them on wagons, and dragged them around town denouncing Catholics on November 5.[38]

The gala balls common to the evening celebrations on such holidays provided a venue for women of gentle birth to demonstrate their political loyalty. Francis Goelet reported that his female companions sang songs known to express loyalty to the Hanoverian regime during the King's Birthday celebrations in New York City at midcentury. During a celebration of the lord proprietor's birthday in Maryland, the ladies present were said to have drunk "the Loyal Healths." It was

37. William Franklin, July 22, 1763, Perth Amboy, in *NJA*, XXIV, *Newspaper Extracts*, V, 210.

38. Charles C. Jones, Jr., *The History of Georgia* (Boston, 1883), I, 517; Shea, "Pope-Day in America"; *South End Forever, North End Forever*. In the 1820s, one old Bostonian recalled, in provincial Pope's Day processions, "boys . . . who danced about the pope, played with the cards and frequently climbed up and kissed the devil. These were called the devil's imps" (Forbes, *Paul Revere and the World He Lived In*, 91).

As runs the *Glafs*
Man's life doth pafs.

My *Book* and Heart
Shall never part.

Job feels the Rod,
Yet bleffes God.

Our *King* the Good
No Man of Blood.

The *Lion* bold
The Lamb doth hold

The *Moon* gives Ligh
In Time of Night.

PLATE 4. "K—Our King the Good—No Man of Blood." 1774. From the New England Primer. The education of children into the empire's political culture began at the earliest ages. They witnessed or participated in the rites of empire in the streets, and they read about the monarch in their primers. The youngest children would learn their letters in a distinctly monarchical manner. In the eighteenth-century New England primer, "K" stood for "king." Courtesy, American Antiquarian Society

in this manner that those not involved formally in institutional politics learned and then expressed their attachment to their royal father and the Hanoverian dynasty.[39]

The importance of such rites to political education in the empire extended beyond the need to shape the views of those not allowed into the formal political community. The creation of a British identity came in response to the extension of the English state beyond its historic confines. Central to this process was the accommodation of the peoples of Scotland, Wales, and Ireland to empire, even the portions of those populations that were moving across the Atlantic. Again, public rites and ceremonies played a critical role in reconciling people to their prince and their place in the empire.

• • •

The Empire Composite

In 1730, a leading Pennsylvania Quaker complained when the colony's growing Irish and Scots-Irish population disturbed "Friends as well as other sober inhabitants" on March 17. The Hibernians, by firing guns and partaking in "revellings

39. Francis Goelet diary, Oct. 30, 1750, NYHS; *Pennsylvania Gazette*, Feb. 22, 1753.

occasioned by the classing together nationally numbers of people under pretence of keeping a day to their . . . St Patrick," disrupted Pennsylvania's public quiet. Governor Gordon denounced them but prophetically told Pemberton to expect more such celebrations. Gordon knew that "strangers" from other parts of Britain and Europe were flooding into the midatlantic through Philadelphia. Their presence presented a challenge to the locale and the empire.[40]

Even as they strove to create a common British imperial identity, royal officials recognized that their empire's many national, regional, and local subgroups could not be completely dismissed. Left as extralegal, popular holidays, the remembrances of national saints' days like Saint Patrick's Day threatened local order and imperial cohesion. What began as informal gatherings were, by the 1730s, being controlled by royal authorities, who incorporated them into the expanded imperial political calendar. Saint George, Saint David, Saint Andrew, and Saint Patrick, the patron saints of England, Wales, Scotland, and Ireland, respectively, became Britons retroactively as remembrances of them were used to celebrate empire.

It was among little populations of immigrants that the first celebrations of the national holidays occurred. These apparently began as private affairs organized by individuals from the respective English, Welsh, Scottish, and Irish (Protestant) nations. They acted on their own initiative, and when the Charleston, South Carolina, "Welch Club" celebrated Saint David's Day in 1735, the royal government chastised them for causing "several Guns to be fired after Sun-set, contrary to an Act of General Assembly." Like Pennsylvania's Scots-Irish, these Welshmen acted outside official control and were seen as disorderly.[41]

The formal integration of these national days into the imperial political calendar was already occurring haphazardly by the time gunfire disturbed Pennsylvania's pious Quakers and Charleston's edgy slaveholders. Officials used decrees and formal activities to define and harness these rites. As early as April 23, 1705, Bay Colony leaders marked Saint George's Day, the English people's national holiday, by firing the guns of Fort William and raising flags throughout the town. In 1733, the celebration of Saint George's Day in Maryland included a sermon and an elaborate celebration "in the Stadt-House . . . where they were honoured with the Presence of my Lord Baltimore." Afterward, the authorities fired the guns of the local fortification as the town's gentlemen drank loyal toasts. In making these national days formal holidays and participating in the festivi-

40. Craig W. Horle, Joseph S. Foster, Jeffrey L. Scheib, et al., eds., *Lawmaking and Legislators in Pennsylvania: A Biographical Dictionary*, II (Philadelphia, 1997), 833.

41. *South-Carolina Gazette*, Feb. 28–Mar. 6, 1735–1736.

ties, authorities expressed a confidence that the subordinate ethnicities were part of and not threatening to an overarching, composite British identity.[42]

As the rites became more formal, participants used toasting and other behaviors to assert their loyalty to the empire. In South Carolina in 1732, a substantial group of gentlemen "drank to the pious Memory of King *William* the 3d, prosperity to the House of *Hannover*, and several other loyal Healths" on Saint George's Day. Such toasting fused the private to the public and reaffirmed the loyalty of the empire's ethnic components to the Protestant monarchy. In 1736 and 1737, some of the leading men in Hanover, Virginia, celebrated Saint Andrew's Day with games and leisure pursuits while demanding that the other participants "behave themselves with Decency and Sobriety." Such behavior expressed acceptance of the established order locally and ultimately the imperial order.[43]

As with the other red-letter days, these national celebrations spread to newly settled areas relatively rapidly. In 1747, the residents at Fort Johnson on New York's northern frontier celebrated Saint Patrick's Day by drinking "So many . . . Healths, that I Can Scarce write," as one participant put it. Sir William Johnson and his family, who dominated the area, apparently kept the holiday there until the Revolution. In so doing, they helped organize the frontier for the empire.[44]

Just how formalized, imperialized, and controlled these ethnic celebrations became by midcentury is evident in an account of Saint Andrew's Day celebrations from New York in 1757. After first giving money to the poor, the assembled gentlemen meeting at "Scotch Johnny's" had a dinner where many "loyal and patriot Healths were drank . . . heartily yet soberly." The group later reassembled at the "King's Arms Tavern" for a ball, with a company of "elegantly dress'd fine Women" and a "great many of his Majesty's Officers . . . several too of the first Rank" joining the Scotsmen. Saint Andrew, like Saint Patrick and Saint David, had now joined the empire's ranks and become one with them.[45]

42. *Diary of Samuel Sewall*, I, *1674–1700*, MHS, *Collections*, 5th Ser., V, 129; *American Weekly Mercury*, May 10, 1733.

43. *South-Carolina Gazette*, Apr. 22–29, 1732 ("Last Sunday [being St. *George's* Day]"). For other examples, see *South-Carolina Gazette*, Dec. 2–Dec. 9, 1731 ("The 30th of November last being St. Andrews Day, and the anniversary Meeting of the St. Andrews Club . . . a Handsome entertainment was provided"); *Virginia Gazette*, Sept. 30–Oct. 7, 1737, quoted in Parent, *Foul Means*, 212. In the 1750s, New Yorkers celebrated Saint Patrick's Day, and the Order of Saint Patrick, composed of Protestants of Irish descent, paraded on March 17, 1768. See Singleton, *Social New York under the Georges*, 309–310.

44. Milton W. Hamilton, *Sir William Johnson, Colonial American, 1715–1763* (Port Washington, N.Y., 1976), 40.

45. *New-York Gazette; or, the Weekly Post-Boy*, Dec. 5, 1757.

Although the London officials wanted to centralize political authority in their far-flung empire, they also accepted the idea of it as an ethnic confederacy held together by the cultural superidentity of "Greater Briton." Rites that celebrated the empire's subordinate ethnic identities also linked the participants rhetorically and visually to the greater state. The rites of empire inculcated affections for the monarchy in the provincial populations and linked them to their distant lord. And yet they also created a sense of local community. Nowhere is this more evident than on the southern frontier, in Georgia.

. . .

William Stephens Brings the Empire to Georgia

April 23 was Saint George's Day, and even the people of the raw settlements that comprised Georgia in 1742 remembered. William Stephens, a career British politician appointed by the Trustees of Georgia as the colony's secretary, ordered the flag hoisted, and "most of the people assembled at Noon, expecting to drink the Kings health." Stephens was pleased to observe that the rite created "a better Concurrence and good temper towards one another (as I thought) than appeared for a while past." In following the empire's political customs, he sought to do more than follow accepted orthodoxies; he hoped to create "that Humour, and promote Unity, if possible, by any way that I could contribute to it." To further this spirit, he ordered a cannon salute and wine for the population.[46]

Diary and newspaper descriptions provide real insight into the imperial rites. Yet the inner dynamic that drove much of it is often much harder to discern in such accounts. For that, we must rely on the Samuel Sewalls, who felt anguish over the changes signified by these rites, and the William Stephenses, who embraced and shaped them as a means of creating community in a new polity. For as surely as Samuel Sewall dreaded them at 1700, by the 1740s British colonists saw the red-letter days as a normal part of life in the provinces, so much so that a leader like Stephens self-consciously turned to imperial rites to bring cohesion to community life on the disorderly southern frontier.

Stephens faced daunting problems in bringing social unity to Savannah. The colony's initial settlements of the 1730s had a utopian character to them. Controlled by idealistic trustees until 1752, Georgia initially resisted slavery, established a land tenure system designed for community cohesion more than efficiency, tried to promote industry, prohibited the sale of alcohol to whites and Native Americans alike, and invited in a spectrum of the unwanted from across Britain and Protestant Europe. By the 1740s, though, these utopian tendencies

46. Coulter, ed., *Journal of William Stephens*, I, 68–69.

were already fading, and officials on the scene struggled to bring order and prosperity to the little colony.[47]

The settlement's diverse and factious population presented a clear problem. When Stephens mustered the Savannah militia in 1742, he described them as "56 Freeholders able men of the Town [many apparently originally from the London area]. . . . A party of . . . German Swiss, consisting of 27. . . . The Trustees German Servants made another body to the number of 22 . . . [and] about 25 Volunteers join'd us, consisting of various Kinds, from the highest to the Lowest Station of life among us." In 1745, he described a minister working, one day, with "the Dutch and Germans. . . . the French and Swiss." There were Lowland and Highland Scots as well as a large number of poor and displaced from the area around London. It was, in other words, an ethnically diverse population that did not even share a language.[48]

This reality, and the war with Spain (the War of Jenkins's Ear) that directly threatened Georgia via a military incursion from Spanish Florida, encouraged Stephens to promote the empire's political calendar. In so doing, he sought to put his world in order, to create a sense of community both localist and imperial in its character. Because the identity of Briton was one designed to transcend ethnicity, it was an especially potent tool for an official in Stephens's daunting situation. For, as strange as it may seem, the localism of both seventeenth-century New England and eighteenth-century Georgia was dependent on transnational, transethnic systems of belief.

Apparently, the Georgia frontier communities had not celebrated the imperial holidays when Stephens's account of Savannah society began in 1741. Named as administrative head of Georgia's newly formed northern county, centered on the Savannah area, Stephens found himself heading a community described by others as seditious and disorderly. He quickly turned to the empire's ritual cycle to bind the settlers together. When, on April 23, 1742, he hoisted the imperial flag and tried to "promote Unity" by celebrating Saint George's Day, Stephens began bringing the empire's shared political culture to Georgia's diverse population.[49]

That fall, Stephens introduced additional imperial holidays. On October 30, Stephens "observed as Customary, by Gun firing, and drinking such healths as

47. For the best short discussion, see Edward J. Cashin, *Governor Henry Ellis and the Transformation of British North America* (Athens, Ga., 1994), 59–72.

48. Coulter, ed., *Journal of William Stephens*, I, 101, II, 222.

49. Phinizy Spalding, "Colonial Period," in Kenneth Coleman et al., *A History of Georgia* (Athens, Ga., 1991), 27; Coulter, ed., *Journal of William Stephens*, I, 68–69.

might be expected" George II's birthday. He asserted the royal origins of his authority by linking the king to the Georgia Trustees during ceremonial toasting. Six days later, he attended "Divine Service[s]" and hoisted the imperial flag on Pope's Day but refused to fire the guns, fearful that they might need the gunpowder for more serious purposes. On November 30 in the same year, Stephens recalled: "This being the Tutilar Saints day of Scotland [Saint Andrew's Day], I order'd the usual Compliment to be paid of hoisting the Flag" at the fortifications in still-tiny Savannah. Soon, the North Britons, as Stephens now called the Scots, "Assembled in the Square, diverting themselves at Cricket etc, with a Barrel of New York Ale placed near, to regale, them . . . and no disorder happen'd." Again, the gentry indulged the North Britons' recreational activities as long as the Scotsmen stayed within accepted social limits and accepted local authority.[50]

Stephens had served in Parliament nearly twenty years before going to Georgia, and he had a political sensitivity that did not fail him as he brought the empire's political rites to Savannah. Since the 1730s, there had been tensions between the colony's considerable Scottish population and the other ethnic groups, particularly the English. A group of dissident Scottish Lowlanders met at a Savannah tavern for some time, and Highlanders settled at Darien repeatedly became enmeshed in the colony's factional disputes. Although Stephens eagerly observed the national days of the empire's constituent nations, he was careful not to allow national holidays to be used for partisan ethnic politics. He celebrated Saint George's Day, but he also was careful to remember "the Tutilar Saints day of Scotland." In 1744, he ordered "the Flag to be hoisted in memory of St. George" on April 23 but refused to fire the guns or provide additional alcohol for drinking healths, not wanting "any preference to be given to it [Saint George's Day] before Saint Andrew."[51]

What is perhaps most noteworthy about Stephens's accounts is the eagerness with which the population embraced national holidays. As in all areas of British America, authorities imposed the rites in the sense that Stephens ordered them and established their form. Yet they would not have been sustainable had the population not wanted them. Part of it was, of course, the feasting, alcohol, and revelry; people were people. But there was more to it. Repeatedly, Stephens noted the "Expectations of our people in taking the usual notice" of such holidays. He tried to limit the Pope's Day celebration to a flag-raising ceremony in 1743 (again

50. Coulter, ed., *Journal of William Stephens*, I, 132, 134, 145. The best overview of early Georgia is Coleman et al., *A History of Georgia*, 9–126.

51. Spalding, "Colonial Period," in Coleman et al., *A History of Georgia*, 35–36; Coulter, ed., *Journal of William Stephens*, I, 145, II, 96.

refusing to fire the guns to conserve gunpowder), but when the townspeople assembled to celebrate, Stephens was forced to expand the activities. He fired the guns and joined them in toasting king and country.[52]

What did the diverse population understand itself to be celebrating? For certain, a Protestant empire that could protect them from their nearby Catholic enemies. And yet there had to be more to it, a level of understanding and attachment whose nuance escapes our detection.

By the mid-1740s, imperial celebrations had become normal in Savannah. In 1744, they apparently added the Welsh national day, Saint David's Day, to the ritual cycle, and the Pope's Day celebration was expanded. Indeed, the cyclical holidays had become so normalized that Stephens recorded in 1745 that, on Saint George's Day, he hoisted the flag, but "considering the many rejoicying days" they now celebrated, he would limit the ceremony to that. Georgia had been made whole with the empire, at least in terms of its public political culture. The trustees' utopian schemes faded, and Georgia began to achieve a greater degree of social coherence and to develop an economy geared to a commercial empire. In 1752, the crown assumed the government.[53]

. . .

The Historic Empire Inverted

The royal celebrations and national holidays spread devotion to the Hanoverian kings throughout provincial society. Newspapers and almanac accounts widened the influence of these rites and expressed the patriotism that the rites were intended to inculcate. The question, of course, is, Just how successful were these efforts, and how deeply did a monarchical mindset penetrate? What kind of empire was it?

The evidence points to deep and real affections for the British monarchy among provincials. The imperial rites and the newspaper accounts helped create these emotional ties. There are simply too many reports of crowds like the "numerous Assembly of Spectators of this and from the Neighbouring Towns" who cheered along with the militia when officials proclaimed George II at Ipswich in Massachusetts in 1727, or those who repeatedly cheered "God Save the King" and drank the royal healths at the opening of the War of Jenkins's Ear in 1739.[54]

The state-controlled press manipulated such descriptions. However, personal

52. Coulter, ed., *Journal of William Stephens*, I, 166, II, 36.

53. Ibid., II, 218.

54. *Boston Weekly News-Letter*, Aug. 24–Aug. 31, 1727; MHS, *Proceedings*, XVIII, 199, 374–375.

accounts from the period are strongly suggestive in the same vein. When Francis Goelet drank the "loyal toasts" in New York City, and his female companions "shewed their loyalty" on the King's Birthday by singing loyal songs, they reaffirmed a happy devotion to their monarch. Bostonian John Rowe called the King's Birthday "a Great Holliday," and no one should doubt he meant it.[55]

Other behaviors suggest true affection but are more difficult to interpret. What were the early Georgians remembering when they demanded cannonades and toasting on Pope's Day in the 1740s? Were Carolina backcountry men who were "so drunk" on the King's Birthday that they could not get to religious services the next day simply happy to have an excuse to drink or truly interested in owning their allegiance to the monarchy? Did those Bay Colonists who braved a "very cold" October 30, 1735, to go to "Dorchester neck to make a Bonfire and play off fireworks" on George II's birthday merely want to relax, or did they celebrate their status as imperial subjects? I suspect the answer is both, and the fact that provincials went to lengths to remember the King's Birthday at all is suggestive of real affection for the British monarchy. Just because people enjoyed themselves immensely during the celebrations does not mean these events did not reflect real political views. The celebrations' rapid geographic spread strongly indicates that emotional attachment to the British king was growing in the eighteenth century.[56]

Perhaps how widespread is suggested in the diary of a simple New Hampshire farmer, Samuel Lane. Among the mundane one-line entries about animals and weather, he recorded, "Oct. 25. 1760. King George the 2nd Died." It seems so incidental, but in that time, given the genre's character, it was an ink and linen monument built in a few words to the central figure in a sprawling empire.[57]

The prevalence of royal rites and public displays of devotion to the Hanoverian monarch in the colonies after 1688 highlights the first British empire's strangest paradox. Even as rites celebrating the monarchy became central in provincial political life, they seem to have declined in England itself. Scholars believe

55. Francis Goelet diary, Oct. 30, 1750, NYHS; John Rowe diary, June 4, 1766, MS, MHS.

56. "June 4. being the Kings Birth Day, all the People round me got drunk so that had but 40 Persons to attend Service on the 5th they being all laid up—A Presbyterian fellow carried off the Key of the Meeting House" (Richard J. Hooker, ed., *The Carolina Backcountry on the Eve of the Revolution: The Journal and Other Writings of Charles Woodmason, Anglican Itinerant* [Chapel Hill, N.C., 1953], 39); Cunningham, ed., "Diary of the Rev. Samuel Checkley," Colonial Society of Massachusetts, *Publications*, XII, *Transactions*, 304.

57. Jerrilyn Greene Marston, *King and Congress: The Transfer of Political Legitimacy, 1774–1776* (Princeton, N.J., 1987), 13; Charles Lane Hanson, ed., *A Journal for the Years 1739–1803 by Samuel Lane of Stratham, New Hampshire* (Concord, N.H., 1937), 38.

that the Glorious Revolution marked a turning point in monarchical ceremony and spectacle in England proper. William and Mary's frugality, the Hanoverians' fear of pro-Stuart crowds, and the populace's general apathy toward their foreign-born rulers are believed to have inhibited royal celebrations.[58]

58. Scholars who have argued that such celebrations were losing their meaning and infrequently celebrated in England include Linda Colley, *Britons: Forging the Nation, 1707–1837* (New Haven, Conn., 1992), 202–203, 231; Tim Harris, "The Problem of 'Popular Political Culture' in Seventeenth-Century London," *History of European Ideas*, X (1989), 53; Ronald Hutton, *The Rise and Fall of Merry England: The Ritual Year, 1400–1700* (Oxford, 1994). Peter Borsay, "'All the Town's a Stage': Urban Ritual and Ceremony, 1660–1800," in Peter Clark, ed., *The Transformation of English Provincial Towns, 1600–1800* (London, 1984), 228–258, discusses the decline of public ceremony associated with the royal calendar. John Brewer has also expressed views in this line in a number of publications. Murray Pittock discusses the prevalence of Jacobite demonstrations in 1714–1716; awareness of them made the Hanoverians wary of public rites or any other large gatherings out of doors ("The Culture of Jacobitism," in Jeremy Black, ed., *Culture and Society in Britain, 1660–1800* [Manchester, England, 1997], 125). The broader context of this aversion is discussed in Paul Monod, *Jacobitism and the English People, 1688–1788* (Cambridge, 1989), and in Nicholas Rogers, *Whigs and Cities: Popular Politics in the Age of Walpole and Pitt* (Oxford, 1989) and *Crowds, Culture, and Politics in Georgian Britain*, especially 21–57 and 215–247; examples of Jacobite crowds' contesting Hanoverian celebrations are on 28–32, 37. Rogers also indicates that demonstrations in favor of the Hanoverians were often top-down affairs sparked by leading men of the realm, particularly in London.

Colonial newspapers would occasionally carry accounts of British celebrations. The celebrations' sporadic character, in my opinion, lends considerable substance to the views of Colley, Harris, et al., but the definitive study remains to be written. T. M. Smollett, *A Complete History of England Deduced from the Descent of Julius Caesar to the Treaty of Aix La Chapelle, 1748* (London, 1757), 437, describes the King's Birthday in 1715 and illustrates the tumult during the succession crisis. Murray Pittock believes that many English celebrants who remembered George II's birthday were brought out by bribery and/or threats. See Pittock, "The Culture of Jacobitism," in Black, ed., *Culture and Society in Britain*, 125–126.

Only recently have scholars examined how monarchical political ceremony worked outside England, in Greater Britain. Bob Harris and Christopher A. Whatley probe the importance of the King's Birthday celebrations in the Scottish Lowlands in "To Solemnize His Majesty's Birthday: New Perspectives on Loyalism in George II's Britain," *History*, LXXXIII (1998), 397–421. In this vein, see also Christine Gerrard, *The Patriot Opposition to Walpole, Politics, Poetry, and National Myth, 1725–1742* (Oxford, 1994); Christopher A. Whatley, "Royal Day, People's Day: The Monarch's Birthday in Scotland, c. 1660–1860,"

As early as the 1720s, colonial writers expressed awareness of this irony. They began commenting on the disjuncture between their own public performances of loyalty to the Hanoverians and the relative lack of them in England itself. "We hear from Manchester," wrote one New Englander to the *Boston Weekly News-Letter*, "That no Notice was taken of her Majesty's Birth Day there, save that some well affected (there being too few of that Sort there) joined in making a Bonfire." The town's bells "never stirred upon the Occasion." Manchester's residents, "who address'd their Majesties upon their Accession, express'd more Loyalty than they are ready to perform." Decades later, exiled loyalist Thomas Hutchinson would comment that, whereas November 5 would be marked in Boston with "great disorders . . . [and] burning Popes," in London all he saw were a few stray boys asking for a halfpenny. The only places in the home islands where these royal holiday rites seem to have played an important role in public political life is on the fringe, in parts of the Scottish Lowlands and Northern Ireland where loyalty to the British monarchy was critical to Protestants living near large populations of questionable loyalty.[59]

By the eighteenth century's first decades, a political marching culture like that in modern Northern Ireland, militantly Protestant and anti-Catholic, was in place in every major provincial American town and village. British Americans in their public performances were more royalist than English contemporaries, and more overtly emotional in their attachment to the throne.

That this should be so is understandable. It has been assumed that the structures of colonial society were antithetical to monarchy, but, given the nature of the eighteenth-century Protestant monarchy, this view needs to be reassessed. By English standards, the colonies were ultra-Protestant, and the Hanoverian kings depended on their Protestantism for their genealogical legitimacy. Provincial pulpits, a primary source of information and means of communication, celebrated these Protestant kings. There was no anti-Hanoverian press; the colleges, as one eighteenth-century writer put it, were "firmly attached to revolution-principles, and the illustrious house of Hanover . . . not one of them . . . hath ever produced (with all humble submission to the famous university of *Oxford*) a single *Jacobite or Tory*." Colonials were loyal to the Protestant monarchy almost

---

in Roger Mason and Norman MacDougall, eds., *People and Power in Scotland: Essays in Honour of T. C. Smout* (Edinburgh, 1992), 170–188.

59. *Boston Weekly News-Letter*, Apr. 25–May 2, 1728; Peter Orlando Hutchinson, ed., *The Diary and Letters of His Excellency Thomas Hutchinson, Esq. . . .* , I (1883; New York, 1971), 280.

without exception. Their divergence from the norms of England are clear, but that certainly made them no less monarchical and no less loyal to the empire.[60]

The first British empire's history has not generally been written as an account of a polity ardently monarchist at its fringes and apathetic or republicanized at its core. Yet some scholars have been aware that, as even the cynical Benjamin Franklin stated in 1754, "the People in the Colonies are as loyal, and as firmly attach'd to the present. . . . reigning Family, as any Subjects in the King's Dominions." But the changes that made them so have been ignored. A royalized public political life is counterintuitive to a degree; by the 1790s, the fringe—North America, Ireland, and the south of Scotland—would be republicanized (at least intellectually), and the English core would be clinging to its monarchy with a marked emotional intensity. That reality, which we have assumed was a constant of Anglo-American political culture in the period, was actually a response to the disorder in the Atlantic world after 1765.[61]

The impetus to make the provinces whole with the empire became a powerful—perhaps the most powerful—transforming force in the period before the Revolution. This royalization did not have a singular meaning to those living through it, though. Nowhere is this ambiguity more prevalent than in the imperial historical identity and understanding embraced on the Atlantic's western shore during the years of British peace.

60. William Livingston, *A Letter to the Right Reverend Father in God, John, Lord Bishop of Landaff* . . . (New York, 1768), 24–25.

61. Franklin to William Shirley, Dec. 4, 1754, Boston, in Leonard W. Labaree et al., eds., *The Papers of Benjamin Franklin*, V (New Haven, Conn., 1962), 444.

3

REMEMBRANCE OF KINGS PAST

HISTORY AND POWER IN

EARLY AMERICA

In the mid-eighteenth century, Robert Strettell Jones was a student at what would become the University of Pennsylvania. As his education advanced, he came to reflect on the origins of knowledge and its relationship to human wisdom. He realized that personal experience would always be limited, but reading history made it possible to "use . . . the Experience of those, who . . . have traveled the Path of Life before us." This allowed the individual to "bring all Antiquity under contribution to us for wisdom. Confining ourselves no longer to a superficial knowledge of Facts, we now strive to trace them up to their Causes and form them into one connected system for the conduct of life." The past, as Jones confided to his diary, provided literate provincials with the tools to reason. "History," agreed Rhode Islander Theodore Foster, "makes men wise." Delaware's Thomas Rodney reached the same profound conclusions. "Man seeth with the Intellectual Eye, Looking on times far off, as with the material eye upon remote objects." This perspective often gave "false judgments," but such reasoning, however flawed, was not "without due honor among wise men." Histories provided "the conclusion of Reason down from probable grounds, they suffice, if not to convince the understanding, yet to give convenient satisfaction."[1]

Jones, Foster, and Rodney reveal a central tenet of provincial America's intel-

---

1. "An Abridgement of Metaphysicks Written March 20, 1761 and a SYSTEM of Rhetoric Wrote Nov. and Dec, 1762," Robert Strettell Jones Papers, APS; Theodore Foster diaries, Nov. 7, 1768, Rhode Island Historical Society, Providence; Thomas Rodney, "The Genoalogy, Being a Historical Account, of the De Rodney, Alias Rodney Family, from the Arrival of the Empress Maud in Great Britain to the Present Time," Manuscript Books, Historical Society of Delaware, Wilmington.

lectual life. History provided valuable instruction to those open to its lessons. The young Marylander Charles Carroll went further still, declaring that all of mankind's knowledge "is acquired from the study of History and personal experience." Most writers would have agreed with these men. Historical precedent informed political decisions, guided the enforcement of English common law, influenced family life, and underlay eighteenth-century philosophy. People reasoned historically, seeking guidance for all that they did and thought.[2]

For British Americans, the past became a way of thinking about empire that, like the British constitution and the monarchy itself, helped establish their commonality with Britons everywhere. A British historical identity, with its roots in an imagined antiquity, became over time a key part of provincials' political culture, related to the imperial political rites that celebrated the Protestant monarchy. The semiautonomous historical identities that existed in the seventeenth-century colonies — the time lines that ran back to the Reformation's early Puritans, to the Netherlands through the Dutch West India Company, to James Nayler, George Fox, and the early Quakers, to real and imagined Cavaliers — were assimilated into and largely supplanted by a comprehensive imperial history. The imperial rites, it came to be understood, celebrated a royal dynasty whose rise to the throne culminated a series of events that ran back into the Middle Ages, to the time of the Anglo-Saxons. It was, by necessity, a version of English history retold to fit a British empire.

Had that imperial history been peaceful and uniformly understood, the first British empire might have been established on a more stable and enduring foundation. British history's chaotic quality, though, prevented a uniform understanding of its meaning from taking hold. In particular, the violent upheavals of the sixteenth and seventeenth centuries provided lessons and highlighted personalities brutally ambiguous in their implications for eighteenth-century observers, who appropriated examples from the turmoil to conflicting ends. Heirs to disaster, the eighteenth-century denizens found it no sin to use the previous century for their own designs. In so doing, these writers and political polemicists unintentionally threatened the empire's stability.

2. "Charles Carroll, May the 16th, 1760, Extracts from the Carroll Papers," *Maryland Historical Magazine*, X (1915), 328.

To "Use . . . the Experience of Those,
Who . . . Have Traveled the Path of Life before Us":
Theories of History, Modes of Reasoning

Few periods in the American past are as neglected as the eighteenth century's early decades. The empire was locked in warfare with its Catholic enemies, and no major "event" marred the internal British peace that stretched from 1689 to the mid-1730s. This superficial quiet masks one of the most profound, if little understood, transformations in provincial political culture: the shift toward the acceptance of an imperial historical identity.

Again, Protestantism acted as the fulcrum for this development. New Englanders' belief in a special millennial mission and the biblically based perceptions of change imported to much of seventeenth-century America by various Puritans, Dutch Calvinists, and Quakers gave way to a dynastically structured history and time line made evident in the period's print culture. A host of officially sponsored and sympathetic writers, encouraged by the Crown's American servants, took up the task of explaining the relationship of particular dynasties to God's holy Protestant design. Provincials accepted this history as a component of their British identity, and it served as the basis of provincial political reasoning until at least 1776. Explanations for events shifted away from a providential and toward a more temporal understanding of change that acknowledged monarchs' role in shaping their societies.

The empire's basic historical-political literature was the calendar almanac. These provided the broadest spectrum of provincial society with a historic education. The most famous in our time is Benjamin Franklin's *Poor Richard's*, but others were as well known in the eighteenth century. Some were closely modeled on English almanacs, whereas others reflected mostly colonial influences. Their content reflected the change in historical understanding between 1650 and 1750.

The original colonial almanacs expressed as malleable a view of historical time as that held by the French revolutionaries who boldly proclaimed 1793 as the Year I. Puritan New England's early almanac writers and editors eliminated the names of months and days because they honored false gods (the origins of Samuel Sewall's complaint with them as well). The seventeenth-century New England almanac writers frequently focused on divine Providence's role in shaping human society. Chronologies included in the almanacs began with Creation and highlighted major biblical events.

Some of these almanac writers linked the major religious events that had occurred since New England's settlement to more distant events in the struggle for a Protestant England. *The New England Almanac for the Year of Our Lord 1686*, for example, noted the passing of New England's founders at the foot of each page, as its author simultaneously retold English history in a manner designed to highlight the Reformation. The reign of good Queen Elizabeth, who established the Protestant religion after the Marian persecutions and defeated the Armada, and the oppression of Puritans that had led to the Great Migration were related to the more recent happenings in New England itself.[3]

The Old Testament and the history of English Protestantism remained a powerful theme in eighteenth-century almanac histories, and this was not confined to New England. The 1741 *Virginia Almanac* had a long time line that began with "The Creation of the World, 5690," and included "The Promise made to Abraham" and "The Birth of Jesus Christ." Such an emphasis celebrated English Protestants' fulfillment of God's holy plan and helped bind the empire together.[4]

The internalization of this Protestant time line is evident in provincial contemporary diaries. Lawrence Hammond's diary noted the English Reformation's major events, such as the Pilgrimage of Grace: when "40000 [Papists] were assembled giving . . . out for a holy pil[g]rimage, on the side of their Ensins, they had hanging only the Cross, on the other side, the cup and bread of the sacrament, as taking arms only for the faith," cloaking their actual design, to enslave the nation for the pope. The habit of keeping diaries in almanacs common in the middle colonies and New England suggests the influence such mass literature had in both regions.[5]

The Glorious Revolution encouraged almanac and popular historical writers

3. David D. Hall, *Worlds of Wonder, Days of Judgment: Popular Religious Belief in Early New England* (New York, 1989), 58–61; Samuel Danforth, *The New England Almanack for the Year of Our Lord 1686* (Cambridge, 1685), esp. 6 of 16. Hall astutely notes the New Englanders' original editing of London's almanacs, the biblical character of the Puritans' own limited almanac production before the eighteenth century, and their changes after 1660. But Hall focuses on astrology and Copernican science in the almanacs. For the restructuring of British almanacs, see Linda Colley, *Britons: Forging the Nation, 1707–1837* (New Haven, Conn., 1992), esp. 20–22. John Miller, *Popery and Politics in England, 1660–1688* (Cambridge, 1973), discusses the impact of Mary I, Elizabeth I, the Armada, and general antipopery on English political culture.

4. *The Virginia Almanac for the Year of Our Lord God . . . 1741* (Williamsburg, Va., 1741). See Nathaniel Whittemore, *An Almanack for the Year of Our Lord. . . .* (Boston, 1717–1728), for examples. Whittemore's Boston almanac frequently noted the time passed from such events as "the Creation of the World" and "Noah's Flood."

5. Lawrence Hammond diary, L. Hammond Collection, 1677–1694, microfilm, P–363, reel 5.3, MHS.

to shift their emphasis to those events that would help establish the legitimacy of Britain's foreign-born Protestant monarchs. Providence was still seen as a force in the world, but it became a force to bolster what was called the Protestant interest in Europe. The focus on the role of Britain in the broader struggle against Catholicism reinforced the rule of first William III and then the Hanoverians, whose claim to the throne was based on their Protestantism. For certain, writers continued to highlight English events. The "Spanish Armada Built," "Gun Powder Plot," and "Bible new Translated" (by King James) were related to a string of events with religious-political meaning that had culminated in the Glorious Revolution. In 1716, Boston minister Benjamin Colman would proudly preach that "neither the bloody Martydoms in the reign of Queen Mary, nor the Spanish Armada . . . nor the Powder Treason," nor the crypto-Catholic Stuarts had been able to enslave Englishmen with popery.[6]

But after 1688, provincial writers linked these events to others across Europe. Key among these events were the Saint Bartholomew's Day massacre in France and Louis XIV's Revocation of the Edict of Nantes. Both had great significance in Britons' worldview, as they illustrated the fate of Protestants in Catholic-dominated absolutist societies. "The Intendant of each Province," colonists were informed, in a detailed description of the Revocation, "with the Bishop, went from Town to Town, and having summoned the Protestants . . . let them know, That it was his most Christian Majesty's Pleasure, that the Roman Catholick Religion only should be professed in his Dominions." They must convert, and those who refused found themselves attacked by soldiers who cried out, *"Die, or turn Roman Catholick!"* Liberty in political and religious matters disappeared; Protestants of all ages were hung "on Hooks in their Chimneys, by their Hair and Feet, and smoaked with Whisps of wet Hay . . . Others were thrown into Fires . . . and after they were desperately scorched, let down by Ropes into Wells." Men and women were stripped and tied together. "But the common Torture," he continued, "and that which seems to be purely of *French* Invention, was the keeping People awake for a Week together." Heavens! The all-too-obvious parallels to the persecutions of Mary I's reign, to Guy Fawkes, and to the Stuart family's absolutist designs were drawn again and again.[7]

These persecutions, at home and abroad, made it essential that Britain have a Protestant prince. As Massachusetts minister Thomas Foxcroft so aptly put it in

6. *Virginia Almanac, 1741*; Whittemore, *An Almanack for the Year of Our Lord*; Benjamin Colman, *A Sermon Preach'd at Boston in New-England on Thursday the 23d of August 1716* . . . (Boston, 1716), 14–15.

7. *Boston Weekly News-Letter*, Sept. 19, 1754.

regard to George I, he seemed "form'd for the happiness of Mankind; rais'd up by a kind of Providence, to be the common Protector of Europe, the Guardian of the Reformation, and the Defense of Britain." The post-1688 rulers acted self-consciously as patrons and protectors of "foreign protestants, who have taken shelter under the shadow of his wings," as one provincial wrote of George II. The British monarchy's role as the protector of "the Protestant interest" throughout Europe shaped provincials' historical understanding and united them with others in the empire.[8]

The Hanoverian succession encouraged a rapid shift to dynastic history as the predominate rendering of the imperial past. Unlike William and Mary and then Queen Anne, George I had heirs who could inherit the throne. In the hands of Anglo-American writers, the pan-European Protestant time line established between 1689 and 1720 became linked to the establishment of this new Protestant dynasty. Writers represented the Hanoverians' assumption of the British throne as the culmination of a series of changes that stretched back to the medieval period and were intertwined with the Reformation. The new, imperial, British past created in this period was actually a reworked English dynastic history that delineated historical eras by reference to the reigning ruling families.

This focus on English dynastic history is significant. Although the empire might tolerate the yearly celebration of a mystical founding saint by its ethnic subgroups, their national histories were too dangerous. Such histories would have been filled with stories of resistance to English power by Welsh, Scottish, and Irish rulers and their subjects. The empire's history became that of English dynasties fused to the struggle of pan-European Protestantism.[9]

This dynastic history spread rapidly after 1715 as merchants carried books, almanacs, and pamphlets to the empire's far corners. The stories of the rise and

8. Samuel Haven, *The Supreme Influence of the Son of God in Appointing, Directing, and Terminating the Reign of Princes* . . . (Portsmouth, N.H., 1761), 20–21; Thomas Foxcroft, *A Sermon upon Occasion of the Death of Our Late Sovereign Lord King George and the Accession of His Present Majesty, King George II, to the British Throne* (Boston, 1727), 26; Benjamin Wadsworth, *Rulers Feeding and Guiding Their People, with Integrity and Skilfulness. . . .* (Boston, 1716), 65.

9. H. Trevor Colbourn, *The Lamp of Experience: Whig History and the Intellectual Origins of the American Revolution* (Chapel Hill, N.C., 1965), 6–8, is the best discussion of the origins of historical debate in the Anglo-American world. Colbourn rightly argues that the dispute over the character of medieval England emerged in the late sixteenth and early seventeenth centuries and was tied to the unsettled question of the power relationship between the monarchy and Parliament. See also Louis B. Wright, *The Cultural Life of the American Colonies, 1607–1763* (New York, 1957), 132–135.

fall of kings, kingdoms, and empires seem to have been the colonial elite's history of choice. Massachusetts and then New Jersey governor Jonathan Belcher had the four-volume *Annals of Queen Anne* in his library, as well as the *Life of Oliver Cromwell* and Gilbert Burnet's *History of His Own Time* (first volume) when he donated his books to the College of New Jersey. In 1755, the library of onetime Virginia burgess Colonel John Waller contained *Memories in the Reign of Queen Anne, History of Charles 2d., Plots vs. King William the 3d, Life of Alexander the Great*, and "three volumes of Artemenes on Cyrus the Great." A variant on this was the history of a realm or part of it. *The History of the Grand Rebellion, Restitution of English Nation, by K. W., England's Remembrance Abt. Powder Plot, Ancient and Present State of England* — these were read and admired throughout the colonies. So deep did they penetrate colonial consciousness that a young John Quincy Adams asked his father for "the History of king and queen" as a gift in the 1770s.[10]

Sketches of realms and dynasties written in almanacs and mass-produced biographies eventually reached the literate populations in the provinces' smallest villages. These histories assigned characteristics to each dynastic lineage and identified the nation with the then-ruling Hanoverian dynasty. Nathaniel Whittemore's *Almanack for the Year of Our Lord, 1717* noted the time passed since "our Deliverance by King William from Popery and Arbitrary Government" and celebrated the "third year of the Happy Reign of our Sovereign Lord, King George." *Whittemore Revived: An Almanack for the Year of Our Lord* for 1738 carried "A Table of the Kings in England from Egbert the last of the Saxon Kings and first of England, to this present Year." They were divided as "the Saxon Line," "The Danish Line," "The Norman Line," etc. The 1741 *Virginia Almanac* carried a list of monarchs going back beyond Alfred the Great to Egbert the Saxon as well as such entries as "London Built by Brutus" and "Caesar first attempted Britain." The 1753 *Virginia Almanac* also contained a list of British rulers that ran back to Egbert the Saxon, and Isaac Bickerstaff's *Boston Almanack* (1769) featured a list of monarchs going back to 821. This time line noted Charles I's beheading and even represented "the common wealth" during the Interregnum as dynastic, with "Oliver and Richard Cromwell, Protector" as the dynasty in place during that upheaval. As late as 1772, the *Pennsylvania Gazette* advertised for sale "The General American Register," which included "A table of the kings and queens of

10. Jonathan Belcher's "Catalogue of Books . . . 1755," Jonathan Belcher's Library, Special Collections and Manuscripts, Firestone Library, Princeton University; "Libraries in Colonial Virginia: Library of Colonel John Waller," *WMQ*, 1st Ser., VIII (1899) (from an inventory, Feb. 5, 1755), 77–80; Jerrilyn Greene Marston, *King and Congress: The Transfer of Political Legitimacy, 1774–1776* (Princeton, N.J., 1987), 14.

England; Genealogical list of the royal family of Great Britain . . . Births, marriages and issue of the sovereign princes of Europe."[11]

Their popularity reflected a general support of the Hanoverians and a powerful identification with the empire and its purported history. But it probably had a social basis as well, reflecting the consolidation of power by local elites early in the eighteenth century. The so-called First Families of Virginia were the most famous of these groups, but there were others in every colony and indeed in most communities. Just as each official was supposed to be the father of his polity in this patriarchal world, each leading family saw itself as a small dynasty.

Dynastic histories influenced thinking at all levels of colonial society. New York gentleman Cadwallader Colden began a formal discussion of the English constitution with William the Conqueror and his relations with the various English barons, tying the ancient constitution to a particular reign. In so doing, he sought to establish the relationship of the legal order to the English nation and the monarchy. New Englander Samuel Chandler, a reader of Nathaniel Ames's almanacs, at one point penned his own time line from William the Conqueror to George I into his diary. He called the Catholic Mary I "a scourge to the nation" and the pope "God Father" to the Spanish Armada that attacked good Queen Elizabeth. James I was a fine king because "he caused the Bible to be translated [and] in his reign was the gunpowder Plot November 5th." And Charles I met his fate because of a popish queen and her intrigues. Just how far interest in these dynasties penetrated down the social order is hinted at by the will of Baltimore iron shaper Joseph Smith. Among his modest effects, he had the first volume of Rapin's *History of England*, a considerable item in an estate that was valued at just four pounds.[12]

Ministers reinforced these historical perceptions in sermons and pamphlets. Even the grand itinerant George Whitefield would talk about God's providential care of the British nation "from the Infant State of WILLIAM the Conqueror, to her present Manhood, and more than Augustan Maturity, under the auspicious Reign of our dread and rightful Sovereign King GEORGE the Second." Whitefield

11. Whittemore, *An Almanack for the Year of Our Lord, 1717*; Whittemore, *Whittemore Revived: An Almanack for the Year of Our Lord, 1738 . . .* (Boston, 1738); *Virginia Almanac, 1741*; *The Virginia Almanac for the Year of Our Lord God . . . 1753* (Williamsburg, Va., 1753); *Bickerstaff's Boston Almanack . . .* (Boston, 1769). In 1774, *Bickerstaff's Boston Almanack* provided a genealogy of George II and George III side by side.

12. *The Letters and Papers of Cadwallader Colden*, IX, *Additional Letters and Papers, 1749–1775, and Some of Colden's Writings*, NYHS, *Collections*, LXVIII (New York, 1937), 251; Samuel Chandler diaries, 1746–1772, microfilm, MHS; Colbourn, *Lamp of Experience*, 12.

and other preachers transmitted this historical worldview into the oral culture and amplified it in the written.[13]

After 1688, the British constitution was formally dependent on the monarch's Protestant genealogy, and this came to be represented in the provinces' popular historical literature as a corollary to dynastic history. *The Loyal American's Almanac for the Year 1715* declared George I's title legitimate "by Fate and due descent." All his family, the author continued, "are PROTESTANTS." Whittemore repeatedly printed George I's genealogy in order to establish the House of Hanover's legitimacy via blood as well as religion. "His Britanick Majesty," he informed his readers, "is descended from Elizabeth, Daughter of James the First, King of England, that Learned and Excellent Prince." James's daughter "was Married to Frederick Count Palatine . . . King of Bohemia . . . whose youngest Daughter Sophia, Princess Palatine, was Married to Ernest Augustus, late Elector of Hannover, and Bishop of Ofmaburg, A Protestant." Ernest was, according to Whittemore, a prince, "who for his Excellent Vertue, was . . . honored with the . . . title of the Standard Bearer of the Empire." George I, "a Prince formed for the Greatest Actions," was the child of Ernest and Princess Sophia and inherited the British throne in "the Line of the Protestant Succession. In this Illustrious house we hope for a Succession of Vertuous Princes, till Time shall be no more." Few provincial Americans, wrapped up as they were in their own Protestant identities, would have disagreed. "Illustrious house": this became the key catchphrase in Anglo-American popular historical literature to describe the Hanoverian dynasty.[14]

This obsession with genealogy became a factor in provincial society's organization. Genealogical research and coats of arms that established real and imagined lineages in the home islands became a rage among provincial gentry by 1740, and in some places, like Virginia, it was an obsession much earlier. Bloodlines maintained over decades and centuries meant legitimacy, and carriages emblazoned with coats of arms patrolled colonial streets, loudly proclaiming the owner's status. We might see this behavior as a response to the consumer revolution; whereas the material symbols of status were becoming more readily available, bloodlines remained exclusive and thus could be used to assert social place. William Alexander, the self-proclaimed "Lord Stirling," provides the most ob-

13. George Whitefield, *Britain's Mercies, and Britain's Duty; Represented in a Sermon Preach'd at the New-Building in Philadelphia on Sunday August 24, 1746* . . . (Boston, 1746), 7.

14. *The Loyal American's Almanac for the Year 1715* (Boston, 1715), inside cover; Whittemore, *An Almanack for the Year of Our Lord, 1717.*

sessive example of this phenomenon. The New Jersey gentleman futilely spent thousands of pounds in the early 1760s trying to establish a genealogical connection to the deceased Scottish Earl of Stirling in order to claim the title and estate. Beyond their assertion of status, genealogies normalized the rule of the local, kin-based oligarchies that dominated provincial society in the eighteenth century.[15]

A shared historical perception came to link the provinces to the home islands in the period that we once simply labeled the era of "salutary neglect." To understand the intensity of this identification and the way it shaped political perception by the eighteenth century's middle decades, one must only read an August 1755 letter to the *Boston Weekly News-Letter*. "In this Time," declared the writer in regard to the looming confrontation with the French that would lead to the Seven Years' War, "when it seems nothing less than the conquest of North America" would assuage the Gallic foe's ambition, "we should cheerfully offer our Swords and Purses for assisting the best of Kings, to verify that heroic and gallant resolution, of not losing a Foot of his American Dominions." This patriot went on to ask, should "the Sons of Britain, A Nation whom neither the Roman Sword . . . nor the unnatural designs of . . . her own Usurping monarchs, could ever reduce to Bondage, tamely behold the Slaves of Lewis, invading the Territories of our gracious Sovereign?"[16]

This writer had come to see himself as a son of Britain, an heir to those ancient Britons who had resisted Roman occupation. His justification for the war and his mode of reasoning were a historically specific defense of a national identity. This identification spread through oral culture as well as written. One of the songs sung in the colonial period was entitled "Great William [III] Our Renowned King," part of a repertoire that, along with the royal rites and print pub-

15. Mary Newton Stanard, *Colonial Virginia: Its People and Customs* (Philadelphia, 1917), 132–135. Apparently, there were quite a few people running around seventeenth-century Virginia with family arms on their silver, rings, and other personal items. Someone even had a quilt with Queen Elizabeth's arms on it. See the quote at the top of 134, concerning a special funeral coach with a Virginia family's arms. See also the description of coat of arms letter seals and rings bearing family coats of arms (134–135). Stanard also claims to have seen 160 headstones bearing coats of arms in an old Virgina graveyard, a claim I find entirely believable. Additionally, she quotes letters from Washington and Jefferson to London asking for family arms and/or genealogical research (135). See also Paul David Nelson, *William Alexander, Lord Stirling* (Tuscaloosa, Ala., 1987), 35–42; Brendan McConville, *These Daring Disturbers of the Public Peace: The Struggle for Property and Power in Early New Jersey* (Ithaca, N.Y., 1999), 41–45. I have benefited greatly from discussions with Karin Wulf on the use of genealogy in early America.

16. *Boston Weekly News-Letter*, Aug. 29, 1755, from the *New-York Mercury*.

lications, educated the mass of semiliterate provincials about their political salvation by monarchs of Protestant descent.[17]

At times it seemed colonial writers were determined to place every event, major and minor, within these historical frameworks. When royal governor William Burnet, the son of Bishop Gilbert Burnet, arrived in Boston in 1728, he was greeted with more than a royal entrance. The *Boston Weekly News-Letter* published a "Gratulatory POEM" placing his arrival in a string of historical developments that had occurred since "Immortal WILLIAM [III] sav'd the British Isle / Groaning in Romish Chains, and Bid it smile." Queen Anne's reign, the crises of 1714 and 1715, the Hanoverian succession, wars with the "Sylvian Salvages, by Rome Enrag'd," George I's death, and George II's coronation were all seen as part of a Protestant imperial progression that had, as one of its threads, the arrival of Governor Burnet in the Bay Colony. That Burnet's own father had helped secure the Protestant succession by making the House of Hanover aware of genealogical data that assured their legitimate right only intensified the sense that dynasty and providential destiny had fused. The writer assumed the colonists shared a British identity, perceived the empire's territory as synonymous with the British king's person, and, most important, believed that owning this identity would mobilize his readers.[18]

In addressing a jury detailed to mete out punishment to the conspirators involved in a supposed slave rebellion in New York City in 1741, William Smith showed how provincials used dynastic history to frame understanding of contemporary events. The "secret springs," as Smith called them, of this "horrible plot" were, not racial oppression, but Rome. It was another manifestation of "popish cruelty" that stretched back across the history of Europe from "the ashes of the ancient Waldenses and Albigenses" to "the massacre at Paris [Saint Bartholomew's Day]," to the Spanish slaughter of Protestants in the Low Countries during the Dutch rebellion; all these "many millions of lives . . . have been sacrificed to the Roman idol." But, as he reminded the jury, they need not look outside the empire for examples of popish conspiracy. The reign of "bloody" Queen Mary; "that execrable design to blow up king, lords, and commons in the gun-

17. *The Letters and Papers of Cadwallader Colden*, VII, *1765–1775*, NYHS, *Collections*, LVI (New York, 1928), 217.

18. "A Gratulatory POEM Received from a Friend the Day after the Arrival of His Excellency Governour BURNET," in *Boston Weekly News-Letter*, July 28, 1728; J. G. A. Pocock, "The Limits and Divisions of British History: In Search of the Unknown Subject," *AHR*, LXXXVII (1982), 318. Pocock comments, "In the seventeenth and eighteenth centuries, the Atlantic seaboard of North America became incorporated in 'English History' and acquired inhabitants with modes of consciousness corresponding to this experience."

powder treason [Guy Fawkes's plot]"; the English Civil Wars and the massacres of Protestants in Ireland; James II's efforts to set up Catholic absolutism—all were "evidences of the destructive tendency of that bloody religion." Smith declared in summation that the fires in the city grew from a "Spanish and popish plot" to massacre Protestants. Smith's charge suggests the hold that an imperial, dynastic Protestant sensibility had on provincial minds. Like the ritual cycle to which it was linked, the imperial time line tied provincials to the empire emotionally, for reading about the struggle between the Protestant good and popish evil could only generate love and fear. Imperial history had any number of subjective understandings. But the danger posed would only become apparent over time.[19]

Such a powerful intertwining of political calendar, dynastic time line, family organization, and constitutional perception should have served as a stable imperial foundation. It was meant to be so. The writing of history—natural, political, social—was, to some degree, designed to "be usefull to my Country," as Cadwallader Colden wrote. But the lessons taught by England's past, particularly its seventeenth-century history, were hardly of a single sort. The violent turmoil of that time reached forward and grabbed at the eighteenth-century empire's very soul.[20]

. . .

*"To All the Years of My Own Life I Have Added
on the Four Years of the Protectorate":
The English Civil Wars in Provincial Political Memory*

In 1745, with the empire facing France from without and Jacobite intrigue from within, a writer to the *American Magazine* drew on the lessons of the nation's past to try to rally the provincial elite against the looming threats. "In King Charles the First's time," he informed them, "the measures of the court were so bad" that most of the "Noblemen and Gentlemen . . . would have taken Arms against him long before the Year 1642, if it had not been for the danger of ruining their Families." Their hesitation "encouraged the Court to increase their Oppressions upon the people. At last the popular Discontents became so general . . . that every one saw, it would be easy to raise an Army against the Government." Still, the gentry hesitated: "Our noblemen and Gentlemen were still afraid of ruining their

19. "Trial of John Ury Alias Jury," in Daniel Horsmanden, *The New York Conspiracy*, ed. Thomas J. Davis (Boston, 1971), 369–370.

20. Cadwallader Colden to Peter Collinson, May 1742, in *The Letters and Papers of Cadwallader Colden*, II, *1730–1742*, NYHS, *Collections*, LI (New York, 1919), 258.

Families; and therefore, when an Army was raised, few of them joined it." The parliamentary army became "composed . . . for the most part, of the lowest Scum of the Nation. What was the Consequence?" he asked. The army "raised in Favor of Liberty, at last destroyed it . . . and invested their General with . . . absolute Power." The danger that those who should take the lead would hold back was again at the door of the imperial house. It was another lesson from an earlier period that eighteenth-century writers constantly turned to for guidance.[21]

It is perhaps difficult for us to imagine that the English Civil Wars once had as strong a hold on colonials as Vietnam and World War II do on contemporary Americans. Yet that seventeenth-century disaster was a powerful historical reference point for all political considerations in the provinces up to 1776. The events between 1640 and 1660 ruptured the dynastic lines central to Britain's imperial-historical worldview and severed God and king. Every form of human behavior and social organization had been called into question, and thus the period offered compelling lessons to its near heirs. The specter of its events, its personalities (Oliver Cromwell, William Laud, Charles I, his sons, Hugh Peter, Prince Rupert, George Monck), and the groups that emerged (the New Model Army, the Rump Parliament, the Fifth Monarchists, the Levelers, the Quakers) were planks in the symbolic-intellectual platform from which eighteenth-century provincials viewed change in their world.

For a people who reasoned historically, though, the English Civil Wars' lessons were often contradictory and potentially threatened the social order. "Everyone," wrote John Wise in 1715, "knows what direful Convultions this [the seventeenth-century struggles over power] has bred in the Bowels of the Kingdom." The meaning of these disorders, though, was open to interpretation. For provincials, the seventeenth century became an obsession, and thus it could not be easily controlled. Parliament had warred with monarch; the parliamentary army had intervened repeatedly and purged Parliament; first the Archbishop of Canterbury and then the king had been executed; new Dissenting Protestant religious groups had appeared (the best known being the Quakers); Cromwell, the protector of liberty, established a military protectorate; and finally the House of Stuart was restored, though that lasted fewer than thirty years before the Glorious Revolution. The larger political danger of this became apparent by the 1740s, when contemporary writers repeatedly invoked competing versions of Civil War figures to frame understanding of the Great Awakening, the rise of the Church of England, and the imperial wars against Catholic France. The historicized lan-

21. *American Magazine* (February 1745), 55–56.

guage that expressed a common British identity came to enable conflicts within colonial society in the eighteenth century.[22]

The events of the English Civil Wars were well known to most seventeenth-century colonists. Many lived through the years of crisis, and after 1660, stories of the Civil Wars and the Restoration saturated both oral and written culture. New England developed a potent oral tradition about Cromwell, the wars, and particularly the three regicide judges and other "men of blood" (those involved in the execution of Charles I) who fled to the Puritan colonies after the Restoration. The Chesapeake colonies, too, had their legends, many of them involving Cavaliers or the Restoration itself.[23]

Late-seventeenth-century writers used examples, comparisons, and metaphors associated with the Civil Wars to carry points in political and religious debate. As early as 1689, Gershom Bulkeley, a critic of New England's Puritan elite, called Boston's revolt against Governor Andros evidence of the "levelling, independent, democratical principle and spirit, with a tang of fifth-monarchy" in the region. All the labels referenced Civil War events or political-religious groups. Charges of a leveling spirit became commonplace in the provincial mainstream whenever an entrenched group felt its power threatened by the "people." Indeed, it is fair to say that such charges were as common as those that warned of the Stuarts' despotism, if not more so.[24]

For eighteenth-century Anglo-Americans, their near history indicated that balance was the key to good order. Their world had none of the celebrations of egalitarianism that ours does. Political theory taught that society was divided between the one, the few, and the many, each of which needed to be kept in balance in the political order. The abstract struggle between liberty and power was supposed to lead to equilibrium between the two, not the triumph of liberty. The Civil Wars had showed that the people could as easily ruin balance from below as a tyrant could from above, and that lesson was not forgotten in the eighteenth century. During political turmoil in South Carolina in the late 1720s and early

22. John Wise, *The Churches Quarrel Espoused; or, A Reply in Satyre, to Certain Proposals Made . . .* (Boston, 1715), 41.

23. Philip F. Gura, *A Glimpse of Sion's Glory: Puritan Radicalism in New England, 1620–1660* (Middletown, Conn., 1984), 222; Jacob Cushing diary, 1749–1772, Microfilm Almanacs, P-79, reel 1, diary in Nathaniel Ames, Almanac, MHS. Ezra Stiles, *A History of Three of the Judges of King Charles I* (Hartford, Conn., 1794), is still the best source for this aspect of seventeenth-century New England's political culture. It is also explored in T. H. Breen's *Character of the Good Ruler: A Study of Puritan Political Ideas in New England, 1630–1730* (New Haven, Conn., 1974).

24. Breen, *Character of the Good Ruler*, 177.

1730s, the assembly's upper and lower houses repeatedly invoked the Civil Wars to legitimate their competing views on the separation of power and the nature of stability within the British constitution. According to an upper house spokesman, the assembly's members possessed "the same turbulent and restless Spirit" that animated "the pretended Parliament of England, in the Year 1649, when they voted the House of Lords useless and dangerous, and afterwards, that Monarchy ought to be abolished."[25]

The Civil Wars' maddening contradictions became apparent as partisans fighting over the Great Awakening, paper money, and the rise of the Church of England in the colonies manipulated the upheavals' lessons to factional ends. Perhaps no figure was more frequently manipulated than the lord protector, Oliver Cromwell. Cromwell's last campaign was a tortured march through the eighteenth century's political culture, directed by the needs of provincials faced with dramatic changes.

Before 1750, disdain for Cromwell ran deep and wide in America. The label of "Cromwellian" was primarily attached to those accused of extreme political behavior. In 1728, a paper libeled a Pennsylvania politician by claiming mockingly that he was familiar with the ways of the "Secretary of State to Oliver Cromwell." The subject of this satire declared it "a vile Abuse." Any show of political militancy might bring forth the charge of "Oliverian" or "Cromwellian" behavior, the undesirable political equivalent of an "enthusiastic" spiritual state. The Virginian William Byrd went as far as to declare it "an abomination to mention the name of Oliver Cromwell" in the Anglo-American world. Byrd reminded contemporaries of Virginia's historic loyalty to monarchy precisely because it still served a political end: to define adherence to the mainstream values of eighteenth-century Anglo-American politics. Provincials used Cromwell to illustrate one type of political deviance, just as they used the deposed House of Stuart to define the dangers of monarchical excess, thus re-creating the German Hanoverian family as the prudent, Protestant, British mean.[26]

Writers also used Cromwell's name as an insult hurled at Presbyterians, Congregationalists, and other Dissenting Calvinists in order to link them to the Civil

25. *South-Carolina Gazette* (Charleston), June 9–16, 1733.

26. *Pennsylvania Gazette* (Philadelphia), Dec. 4, 1728. For a basic discussion, see Alfred F. Young, "English Plebeian Culture and Eighteenth-Century American Radicalism," in Margaret Jacob and James Jacob, eds., *The Origins of Anglo-American Radicalism* (London, 1984), 187–212. See also Peter Karsten, *Patriot-Heroes in England and America: Political Symbolism and Changing Values over Three Centuries* (Madison, Wis., 1978), 21; Marion Tinling, ed., *The Correspondence of the Three William Byrds of Westover, Virginia, 1684–1776* (Charlottesville, Va., 1977), 535; *Virginia Almanac, 1741*.

War period's radical sectarians. New Yorker Archibald Kennedy declared early in the 1750s that "in party Politicks, the Affair is soon over, and commonly ends only in a few sour Looks; whereas those in Religion, last from Generation to Generation, and commonly end in Fire and Faggot. . . . And did not Cromwel, upon the very same Principles, overturn one of the best Constitutions under the Sun." An Anglican cleric in New London, Connecticut, called the area's Dissenting majority "the bigotted Relics of the Oliverian spawn in the Novanglican Part of the world." These writers sought to portray their religious antagonists as extremists of the sort that executed a king.[27]

This vilification intensified at midcentury in some circles. In 1762, Massachusetts governor Francis Bernard accused Jonathan Mayhew of Cromwellian tendencies during a nasty confrontation sparked by the recurring issue of whether the colonies should have an Anglican bishop. One satirist, in a 1764 tract denouncing the violent activities of the Scots-Irish Paxton Boys on the Pennsylvania frontier, sarcastically declared of their behavior that it was "agreeable to my Forefathers Oliverian spirit." The same writer went on to claim that if "you know Olivers Schemes took effect; more through Policy and Cunning than Force, we must keep on our Guard, or we shall be in the sudds." Anglican minister Charles Woodmason described the Carolina backcountry Presbyterians who were tormenting him as "a Pack of vile, levelling common wealth Presbyterians In whom the Republican Spirit of 41 yet dwells."[28]

Even as this denigration of Cromwell increased, a rhetorical rehabilitation of the lord protector began. This colonial march to acceptance was born, not in a desire to republicanize the provincial world, but rather to buttress a monarchy in conflict with Europe's Catholic powers, particularly France. In the 1740s and 1750s, as the intermittent one-hundred-year war against that hated national enemy reerupted, Cromwell's metaphoric restoration began, in large part to justify a more assertive use of royal prerogative to fight France.

Cromwell's military bearing, his willingness to use force against all who opposed him, and his success in dealing with France's Bourbon rulers a century

---

27. [Archibald Kennedy], *A Speech Said to Have Been Delivered Some Time before the Close of the Last Sessions, by a Member Dissenting from the Church* ([New York], 1755), 4–5; "Ecclesanglicus to Jos. Harrison, Esq., Collector, 1764," Sparks Collection, I, fol. 10, no. 89, Houghton Library, Harvard University, Cambridge, Mass.

28. Colin Nicolson, *The "Infamas Govener" Francis Bernard and the Origins of the American Revolution* (Boston, 2001), 77; *The Paxton Boys: A Farce, Translated from the Original French* ([Philadelphia], 1764), 7–8; Marjoleine Kars, *Breaking Loose Together: The Regulator Rebellion in Pre-Revolutionary North Carolina* (Chapel Hill, N.C., 2002), 127.

earlier recommended him to frightenened colonists faced with the threat of French invasion from Canada. In July 1742, the *Boston Weekly News-Letter* reported that a privateer captain named Frank, "grandson of Oliver Cromwell," had inherited "the Virtues of that Hero without his Vices" and captured nine Spanish ships during the War of Jenkins's Ear.[29] In 1743, writers for the *American Magazine* recalled how the lord protector dealt with a French threat a century earlier: "Cromwell sent one Morning for the French Ambassador . . . and upbraided him publickly for his Master's designed Breach of Promise, in giving secret Orders to the French General to keep Possession of Dunkirk, in case it was taken [by the English and French, cooperating against the Spanish]." According to the magazine, "the Ambassador protested he knew nothing of the matter. . . . Upon which Cromwell . . . (says he). . . . that if he [the French ambassador] deliver not up the Keys of the town of Dunkirk . . . within an Hour after it shall be taken, I'll come in Person and demand them at the Gates of Paris. The Message had its effect." The struggle with France so elevated Cromwell that a privateer operating from New York during the Seven Years' War carried his name.[30]

The identification with Cromwell as a warrior against Catholic hegemony was strong in New England. There, writers measured soldiers and even public officials against Cromwell or described them as Cromwellians in a new age. This reference came to carry positive meanings in most contexts, as it did in a poem composed by Boston almanac writer Nathaniel Ames at the Seven Years' War opening. "I have just heard," wrote Ames, "how the proud Gallic Pow'rs / Prostrate themselves before the leaden Show'rs / Which our Cromelians with just Rage possest / Aim'd sure and fatal at each bleeding breast." Cromwell seems to have been particularly popular in Connecticut; this might have grown from the widely known story that Cromwell intended to remove to the colony on the eve of the Civil Wars. John Adams remembered hearing a rural New England preacher speak positively of Cromwell in the early 1760s.[31]

Had Cromwell's rehabilitation merely been tied to the cycle of imperial wars, it no doubt would have slackened when the wars ended. However, changes in

29. *Boston Weekly News-Letter*, July 8–15, 1742.

30. Tinling, ed., *Correspondence of the Three William Byrds*, 535; *American Magazine* (October 1743), 61; I. N. Phelps Stokes, *The Iconography of Manhattan Island, 1498–1909*, IV (New York, 1922), 691.

31. Nathaniel Ames, *An Astronomical Diary; or, An Almanack for the Year of Our Lord Christ, 1756* (Boston, [1755]); Young, "English Plebeian Culture and Eighteenth-Century American Radicalism," in Jacob and Jacob, eds., *Origins of Anglo-American Radicalism*, 194–200, esp. 197.

colonial religious life also helped remake Cromwell's reputation in the provinces. Surprisingly, his unwitting ally in this moment of triumph was his old antagonist, Charles I, England's long-since-beheaded monarch.

It is impossible to understand Cromwell's historical rehabilitation at midcentury apart from the hostility provoked by the Church of England's rise in the colonies. Historical antagonisms between the state church and the various colonial Dissenters dating back to the seventeenth century were dredged up first when William and Mary and then Queen Anne encouraged Church of England missionaries to evangelize in the American provinces. Many Dissenters feared that the state church would be established universally in the empire, which explains in large part their explosive hostility to the appointment of an American bishop when that issue arose periodically throughout the eighteenth century. The planting of the Church of England in the colonies threatened to "make us Dissenters in our own Countrys. . . . a Designe Barbarous as well as unjust, Since it was to be Free of her . . . [that] we went so farr," as a worried William Penn aptly put it as early as 1704.[32]

By midcentury, the Protestant churches had been fighting for the soul of provincial America for decades. The Anglicans had organized four hundred congregations in the mainland provinces and repeatedly agitated for their own bishop. When Anglicans began to remember the "blessed martyr" Charles I on January 30, the anniversary of his execution, it was more than some colonials could stomach, and it was then that they turned to the lord protector, Oliver Cromwell, for aid against those who would celebrate a royal tyrant.[33]

32. Richard S. Dunn, Mary Maples Dunn, et al., eds., *The Papers of William Penn*, IV, *1701–1718* (Philadelphia, 1987), 259.

33. For additional insight into religious conflict in the earlier period, see Lord Cornbury to the Society for the Propagation of the Gospel (hereafter cited as SPG), Mar. 24, 1703/4, New York, SPG microfilm, reel 13; John Chamberlain to SPG, Oct. 9, 1703, Nassau Island, Hemstead, New York, SPG microfilm, reel 13. The New Englanders on the eastern end of Long Island were said to "hate the name of the Church of England," an "independent minister, who have poisoned the minds of the People soe far" (Cornbury to SPG, Oct. 22, 1705, New York, SPG microfilm, reel 13). McConville, *These Daring Disturbers of the Public Peace*, 68–73, addresses the actions of Anglican itinerants in New Jersey. Patricia U. Bonomi, *Under the Cope of Heaven: Religion, Society, and Politics in Colonial America* (New York, 1986), esp. 42–50, 52–54, 56–57, 64–65, 119–121, 202–203, gives a more extensive and thorough overview. For examples of the itinerants' activities, see John Brooke to SPG secretary, 1706, American Papers, XII, NYHS. John Frederick Woolverton, *Colonial Anglicanism in North America* (Detroit, 1984), provides a general overview of the development of the Church of England in America; Carl Bridenbaugh, *Mitre and Sceptre: Transatlantic*

As these remembrances became more pronounced, two of provincial America's leading thinkers, the New Englander Jonathan Mayhew and the New Yorker William Livingston, established another framework for Cromwell's historical rehabilitation, as someone who sought, at least initially, to keep the national constitution in balance. Mayhew was the more strident of the two. Early in 1750, in *A Discourse concerning Unlimited Submission and Non-Resistance to the Higher Powers*, Mayhew asked a loaded historical question: "If it be said," he declared, "that although the parliament which first opposed king Charles's measures, and at length took up arms against him, were not guilty of rebellion; yet certainly those persons were, who condemned and put him to death; even this perhaps is not true." Charles, Mayhew insisted, had dethroned himself by repeatedly breaching his realm's fundamental constitution. Cromwell and his associates "might possibly have been very wicked" men. There was, Mayhew acknowledged, "male-administration during the Interegnum." Nonetheless, "Cromwell and his adherents were not, properly speaking, guilty of rebellions because he, whom they beheaded was not, properly speaking, their king; but a lawless tyrant."[34]

What did Cromwell and his contemporaries signify to those who thought like Mayhew and Livingston? Anglo-American political imperatives in the period between the Spanish Armada and the American Revolution might be summarized thus: normalize and preserve the Protestant succession in England, maintain the society's delicate religious equilibrium, defeat the realm's Papist enemies, and safeguard the vaguely defined liberties and properties of Englishmen — and Britons. Such disparate goals called for a ruler with seemingly contradictory political characteristics: firm, decisive, and militaristic in foreign affairs; gentle, legalistic, and restrained in domestic matters; militantly Protestant but also somehow malleable in his faith.

The tensions caused by these demands help explain why England went through three ruling dynasties in a little more than one hundred years, and they

---

Faiths, Ideas, Personalities, and Politics, 1689–1775 (New York, 1962), provides a detailed examination of the conflict over American bishops in the 1760s. Bruce E. Steiner, "New England Anglicanism, A Genteel Faith?" *WMQ*, 3d Ser., XXVII (1970), 122–135; Jon Butler, *Awash in a Sea of Faith: Christianizing the American People* (Cambridge, Mass., 1990).

34. Jonathan Mayhew, *A Discourse concerning Unlimited Submission and Non-Resistance to the Higher Powers: With Some Reflections on the Resistance Made to King Charles I.* ... (Boston, 1750), esp. 47–48. "An Independent," *A Discourse on Government and Religion, Calculated for the Meridian of the Thirtieth of January* (Boston, 1750), 11–12, also attacked the remembrance of this anniversary and legitimated the behavior of the regicides.

also help to explain why Cromwell survived as a political symbol of merit. For some provincial writers, Cromwell and his compatriots represented a strain of political-historical thought having commonwealth, Puritan, constitutional monarchical, and absolutist monarchical characteristics. This perceptual pattern was (obviously) rife with inconsistencies and existed below the level of a coherent political philosophy, having strong emotional as well as rational components.

Cromwell's figure remained equivocal even through the revolutionary crisis. The ambiguity of the Civil Wars and their figures — Oliver, Charles, and the other long-dead combatants — threatened the empire's stability. History should provide clear lessons, but it could not if civil war was the reference point. Trifling provincial political battles became linked to that larger struggle for the nation, fought and refought on the pages of colonial print culture. What was now could always be called into question because of the turmoil in the past. And the questions raised should not be understood as occurring just on the macro or abstract level of political debate. The events of the past shaped how individuals understood themselves.

. . .

Memories of a Violent Past

The shift to an imperial perception of history centered on the English Civil Wars seems another academic abstraction created by a willful reading of eighteenth-century print culture. That shared imperial past, though, was real and operated in intensely personal ways to shape specific lives. In particular, the Civil Wars marked participants with an indelible imprint of blood and trauma still visible in all areas of British America decades, even a century, later.

In 1706, a man named John Pearce wrote to the Woodbridge, New Jersey, Quaker meeting to confess his sins. "Whereas, I do hear that some dear friends do hear that I am like to be lead away after a separate party called Ranters." It was "true, for I have been mislead too much by their fair words and fine appearances like Angels of light." However, he now realized that they intended to destroy all order in the world and in particular the Quaker meetings. He thanked God for delivering him from the Ranters' clutches and pleaded with the Quakers to accept him again as a member.[35]

As a distinct document, John Pearce's confession is simply a statement of theological confusion by a man living in a small midatlantic province. Read in context, however, the confession suggests the hold that the Civil Wars and the

35. Minutes, Monthly Meetings of Friends, Oct. 19, 1706, Woodbridge, New Jersey, Friends Historical Library (microfilm), 33–34, Swarthmore College, Swarthmore, Pa.

resulting social dislocations had on provincials in the eighteenth century's first decades. Ranter and Quaker, royalist and regicide, parliamentarian and Fifth Monarchist — the war's political and spiritual protagonists remained a real presence to them fifty-plus years after the upheaval ended.

What we know of John Pearce's story is as potent an example of this as any. Born poor, probably not native to New Jersey, he had been in the colony's eastern division since the 1680s. He somehow became attached to the Quaker meeting in that decade, and in 1687, he petitioned it for a cow.[36] By 1701, the year Queen Anne royalized New Jersey's government, Pearce was caught in the middle of a theological divide that had originated in England in the 1650s. The upheavals of the 1640s had encouraged the appearance of new Christian sects in England. The Religious Society of Friends, or Quakers, is the best known of these, in large part because it has endured until today. But there were others, none more notorious than the Ranters.

The Ranters, if indeed they ever existed as a coherent movement or tendency in England, were rivals to and yet closely associated with the Quakers. Both began as antinomian movements driven by a belief in an inner-dwelling Holy Spirit and some form of direct divine revelations.[37] "Ranter" quickly became a term synonymous with "heretic" and "religious deviant" in the Anglo-American world. And it came to shape the lives of dispossessed or marginalized figures like John Pearce. He could not escape this historical-religious label that pushed him to the edge of Anglo-American society, and ultimately it formed his self-perception. Nor could he completely draw himself away from the New Jersey Ranters, whose

36. Ibid., Feb. 13, 1687, meeting held at Amboy.

37. Christopher Hill, *The World Turned Upside Down: Radical Ideas during the English Revolution* (London, 1972); A. L. Morton, *The World of the Ranters: Religious Radicalism in the English Revolution* (London, 1970). This line of interpretation was challenged by J. C. Davis, *Fear, Myth, and History: The Ranters and the Historians* (Cambridge, 1986), bringing on a remarkably heated debate. See Mark Goldie, "Review of Fear, Myth, and History: The Ranters and the Historians," *Journal of Ecclesiastical History*, XXXIX (1988), 150–151; David Underdown, "Review of Fear, Myth, and History: The Ranters and the Historians," *Journal of Modern History*, XLI (1989), 592–594; Edward Thompson, "On the Rant," in Geoff Eley and William Hunt, eds., *Reviving the English Revolution: Reflections and Elaborations on the Work of Christopher Hill* (London, 1988), 160; Barry Reay, "The World Turned Upside Down: A Retrospect," ibid., 66–69; and J. C. Davis, "Fear, Myth, and Furore: Reappraising the Ranters, Reply," *Past and Present*, no. 140 (August 1993), 194–210. For overviews of early antinomian movements in colonial America, see Gura, *A Glimpse of Sion's Glory*, 63, 237–275; and Stephen Foster, *The Long Argument: English Puritanism and the Shaping of New England Culture, 1570–1700* (Chapel Hill, N.C., 1991), 138–175.

"fair words" he repeatedly found so seductive. He was, in other words, a man marked by the past for his entire life. His letter to the Woodbridge Quaker meeting was followed by an additional letter declaring that he had indeed become one with "his dear friends. . . . and justifying the s:d separate Party." He accepted this persona and the condemnation that came with being identified with the kinds of sectarians that appeared in the years of civil war.[38]

The past's hold was not always so indirect. Memories of the Civil Wars defined lives into the eighteenth century. When Boston's William Parsons died in 1702 after eighty-eight years of life, Samuel Sewall marked him as a man of the tumultuous past whose most noteworthy moment came with his participation in "the fifth-monarchy fray in London" in 1661, a religiously inspired putsch against Charles II designed to bring on the rule of God on earth. These Fifth Monarchists believed that the reign of Jesus Christ was upon them, and in the wake of their failed coup, they were suppressed. Since then, Parsons had lived in exile on the empire's fringe, noteworthy only for that moment of millennial defiance four decades before.[39]

There were others still tied to that past, like "Edward Wale," who lived on Maryland's Eastern Shore until 1718. "Wale" was believed erroneously to be somehow connected to the regicide Edward Whalley (some even thought him the same man), and he apparently lived out his life the subject of local gossip about his imagined connections to the past. East-Hampton, New York's William Fithian was believed to have served in the New Model Army, seen Charles I executed, and come to America at the Restoration in order to avoid retribution. Often, these rumored historical connections are all we know of these lives.[40]

What is most amazing is the way that past held on in individual lives, refusing to lose contact with the present as it stretched forward. What weight did New Jersey governor Lewis Morris place on his father's service in the New Model Army during the Civil Wars and his namesake uncle's conversion to the Society of Friends long before it was fashionable? We are unsure, but he was well aware

38. Minutes, Monthly Meetings of Friends, Oct. 19, 1706, 33–34; "At a Monthly Meeting at Nathaniel ffitz-Randolph's in Woodbridge the 16th Day of the 7th. Month 1708," ibid.

39. *The Diary of Samuel Sewall*, II, *1699–1714*, MHS, *Collections*, 5th Ser., VI (Boston, 1929), 52.

40. J. Weeden, S. Johnpeter, and R. Nelson, "Records Are Remorseless as Regards Theory," paper published online, August 1998 (www.smokykin.com/regicide.htm); Robert Patterson Robins, "Edward Whalley, the Regicide," and "The Will of Edward Whalley," both in *Pennsylvania Magazine of History and Biography*, I (1877), 55–66; *Records of the Town of East-Hampton, Long Island*, III (Sag Harbor, N.Y., 1889), 2–3.

of both facts. Benjamin Rush claimed that knowledge of his ancestor who served in the New Model Army led him to explore republican ideas in Scotland in 1766. The son and grandchildren of the regicide judge John Dixwell, who had fled into hiding in New Haven, continued to struggle with the legacy of his actions into the time of the revolutionary crisis, when Massachusetts's last civilian royal governor, Thomas Hutchinson, made note of them. Hutchinson himself knew his ancestor, the famous antinomian Anne, had suffered public humiliation in Boston in the 1630s and drew comfort from her persecution when he faced his own political trials during the 1760s and 1770s. For them, the seventeenth century's tortured past was real, instructive, reprimanding, shaping, alive. It gave social meaning to these lives and countless others, reasserting itself again and again in unexpected ways.[41]

. . .

Oliver and Charles, William and Mary . . . and Empire

Eighteenth-century New York's prolific chronicler Cadwallader Colden understood both the promise of the identity of Briton and the danger that the British nation's history posed to a stable order. The former united the diverse and dispersed peoples of the empire in a common understanding of themselves. The latter, though, posed a threat to the empire, particularly the near past. "Our History," he wrote, "is not so well established as to serve as a Basis for such an enquiry." A "little away beyond our present times and so many will be found Interested in the Relation of Facts, that it will not be easy to agree on the Truth." The Civil Wars' ambiguous moral lessons and the inability to agree on a common understanding of events weakened the empire's conceptual foundations.[42]

By the 1740s, the colonies had come to be situated within a national historical framework that stretched back to Roman times. This history portrayed the Protestant Reformation and the arrival of the Hanoverian dynasty as the logical conclusion of Britain's development. The embrace of this history did not, however, bring stability to colonial political life. The near past's violent upheavals and

41. Eugene R. Sheridan, *Lewis Morris, 1671–1746: A Study in Early American Politics* (Syracuse, N.Y., 1981); Alan Craig Houston, *Algernon Sidney and the Republican Heritage in England and America* (Princeton, N.J., 1991), 225–226. The Dixwell Papers, contained within the Wigglesworth Papers, MHS, contain correspondence from the regicides' descendants. See also Hutchinson to [?], Thomas Hutchinson Letterbook, II, 12, microfilm, MHS.

42. *Letters and Papers of Cadwallader Colden*, IX, *Additional Letters and Papers, 1749–1775, and Some of Colden's Writings*, NYHS, *Collections*, LXVIII (New York, 1937), 253.

disorders could provoke a wide range of emotional responses in the eighteenth century, which is why writers and politicians invoked them. Such manipulations were especially dangerous in the first British empire because it was the passions, expressed in the written and spoken word as well as in political rites, that held the extended nation together.

4

THE PASSIONS OF EMPIRE

AFFECTION, DESIRE, AND THE BONDS OF
NATION IN THE BRITISH ATLANTIC

. . . .
. . .
. .
.

In the Stamp Act's aftermath, Parliament investigated the provincials' violent response to the legislation. By English standards, the stamp tax was mild, and the
London government assumed that the unrest must have had some other origins.
Like historians two hundred years later, members of Parliament sought answers
to this troubling question in the past, in the years before 1765. In their case, they
picked as trenchant and treacherous an informant as one could possibly imagine: Benjamin Franklin — scientist, diplomat, printer, writer, inventor, "Franklin,
of Philadelphia" as he referred to himself with studied restraint at the opening
of his interview. For several hours, MPs questioned Franklin about those now-
unsettled provinces on the British Atlantic world's far rim. At a critical moment,
they asked about provincial political attitudes in the decades before the outbreak
of resistance to parliamentary authority. The Sage of Philadelphia assured the
members that the Americans' temper toward Britain was the "best in the world.
They submitted willingly to the government of the Crown." In fact, he insisted,
"they were led by a thread. They had not only a respect, but an affection, for
Great-Britain, for its laws, its customs and manners."[1]

Franklin had voiced one of the empire's central truths: the passions, focused
and tempered by political rites and print culture, gave the first British empire
coherence. Protestant political culture rested on love for the king, fear of Catho-

---

1. *The Examination of Doctor Benjamin Franklin, before an August Assembly, relating
to the Repeal of the Stamp-Act, Etc.* ([Philadelphia, 1766]), 3–4. Passion in the eighteenth
century has been explored by a number of scholars. See Roland Greene, *Unrequited Con-
quests: Love and Empire in the Colonial Americas* (Chicago, 1999), as well as the work
of Julie Ellison. See also Paul Downes, *Democracy, Revolution, and Monarchism in Early
American Literature* (Cambridge, 2002).

lics, and the desire to consume in emulation of the British gentry. The imperial contract, the elaborate monarchical rites, and the unique historical time lines constructed in the print culture channeled these imperial passions. This is what those aspects of the British state were designed to do—link provincial emotions to the empire's motifs and symbols. The passions of empire were visualized in political spectacle; historical and political writers gave meaning in time to those emotions. The appeal to these feelings became part of formal governmental and political discourse through official decrees and proclamations.

Although the troika of love, fear, and desire proved a powerful imperial foundation, it was markedly different from the emotional structures created in the home islands by a political order dominated by extensive patronage ties, the state church, long established custom, and a tightly controlled land tenure system. In the most abstract sense, it may be said that, in the provinces, attachment to the monarchy was passionate, created by rites and print culture, whereas in England it was "normal," meaning the social structure, land tenure system, and customs supported it. This divergence left the monarch's person and political character open to a spectrum of subjective understandings in the colonies and the empire in aggregate.

. . .

"This Celestial Venus": The Empire of Love, the Love of Empire

John Wise looked deeply within his own soul during his emotional efforts to reconcile the New England Way to metropolitan expectations. Surveying the jumbled riot of institutions that together amounted to the first British empire early in the eighteenth century, Wise expressed the hope that something more would unite the dispersed dominions than the institutional similarity that some imperial officials hoped to impose on the colonies. He publicly prayed that "the Great ANNE, our Wise and Protestant Princess," would live to see "all the *Protestant Churches* thro' her vast Empire, more vertuous and more united." That unity, he thought, could only be achieved if their common focus became "their Love and Loyal Actions in Her Person and Government. Let Her Most Excellent Majesty, next to Christ, continue absolute in Her Empire over their hearts." Only in that manner would she win "all the Fame of Rule and Soveraignty from her Royal Progenitors, who could never so charm such Mighty Nations."[2]

We have been conditioned by our modern society to understand love as a personal emotional tie and empire as the end product of institutional violence

---

2. John Wise, *The Churches Quarrel Espoused; or, A Reply in Satyre, to Certain Proposals Made . . .* (Boston, 1715), 24–25.

and cultural hegemony. Love of country is often derided as a manifestation of false consciousness. But emotions in the first British empire worked differently. As they embraced a Protestant, British identity and the Protestant succession, provincial Americans shifted their perception of the monarch from a dreaded ruler to an object of affection who would arbitrate all imperial relationships. Love came to be seen as a governing principle expressed in public behaviors throughout the society. The tie between master and subordinate was explained as an affectionate one; love of country was seen as the highest social virtue, and rulers were believed to be devoted to their charges. Theoretically, a loving bond came to exist between every subject and the monarch, a tie that held the empire together.

If the seventeenth-century upheavals taught just one lesson, it was that kings could not be trusted. The settlement of the Glorious Revolution reflected this. By situating sovereignty in Parliament and invoking the ancient constitution that stretched back to Magna Charta, the expanding British nation sought to control royal prerogative and stifle royal personalities bent on the sins of constitutional innovation or absolute power. In the decades immediately after 1688, provincials retained this fear of their monarch, even their deliverer from popery, William III. In fact, the legitimating of William by his military prowess, stern Calvinism, and his supposed providential connection encouraged distance rather than affection. He was still the "dread soveraigne" imagined in colonial petitions to monarchs before and after 1688. And yet, by the end of George I's reign, the primary bond of empire was no longer fear, but a love shared between ruler and subject.[3]

The imperatives conveyed by Protestant theology and political theory lay at the root of the empire's political-emotional transformation. One early-seventeenth-century English writer summed up succinctly the relationship between Protestant Christianity and this socially binding love when he wrote, "There is in us by nature no spark of love at all, if Christ by his loving of us did not first instill love into us." Seventeenth-century colonists prided themselves on the Protestant Christian love that held them together. As religious imperatives in whole or part structured their societies, this ideal became the subject of frequent public discussion. Robert Barclay, writing from Boston in 1677, entitled his meditation on Christian order *Universal Love Considered, and Established upon Its Right Foundation*. "Christian Love," he wrote, "and Charity is fully . . . described in the Holy Scriptures, where it is preferred before all other Virtues and prop-

3. J. G. A. Pocock, *The Ancient Constitution and the Feudal Law: A Study of English Historical Thought in the Seventeenth Century* (Cambridge, 1987); Richard L. Bushman, *King and People in Provincial Massachusetts* (Chapel Hill, N.C., 1985), 47. Bushman discusses the character of petitions to the monarchy at some length (46–54).

erties." Virtue "proceedeth from Love; hence God himself is called *Love* . . . By this *Love* we are Redeemed from the Corruption of our Nature." The true Christian spent his time loving God. This love was above "the Love of Self, the Love of the World, the Love of any Creature." In the colonies, at least, the transference of this emotional language into the Protestant political culture would alter understanding of the monarchy. By 1740, colonials saw the king as a caring figure who expressed his affections to them in royal proclamations, in political rites, and in his behavior as reported by the colonial newspapers.[4]

This Protestant affection became a powerful strut that supported the Glorious Revolution's settlement. As Anglo-American political culture defined itself in opposition to fearsome, absolutist Catholic monarchs, it created an imperative for Protestant British monarchs to invoke love to explain their rule. Law and custom supposedly bound these Protestant monarchs, who were seen to be paternalistic and somehow emotionally open. When George II took the throne, the *American Weekly Mercury* reported that he "express[ed] the Sentiments of My Heart . . . by all possible means, to Merit the Love of my People, which I shall always look upon as the best Support and Security of My Crown." When George's son Frederick died at midcentury, the *Boston Weekly News-Letter* described him as "heartily convinced the Felicity of a Prince depends on the Love and Affection of his People." Frederick strove to "cultivate that Love and Affection" with his every action, according to this Boston writer. The monarch, this beloved figure, would protect the empire, preserve the Protestant political culture, and arbitrate the imperial constitution for the good of his loving subjects.[5]

Official actions were explained in this affectionate rhetoric as love supposedly guided officials. Each provincial official acted as patriarch of his own trust, right down to the town fathers in the rawest frontier community, and each was supposed to cultivate the love of those in his charge. As early as 1689, John Blackwell commented to Pennsylvania proprietor William Penn that "you desire me to Rule by love and persuasion (the Rationall Sceptre and Empire) rather than by Rigour" over the new Quaker colony in America.[6]

The inclusion of the trope of love in imperial decrees amplified its impact and

---

4. Conrad Russell, *The Causes of the English Civil War: The Ford Lectures Delivered in the University of Oxford, 1987–1988* (Oxford, 1990), 64; Robert Barclay, *Universal Love Considered, and Established upon Its Right Foundation* . . . ([Boston], 1677), 4–6.

5. *American Weekly Mercury* (Philadelphia), Sept. 7–14, 1727; *Boston Weekly News-Letter*, June 13, 1751.

6. John Blackwell to William Penn, Jan. 13, 1689, Philadelphia, John Blackwell Letters, 1688–1690, HSP.

gave it formal meaning. In 1733, Viscount Howe assured the Council of Barbados that George II's "gracious Love extends to all his Subjects." Howe intended to act as the agent of that affection in the sugar islands. Imperial addresses and decrees like this, in their actual deliveries and subsequent reproduction in print, were the primary means by which people received the king's affections. Typical in this regard was the rationale purported to be George II's for the War of Jenkins's Ear in 1739. "I have," he said to Parliament, "upon all Occasions, declared, how sensibly I have been affected with the many Hardships and Injuries sustained by my Trading Subjects in *America*." The true interests of his people were "to[o] much at Heart" to allow them to continue to suffer Spanish abuses. At the opening of hostilities, the London government linked this love to action when it instructed Maryland's Governor Ogle to "grant commissions of Marque and Reprisal to any of Our loving subjects" so that they might raid Spanish shipping.[7] Nathaniel Ames's *An Astronomical Diary; or, An Almanack for the Year of Our Lord Christ, 1752* summed up the role of these affectionate links in the imperial order: "Look round our World; behold the Chain of Love / Combining all below, and all above." Such was the expectation and the hope of authority in the eighteenth-century empire. So successfully had this trope been planted that, at the Seven Years' War's end, Thomas Pownall would write that "nothing can eradicate from their [provincials'] hearts their natural, almost mechanical, affection to Great Britain, which they . . . call . . . home."[8]

The ability of this emotional language to shape perception was evidenced in 1765, when the delegates at the Stamp Act Congress wrote to their king of their devotion and "affection." Their hearts were "impressed with the most indelible Characters of Gratitude to your Majesty, and to the Memory of the Kings of your Illustrious House." The Hanoverians' actions across the eighteenth century gave repeated proof "of your Majesty's Paternal Love to all your People." In the same moment, the governor and council of Pennsylvania sent their "unfeigned Assurances that our Hearts" remained bound to king and country. Even the rioters who broke into South Carolinian Henry Laurens's home searching for stamped paper in 1765 expressed their "love" for him after finding nothing. Love bound the empire, and love governed it.[9]

7. *American Weekly Mercury*, June 7–14, 1733; *New-York Weekly Journal*, Apr. 30, 1739; "Colonial Militia, 1740, 1748," in *Maryland Historical Magazine*, VI (1911), 44.

8. Nathaniel Ames, *An Astronomical Diary; or, An Almanack for the Year of Our Lord Christ, 1752* (Boston, [1751]); [Thomas Pownall], *The Administration of the Colonies* (London, 1764), 25.

9. Bushman, *King and People*, 48–49; George Edward Reed, ed., *Pennsylvania Archives*,

The love that bound the empire was supposed to be tempered, ensuring monarchical control in the polity. As one Jerseyman declared in 1747, left to themselves, "the hearts of Men Naturally are filled with perverse and Rebellious principles." Thus the heart needed to be harnessed to the cause of good order in a just empire. "The Passions," one observer noted, "are all good in themselves, if directed to proper Objects, and do not exceed in Measure, the Excellency of their Objects." The passions "and Affections are not to be Eradicated . . . but Regulated." Only such a tempering could produce a natural, ordered society. Presbyterian minister Samuel Davies concurred, believing, as he preached in Delaware in 1748, that all man's *"Affections must be regular and governable,* otherwise he *cou'd not keep* the Law." The monarch was, as John Wise noted, the highest object of appropriate affection on earth, and each level of society should receive its proper measure of love. Indeed, political society was designed to allow the passions to flow in channels that reinforced rather than eroded the established order. Language and ritual assured that emotions did not swamp good order.[10]

From 1688 to 1775, colonists used affectionate tropes to describe key imperial relationships. But to shape meaning, this rhetoric needed to have physical expression in human behavior. Certainly, political rites played a key role in asserting the royal family's goodness. That these rites celebrated the Hanoverians' life cycle and the development of Protestantism in England only heightened their emotional impact. Beneath the macro level of public rites, though, a host of social conventions encouraged provincials to understand the imperial power structure as one of affection. These customs normalized access to resources, to positions of respect and honor, and to one's fellow subjects. The imperial emotional structure, like the social structure, looked like a wedding cake, with clear hierarchies. The social customs that expressed these affections made clear the ordering of society.

Perhaps the most important act of affection in colonial political society was treating. The king's government provided treats on royal holidays, on days of legal or political ceremony, or after military victories. For a social superior to give entertainment to inferiors in order to express gratitude for political, military, or economic support became a universal custom. In September 1733, the government of Antigua treated the island's white population to "Bonfires and Illuminations . . . Two Oxen Roasted Whole, and . . . a great Quantity of Liquor"

4th Ser., III, *Papers of the Governors, 1759–1785* (Harrisburg, 1900), 320; Gordon S. Wood, *The Radicalism of the American Revolution* (New York, 1991), 91.

10. *NJA,* VII, 71–72; *American Weekly Mercury,* Sept. 11–18, 1729; Samuel Davies, *A Sermon on Man's Primitive State; and the First COVENANT. Delivered before the Reverend Presbytery of New-Castle, April 13th, 1748* (Philadelphia, 1748), 18–19.

in the form of "several Hogsheads of Beer and Wine" after Parliament repealed a sugar regulation that was damaging the island's economy. "J. Brenton, Esq.," of Newport, Rhode Island, treated the town's artillery company (of which he was a captain) to a "handsome Dinner" after they "made their first publick Appearance in their Dress . . . [and] . . . performed the Manual Exercise . . . to the Satisfaction of a great Number of Spectators." Captain Brenton used public training as an opportunity to show his devotion to those beneath him. In return, he expected acceptance of his status as community leader. All the colonial gentry followed this practice; when the New England militia won its miraculous 1745 victory at Louisbourg, Bostonians celebrated all day. In the evening, the royal government provided a bonfire, fireworks, and casks of wine to the assembled mass.[11]

If treating expressed the social contract on a local level, hand kissing made visible the role of affection in establishing one's place in the imperial order. Colonial newspapers actually carried accounts of those who earned the ultimate honor, kissing the monarch's hand. In 1706, the *Boston News-Letter* reported that London's mayor and councilmen received an audience with Queen Anne, who "very graciously . . . admit[ted] them to the Honour of kissing Her Hand." In 1708, Bay Colonist Jonathan Belcher wrote breathlessly to his brother that he had journeyed to Hanover and met with Princess Sophia, heiress to the British throne by virtue of Protestant genealogy. The princess "called me by my name" and then "pulled off her Glove" so that he might kneel and "kis's her Hand." He remembered this thrill clearly forty years later. The princess had recognized him, and he had been allowed to express his subordination. In 1721, the much traveled royal retainer Sir Francis Nicholson, appointed governor of South Carolina, "had the Honour to kiss His Majesty's Hand" when he formally received his posting. Such acts upheld the perception that affection as much as power maintained hierarchy in the British polity.[12]

The centrality of such affectionate acts to the political order is nowhere more apparent than in the actions of the father of our country at the dawn of his public life. George Washington's role in the Seven Years' War established his reputation as a military leader. Close examination of his activities in that sprawling conflict provides us with a view of a Washington very different from the one we know, of a provincial man with aspirations to rise in the imperial power structure. And,

---

11. *Boston Weekly News-Letter*, Sept. 13–20, 1733, Sept. 27, 1744, July 4, 1745.

12. *Boston News-Letter*, Nov. 11–18, 1706; Jonathan Belcher, Sr., to his brother and Captain Foster, Nov. 16, 1708, London, Belcher Papers, General MSS Collection, Special Collections, MHS; *Boston News-Letter*, July 17–24, 1721. For another example, see William Logan to John Smith at Burlington, [1760s?], John Smith Letterbook, HSP.

if we understand that love helped hold the empire together, it should come as little surprise that we find him writing to Virginia's lieutenant governor, Francis Fauquier, in late 1758, anxious to earn the "honor of kissing your hand, about the 25th instant." As Washington well knew, to rise in the empire, one sometimes needed to kneel and kiss authority's hand.[13]

Love, the celestial Venus, bound one subject to another and helped to structure social relationships in a Protestant political culture. Bound in affection, Britons on both sides of the Atlantic were supposed to be free to enjoy their liberties and properties. But the eighteenth century was not the Age of Aquarius. Love governed, but fear ruled. The two, love and fear, held the empire together.

• • •

Romaphobia: The Fear of Catholics and the Character of British Liberty

In 1754, the king's loyal subjects in Maryland moved to deal with a dangerous element among them: Catholics. "Some Measures," it was reported, "were thought necessary to be taken in order to put a Check to the Papists within that Province." The situation seemed urgent, "as the French are encroaching on all his Majesty's Territories on this Continent, and spiriting up the Indians to make Incursions and commit Hostilities on his Majesty's Subjects." Two men particularly concerned the assemblymen, who determined that "an exact Enquiry may be made into the Matter contained in certain Depositions therewith delivered, against one Gerard Jordan, jun., and Joseph Broadway, of St. Mary's County." Their apparent crimes were "obstructing the raising his Majesty's Levies" and toasting the Stuart Pretender. Prodded by his assembly, the province's governor offered a twenty-pound reward for the two Papists' capture.[14]

The idea that a provincial governor and assembly would devote such attention to two men accused essentially of toasting seems strange to us today. But the toast, like hand kissing, played an important public role in displays of political loyalty, and to British Americans, drinking to the Stuart Pretender was deadly serious business. The intense fear that permeated provincial society — of Catholics, popery, the Pretender, the European Catholic powers and their Indian allies — also helped hold the empire together. Initially, this fear legitimated Brit-

13. George Washington to Francis Fauquier, Dec. 9, 1758, in George Reese, ed., *The Official Papers of Francis Fauquier, Lieutenant Governor of Virginia, 1758–1768*, I (Charlottesville, Va., 1981), 130–131.

14. *New-York Gazette; or, the Weekly Post-Boy*, June 24, 1754. For a modern study of English anti-Catholicism, see Colin Haydon, *Anti-Catholicism in Eighteenth-Century England, c. 1714–80: A Political and Social Study* (Manchester, 1993).

ain's Dutch- and German-born rulers and rallied the empire against its foreign enemies. Over time, though, provincial elites also used antipopery and anti-Catholicism as instruments of social control. In the first, royal America, the expansive liberty that provincials believed their birthright was realized in religious intolerance, ethnic suspicion, and political fear. It was an empire of demons as much as one of love.

Fear of Catholics grew from the dynastic and religious problems of sixteenth-century England. The bitter seventeenth- and eighteenth-century conflicts amplified these feelings and made denouncement of popish governments and Catholics a stock-in-trade of English print culture. Anti-Catholic feelings expanded dramatically in the period from the massacres of Protestansts in France through the time of the Spanish Armada, and antipopery played an important and apparently underappreciated role in provoking the English Civil Wars.[15]

The particular themes of eighteenth-century antipopish literature that became common in the provinces can be traced to England in the period between 1679 and 1689. In that decade, the realm went through the fears of a Popish Plot, the Exclusion Crisis, the expulsion of Protestants from France, and the Glorious Revolution. A massive upwelling in antipopish literature began as the ascent of James, Duke of York, Charles II's Catholic brother, took on the air of inevitability. Speakers denounced the sins of Rome as mobs burned papal effigies. Pamphlets, broadsides, and sermons came pouring out of London's publishing quarters, each trying to outdo the other in highlighting Catholicism's seditious and subversive nature. James's subsequent overthrow did nothing to dampen this trend. Lurid antipopery, for lack of a better term, flooded the empire's print culture after 1688–1689.[16]

15. Russell, *Causes of the English Civil War*, 73–74.

16. Tim Harris, *Politics under the Later Stuarts: Party Conflict in a Divided Society* (London, 1993), 80–116; J. R. Western, *Monarchy and Revolution: The English State in the 1680s* (London, 1972). *Historical Journal* carried a number of articles on these themes in the 1980s and 1990s. The burning of papal effigies actually had its origins in the celebration of Saint Hugh's Day, November 17, which was also the day of Elizabeth I's coronation. It was then adopted as a practice on November 5. See Peter Shaw, *American Patriots and the Rituals of Revolution* (Cambridge, Mass., 1981), 204–207. The discussion of antipopery in the American provinces, particularly in the seventeenth century, is limited. For the impact in New York, the best statement is John M. Murrin, "English Rights as Ethnic Aggression: The English Conquest, the Charter of Liberties of 1683, and Leisler's Rebellion in New York," in William Pencak and Conrad Edick Wright, eds., *Authority and Resistance in Early New York* (New York, 1988), 56–94. For a very useful discussion, see also J. C. D. Clark, *The*

A broadside that circulated in provinces in 1689 captured perfectly the intensifying anti-Catholicism and the perception that the new monarchs, William and Mary, had saved the nation from popery. *Popery Pickled; or, The Jesuits Shooes Made of Running Leather* assured its readers and listeners that "Would you have a new Play acted / Would you see it just begun / Popery is run Distracted / And the Priests are all undone / Now you'll see their Beads and Crosses / All lie Prostrate on the Ground." In 1698, a Yorker declared that, had not William and Mary seized the throne, Papists would have "fetter'd all Europe," and pan-European Protestantism would have been undone. Bay colonist John Marshall, who labeled William III's death a "grave blow to all Europe" in his diary because the Anglo-Dutch monarch was the Protestant interest's chief defender, suggests colonials' internalization of these views. Nathaniel Whittemore's Boston almanac asked heaven to protect George I from "Popish Plots and all his Foes may Heaven him secure / That he and his for Protestants while Sun and Moon indure." Skulking Catholics, foreign Catholics, Jesuits, Jacobites—these were the agents of fear in the empire. They encouraged Protestant subjects to cling to one another and to their Protestant ruler.[17]

Anglo-American writers used comparison to the Catholic kingdoms to help define the new identity of Britishness. Catholic rulers and Catholicism were so bad, maintained Robert Stevens of South Carolina in 1711, that the Yamassee Indians returned to their "Ancient Atheism" after "they had been instructed by the Spainards in the principales of the Popish Religion from whence they fled ... to live under the mild Government of the English." Anglo-American writers constantly drew such contrasts without any sense that their own persecutions of Catholics mirrored those suffered by Protestants in Catholic lands.[18]

Although France and Spain were the primary points of comparison, provincial writers obsessed about the persecution of Protestants anywhere. The *American Weekly Mercury* reported in March 1720 on the "extreme Violences" launched by Catholic bishops against Polish Protestants in several provinces. The persecutions were supposed to have been reported to "his *Britannick* Majesty," who,

---

Language of Liberty, 1660–1832 (Cambridge, 1994). Also helpful is David S. Lovejoy, *The Glorious Revolution in America* (New York, 1972). But the entire topic is underexplored.

17. *Popery Pickled; or, The Jesuits Shooes Made of Running Leather* (London, 1689); Isaac Addington, *An Answer to a Letter from a Gentleman of New Yorke* (Boston, 1698), 2; John Marshall diary, May 1702, Braintree, Mass., MHS; [Nathaniel Whittemore], *An Almanack for the Year of Our Lord, 1716* ([Boston], 1716).

18. Robert Stevens to the Society for the Propagation of the Gospel (hereafter cited as SPG), [1711?], South Carolina, SPG microfilm, reel 17.

as a leader of the Protestant cause, expressed his appropriate outrage. Colonials read into every such incident their own fate if the Hanoverians should fall.[19]

The permeation of such thinking about Catholics and Catholic princes into everyday life is nowhere more evident than in the tutor Philip Fithian's account of an evening of casual diversion in prerevolutionary Virginia. After drinking and dancing, the group decided to engage in one of its favorite activities, playing "Break the popes neck." Colonel Philip Lee was "chosen *Pope*, and Mr Carter, Mr Christian, Mrs *Carter*, Mrs *Lee*, and the rest of the company were appointed Friars. . . . Here we had great Diversion." It is hardly surprising that they should enjoy such games. From early childhood, provincials were taught to mock the pope, deride his image, and denounce his behavior. It wasn't just the little boys who dragged hideous pope effigies through the streets. Peter Oliver remembered that every child who learned to read from the *New England Primer* each morning faced a drawing of the pope with darts on his face on the cover. In this world-view, all destructive or antisocial behavior could be construed as either coming from Catholics, having Catholic characteristics, or threatening to bring Catholicism somehow back to Britain.[20]

The creation of an ethnically compound empire intersected with this intense "Romaphobia" and, over time, antipopish language came to express anxiety about British America's ethnic strangers. It was a double-sided blade. Provincials imagined the empire as a haven for Protestants across Europe fleeing, as one German from Strasbourg put it, "the civil and religious oppressions which my country is subject to under an arbitrary and Romish government." Yet Protestants seeking asylum arrived as cultural aliens. Such strangers appeared subversive to the British identity feverishly being inculcated in the empire. William Smith reported in his *Brief State of the Province of Pennsylvania* that the Germans who had entered the colony between 1700 and 1750 were in danger of being corrupted by French priests determined to introduce "the Horrors of *Popish* Slavery" into the backcountry. Smith demanded immediate language and civic instructions to bring them into a British identity. Virginia's Governor Dinwiddie warned Robert Hunter Morris in 1755 of the serious "Dangers we are in from the German Roman Catholicks" living on the Pennsylvania frontier.[21]

19. *American Weekly Mercury*, Mar. 1, 1719/20.

20. Hunter Dickinson Farish, ed., *Journal and Letters of Philip Vickers Fithian, 1773–1774: A Plantation Tutor of the Old Dominion* (Williamsburg, Va., 1957), 34; Douglass Adair and John A. Schutz, eds., *Peter Oliver's Origin and Progress of the American Rebellion: A Tory View* (Stanford, Calif., 1961), 94.

21. John Richard Alden, *John Stuart and the Southern Colonial Frontier* (Ann Arbor,

The oaths given to culturally alien immigrants expressed these fears and became a means of controlling outsiders. Each immigrant was supposed to own the new imperial mean given voice by Jacob Smith, a German settler in Pennsylvania. During his naturalization oath, he swore he was "a Protestant" and would be "true to our Sovereign Lord King GEORGE." In an extreme form of such vows, German settlers in rural New York affirmed, "I do from my Heart abhor, detest, and abjure as . . . Heretical that damnable doctrine. . . . that Princes excommunicated . . . [by] . . . the See of Rome, may be deposed and murthered by their Subjects." The same oath called on its takers to denounce "any of the Descendents of the person who pretended to be Prince of Wales during the life Time of the late King James the Second" and deny that they had any right to the throne. Finally, and most startlingly, the oath takers were forced to swear that they did not believe in transubstantiation and that they did not adore the Virgin Mary or engage in any other "Idolatrous" practices.[22]

Over time, the anti-Catholic rhetoric came to be used to control native-born British Americans as circumstances demanded it. Real Jacobite conspiracies in the home islands reinforced this fear of popish subversion from within. Authorities used such fears to encourage the population to examine and if necessary alert them to anyone or anything that seemed Catholic and thus dangerous.[23]

An example of the use of antipopery for social policing occurred in New York City in 1741. The authorities attributed a series of fires in the city to a Catholic-tainted slave conspiracy. At the plot's center, officials declared, stood a priest who had entered New York covertly, "a principal promoter" of the "most horrible and Detestable" conspiracy "brooded in a Conclave of Devils, and hatcht in the Cabinet of Hell." The lower orders both black and white were purportedly drawn in by an "infamous Oath." Ominously, a woman allegedly kissed a book, a sure sign of impending Catholic tyranny. As one provincial reported, without any sense of irony, during the aftermath, "the Old proverb has herein also been verifyed That there is Scarce a plot but a priest is at the Bottom of it."[24]

1944), 353; [William Smith], *A Brief State of the Province of Pennsylvania* (1755; rpt. New York, 1865), 32–34, 34n; "Governor Dinwiddie to Governor Morris, September 20th, 1755," in R. A. Brock, ed., *The Official Records of Robert Dinwiddie . . .* , II, Virginia Historical Society, *Collections*, N.S., IV (Richmond, Va., 1884), 207.

22. Shippen Family Papers, box 1, APS; Milton W. Hamilton, ed., *The Papers of Sir William Johnson*, VIII (Albany, 1933), 653–656.

23. See *New-England Courant*, Oct. 1–8, 1722; *Boston Weekly News-Letter*, Feb. 20, 1752.

24. Daniel Horsmanden to Cadwallader Colden, Aug. 7, 1741, *The Letters and Papers of Cadwallader Colden*, II, *1730–1742*, NYHS, *Collections*, LI (New York, 1919), 225; Horsmanden, *The New York Conspiracy*, ed. Thomas J. Davis (Boston, 1971), 60.

Some of the slaves were actually sailors captured by New York privateers in the Spanish Caribbean. Thus nationality and religion as well as race made them suspect. The New York authorities believed these bondsmen retained their affections for Spain and Catholicism. In actuality, they had been free men as Spanish subjects and bitterly resented being sold into slavery. Fear of them ran so deep in the general population that, at one point, frightened New Yorkers had chanted *"the Spanish negroes; the Spanish negroes"* in the city's streets to force the authorities to suppress them. Authorities interrogated dozens of slaves, servants, and poorer whites and placed strict controls on them. Officials searched homes for stolen goods and passed legislation against those who might sell slaves liquor. Executions followed; authorities burned thirteen slaves and hanged seventeen more, along with four whites. Others were transported, and across the Hudson, in Hackensack, New Jersey, freeholders burned several slaves who reputedly set fires.[25]

The incident (real or imagined) also led the city's aldermen and Governor George Clarke to order a closer watch on all immigrants and strangers, who might be secret Catholic agents. The aldermen approved a house-to-house search designed in part to uncover strangers who might be trying to incite rebellion. Governor Clarke ordered the militia to assist this search and encouraged the king's subjects to "inquire concerning all . . . Strangers . . . obscure People that have no visible way of Subsistence." He feared that "popish emissaries" had been sent to the city "under disguises, such as DANCING MASTERS, SCHOOL MASTERS, PHISICIANS, and such like" so that "they may easily gain admittance into Families" and seduce the young and the weak. Cadwallader Colden wrote a detailed account of just such a "teacher" who "called himself Luke Barington," a "Stranger in this Neighbourhood at the time of the Negro Conspiracy." An Irishman, he had "traveld into Italy . . . there turn'd roman Catholick." He had set himself up in New York City as a schoolteacher shortly before the conspiracy, cavorted with Irish Catholic servants, refused to drink George II's health, and reportedly pledged his allegiance to Philip of Spain. It was feared that such actions would encourage others, and Catholicism and absolutism would replace an empire of Protestant love. In the end, Barrington turned out to be the failed son of a minor gentleman in the home islands, a threat solely to his family reputation, nothing more.[26]

25. Horsmanden, *The New York Conspiracy*, ed. Davis, 28, 39, 50, 386.

26. Ibid., 33; *New-York Weekly Journal*, Aug. 9, 1742; Colden to Daniel Horsmanden, July 29, 1742, in *The Letters and Papers of Cadwallader Colden*, VIII, *Additional Letters and Papers, 1715–1748*, NYHS, *Collections*, LXVII (New York, 1937), 288–289.

Similar reasoning created doubts about Maryland's Catholics during the wars with the French at midcentury. In 1745, at the outbreak of King George's War, Maryland's Governor Thomas Bladen expressed fears about his colony's Catholic population. Specifically, he believed that Jesuit emissaries were working among the Native Americans deep in the province's interior to turn them to the French interest. He demanded action to control those populations and assure their loyalty to the British cause. In 1754, Virginia's Governor Dinwiddie reported to the London authorities that Catholics constituted more than one-third of neighboring Maryland's population. "I fear," he continued, "they w'd be glad of any Conquest [of the Chesapeake by the French and Indians] y't w'd establish their religion."[27]

It was not the actual number of Catholics that in the end frightened imperial officials. The fear of internal subversion, of Britons turning to Catholicism and Catholic ways, expressed a starkly Calvinist view of the human soul. In that worldview, Protestantism and British Protestant liberty demanded much. It should not be confused with the ultralibertarianism of postmodern society. There was always a danger that that which was asked was too much, that the individual soul might be seduced by Catholic spectacle and the range of emotions it could create. Awe seems to have been the most dangerous of these emotions, coupled to a craving for idolatry. One of those condemned as a secret Catholic during the New York unrest in 1741 asked of his accusers, "Now how come these persons to know so much, to be acquainted with priests and their secrets?" Although shouted in desperation, it was a question they asked themselves (in an abstract sense) more than we might now acknowledge. Fear of the empire's Papist enemies expressed an anxiety about themselves and their own innate depraved tendencies.[28]

As strange as it may now seem in our world of unchecked democracy, religious bigotry helped define British liberties. Exclusion of Catholics from the empire's political and social council framed the parameters of British liberties and properties. Difference was suspect and the absorption of cultural aliens into the em-

27. "Proceedings of the Council of Maryland, 1745/6. At a Council Held at the House of His Excellency the Governor in the City of Annapolis . . . ," Feb. 24, 1745/6, *Proceedings of the Council of Maryland, 1732–1753*, XXVIII, Archives of Maryland Online, 353; Dinwiddie to Secretary Robinson, Sept. 23, 1754, in R. A. Brock, ed., *The Official Records of Robert Dinwiddie . . .* , I, Virginia Historical Society, *Collections*, III (Richmond, Va., 1883), 323.

28. Horsmanden, *New York Conspiracy*, ed. Davis, 367. Russell, *Causes of the English Civil War*, cogently comments that England's sixteenth-century iconoclasts feared the seductive powers of the images they destroyed (77).

pire's shared identities—Protestant, Briton, free—was the highest goal of those who generated political print culture. Internal deviance, particularly of a political nature, was referenced to Catholicism, France, and the Stuart Pretender as a means of controlling it.[29]

This fear insinuated itself into the epistemological base of provincial thinking where reason meets passion, and it never let go of those who lived within its grasp. One New Yorker writing in 1810 vividly remembered that the power "the English government" got from fear of Catholics led them "to cherish this animosity." Those who had lived before the war, he continued, were "religiously" taught to "abhor the Pope, Devil and Pretender." Visualized in the effigies of November 5, blamed for every historical disaster that had overtaken Protestants, denounced in oaths, in print, and in toast, the Protestant apocalypse's three riders were among the empire's strongest supports. It is critical to understand the passions of empire as real things that shaped behavior. People loved the king and feared his enemies in large part because they participated in a ritual cycle that encouraged these emotions. They read a print culture saturated with words of affection for the monarch and a dread of Catholics. And they spoke in a political-religious idiom that incorporated these emotions.[30]

Material desires made these emotional ties to empire part of everyday life. Over time, the consumption of British goods took on overt political meaning as products linked to the monarchy became common in the American colonies. These goods allowed provincials to visualize the passions of empire in their own lives.

• • •

Envy, Desire, and the Commodification of Monarchy

In 1772, the *Massachusetts Gazette and Boston News-Letter* carried an ad aimed at combating one of the eighteenth century's worst tyrants: tooth decay. The era was, among other things, a time of great dental misery. Doctors and merchants answered the demand created by disfigurement and pain. One such pseudo-dentist, Jacob Hemet, recommended to the Boston public "his newly discovered Essence of Pearl, and Pearl Dentifrice, which he has found to be greatly superior . . . in elegance . . . also in efficacy, to any thing hitherto made use of for complaints of the Teeth and Gums." But Hemet realized that his product's strongest draw was the teeth of his most famous clients, "her Majesty, and the Princess Amelia."[31]

29. *Boston Weekly News-Letter*, Jan. 9, 1755.
30. Horsmanden, *New York Conspiracy*, ed. Davis, 2.
31. *Massachusetts Gazette and Boston News-Letter*, Apr. 16, 1772.

It is hard to imagine that essence of pearl might play as meaningful a role in instructing us about the provincial order and empire as court records, a preacher's sermon, or an Enlightenment writer. Scholars, however, have correctly established that provincials consumed British goods with abandon, that gender differences shaped consumption and were shaped by it, and that commercial demands set off ripple effects throughout the imperial economy. Imperial trade lay at the foundation of eighteenth-century political economy.

The efforts to link these changes to political transformation in the empire have, however, been fraught with difficulty. The intersection of consumption and change in the period seems obvious. Printed materials moved along trade networks as both product and vehicles of advertisement. The bitter paper money disputes that wracked the colonial polities in the eighteenth century were tied directly to increased consumption. The initial conversion experiences in the Great Awakening have been convincingly linked to a guilty reaction to the spread of consumer culture, and consumer boycotts were at the core of imperial protest until 1774. But consumption of British goods also integrated the empire economically and culturally, even as commercial ambitions created real social disruptions.[32]

32. The most important study to date is that of T. H. Breen; see Breen, *The Marketplace of Revolution: How Consumer Politics Shaped American Independence* (New York, 2004); Breen, "An Empire of Goods: The Anglicization of Colonial America, 1690–1776," *Journal of British Studies*, XXV (1986), 467–499; and Breen, "'Baubles of Britain': The American and Consumer Revolutions of the Eighteenth Century," in *Past and Present*, no. 119 (May 1988), 73–104. See also J. E. Crowley, *This Sheba, Self: The Conceptualization of Economic Life in Eighteenth-Century America*, Johns Hopkins University Studies in Historical and Political Science, Ser. 92, no. 2 (Baltimore, 1974). The literature on consumption in the Anglo-American world in the eighteenth century is extensive and growing. Some of the most important studies since the 1960s are Ralph Davis, *A Commercial Revolution: English Overseas Trade in the Seventeenth and Eighteenth Century* (London, 1967); W. E. Minchinton, ed., *The Growth of English Overseas Trade in the Seventeenth and Eighteenth Centuries* (London, 1969); Winifred B. Rothenberg, "The Market and Massachusetts Farmers, 1750–1855," *Journal of Economic History*, XLI (1981), 283–314; Joan Thirsk, *Economic Policy and Projects: The Development of a Consumer Society in Early Modern England* (Oxford, 1978); Carole Shammas, "How Self-Sufficient Was Early America?" *Journal of Interdisciplinary History*, XIII, no. 2 (Autumn 1982), 247–272; Neil McKendrick, John Brewer, and J. H. Plumb, eds., *The Birth of a Consumer Society: The Commercialization of Eighteenth-Century England* (Bloomington, Ind., 1982); Lorena S. Walsh, "Urban Amenities and Rural Sufficiency: Living Standards and Consumer Behavior in the Colonial Chespeake, 1643–1777," *Journal of Economic History*, XLIII (1983), 109–117; J. G. A.

To address this paradox, we need to rethink consumption. It expressed and continues to express emotions—hope, fear, love, anxiety—that are tied to power and personal relationships. "That which men Desire," Hobbes wrote, "they are also sayd to LOVE . . . so that Desire, and Love, are the same thing; save that by Desire, we always signifie the Absence of the Object." The spread of one category of goods, those that appropriated the royal families' names and images for commercial or artistic ends, suggests both the ways commerce normalized the Hanoverian regime and the danger inherent in a commercial empire based on the passions. Products that bore the royal seal, advertisements for goods that invoked the monarchy, and mass-produced royal images helped express and shape the personal emotional ties that acted as imperial filament in the British Atlantic. These products became commonplace in the eighteenth century, and as they did, more and more provincial homes came to contain images of the monarch or royal family. This royalization of private life expressed a swelling loyalty, but it also allowed provincials to imagine the empire as a personal, emotional relationship between individuals and their king.[33]

The rising affluence that made these purchases possible threatened the assumption of social immobility and material limits upon which the early modern order rested. Affluence was supposed to be for the few and thus connected to power. In a letter to the home islands in the mid-eighteenth century, Georgia Council president James Habersham provides us with an illustration of how material display was supposed to reinforce the existing power structure. He complained to his London correspondent William Knox that, while the ship from the empire's capital had arrived in Savannah, "I received my Cloths, tho' too late for the King's birth day, and so was the Governor's." To wear fine cloths from London during royal rites honored the monarch and at the same time asserted one's own status in the local power structure. Habersham knew that clothing marked mutuality between gentlemen, and he was quick to add, "I much approve of your

---

Pocock, *Virtue, Commerce, and History* (Cambridge, 1985); Robert Blair St. George, ed., *Material Life in America, 1600–1860* (Boston, 1988), particularly the essays in section three, and Rodris Roth, "Tea-Drinking in Eighteenth-Century America: Its Etiquette and Equipage," 439–462; Graham Hood, *The Governor's Palace in Williamsburg: A Cultural Study* (Chapel Hill, N.C., 1991); John J. McCusker and Russell Menard, *The Economy of British America, 1607–1789* (Chapel Hill, N.C., 1991); John Brewer and Roy Porter, eds., *Consumption and the World of Goods* (New York, 1993); Stephen Innes, *Creating the Commonwealth: The Economic Culture of Puritan New England* (New York, 1995); Jon Butler, *Becoming America: The Revolution before 1776* (Cambridge, Mass., 2000), 50–88, 131–184.

33. Thomas Hobbes, *Leviathan*, ed. Richard Tuck (Cambridge, 1991), 38.

Taste . . . but how you send so gay a Waistcoat, however to shew my respect to you, I wore it."[34]

The spreading consumer revolution gradually unhinged the fusion of material goods with status. But to understand how that occurred, it is critical to put aside the debates over a liberal or republican colonial past or a premodern versus modern worldview. The problem was not the antimaterialistic streak within Puritanism, evangelical culture, or republicanism. Nor was it materialism per se. It was, rather, the envy-driven wishes for increasingly available material goods that had been, within living memory, limited to a certain social stratum. Abundance threatened all that the colonial gentry aspired to; it scrambled the link between possessions and social status. When that abundance was wrapped in a royal package, consumption became a vehicle, figuratively and in some cases literally, for the internalization of authority that ultimately created a new political logic in North America. Such objects personalized the relationship between monarch and imperial subject. The nature of consumption obscures that critical change to a large degree, and yet the sources provide just enough evidence for speculation on its character.[35]

Eighteenth-century observers fixed on envy and desire as the cause of a kind of rolling crisis of status they perceived around them. They understood these feelings to create faction, feared by eighteenth-century political and social theorists of all stripes. In the 1720s and 1730s, with royal rites' being passed along seamlessly to new generations and social immobility firmly at the core of provincials' American dream, a host of widely dispersed commentators began to complain about the power of envy to rupture the social body's harmony. A writer to the *American Weekly Mercury* stated that, of all the passions, "Envy . . . proceeds from an inward Grief and Disatisfaction at the good of another. . . . Envy sooner exerts its Fury upon its own Bowels, than on the Honour of its Neighbour. . . . Men are naturally apt to look with an ill Eye on anothers Happiness, and desire to reduce the Fortunes of none more than those whom they have once seen upon the Level with themselves." A 1733 correspondent to the *South-Carolina Gazette* declared that "the Passions which most disturb the human Mind, are *Lust* and *Anger* . . . but vehemence of Passion is not so dreadful a Distemper of the Mind, as *Envy*

---

34. James Habersham to William Knox, July 12, 1768, Georgia, in *The Letters of Hon. James Habersham, 1756–1775*, Georgia Historical Society, *Collections*, VI (Savannah, 1904), 75.

35. Very useful in this regard is Joyce Appleby, "Consumption in Early Modern Social Thought," in John Brewer and Roy Porter, eds., *Consumption and the World of Goods* (London, 1993), 162–173.

and hidden *Malice*." Envy, he continued, "inflames us against others, who, in *our Opinion*, are *happier* than we." Envy threatened the dream of social immobility that was also a hope of a conflict-free society.[36]

It became a trope of provincial literature to denounce those who had made their fortunes and put on the airs of a superior rank. The Philadelphia writer "Busybody" used his essays to urge the ambitious to act in a manner as "to cause all his Acquaintaince to wish his Prosperity and Advancement in the world." He particularly instructed them to be patient but feared "that the Persons I am endeavoring to instruct, will think that nothing short of Grandeur can be worth their pressing after." Few men, he continued, "know how to demean themselves, whose Industry has been crowned with success; and we more frequently see the Man, vain and full of himself that from a mean Birth and little stock has shot up."[37]

The traveling Maryland doctor Alexander Hamilton, who provided a detailed account of the American provinces in the 1740s, described just such a pretend gentleman. Hamilton mocked this William Morison, "a very rough spun, forward, clownish blade" he encountered in Pennsylvania, for attempting to "pass for a gentleman." Morison couldn't pull it off, despite his repeatedly telling his road companion that he "had good linnen in his bags, a pair of silver buckles, silver clasps, and gold sleeve buttons . . . that his little woman att home drank tea twice a day."[38]

This interesting account reveals the threat consumption posed to the system as a whole. More and more Morisons began to appear in provincial America, convinced they could somehow purchase gentility and all that came with it. Although Hamilton might note the disjuncture between Morison's material refinement and his personal gentility, between his goods and his manners, for many others, boundaries began to blur. Of course, the denunciation of such people itself became a vehicle to social mobility, an opportunity to display one's own learning and discretion. Those like Hamilton who instructed others asserted their own superiority.

In the 1730s and 1740s, provincial observers increasingly denounced the social disruptions caused by wanton material desire. In South Carolina, the heightening fear of a black majority was apparently paralleled by considerable anxiety over

36. *American Weekly Mercury*, June 22–29, 1732; *South-Carolina Gazette* (Charleston), Aug. 11–18, 1733.

37. *American Weekly Mercury*, May 1–8, 1720.

38. Carl Bridenbaugh, ed., *Gentleman's Progress: The Itinerarium of Dr. Alexander Hamilton, 1744* (Pittsburgh, 1948), 13–14.

those growing numbers within white society who would grasp at a higher social status. "Blackamore," writing in 1733, conflated the problems of racial identity with the problem of status in an inflationary economy where social mobility was more prevalent than many were comfortable with.

Blackamore feared status amalgamation, a social sin he saw equal to racial amalgamation. Physical lust produced the latter; the former grew from the twin ills of envy and emulation. After a long description of "mulattoes," Blackamore launched into an assault on those who "from mean Beginnings find themselves in Circumstances a little more easy." Such people, he complained, had ambitions beyond their station. But it was impossible for such a person to affect "the natural and easy Manner of those who have been genteely educated." After saluting those real gentlemen who could "converse freely . . . with honest Men of any Degree below him, without degrading or fearing to degrade himself in the least," Blackamore declared himself (improbably) as an "ordinary Mechanick." He hoped to always know his "Station." Those who did not know their station, "a Man well dress'd . . . mighty cautious how he mixes in Company" and a "young Woman Mistress of a newly fine furnished House, treating me with . . . a high Manner of Condescension that might become a Governor's Lady," made fools of themselves and confused the society's lines of authority.[39]

These parvenus he thought of as "Mungrel," the man a kind of half-gentleman, the woman "not long since . . . somebody's Servant Maid." Blackamore concluded his remarks by declaring that nothing was as "monstrously ridiculous as the *Molatto Gentleman*." The "ridiculous" figures grew from the disjuncture of their material possessions—the fine clothes and furniture that marked gentile status—with their education, birth, and manners. The socially amalgamated figure made a mockery of the status that he or she aspired to.[40]

The material appropriation of royalty should be viewed against this backdrop of desire and anxiety. When this use of royalty for commercial ends in the colonies began is difficult to determine. It had not begun in earnest in the provinces before William III's death; the throne was too precarious, as it would be again in the reign of George I, to allow for uncontrolled consumer appropriation. Newspapers did not appear in the colonies with regularity until early in the eighteenth century, and the commercial ad as a literary genre did not become normalized until the 1730s. We can date the monarchy's commercialization firmly to that decade, when the *Boston Weekly News-Letter* advertised Dr. Boylston's *History of the Small Pox Inoculation in New-England*, dedicated to "Her Royal Highness

---

39. *South-Carolina Gazette*, Mar. 5–22, 1734/5.
40. Ibid.

the PRINCESS of WALES." Similar ads appeared in other colonial publications as consumer goods became more widely available.[41]

This brief ad for Boylston's *History* suggests the origins of this particular form of monarchical appropriation. It seems to be related to dynastic stability. By 1730, George II was securely on the throne, and thus appropriation of royal authority for commercial ends would have seemed less threatening. The sellers' intent, one suspects, was in no way to denigrate royal authority. Rather, they sought to take advantage of the tremendous affections being generated for the monarchy in the broader political culture. For consumers, such goods offered social status but also affirmed their ties to the empire and linked them emotionally to the royal family.

The association with medical science obvious in many of the royally oriented ads grew from the Hanoverians' patronage of science and the medical arts. George II and Queen Caroline kept busts of Newton handy in their residences, desperately seeking to be seen as a progressive monarchy attuned to the eighteenth century's new sciences. Their approval of scientific progress laid them open to the appropriation of imperial crests for commercial ends, and although they attempted to control it, the Hanoverians never stamped it out. To control the language to that degree would have been too difficult in the sprawling commercial empire.[42]

One after another colonial ad writer managed to suggest royal approval of medical and even what we would consider personal hygiene products. Initially, this was done indirectly, as when the *New-York Gazette; or, the Weekly Post-Boy* advertised "The Princely Beautifying Lotion . . . [which] beautifies the Face, Neck, and Hands, to the utmost perfection" or when an ad in the *Pennsylvania Gazette* proclaimed the value of "the great and learned Doctor SANXAY's Imperial Golden DROPS," which had been developed in the course "of private practice with the . . . most delicate constitutions, the first nobility . . . in Great Britain, Ireland, and many persons eminent for fortune and character in America."[43]

Eventually, the ads turned to direct linkage in one form or another. In 1753, the *New-York Gazette; or, the Weekly Post-Boy* advertised "by the King's Patent . . . West's ASTMATICUM MIRABLE, or wonderful Pectoral ELIXIR . . . [which] cures all colds, Hoarsness . . . Wheezing, Ratling in the Throat, or Difficulty of

41. *Weekly News-Letter* (Boston), Feb. 5–12, 1730.

42. Ibid., Oct. 12–19, 1732. "*London, August* 10. Her Majesty having built a fine Grotto or Hermitage at Richmond and adorned it with the Bustoes of Mr. Locke, Sir Isaac Newton, Mr. Woolaston (Author of *The Religion of Nature Delineated*) and the late Dr. Clarke."

43. *New-York Gazette; or, the Weekly Post-Boy*, Feb. 26, 1753; *Pennsylvania Gazette* (Philadelphia), Feb. 28, 1771.

Breathing." With the king's approval, all things were possible, even a cure for the common cold.[44]

In this same period, royal likenesses, crowns, or royal arms came to adorn mass-produced glass and earthenware. Fragments of plates bearing the likeness of William and Mary have been unearthed at Jamestown in Virginia, though dating their exact arrival is impossible. Virginia archaeological sites have also yielded delftware emblazoned with the royal arms and the Hanoverian mottos "Dieu Et Mon Droit" and "Honi Soit Qui Mal Y Pense." Platters showing a cavalier presenting a woman a flower and a plate with a crowned "GR" (representing Georgius REX) and a royal figure in robes that celebrated the Hanoverian succession in 1714 have been found in the same sites.[45]

New England's glass, slipware, and delftware also carried imperial themes, though there, tastes more obviously reflected the accommodation of local political cultures with the empire. Products that mixed imperial and Protestant themes were available throughout the empire, but New Englanders seem to have been especially fond of them, reflecting their creolization. Early in the eighteenth century, Maine settlers owned gray stoneware with the crowned initials "GR" over a cherub's head, and gray stoneware jugs carrying an equestrian seal with "William III by the grace of God King of Great Britain, France and Ireland" were present in New England.[46]

Other glass, earthenware, slipware, delftware, and tiles carried imperial themes or expressed aspects of the Protestant political culture. As early as the 1680s, London tile makers produced Popish Plot tiles that charted the course of the purported Catholic conspiracy at the end of the 1670s and offered the opportunity of symbolically sharing the home with the informer Titus Oates. Although we cannot determine with certainty how many colonials, if any, had these tiles, by the time of George III's ascension to the throne, Wedgwood was mass-producing ceramics with the royal likenesses and imperial themes for the Atlantic markets. Even Benjamin West's famous painting of General Wolfe's death at the Battle of Quebec in 1759 was transferred to ceramics and sold in the provinces.[47]

44. *New-York Gazette; or, the Weekly Post-Boy*, Jan. 29, 1753.

45. Ron Fuchs, Assistant Curator of Ceramics, Winterthur Museum, relayed by Leslie Grigsby; Grigsby, *English Pottery: Stoneware and Earthenware, 1650–1800* (London, 1990), 104–105, 156, 423; Grigsby, *English Slip-Decorated Earthenware at Williamsburg* (Williamsburg, Va., 1993), 48. I am extremely grateful to Leslie Grigsby for her advice and assistance in understanding imperial delftware.

46. *Unearthing New England's Past: The Ceramic Evidence* (Lexington, Mass., 1984), 18, 47, 67.

47. Michael Archer, *Delftware, The Tin-Glazed Earthenware of the British Isles: A Cata-*

PLATE 5. *Stoneware tankards with "AR" and "GR" ciphers. Monarchical images and symbols could be found in both homes and more public settings like taverns, where mugs with royal arms or symbols were hoisted to toast the monarchy and Protestant political culture on any number of red-letter days. "AR" stood for "Anne* REX," *and "GR" was "George* REX." *The Colonial Williamsburg Foundation*

Purchasing such goods allowed for the royalization of the household. Those who selected imperially themed goods affirmed their place as British subjects in the privacy of their own homes. They proclaimed British patriotism and established a visual connection to the empire. Perhaps the best evidence of this admittedly semi-hidden process of domestic royalization in the provinces comes from the consumption of royal images.

logue of the Collection in the Victoria and Albert Museum (London, 1997), 429. In the 1680s, there was a "Popish Plot Nine Tiles relating to the Titus Oates Conspiracy" line of painted ceramic tiles made in London. Leslie B. Grigsby, *The Longridge Collection of English Slipware and Delftware*, 2 vols. (London, 2000), esp. 62, contains numerous examples of politically themed slip and delftware. The demand for Saint George slipware was apparently high in the eighteenth century. Saint George was the patron saint of England. See David Drakard, *Printed English Pottery: History and Humour in the Reign of George III, 1760–1820* (London, 1992), 146, 148–151.

The Consumption of Images and the Problem of Representation

In February 1750, the *New-York Weekly Journal* carried a description of a newly planned capital for His Majesty's province of Nova Scotia. "That City," the paper reported, "is at the first to consist of 2000 Houses, disposed in fifty Streets of different Magnitudes." At the town's center was to be a "spacious Square, with an Equestrian Statue of his present Majesty in the Center of it." The streets were "all built in straight lines, crossing one another at right angles." In this town, all roads would lead to the king.[48]

But a year earlier, the same New York papers called attention to a king on the road, literally. Wax "'Effigies of the Royal Family of England' and others, to the number of fourteen wax figures, are advertized to be seen from 7 a.m. to 6 p.m." On October 9, 1749, the wax figures and a "Puppet Shew" were exhibited for poor debtors' relief, with the royal figures to be displayed before the "shew."[49]

The empire's physical and demographic expansion created a subtle problem of aesthetic authority. How would the king be represented to these growing populations who would never see the royal person? How would they come to know and love the Hanoverian monarchy? Royal celebrations and a royal political calendar, a restructuring of language conventions and public behavioral norms, and religious invocations designed to assert monarchical supremacy to an unprecedented degree all provided an education. But there was more, as the plan for Halifax and the touring wax show suggest. Between 1690 and 1776, provincial officials used visual representations of royalty to normalize their authority. But the gradual spread of the monarch's commodified likeness in the form of prints, mass-produced portraits, glassware, and even wax museums and puppet shows undermined the efforts to control how American subjects saw their kings' likenesses. Private representations ultimately helped create contradictory understandings of the monarchy and by extension the entire empire.[50]

Imperial officials sent formal monarchical portraits to the American prov-

48. *New-York Weekly Journal*, Feb. 27, 1749/50.

49. I. N. Phelps Stokes, *The Iconography of Manhattan Island, 1498–1909*, IV (New York, 1922), 616.

50. The best short discussions of the rise of colonial consumption of portraits are Margaretta M. Lovell, "Painters and Their Customers: Aspects of Art and Money in Eighteenth-Century America," in Cary Carson, Ronald Hoffman, and Peter J. Albert, eds., *Of Consuming Interests: The Style of Life in the Eighteenth Century* (Charlottesville, Va., 1994), 284–306; and Lovell, "Reading Eighteenth-Century American Family Portraits: Social Images and Self-Images," *Wintherthur Portfolio*, XXII (1987), 46–71.

inces as gifts to colonial governments designed to solidify royal authority. Public likenesses of the monarch had become commonplace in parts of Britain during Queen Anne's reign. The importance of such portraits to imperial relationships was demonstrated early in the eighteenth century in Massachusetts Bay. In 1705, Jonathan Belcher returned from a visit to Hanover in Germany with a portrait of Princess Sophia, Protestant heir to the throne and mother of George I. The painting was a gift to Massachusetts Bay, and Joseph Dudley ordered it displayed with the portrait of "her Majesties [Queen Anne]." He asked Belcher to attend the province's "Council and the Officers" in order that he might see the portrait hung in the council chamber and "drink her Majesties and Royal Highness health, it being her Majesties birthday."[51]

Strangely, provincial officials did not immediately thank Sophia, an oversight that caused a panic when it was recognized. Dudley desperately sought to make "an acknowledgement of this Honour and Favour done to the Province," but, "having no Correspondent, nor acquaintance in Her Highness's Court," he could not rectify so grievous an error alone. Dudley turned to Belcher to recoup the situation, which the young man did by again journeying to Hanover "to Apologize" for his and the province's mistake. He threw himself "at Your Royal Highnesses feet and Humbly ask[ed] forgiveness." He begged the princess to accept atonement from "Her Majesty's Governour in N. England" in the form of "candles . . . and An Indian Slave [a young boy], A native of my countrey." That the colony would assuage its fears at the expense of an Indian boy may be surprisingly brutal to us, but, as Belcher's note to Sophia suggests, they saw him as symbol, property, and human being, a representation of their province, just as the portrait depicted both the princess's person and the Protestant succession.[52]

In the same period, portraits and royal representations became part of diplomatic initiatives to the Five Nations in northern New York. In August 1710, Governor Robert Hunter presented medals with Queen Anne's "Royal Effigie on one side" to be kept at the Five Nations' main villages. Hunter further presented each of the nations with twenty pictures of the queen in silver, "to be given to the Chief Warriors" to wear around their necks so they would "allways be in a readiness to fight under her Banner." The queen's image realized her authority on the empire's far rim by establishing personal-political ties to the Five Nations' head-

51. Paul Kléber Monod, *The Power of Kings: Monarchy and Religion in Europe, 1589–1715* (New Haven, Conn., 1999), 294–295; Joseph Dudley to Jonathan Belcher, Feb. 6, 1705/6, Miscellaneous, Frederick Lewis Gay Transcripts, I, 172, MHS.

52. Dudley to John Chamberlayne, Mar. 1, 1707/8, and Belcher to Princess Sophia, Sept. 12, 1708, Gay Transcripts, I, 173, 174.

men. What must the recipients have thought as they wore this image in the deep woods of northern New York?[53]

Southern governments placed equally high importance on royal portraits and emblems. In 1721, South Carolina leaders ordered their agents to request portraits of George I and his consort, the royal arms, and silver plate for the Charleston Anglican church. In 1739, Caroline County, Virginia, paid a visiting English artist 1,600 pounds of tobacco to paint the king's arms on the side of their new courthouse, to remind them of the king's power and justice. When the capital building at Williamsburg, Virginia, burned to the ground in January 1747, the colonial papers reported that officials fortuitously saved both the all-important records and "the Pictures of the Royal Family." The efforts to save the portraits and the widespread reports of their salvation reflected their worth.[54]

In most colonies, officials installed royal portraits in government buildings in ceremonies that coincided with royal birthday celebrations or other imperial holidays. The practice was evident as early as the arrival of Sophia's portraits in Boston in 1706, but as the celebrations themselves became more elaborate, so did the images' role in them. On June 6, 1765, the *Pennsylvania Gazette* reported on the King's Birthday celebration at Burlington, West New Jersey. The paper's description shows the relationship of royal portraits to royal rites and the articulation of power. The reporter declared that "the Gentlemen of the Council, and General Assembly, together with the Mayor and Corporation . . . and many of the Magistrates and principal Inhabitants, went at Noon in Procession to the House of his Excellency our Governor." William Franklin greeted them, and they drank the royal healths as small cannons fired a salute.[55]

---

53. "Colden's History of the Five Indian Nations, Continuation, 1707–1720," in *The Letters and Papers of Cadwallader Colden*, IX, *Additional Letters and Papers, 1749–1775, and Some of Colden's Writings*, NYHS, *Collections*, LXVIII (New York, 1937), 391.

54. Edward McCrady, *The History of South Carolina under the Royal Government, 1719–1776* (New York, 1899), 40. George I had locked his consort away years before. Apparently, the colonial government was unaware of this. I would like to thank John Murrin for this observation. On the courthouse and the king's arms, see T. E. Campbell, *Colonial Caroline: A History of Caroline County, Virginia* (Richmond, Va., 1954), 125. On the burning of the capital building, see *New-York Evening-Post*, Apr. 6, 1747. Twenty years later, William Tryon would report to the Earl of Hillsborough that he had incorporated "Medals of the King and Queen on the Frieze over the Columns" in the governor's mansion house he was building in North Carolina. See William Tryon to the Earl of Hillsborough, Jan. 12, 1769, in William S. Powell, ed., *The Correspondence of William Tryon and Other Selected Papers*, II, *1768–1818* (Raleigh, N.C., 1981), 292.

55. *Pennsylvania Gazette* (Philadelphia), June 6, 1765.

PLATE 6. *George II. 1752.
From the* New England Primer.
*Beginning in the 1730s, portraits
of the British monarchs began
circulating widely in the colonies.
They were included in children's
books, sold for the decorating
of private homes, and placed in
taverns and other public places.
Courtesy, American Antiquarian
Society*

But the day's climax was still to come. "The Company," the *Gazette* continued, "had likewise the Pleasure of seeing the fine Portraits of their Majesties (drawn at full Length, in their Coronation Robes . . .) which were lately sent over as a Present from the Crown to his Excellency." By placing and displaying the portraits within government buildings, royal officials linked visually their power with the larger imperial order.[56]

If formal viewings in controlled situations had been the only way that provincials saw portraits of their monarchs, perhaps such representations would have enhanced the colonial gentry's status and helped permanently stabilize the imperial order, as they were designed to do. Whatever way colonials understood them, such spectacles reinforced the imperial order. However, at the dawn of the era of mass production, royal images began to be produced for commercial ends. The consumption of these images allowed the purchasers to bring the monarch and the empire quite literally into the home.

Mass-produced prints of the monarchs first appeared in the provinces early in the eighteenth century. Print portraits of Queen Anne apparently circulated in the colonies after 1702, and prints of George I and George II seem to have been sold in the port towns by the 1720s or the early 1730s. In April 1746, the *Pennsyl-*

56. Ibid.

PLATE 7. *George III copper medal. 1762. Miniatures and medals bearing the monarch's likeness arrived in the colonies as early as Queen Anne's reign. Worn on the person or displayed in the home on a mantle or in another prominent place, these signaled personal allegiance to the monarch and loyalty to the Protestant succession. Courtesy, Massachusetts Historical Society*

vania Gazette advertised imported pictures of the royal family for sale. The same bundle contained other prints with imperial themes, including some of "Consultations between the Pope, the king of France, the Old Pretender, Young Pretender, a Highlander and the Devil," produced in response to the '45 Jacobite rebellion in Britain. Certainly by the 1760s, such portraits were being sold beyond the ports. Joseph McAdams of Northumberland County, Virginia, offered "200 prints, or pictures, representing all the persons and characters of note in Europe, viz., Crowned Heads" for sale to his neighbors. Merchants also sold medallions, like the "Sundry Medals of his present most Sacred Majesty GEORGE III struck on a fine white Metal." One side contained a "Portrait of His Majesty," the other "a Heart encircled with Oak and Laurel Branches; the Motto, ENTIRELY BRITISH." By the time the imperial crisis erupted, such prints and portraits were widely distributed.[57]

The flood of prints allowed for a royalization of domestic life. Contemporary commentators noted that the English-speaking people had a tendency to decorate their homes with portraits of family and friends. People of high and even middling status gave face portraits and miniatures of family members as gifts.

57. *American Weekly Mercury*, Apr. 24, 1746; Lovell, "Painters and Their Customers," in Carson, Hoffman, and Albert, eds., *Of Consuming Interests*, 301; *Virginia Gazette* (Williamsburg), Oct. 17, 1766; *Boston News-Letter*, June 25, 1761.

They decorated the interior chambers of provincial homes or were carried on the person. Although this was obviously much more common among the British aristocracy, the colonial gentry adopted portrait decoration at least as early as the 1720s.

It is against this backdrop that we should view the inclusion of royal portraits and imperially themed paintings in provincial homes. In 1728, Virginian Colonel Maximilian Boush had portraits of Queen Anne and Prince George in his home. A more vivid example of this familiarization occurred in Benjamin Franklin's Philadelphia home. At one point in his extended travels, his wife, Deborah, wrote to him that she had decorated the family sitting room with "brother John's picture, and one of the King and Queen." The portraits united family and monarch in Franklin's home and, no doubt, in others.[58]

The maudlin emotions such portraits could bring forth are evident in the will of Franklin's loyalist son, William, who lived in a bitter exile in London. Writing in 1813, he gave everything he had to family and friends without stipulation, except "the family pictures and those of the King and Queen" and "likewise the glass out of which the Queen drank at the Coronation Dinner"; the fate of these, he was very careful to control. Their value was heightened by his exile, his alienation from his father, and his other sufferings as a loyalist. He wrote long after the Revolution, but it is powerfully telling that he would single these things out and link family portraits with those of the monarchy.[59]

Some British Americans actually carried the monarch's image with them on their person. This practice, too, underwent a shift shaped by the spread of the cult of Protestant monarchy and industrial production. Initially, only a select few with direct access to the monarchy carried such images. Virginian Daniel Parke, who eventually became the governor of Antigua, wore a miniature of Queen Anne presented to him by the last Stuart queen herself when he brought her news of the Duke of Marlborough's great victory over the forces of Louis XIV at Blenheim. When Jonathan Belcher visited the court of Hanover in 1706, he reported with pride to his brother that the Princess Sophia "gave me a pretty pocket piece with her face on one side, which desir'd I would accept as a mark of her respect

58. John Brewer, *The Pleasures of the Imagination* (Chicago, 1997), 209–213; Mary Newton Stanard, *Colonial Virginia: Its People and Customs* (Philadelphia, 1917), 317; John F. Watson, *Annals of Philadelphia, and Pennsylvania in the Olden Time . . .* (Philadelphia, 1909), I, 206.

59. Last will and testament of William Franklin, Apr. 15, 1813, William Franklin Papers, box 1, APS.

and thanks" for Belcher's having twice visited her. So deeply did he value this piece that he passed it to his son in 1749 as a special mark of his love.[60]

By that latter date, wider populations could experience the same sort of tie as mechanical reproduction allowed miniatures and miniature engravings of the king to be sold in the provinces. These were small enough to fit inside a watch cover or a carrying case. The inscription below one such miniature told "BRITONS" to "BEHOLD the Best of KINGS. Beloved by the Bravest of People. Justly admired by all, By his Enemies Dreaded." To carry the king's likeness was to own one's allegiances in a most intimate fashion.[61]

The power such prints and portraits had to inculcate loyalty is evident in an account of one given by Philip Fithian in Virginia in 1774. Even at that late date, he described in great detail a print of the West painting portraying General Wolfe's death at Quebec at the height of the Seven Years' War. He found the "two Lions couchant, the Emblems of the british Nation, supporting the Sarcophagus or marble Urn, and intended to express the gratitude of his native country for his eminent Services" to be especially noteworthy and appropriate.[62]

People in every colony had royal portraits and imperial prints by 1765. From the numbers mentioned in newspaper ads, it seems probable that at least thousands of households had prints or portraits of the royal family by that date, although that number is simply a guess. It was possibly much higher, into the tens of thousands, but not likely much lower. These representations, along with the tiles, delftware, slipware, and glassware, allowed for an imperialized household.

To fully understand the power of this widespread personalization of royal images, we have to do one of the most dangerous things a historian can do: read backward and, worse yet, do so through the revolutionary crisis. Although formal representations of the king were destroyed as part of a spectacular iconoclasm in 1776 that expressed deep anger at a rogue political father, some of the mass-produced portraits suffered a different fate. In February 1777, John Adams was in Baltimore with other members of the Continental Congress. As he visited homes in the city, he noticed that "they have a Fashion in this Town of reversing the Picture of King G. 3, in such Families as have it." One evening he came across one

60. David Hackett Fischer, *Albion's Seed: Four British Folkways in America* (New York, 1989), 319; Belcher to his brother and Captain Foster, Nov. 16, 1708, London, Belcher Papers.

61. E. McSherry Fowble, *To Please Every Taste: Eighteenth-Century Prints from the Winterthur Museum* (Alexandria, Va., 1991), 86–87.

62. Farish, ed., *Journal and Letters of Philip Vickers Fithian*, 71.

of these "Topsy Turvy Kings," as he called them, with a poem mounted beneath it. The poem mocked the ruler who, as they noted, had once had the power to create both fear and love in his subjects:

> Behold the Man who had it in his Power
> To make a Kingdom tremble and adore
> Intoxicate with Folly, see his Head
> Plac'd where the meanest of his Subjects tread
> Like Lucifer the giddy Tyrant fell
> He lifts his Heel to Heaven but points his Head to Hell.[63]

A similar, though less public, statement was made by Georgia whig William Ewen. Rewriting his will at the Revolution's outbreak, he carefully enumerated his possessions, including twenty-nine portraits, and listed their value. On a separate sheet, he then listed just his portrait of George III and gave its value as worthless. In New Hampshire, crowds defaced official portraits of the royal family, and "pictures and escutcheons of the same kind in private houses were inverted" much as they had been in Baltimore.[64]

Adams, the Baltimore poet, and Ewen realized that the pictures still had, at that late date, a powerful but unfixed meaning that could be manipulated because the attachment to them had such an intense, personal quality. Although the Revolution made this apparent to many, it had hardly begun the process. Rather, the images themselves expressed a personalization of the relationship between subject and monarch that had been encouraged by a political culture rich in ritual and imperial rhetoric but truncated institutionally. Only such personalization can explain why Baltimore residents satirized rather than destroyed the portraits of a king who had once been able to make his subjects "tremble and adore." Such actions reflected a sense of long-standing emotional ties violated.[65]

63. L. H. Butterfield, ed., *Diary and Autobiography of John Adams*, II, *1771–1781*, Feb. 16, 1777, The Adams Papers, Series 1, Diaries (Cambridge, Mass., 1961), 259.

64. Harold E. Davis, *The Fledgling Province: Social and Cultural Life in Colonial Georgia, 1733–1776* (Chapel Hill, N.C., 1976), 189; Jeremy Belknap, *The History of New-Hampshire* (New York, 1970), 368.

65. Letters of Colonel John Murray of Rutland, Massachusetts, in Brinley Family Papers, box 1, HSP. According to family tradition, a mob near Worcester, Mass., ran his portrait through the wig in 1774 after he was named a Mandamus Councillor and fled to Boston (ibid.). The Rev. Jeremiah Leaming, Anglican, graduated from Yale and was an Anglican minister in Newport, R.I., and Norwalk, Conn. At the outbreak of the Revolution, whigs took his portrait, defaced it, and nailed it upside-down on a signpost. See

Although they were commodities, the portraits, prints, and medallions displayed in the colonies before the Revolution conveyed the same sense of respect and affection for the monarchy that the formal visualizations did. They were placed in positions of honor within homes. Over time, however, monarchical representations designed overtly for profit appeared in the American provinces. They, too, tapped into the emotions generated in the broader political culture, but in a manner that, in retrospect, made the monarch too familiar, too close, too much a commodity.

There are a number of such examples, but perhaps none is as surprising as the royal wax figures. Charleston, South Carolina, planters saw wax figures representing "their present most Sacred Majesties" exhibited in August 1737. Touring groups displayed similar figures at midcentury, and in 1749, New York City's papers announced that "the Effigies of the Royal Family of England" would be displayed, along with fourteen others. Eventually, a Mrs. Wright established a wax museum of sorts. She displayed the figures for profit until boys playing with candles burned the museum down, excepting of course saintly George Whitefield's wax figure, which miraculously survived the fire.[66]

People found further emotional and political meaning in such wax figures. Although we have no detailed account of a reaction to the touring figures or the New York museum, Francis Goelet, visiting London in 1750, saw images of "the maiden Queen Elizabeth, with the Lady Margaret Russell," as well as "the happy union of the red rose and the white in the healing marriage of King Henry the Seventh of the House of Lancaster" and "Their excellent Majesties, King William and Queen Mary, sitting in their royal robes . . . Queen Anne Lying in state, surrounded with pious mourners, lords spiritual and temporal with guards and attendants." Although such displays supported the Protestant succession, they were commercial spectacles foremost designed to gain an immediate emotional response.[67]

Before the Revolution, no political figure was more hated by the colonists than France's Sun King, Louis XIV. He stood in life and death as the feared embodiment of the type of Catholic, arbitrary power the colonists never ceased to denounce. But Louis XIV knew a lot about the projection of royal dignity, and he

Lorenzo Sabine, *Biographical Sketches of Loyalists of the American Revolution, with an Historical Essay*, II ([1864]; rpt. Port Washington, N.Y., 1966), 7.

66. *South-Carolina Gazette*, Aug. 13, 1737; Stokes, *Iconography of Manhattan Island*, IV, 616; Esther Singleton, *Social New York under the Georges, 1714–1776* (New York, 1902), 318–319.

67. Francis Goelet diary, Dec. 21–25, 1750, NYHS.

could have told the Hanoverians that if your likeness was the warm-up act for a "puppet shew" touring provinces distant from the throne, trouble lay ahead. For eighteenth-century kings, popularity and authority were by their natures different things.[68]

It has been said by more than one historian that the colonists who expressed affection for the three Hanoverian Georges did so because they did not know them. But perhaps the opposite was true; perhaps the colonists knew the king intimately, emotionally, and visually. The rites, and writings, and imperial goods imparted just such an emotional education. That knowledge allowed for a freedom of understanding that would ultimately problematize imperial institutional control. In an empire of emotions, imaginations created many monarchs and constitutions.

. . .

Of Ralph and Will, of Empire and Province, of King and People

The changes in provincial political culture that occurred in the era that was once known as the period of "salutary neglect" firmly planted imperial perceptions and loyalty to the monarchy in British America. By 1774, a visitor to South Carolina could comment that "most people that are born in Carolina" called England "their home tho' they have never been there." Key among the perceptions created to sustain this identification was that a powerful, benevolent Protestant prince concerned primarily with the welfare of his far-flung subjects ruled the empire.[69]

Colonial print culture strongly reinforced these positive perceptions. The same newspapers that amplified the royal political rites' power by persistently reporting on them also educated colonists about the royal family's character and the historical developments that led that family to the throne. Those presses described the three Georges as "the best of KINGS" day in and day out for five decades. Distance from the corrupt bureaucracy that controlled the empire reinforced provincials' belief that they had been blessed with the greatest kings that a monarchical world had to offer. Little wonder, then, that they should purchase the royal likeness or products seemingly carrying the royal family's endorsement. It would have been surprising if the colonists did not love the British monarchy, and perhaps we should take at his word the Pennsylvania writer who declared during the Seven Years' War, "All His Majesty's loyal Subjects among us (and in-

68. Stokes, *Iconography of Manhattan Island*, IV, 616.

69. Robert Olwell, *Masters, Slaves, and Subjects: The Culture of Power in the South Carolina Low Country, 1740–1790* (Ithaca, N.Y., 1998), 40–41.

deed where is there a disaffected One) felt for his Majesty" in that moment of crisis.[70]

A strange paradox emerges from this understanding. It seems that eighteenth-century America became more overtly monarchical than England itself. Glimpses, fragmentary images, really, of the imperial polity's true character have emerged from time to time, but their full meaning has been obscured by the historiography's general orientation toward the Revolution. Overall, the image that has remained current in popular and many scholarly imaginations is of an English core that was monarchical, Protestant, and hierarchical. Clannish Scottish Highlanders, Papist Irishmen, scarcely more civilized Scots-Irish Presbyterians in Ulster, and nascent Americans in one form or another scattered along the eastern seaboard inhabited the imperial fringe.[71]

In fact, though, by 1740, the empire's political culture seems to have been the mirror image of what we had imagined. Many in the fringe areas of Greater Britain — Scotland, Ireland, and the American colonies — were ardently, publicly monarchical. Even the Jacobite sympathizers in the Highlands and in Ireland can be conceived this way, though they were obviously loyal to the Stuart dynasty. The core population — the English — seems to have been apathetic about the Hanoverians, and it was British thinkers who were enthralled with aspects of the radical Enlightenment. As one provincial put it, "Old England, and not New, must be the land of deists and freethinkers." The political and religious implications of this remark are clear. The fringe was far more royalist in terms of public life

70. *Pennsylvania Gazette*, Oct. 4, 1759.

71. The anglicization thesis was originally formed by John M. Murrin in the mid-1960s. He postulated the norming of colonial institutions along the models provided by England, particularly the bench and the bar. He later suggested that the land tenure system was in the process of anglicization during the imperial crisis.

In the 1980s and 1990s, Jack Greene and T. H. Breen reexamined aspects of the empire and provincial America in light of the anglicization thesis. Greene postulated that the colonies were becoming more like one another and more like the cosmopolitan core across the eighteenth century. This integrated empire, he believed, rested on an increasingly liberal political economy of self-interest and acquisition. Breen has focused on the consumption of British goods in the colonies through to the boycotts of the imperial crisis. Like Greene, Breen sees America as essentially liberal from its origins.

J. G. A. Pocock, Bernard Bailyn, Gordon Wood, and a host of others have examined the transmission of ideas and patterns of reasoning from England to America. Essential to their project was the belief that these concepts, marginalized or peripheral in England, flowered once transferred to American soil, encouraging the gradual republicanization or democratization of American society and politics.

than we have imagined, and the prevalence or lack of political celebrations of the Hanoverian dynasty is one way to trace the contours of the empire's overarching political culture.[72]

Acceptance of this understanding of the empire's political culture at mid-century makes much of the later eighteenth century's turbulent history more understandable. Republican revolutions occurred in two of the most monarchical societies in the Atlantic world, British America and Bourbon France. Their political cultures were more alike, particularly in their visualization, than we have been comfortable admitting, even as we must continue to acknowledge the profound differences between these societies in other arenas. The most apathetic and republicanized society, England proper, not only retained its monarchy but also enhanced his prestige as revolution, war with France, and George III's own illness led the nation to rally around its symbolic head. That combination, of earlier republicanization followed by a renewed royalism, encouraged change and accommodation without revolution. We will better understand eighteenth-century America if we accept that monarchy, hierarchy, and patriarchy were primary forces of change and subversion in certain contexts.[73]

A satirical dialogue between two brothers published in 1742 suggests how the society's royalization potentially endangered the empire. Almanac writer Nathaniel Ames printed this purported exchange between two Massachusetts brothers, Ralph and Will. The former was a "Freshman at College [Harvard]," whereas his brother Will was "an Ignorant Rustick" in need of instruction about the province's political affairs. As Ralph tried to explain the intricacies of the financial problems that rocked the Bay Colony in the 1740s to his uneducated brother, he mentioned that the issue had finally been sent to Parliament for settlement. "The Barlemend," the country brother responded, "Whad's that?" His Harvard-educated brother called it "The Place where Noble-men resort / And make the Nation's highest Court." When he explained the Parliament's powers, his country brother, in shock, declared, "Hold, Brother *Ralph*, pray give me leave / I by your Dalk thus much berceive / This Barlemend's a dreadful Thing / As great and powerful as a King."[74]

---

72. Andrew Croswell, *Observations on Several Passages in a Sermon Preached by William Warburton, Lord Bishop of Gloucester* . . . (Boston, 1768), 29.

73. Linda Colley, *Britons: Forging the Nation, 1707–1837* (New Haven, Conn., 1992), 206–210, discusses the resurrection of the monarchy in Britain in the early decades of George III's reign.

74. Nathaniel Ames, *An Astronomical Diary; or, An Almanack for the Year of Our Lord Christ, 1742* (Boston, 1742).

It was, of course, only a satire in an almanac, yet it revealed an emerging truth about provincial Americans and their imperial perceptions. Whereas some among the educated, Atlantic-facing elite understood the empire and the constitutional settlement as those in London did, with "The King the Parliament . . . join'd to / And they do all things they've a mind to," as Ralph said, others, who had learned of the empire via rites, almanacs, and decrees, understood the king alone as the ultimate location of power in the Anglo-American political universe.[75]

It was not, strictly speaking, a perception limited to the yeomanry. As well-read a gentleman as Lewis Morris, who purportedly had the largest library in America in the 1730s, conceded that "the King has Powers and Prerogatives in *America* that he has not in *England*," in large part because the colonial charters originated with the crown, even as he insisted that the monarchy was still bound by the British constitution. The confusion over the provincial charters' fundamental character and the nature of British liberties in the colonies that prompted Morris's statement only reinforced the message of political rites and historical writers that the king was somehow supreme and apart from Parliament in the empire.[76]

By the 1740s, the predominant political ideology in the provinces was a kind of benevolent royalism that grew from the broader Protestant political culture. Given everything we have been told about eighteenth-century America, it is difficult to even imagine such an ideology. But if we look at some East Asian societies today, we see political-religious cults of political personality in polities with dynamic commercial growth. It is logical that such a situation should develop in the colonies. Parliament and other imperial institutions were diminished in public rites and political discussion or unknown altogether to the yeomen in the countryside. The political rites, the language of power and imperial representation, the emotional structure of imperial rhetoric, and even consumer goods and visual representations all encouraged provincials to think like Will even as their betters put on the airs of Ralph and adopted a more sophisticated worldview.

A multiplicity of monarchs came to exist because building a political state out of Britain's disjointed, transatlantic empire was simultaneously successful and a distinct failure. In the period between 1688 and the 1740s, the iconography, rites,

75. Ibid.

76. Eugene R. Sheridan, *Lewis Morris, 1671–1746: A Study in Early American Politics* (Syracuse, N.Y., 1981), 150; Lewis Morris, *The Opinion and Argument of the Chief Justice of the Province of New-York concerning the Jurisdiction of the Supream Court of the Said Province, to Determine Causes in a Course of Equity* (New York, 1733), 2.

and history that explained the nature of power in the empire won wide acceptance. But state patronage, the land tenure system, and financial structures that conditioned behaviors in the home islands were largely missing. Half a state had been very firmly established. This disjuncture created a wildly royalist society whose institutions and property system remained immature and unsettled when compared to those of western European monarchies.

When, like the two brothers in Ames's almanac, provincials increasingly fell into quarreling over place, money, land, and institutional power beginning in the 1730s, the British peace began to give way to more troubled times. The parties to these conflicts turned to their imagined rulers for support against their opponents. In so doing, they exposed growing contradictions in the understanding of king and constitution in the American provinces. Passionate ties encouraged subjective understandings of the empire, the constitution, and the monarch's nature. And it was thus that an empire of many peoples came to be ruled by a king with many faces.

PART TWO
THREE FACES

. . . .
. . .
. .
.

The growth of a political culture focused on the monarchy brought stability to the settler colonies in the four decades after the Glorious Revolution. Whereas institutional structures continued to vary between proprietary, charter, and royal colonies, political language, ceremony, and rites became remarkably standardized. Provincials accepted British historical identities and venerated the Hanoverian dynasty as their protectors against French conquest from without and Catholic subversion from within. Political and commercial ties between the home islands and British North America grew. It seemed that the foundations of an enduring and peaceful empire had been established. But it was not to be.

The successful royalization of provincial political culture created a problem of authority that was ultimately unresolvable. As the population continued to expand and diversify ethnically and racially, the disjuncture between the emotional ties generated within the political culture and its institutional truncation became more pronounced. Across the entire social order, from its haughty gentlemen to enslaved African-Americans, individuals and groups repeatedly reconceived their relationship to the king and the British constitution.

By the 1740s, at least three conceptions of the king and the empire were manifesting themselves in the American provinces. The spectrum ran from forms of divine-right monarchy to belief in an extralegal, extrainstitutional monarch at one with his meanest subjects.

5

THE PROBLEM WITH PATRIARCHY

INSTITUTIONS, EVENTS, AND EMPIRE

RETHOUGHT

By the 1730s, the cult of monarchy had muscled its way to the center of public life. The empire's main iconography was very firmly established; the state's symbolic structure had been successfully planted in British America. States, though, are founded upon more than rites and icons and the emotions they create. The system of offices and patronage appointments that composed the early modern realm's institutional architecture remained immature in the American colonies. In the demographic, social, and political context that began to emerge, the imperial state's disjointed character became a threat to public order.

Encouraged by a patriarchal political culture to assume the role of community fathers, propertied men at all social levels sought institutional acknowledgment of their status, only to find themselves often frustrated. A remarkable rate of population increase assured that more and more people competed for a limited number of places in provincial power structures. The creation of new institutions never kept pace with this population growth; new counties and colonies appeared far too slowly to satisfy the need for honor and place. The result was a series of public conflicts that revealed the subversive danger of patriarchal desire and the subjective understanding of king and constitution.

Our libertarian traditions have led historians to believe that these conflicts undid imperial bonds or created more individualistic or republicanized polities. In fact, though, the many events that form the earliest part of the American story are best understood as struggles to get into the empire in the role of local patriarch. Maximum individual liberty had yet to be proclaimed a cultural godhead. Kafka's *Castle* had yet to be written; "organization man" had yet to be born. Institutional participation was linked to social status and brought emotional fulfillment in a manner that our more cynical age finds mystifying. Conflicts like the Zenger Crisis in New York that have been traditionally understood as part of the liberalization or republicanization of America in fact occurred in an imperial context that fundamentally changes their historical meaning, once we acknowledge it.

. . .

Anglicization in the Imperial Marches

Sometime in the 1760s, a minor imperial official considered the problems created by explosive poulation growth in the American provinces. "The British colonies in . . . America notwithstanding their present growth and importance were at first undertaken by Private Adventurers. . . . They have from very trifling Beginnings, most unexpectedly increased in little more than a century to [a] Million and a half of people." This increase grew from "Foreign Accession and Propogation . . . Where the Means of life are so attainable that none are restrain'd from Marriage . . . no devastations have ever been made by Pestilence or Famine, the natural increase Must Exceed prodigiously." As this man knew, the growth strained the empire's institutional structures. It wasn't that the colonists weren't loyal—they were, intensely and passionately. They had no dreams but of being British and of the empire. But no one had anticipated their numbers as Protestants from across Europe flooded to America, the continent being "layed open as it were a great Common."[1]

Around the same time, Robert Livingston, Jr., wrote to his son-in-law, the New York attorney James Duane, about his family's struggle against the colony's Delancey faction. Although the parties to the struggle had been given religious labels and indeed argued over religious issues, for Livingston, the fight was not about religion. They, Livingston wrote, meaning the Delancey family, "do not value the Presbyterian, nor even their own church, where it happens to be in opposition to their favoured Scheem of Ruling over all the familyes in the Country [meaning the colony of New York]."[2]

The two passages reveal contemporary awareness of two of the most powerful forces of change in the late empire, population growth and family rivalries for power and place. As the British official noted, the opening of a continental super-commons for displaced Protestants coupled with reproduction that "must Exceed prodigiously" had accelerated the mainland colonies' demographic growth to unprecedented levels for European-dominated populations. Like rising water,

1. "Observations on the British Colonies in America, Received from Malaga in 1769, Thought to Be Wrote by the Late Comptroller Wair Who Died Consul in Malaga," NYHS.

2. Edward P. Alexander, *A Revolutionary Conservative: James Duane of New York* (New York, 1938), 47.

provincials pushed on the society's boundaries, unintentionally, often unconsciously, but still forcefully. The ruptures caused by their actions are familiar to historians, and the myths surrounding this mass of colonial yeomen form the core of our national story. The rivalries between elite family groups in various colonies are also well known, but the relationship between these two developments has remained partially hidden.

It has been assumed that population pressures helped undo the empire and create a liberal society by loosening traditional and social conventions. There is a logic to this supposition, and in retrospect, if we look back through the Revolution, it makes good sense. If we read forward from the seventeenth century, though, the petty squabbles, conflicts, and events of this period suggest another pattern. Provincials seeking place in the government—town, county, or imperial—drove many political changes. Before the Revolution, Americans wanted more patriarchy and more empire, not less, and, strangely, such desires, held by more and more people, helped unravel the imperial state. The growth of institutional structures that conveyed honor, power, or simply public voice to those who served them never kept pace with population growth. The scarcity of patronage positions repeatedly caused conflict as those who received them earned the disdain of those who, like Robert Livingston, Jr., felt themselves excluded or threatened. The desperate desire for place intensified as the imperial cult of monarchy spread the idea of the polity as a series of ruling fathers headed by a benevolent king, and the budding consumer revolution diluted the power of material goods to reaffirm status. This was one of the first empire's central truths, its strange equation—the ever-growing number of colonists wanted into the empire and wanted more patriarchy until the empire collapsed, a failure that grew in part from their desires.

In the decades after the Glorious Revolution, the London bureaucracy gradually addressed the lack of uniformity in civil institutions that had so troubled the later Stuart kings. Early in the eighteenth century, as imperial rites were introduced and imperial history written, officials haltingly remade provincial governments and legal systems along English lines. The models provided by London and England's southern counties became the template for the colonies' restructuring, a transformation designed to ease imperial control. Anglicization, as this process has come to be known, gradually made the empire more coherent institutionally.

Simply looking at imperial institutional structures in the 1730s, one sees a cumbersome but by no means unworkable institutional architecture designed to answer any challenges in British America. Agents appointed by colonies as a whole, by assemblies, and even by private interests within each province linked the colonial governments to the London bureaucracy. These brokers solicited the Board of Trade, the central imperial institutional control over the provinces. They also approached members of both houses of Parliament, aristocrats, and even the monarch if circumstances demanded it. This unwieldy system was rife with delays and corruption. Yet for seventy-five years, in various incarnations, it kept the empire together.[3]

Governors headed the colonies. London authorities, either royal bureaucrats or proprietary owners, in the case of Pennsylvania and Maryland, appointed them. By the 1730s, the only remaining exceptions to this were the charter governments of Connecticut and Rhode Island, whose populations elected their governors. The governors themselves seem to fall into three categories: placemen related to prominent aristocrats in the home islands; prominent provincials with connections in London; and military officers rewarded for service. They all hoped for wealth gained from a royal salary, gifts from their respective assemblies, and fees.[4]

Acting with the advice of a colony's leading men or governor, London also appointed most of the major administrative officials. Such appointments were based upon the man's "Birth, his property, his Friends and his own Merit," as Virginia's lieutenant governor Francis Fauquier explained in relation to a member of the Fairfax family selected to be the province's attorney. These factors, according

3. The Ferdinand St. John Paris Papers, NJHS, provide an unusually complete look at the work of a colonial agent in the mid-eighteenth century. Michael G. Kammen's study, *A Rope of Sand: The Colonial Agents, British Politics, and the American Revolution* (Ithaca, N.Y., 1968), remains the standard study of the colonial agencies. See also David Hancock, *Citizens of the World: London Merchants and the Integration of the British Atlantic Community, 1735–1785* (Cambridge, 1995). For the uses of imperial authority in the colonies, see Timothy Shannon's insightful study, *Indians and Colonists at the Crossroads of Empire: The Albany Congress of 1754* (Ithaca, N.Y., 2000); see also Winfred T. Root, "The Lords of Trade and Plantations, 1675–1696," *AHR*, XXIII (1917), 20–41.

4. Beverly McAnear, *The Income of the Colonial Governors of British North America* (New York, 1967), 10; John W. Raimo, *Biographical Directory of American Colonial and Revolutionary Governors, 1607–1789* (Westport, Conn., 1980); Leonard Woods Labaree, "The Early Careers of the Royal Governors," in *Essays in Colonial History Presented to Charles McLean Andrews by His Students* (New York, 1931); Labaree, "The Royal Governors of New England," Colonial Society of Massachusetts, *Publications*, XXXII (1937), 120–131; Michael C. Batinski, *Jonathan Belcher, Colonial Governor* (Lexington, Ky., 1996); Edward J. Cashin, *Governor Henry Ellis and the Transformation of British North America* (Athens, Ga., 1994); Marshall Delancey Haywood, *Governor William Tryon, and His Administration in the Province of North Carolina, 1765–1771* (Raleigh, N.C., 1903); Mary Lou Lustig, *Robert Hunter, 1666–1734: New York's Augustan Statesman* (Syracuse, N.Y., 1983).

to Fauquier, provided one with "a just claim to the honor." Honor: this was the return on many of the empire's lesser offices, because the fees paid to them were negligible. Such appointments confirmed one's place in an endlessly hierarchical order. As the political structure reflected the social structure and the distribution of material wealth, holding office influenced all social relationships.[5]

The various provinces' legislative structures also became more similar to one another in the eighteenth century and tried to emulate Parliament in their procedures. Upper houses whose members were appointed from London were joined to elected lower houses whose members held substantial property in their home locales. Pennsylvania's structure differed significantly, since its upper house played largely an advisory role. In Massachusetts, the outgoing upper house and the incoming lower house elected the upper house, subject to the royal governor's negative. These upper houses also acted as the highest court in some colonies and as the royal governor's advisers. Usually numbering ten to twelve men, the councillors were among the wealthiest men in their respective colonies.[6]

As the eighteenth century progressed, colonials also remade their courts along the lines of those in England. Lawyers and judges increasingly received formal training of some type modeled on that given at the Inns of Court in London. Some actually went to London for training or studied there before removing to the colonies. Under the influence of such judiciaries, court structure became more uniformly anglicized, and the courts sat in the monarch's name. The county courts of sessions that met four times a year, the justice of the peace (JP) courts that assembled monthly, and local sheriffs dominated legal matters in the empire's far marches. Portraits of the kings and queens, royal arms, and other monarchical insignia decorated courtrooms in many colonies, reinforcing the power of courts by linking them to the human embodiment of empire.[7]

5. "To the Earl of Shelburne, York, July 30th 1767," in George Reese, ed., *The Official Papers of Francis Fauquier, Lieutenant Governor of Virginia*, III, *1764–1768* (Charlottesville, Va., 1983), 1491.

6. Alan Tully, *Forming American Politics: Ideals, Interests, and Institutions in Colonial New York and Pennsylvania* (Baltimore, 1994), 365–370, 387–389, discusses the oligarchic nature of the New York and Pennsylvania legislatures; see also Thomas L. Purvis, "High-Born, Long-Recorded Families: Social Origins of New Jersey Assemblymen, 1703 to 1776," *WMQ*, 3d Ser., XXXVII (1980), 599; Bruce Daniels, "Family Dynasties in Connecticut's Largest Towns, 1700–1760," *Canadian Journal of History*, VIII (1973), 99; Leonard Woods Labaree, *Conservatism in Early American History* (New York, 1948), 4–5. The meeting of the Virginia Burgesses was often a family reunion for the First Families of Virginia.

7. John M. Murrin, "Anglicizing an American Colony: The Transformation of Provincial Massachusetts" (Ph.D. diss., Yale, 1966); James A. Henretta, *"Salutary Neglect"*: *Colo-*

The courts brought the king's justice and prerogative (rhetorically free of both assemblies and Parliament) to every community in North America. Virginia's magistrates opened court with "Oyez, oyez, oyez, silence is commanded in the court while his Majesties Justices are sitting. . . . God Save the King." The tendency to invoke the king as the origin of authority in the empire was especially pronounced in the legal system.[8]

The empire touched people in their other governing institutions as well. The county, town, and township were key among these. From New Jersey north, the town dominated; to the south, the county was central, though not exclusively so in South Carolina and Georgia, where parishes also played significant institutional roles. Local institutions tied the yeomanry to their king; appointed or elected officers organized them in their militias for imperial defense; and the yeomen voted for their assembly legislators in town- or countywide elections (depending on the region).

Anglicization was chronologically staggered, even within regions. In New York, particularly New York City, imperial institutions became entrenched after Leisler's Rebellion. All the colony's political factions accepted the monarchy and imperial norms without real question. New York's polyglot Dissenting populations welcomed a monarch legitimated in part by the claim to defend pan-European Protestantism. Intermarriage after 1710 eventually united the province's warring families, who became champions of royal authority and controlled its institutions and rituals even as they continued to squabble bitterly.[9]

---

nial Administration under the Duke of Newcastle (Princeton, N.J., 1972); Bruce H. Mann, Neighbors and Strangers: Law and Community in Early Connecticut (Chapel Hill, N.C., 1987); Ian K. Steele, "The Anointed, the Appointed, and the Elected: Governance of the British Empire, 1689–1784," in P. J. Marshall, ed., The Oxford History of the British Empire, II, The Eighteenth Century (Oxford, 1998), 113. See also the work of A. G. Roeber, Cornelia Hughes Dayton, Jack P. Greene, Alan Tully, and the older imperial school literature.

8. A. G. Roeber, Faithful Magistrates and Republican Lawyers: Creators of Virginia Legal Culture, 1680–1810 (Chapel Hill, N.C., 1981), 78–79. The drama of court day is described by Roeber, esp. 73–83, and by Rhys Isaac, The Transformation of Virginia, 1740–1790 (Chapel Hill, N.C., 1982).

9. Beverly McAnear, "Politics in Provincial New York, 1689–1761" (Ph.D. diss., Stanford University, 1935), II, 1000–1002; Patricia U. Bonomi, A Factious People: Politics and Society in Colonial New York (New York, 1971), 56–86; Lustig, Robert Hunter, 64–140; Philip S. Haffenden, New England in the English Nation, 1689–1713 (London, 1974); Donna Merwick, Possessing Albany, 1630–1710: The Dutch and English Experiences (Cambridge, 1990), 220–285.

In Pennsylvania, Quaker resistance inhibited acceptance of many imperial norms for decades. Pennsylvanian James Kenny threw into high relief the colony's problematic relationship with imperial norms when he recalled a trip to the interior with a British-born Lieutenant Lim during the Seven Years' War. After reading "Barchleys Apollogy," the lieutenant confronted Kenny about "how much we [the Pennsylvanians] were against excess, and calling the Days and months by the heathen names." Lim "strove to vindicate both arguing that the use of many things that we counted excess helped to promote Trade and augmented the Revenues of the Crown." Kenny refused to concede and told him, "Excesses . . . was a means to deprive the Subjects of an Heavenly Crown would by no means of gaining a blessing to the Earthly Crown." It was a defense that would have made Samuel Sewall proud, had a New England Congregationalist uttered it.[10]

As these men knew, Pennsylvania's institutional structure differed somewhat from that of the metropolis. The assembly's power compared to the upper house was greater than that of the House of Commons in relation to the House of Lords. Even Pennsylvania, however, acknowledged royal authority. Driven by the demands of the imperial wars against France, a hybrid creolized political culture came into existence. As elsewhere, the language of authority in Pennsylvania was royalized. For example, Governor James Hamilton, attempting to raise troops in 1761, told the assembly he "had the Honour to receive from one of his Majesty's principal Secretaries of State, the King's Command" to act in this manner. Hamilton personalized the request, telling the legislators that "the King is pleased to furnish all the men so raised. . . . with Arms, Ammunition, and Tents." Within a few years of this speech, there would be a concerted (though ultimately unsuccessful) drive headed by Ben Franklin, among others, to place the province's government in the king's hands.[11]

In all the colonies, local leaders, almost invariably the towns' and counties' largest property holders — the councillors and assemblymen, session judges, and other officials — were the political fathers. A man like this, as one Bostonian noted about an imperial governor, was supposed to "imitate his Master in his Royal Vertues, his Courage, Justice, Clemency and other Ennobling Qualifications." It was a social and political structure congruent with the broader royal political culture that celebrated the empire's political father and his family, which helps

10. James Kenny, Dec. 22, 1758, Journal to the Westward, 1758–1761, HSP.

11. "Opening Speech to the Assembly concerning the Raising of Troops for His Majesty's Service," in George E. Reed, ed., *Pennsylvania Archives*, III, 4th Ser., *Papers of the Governors, 1759–1785* (Harrisburg, 1900), 65.

explain its durability. In England, similar structures had maintained community stability since the sixteenth century and steadied the realm after 1688.[12]

At midcentury, the provinces seemed to be developing the same way. Groups of prominent families controlled the governing apparatus in each colony, soliciting a severely limited number of official positions for their relations and friends. They were like vines on a tree, seemingly indistinguishable from the power structure they came to inhabit. In this manner, colonial power structures came to resemble the county communities that dominated life in the English countryside. It should have been the beginning of a stable, anglicized British America. But it was not. This process of remodelling along English lines occurred in a society experiencing explosive population growth, and the combination proved dangerous to the social order.

. . .

Population and the Problem of Patriarchal Desires

The anglicization of colonial institutions came to bear on a strange equation shaped by population growth, widespread freehold land tenure, and political royalization that, taken together, inhibited the stabilization of the first British empire. The problem was the divergent functioning of patriarchy in the British Atlantic. In Britain, freeholders were fewer and far between. Those who owned substantial acreage could expect to play an active role in local politics, especially eldest sons. Primogeniture remained current throughout the British Isles.

In the colonies, the situation was different. Royal ceremonies and print culture spread the cult of monarchical patriarchy everywhere. But in America, freeholders abounded, while new colonies, counties, towns, and even churches came into being only fitfully and totally out of sync with the yeomen freeholder population's growth. It was in just such a situation that patriarchal expectations could become a powerful force for change.

By 1740, this strange problem in the British peace was already becoming apparent. The royalization of the yearly political calendar and print culture in a demographically expanding society helped create desires for place and authority that threatened the established order. The situation was particularly severe in relationship to political structures. On the mainland south of Canada, only one new colony, Georgia, was founded between 1700 and 1763, and its government was not royalized until 1752. That colony's institutional layout highlights the problem of institutional creation. The county structure was never successfully

12. Amicus Patrie, *A Word of Comfort to a Melancholy Country; or, The Bank of Credit Erected in the Massachusetts-Bay* (Boston, 1721), 3.

extended, and in 1776, Georgia would still consist of one county (parishes were subordinate entities within the county) with a royal governor and legislature on top of it. As with many colonies, London authorities appointed the governors (the most notable being the Scot Henry Ellis and James Wright) and the Legislative Council. This left precious few places of honor and authority for the local white male population to aspire to.[13]

This same problem, in various guises, intensified across British America as the population grew and expanded and institutional development failed to keep pace. Population figures for the period are sometimes sketchy, but the trends are clear. New York's population grew by 3.1 percent annually in the eighteenth century. By 1771, 168,000 Yorkers of European and African origins shared the colony's lands, up from about 18,000 in 1698. New Jersey's population grew 3 to 4 percent per year in the eighteenth century, and by the 1770s, approximately 110,000 colonists lived there. Rhode Island began the century with 7,181 souls and had nearly 60,000 in 1774, a growth rate of 3.2 percent for European and African populations. Maryland grew from 32,258 black and white residents early in the century to 164,000 by 1763. There were variations, of course, and dips in growth in some locales. Certainly, in the southern colonies, the rapid importation of slaves complicates the broader meaning of the growth. But the overall trend was a stunning expansion that quickly began to outstrip the institutional structure's ability to serve the population.[14]

Proprietary Pennsylvania offers a telling example of how a rapid population increase without corresponding institutional growth could strain a society. Between around 1725 and 1755, 77,000 immigrants arrived in Philadelphia, and natural reproduction increased apace. By 1775, around 300,000 people of Euro-

13. Harold E. Davis, *The Fledgling Province: Social and Cultural Life in Colonial Georgia, 1733–1776* (Chapel Hill, N.C., 1976); Paul S. Taylor, *Georgia Plan: 1732–1752* (Berkeley, Calif., 1972); W. W. Abbot, *The Royal Governors of Georgia, 1754–1775* (Chapel Hill, N.C., 1959). See also P. M. G. Harris, "The Social Origins of American Leaders: The Demographic Foundations," in Donald Fleming and Bernard Bailyn, eds., *Perspectives in American History*, III (Cambridge, 1969), 159–344; James Kirby Martin, *Men in Rebellion: Higher Governmental Leaders and the Coming of the American Revolution* (New Brunswick, N.J., 1973); Stanley Elkins and Eric McKitrick, "The Founding Fathers: Young Men of the Revolution," *Political Science Quarterly*, LXXVI (1961), 181–216; Philip J. Greven, Jr., *Four Generations: Population, Land, and Family in Colonial Andover, Massachusetts* (Ithaca, N.Y., 1970).

14. The figures are drawn from Robert V. Wells, *The Population of the British Colonies in America before 1776* (Princeton, N.J., 1975). For New York, see ibid., 111–113; for New Jersey, 134–135; for Rhode Island, 97–98; for Maryland, 146–147.

pean descent lived in the colony, and many of the immigrants and young settled on the colony's frontier. Begrudgingly, over time, five new interior counties were created, but they were only assigned ten assembly seats despite having, by the 1750s, half the colony's population. The three eastern counties, dominated by a long-settled elite, retained twenty-six seats.

Worse yet, the ratio of assemblymen to population climbed alarmingly throughout the period. In the eighteenth century's third decade, that ratio was one assemblyman for approximately every 340 white males. By 1770, it was approximately one assemblyman for every 1,300 white men. The lack of representation for the interior became a major point of contention during the march of the Paxton Boys in 1764 and in the political crisis in the colony in the spring of 1776 that led to the pro-independence party's ascent to power.[15]

The same sort of denial of place and respect to portions of rapidly growing populations occurred everywhere. For decades, the coastal elite in the Carolinas prevented the ever-mounting number of interior settlers from having effective political representation and institutional access. Legislative attempts to create new counties and towns at midcentury were disallowed by the Crown in 1754 because they were seen as an assault on prerogative. Tensions boiled over in both North and South Carolina and continued for decades until new royal institutional structures were created shortly before the Revolution.

In New Hampshire, the lack of a county structure caused repeated disputes throughout the provincial period. Governor Bennington Wentworth refused to erect courts outside the capital of Portsmouth, and in 1767 the colony still had only one county. Conflicts exacerbated by population growth continued to disrupt the polity until 1771, when Governor John Wentworth finally established five counties in the interior. By then, events had already begun to erode royal authority in the colony. There was not enough government to go around in the little colony or, indeed, anywhere in British America.[16]

15. Ibid., 143; James T. Lemon, *The Best Poor Man's Country: A Geographical Study of Early Southeastern Pennsylvania* (Baltimore, 1972); David Hawke, *In the Midst of a Revolution* (Philadelphia, 1961), 17–22; Gordon S. Wood, *The Radicalism of the American Revolution* (New York, 1991), 128; Jack P. Greene, "Legislative Turnover in British America, 1696 to 1775: A Quantitative Analysis," *WMQ*, 3d Ser., XXXVIII (1981), 442–463. New York went from a ratio of 1 legislator for every 320 white males in 1730 to a 1 to 1,065 ratio shortly before the Revolution. This change may in part help explain the breakdown of order in the New York countryside after 1750, although other factors were clearly in play in that disorder.

16. Charles Lee Raper, *North Carolina: A Study in English Colonial Government* (New

The overwhelming tendency to continue older leading men in office aggravated this situation again and again. Such men traditionally kept their positions for decades, and, unrestrained by law or custom, added offices to their portfolios whenever possible. Lancaster, Virginia, patriarch Edwin Conway, for example, served forty years on the Court of the Quorum before the grim reaper removed him from office in 1752. Men elected to their respective assemblies would serve term after term until they retired or death overcame them. Twenty-four New York Council members died while serving, and another ten went to their maker shortly after leaving office. Daniel Horsmanden gave thirty-five years to that body, and the legendary Cadwallader Colden held on for fifty-five, serving in a number of other offices simultaneously![17]

The tendency to see possession of such offices as a kind of right led leading men to try to pass offices on to their younger relatives. They thus sought to secure the place of their dynasty at the expense of other families. William Smith, Sr., did exactly this when he resigned from the New York Council in favor of his namesake son in 1767. Founding father Benjamin Franklin did the same thing; after serving ten years as Pennsylvania Assembly clerk, he was elected to that body and resigned the clerk position in favor of his son William. Later, the elder Franklin would use his influence with Lord Bute to get William appointed royal governor of New Jersey.[18]

York, 1904), 226; Marjoleine Kars, *Breaking Loose Together: The Regulator Rebellion in Pre-Revolutionary North Carolina* (Chapel Hill, N.C., 2002); Richard Maxwell Brown, *The South Carolina Regulators* (Cambridge, Mass., 1963); Paul W. Wilderson, *Governor John Wentworth and the American Revolution: The English Connection* (Hanover, N.H., 1994), 115–117; Jeremy Belknap, *The History of New-Hampshire* (New York, 1970), 343–344; Bernard Bailyn, *The Origins of American Politics* (New York, 1968), 99. A general discussion of the demographic structure is Philip J. Greven, Jr., "Historical Demography and Colonial America," *WMQ*, 3d Ser., XXIV (1967), 438–454. The best effort to situate the demographic structure of the society to leadership selection and patterns is P. M. G. Harris's "Social Origins of American Leaders," in Fleming and Bailyn, eds., *Perspectives in American History*, III, 159–346.

17. Roeber, *Faithful Magistrates and Republican Lawyers*, 76; Jessica Kross, "'Patronage Most Ardently Sought': The New York Council, 1665–1775," in Bruce C. Daniels, ed., *Power and Status: Officeholding in Colonial America* (Middletown, Conn., 1986), 218–219.

18. Leslie Francis Stokes Upton, "William Smith, Chief Justice of New York and Quebec, 1728–1793" (Ph.D. diss., University of Minnesota, 1957); Sheila L. Skemp, *William Franklin: Son of a Patriot, Servant of a King* (New York, 1990), 15; Edmund S. Morgan, *Benjamin Franklin* (New Haven, Conn., 2002), 126.

These practices helped create interrelated local oligarchies with a tight grip on status. By the 1720s, about forty intermarried families ran the middle colonies. They passed power from one generation to the next seamlessly and largely without external challenge even as they squabbled bitterly among themselves. In 1763, Cadwallader Colden wrote to the Earl of Egremont that the colony had "a set of Lawyers . . . as Insolent, Petulant, and at the same time as well skilled in all the chicanerie of the Law as perhaps is to be found anywhere else." Colden knew that the appointment of disinterested judges would have done much to squelch the bar's influence, but he also knew the impossibility of finding such judges. It was, he explained, a fact of life that "the distinguished Families in so small a Country are so united by intermarriage and otherwise" that to move against their interest was impossible, even in legal matters. Few cases could be brought before a judge who "is free from connections with those interested either in the Case or in other Cases similar to it."[19]

Colden might have added (though he probably didn't have to) that he had used his own political influence to assist his numerous offspring in getting positions. Governor George Clinton had enlisted Colden's aid against the powerful Delancey kin-patronage network in the late 1740s, and Colden's kin received patronage from the governor. By 1750, two of Colden's sons had been appointed to important posts in New York's imperial structure. His other sons received military or imperial-logistical appointments. Colden's description of New York's

19. I. N. Phelps Stokes, *The Iconography of Manhattan Island, 1498–1909*, IV (New York, 1922), 737. For the best discussion of this structure, see John M. Murrin and Gary J. Kornblith, "The Making and Unmaking of an American Ruling Class," in Alfred F. Young, ed., *Beyond the American Revolution: Explorations in the History of American Radicalism* (Dekalb, Ill., 1993), 27–79. See also Brendan McConville, *These Daring Disturbers of the Public Peace: The Struggle for Property and Power in Early New Jersey* (Ithaca, N.Y., 1999), 111–115; Roger Champagne, "Family Politics versus Constitutional Principles: The New York Assembly Elections of 1768 and 1769," *WMQ*, XX (1963), 57–73; and especially the essays in Daniels, ed., *Power and Status*, particularly the essays by Ronald K. Snell, "'Ambitious of Honor and Places': The Magistracy of Hampshire County, Massachusetts, 1692–1760" (17–35), Bruce C. Daniels, "Diversity and Democracy: Officeholding Patterns among Selectmen in Eighteenth-Century Connecticut" (36–52), Lorena S. Walsh, "The Development of Local Power Structures: Maryland's Lower Western Shore in the Early Colonial Period" (53–71), Richard Alan Ryerson, "Portrait of a Colonial Oligarchy: The Quaker Elite in the Pennsylvania Assembly, 1729–1776" (75–105), and Grace L. Chickering, "Founders of an Oligarchy: The Virgin Council" (255–274). Chickering provides a simple but informative chart of the intermarriage among the member families of the Virginia Council on 261.

bench and bar, even allowing for his relentless cynicism, provides an illuminating description of provincial politics.[20]

It was the same north and south. In Virginia, nine families provided one-third of the members of the colony's council in the period between the Glorious Revolution and the American Revolution. These nine families were tightly intermarried and also related by blood to the other two-thirds. In fact, one-sixth of the members of the Council of the Virginia House of Burgesses in the period after 1688 had the same grandmother, a woman named Lucy Higginson who married often and well in the mid-seventeenth century. In New Hampshire, the Wentworth family controlled the major offices from the 1740s until they were overthrown in the revolutionary crisis. John Wentworth was made lieutenant governor in 1717, when New Hampshire and Massachusetts still shared the same royal governor. His son Benning followed him in 1741, becoming New Hampshire's first independent royal governor, and his nephew John, in turn, followed his uncle into the governorship. They were never lonely, as family members served in the colony's assembly and council throughout the period. The custom of relatives in office reached its logical extreme during John the younger's regime: his initial Council consisted of three uncles (two by marriage), his own father, three cousins, and the husband of another cousin.[21]

Colonials everywhere knew of these developments. Massachusetts governor Francis Bernard recognized the problems such a monopoly of position created. He appointed an enormous number (462) of county justices in the Bay Colony and further avoided appointing friends to office, only to see his efforts to extend state patronage unravel during the imperial crisis. His eventual successor, Thomas Hutchinson, repeatedly commented on kinship as a reality of New England's political life. The same families controlled churches, militia units, towns, and counties for generations. These little oligarchies were usually based on seventeenth-century families, along with some members of the merchant elite (the Hancock family in Boston, for example). Hutchinson's own family became one such extended kin group through intermarriage and dominated politics in the Bay Colony in the 1760s and 1770s before they were overthrown.[22]

20. Stanley Nider Katz, *Newcastle's New York: Anglo-American Politics, 1732–1753* (Cambridge, 1968), 178.

21. Labaree, *Conservativism in Early American History*, 7–8, 19; Belknap, *The History of New-Hampshire*, 344–345; Colin Nicolson, *The "Infamas Govener" Francis Bernard and the Origins of the American Revolution* (Boston, 2001), 72. Wilderson, *Governor John Wentworth and the American Revolution*, is an excellent discussion of that member of the family and the English context of his appointment.

22. Nicolson, *The "Infamas Govener,"* 72. The best discussion of Hutchinson is still

If provincial America had been a demographically stable, geographically contained society with a settled European-style land tenure system, the strange equation would never have arisen. America might well have found imperial equilibrium politically, a comfortable place in the empire akin to Canada in the nineteenth century. But the ability to realize authority commensurate with economic and social status was severely restricted in eighteenth-century America. The ever-increasing number of eldest sons would have been especially troubled, since a truncated form of primogeniture retained a powerful hold over their social imaginations. As these men got older, they assumed they would have a place of respect and authority in the community. All too often, these expectations failed to be met.[23]

Over time, the inability to realize position shaped the political behavior of men at every level of the social order. When a New York loyalist sought to explain how a conservative lawyer like James Duane could become a revolutionary, he declared that, in Duane's case, the deciding factors were "being married in the Livingston family, disappointed in an application to Lord Dunmore, and in another to Genl. Tryon, to be made one of his Majesty's Council, and his determination to be a great man, all combined to hurry him down the stream to rebellion." This problem, the slow-burning crisis of the three "P's"—patronage, population, and patriarchy—ran back far deeper into the provincial past and indeed manifested itself in some of the period's famous episodes.[24]

The Zenger Crisis specifically, historically enshrined in the whig political traditions as a moment of birth for various forms of modern freedoms, allows us to see clearly these factors at work on colonial society. For, as much as we would

Bernard Bailyn, *The Ordeal of Thomas Hutchinson* (Cambridge, Mass., 1974). Hutchinson's own history of the Bay Colony is a potent source of information on the origins of this oligarchic control. Richard S. Dunn, *Puritans and Yankees: The Winthrop Dynasty of New England* (Princeton, N.J., 1962), is a valuable discussion of the most famous of the seventeenth-century family dynasties. Daniel Scott Smith, "'All in Some Degree Related to Each Other': A Demographic and Comparative Resolution of the Anomaly of New England Kinship," *AHR*, XCIV (1989), 44–79; see also Edward M. Cook, Jr., *The Fathers of the Towns: Leadership and Community Structure in Eighteenth-Century New England* (Baltimore, 1976).

23. For primogeniture in New England, see Toby L. Ditz, *Property and Kinship: Inheritance in Early Connecticut, 1750–1820* (Princeton, N.J., 1986); for Virginia, see C. Ray Keim, "Primogeniture and Entail in Colonial Virginia," *WMQ*, XXV (1968), 545–586; Carole Shammas, Marylynn Salmon, and Michael Dahlin, *Inheritance in America from Colonial Times to the Present* (New Brunswick, N.J., 1987).

24. Alexander, *A Revolutionary Conservative*, 105.

like to see ourselves somehow intellectually connected to the actors in that mini-drama, they knew they lived in an empire where the most important tie was to the king.

· · ·

Zenger Reconsidered

The Zenger Crisis. Freedom of the press, jury nullification, Country ideology's introduction to America, the beginnings of a bourgeois "public sphere," and the beginnings of American democracy itself have all been attributed to this squabble in New York politics that began over salary money and patronage positions. Placed within its appropriate, imperial context, though, the crisis looks quite different than we have imagined. The royalization of political rites and public rhetoric enabled a factional fight over place within the giant, oligarchic superfamily that ruled that colony. Because the royalization of British America allowed for incredible latitude in understanding of the central motifs of order, colonials on both sides of the dispute were able to invoke the king against their political opponents. Writers discussed the tension between liberty and power as part of this debate, but they linked that discussion to dynastic history and imperial themes that grew from the efforts to legitimate the Hanoverian dynasty.[25]

The Zenger Crisis grew from a long-running dispute that pitted a group of New York politicians led by Lewis Morris, James Alexander, and Rip Van Dam against a faction that was eventually supported by a newly appointed royal governor, William Cosby. Morris's supporters included New York's agrarian interest and also many of the Scottish gentlemen who had been settling in the midatlantic since the 1680s. Morris himself had married the daughter of a leading Scotsman, James Graham. Their opponent, William Cosby, was a placeman and former sol-

25. Michael Warner, *The Letters of the Republic: Publication and the Public Sphere in Eighteenth-Century America* (Cambridge, Mass., 1990), Bailyn, *Origins of American Politics*, and the body of scholarship produced by Leonard Levy use this approach. Tully's solid study of midatlantic politics (*Forming American Politics*) — as solid as a study of the midatlantic can be that takes no account of New Jersey — is a case in point. He entitles his section on Zenger "Freedom of Speech and the Zenger Trial." More egregious in this regard are Bailyn's *Origins of American Politics* and *Ideological Origins of the American Revolution* (Cambridge, Mass., 1992), both of which are sophisticated restatements of the whig tradition and teleological in the extreme. As early as 1960, Leonard Levy established that the Zenger trial did not secure freedom of the press as was once believed. See Levy, "Did the Zenger Case Really Matter? Freedom of the Press in Colonial New York," *WMQ*, 3d Ser., XVII (1960), 35–50.

dier who had married the Earl of Halifax's sister, a cousin of the powerful Duke of Newcastle. Some merchants, several members of the important Delancey family, and some imperial officials supported Cosby. Passions ran high for years as the factions struggled for power and imperial patronage.[26]

The dispute actually ran back a number of years before Cosby arrived in the colony in August 1732. The thread of continuity uniting events in New York that stretched from the late 1720s to 1736 is that, in each episode, conflict flared, not over major policy issues, but rather over control of the limited places of authority and political patronage. Both the Morrisites and their opponents were highborn men of property who felt they had the right to rule. Lewis Morris, the struggle's protagonist, held vast properties in New Jersey and New York. But the truncated imperial state that existed in New York could only accommodate a few such great men seeking institutional acknowledgment of their authority, locking out others of similar status. It is telling that the crisis would not be resolved until more such places were created by the London government by granting New Jersey a separate executive (it had shared governors with New York since 1702) and appointing Lewis Morris governor.

The problem began with Morris's loss of place. He had gained real influence in New York through his close alliances with Governor Robert Hunter (1709–1719) and then Governor William Burnet (1720–1728), who shared his views that those who held landed property were most fit to rule. Morris had acted as legislative ally of these governors from his Westchester assembly seat, in the process securing patronage positions for his supporters.[27]

After Burnet's departure, though, Morris gradually lost power. Burnet's replacement, John Montgomerie (1728–1731), became embroiled in a salary dispute with Morris, who remained a New York supreme court justice. The dispute, which foreshadowed the Zenger Crisis in many ways, saw Morris's son suspended from the Governor's Council for defending his father's honor. By the early 1730s,

26. Bonomi, *A Factious People*, 106; Murrin and Kornblith, "The Making and Unmaking of an American Ruling Class," in Young, ed., *Beyond the American Revolution*; Tully, *Forming American Politics*. Lustig, *Robert Hunter*, 78, 109, 118–119, gives ample evidence of Morris's involvement with the Scottish gentlemen of New York. Morris was related to the Scots through his marriage to Isabella, the daughter of James Graham, a leading Scottish-born politician active in New York in the 1690s (Eugene R. Sheridan, *Lewis Morris, 1671–1746: A Study in Early American Politics* [Syracuse, N.Y., 1981], 24).

27. Tully gives a good, brief account (*Forming American Politics*, 95–96). For an equally solid extended treatment, see Sheridan, *Lewis Morris*, 91–180. Morris's relationship with Hunter is explored by Lustig, *Robert Hunter*, 78–79. For Hunter's use of patronage, see ibid., 110–111.

the elder Morris was barely holding on to his place, and then only because of a vacuum in the governor's chair caused by Montgomerie's death. When the London government filled that vacuum by appointing William Cosby, Morris and his ally James Alexander quickly lost their places in the power structure. On his arrival, Cosby demanded fees collected by New York's acting governor Rip Van Dam, a political ally of Morris's. Cosby moreover tried to influence the legal proceedings in the matter in a way that threatened Morris's position as head of the supreme court. Cosby eventually removed him from office and replaced him with James Delancey. When a Delancey supporter challenged Morris for the seat in the New York legislature from Westchester County in the election of 1733, the Zenger Crisis began.[28]

From the beginning, imperial themes and motifs linked to the monarchy dominated the struggle. On election day in 1733, Morris's supporters rode in procession onto the green at the village of Eastchester: "first rode two Trumpeters and 3 Violins; next 4 of the principal Freeholders, one of which carried a Banner, on one side of which was affixed in gold Capitals, KING GEORGE, and on the other, in like golden Capitals LIBERTY and LAW; next followed the Candidate Lewis Morris, Esq. then two colours." After intense political infighting revolving around the eligibility of Morris's Quaker supporters to vote (because they would not swear a loyalty oath to George II due to religious scruples), he took the election. Morris's supporters greeted him like an arriving imperial governor when he returned to New York on October 31, "saluted by a general Fire of the Guns from the Merchants Vessels; and . . . receiv'd by great numbers of the most considerable Merchants and Inhabitants . . . and by them with loud Acclamations of the People . . . conduct'd to the Black Horse Tavern." There "was fix'd a Tabulet with golden Capitals, KING GEORGE, LIBERTY AND LAW."[29]

That tablet suggests the Zenger Crisis's most underappreciated aspect. The debate over monarchy's character current in the empire in the eighteenth century's first decades provided the broader context for the Morrisites' eventual use of so-called radical Country thought. Initially, they situated their struggle for place in terms of the conflict between the deposed House of Stuart and the Hanoverians. During the confrontation at the Eastchester election, Morris and his supporters cried out, "No Excise . . . no Pretender," and accused "William Foster, Esq., the Candidate on the other Side, with being a Jacobite," an advocate of the House of

28. Sheridan, *Lewis Morris*, 140–180, esp. 141, 144.

29. *New-York Weekly Journal*, Nov. 5, 1733. Morris's Quaker support originated with his by-then-deceased uncle, Lewis Morris, who was a leading Quaker in New York in the 1670s.

Stuart and absolutist government. The Morrisites declared themselves champions of balanced monarchy.[30]

In a newspaper piece published after the election, a pro-Morrisite writer said, "There are two Sorts of Monarchies, an absolute and a limited one." Clearly thinking ahead, the writer declared that "in the first, the liberty of the Press can never be maintained; it is inconsistent with it; for what absolute Monarch would suffer any subject to animadvert on his Actions, when it is in his Power to declare the Crime." Identifying his own cause with "limited Monarchy, as England," the writer argued for the rule of law as "the sure Guide to direct the King, the Ministers, and others his Subjects."[31]

Writers in support of Morris placed the disputes within the context of the Stuart family's seventeenth-century political battles, particularly the controversies before the English Civil Wars. Those disputes played a crucial, living part in the royal political culture, as they helped legitimate deposing the Catholic line of the House of Stuart in 1688. One such writer, "Independent Whig," stated in a 1733 letter to the *New-York Weekly Journal* that, "by an independent Whigg," he did not mean some kind of republican but rather "one whose Principles lead him to be firmly attached to the present happy Establishment, both in Church and State, and whose Fidelity to the Royal Family [the Hanoverians] is . . . not to be called into question." He encouraged use of satire against New York's placemen; such writings "were of great Service to the Patriot Whiggs" against the Stuarts, particularly "in the Reign of King Charles and King James the Second, as well as in that of Queen Anne. They asserted the Freedom of Writing against wicked Ministers."[32]

Several months later, another writer to the same paper referenced the supposed persecution of Morris to the tyrannical period of Charles I's personal rule in the 1630s. The writer declared that "Mr Hampden [a parliamentary leader]" was "one of the most bright . . . Characters that acted upon the Stage of those times; but the Opposition he gave in the Case of Ship Money [the tax collected by Charles I without the approval of Parliament in the 1630s], is by [no] meanes to be forgiven, by Men of Laudean [meaning absolutist] Principles." As was the case with Morris, "one of the best" of men was being portrayed "as one of the Worst of Men." These writers sought to identify Morris with the Protestant succession and his opponents with the previous century's Stuart excesses.[33]

30. Ibid.
31. Ibid., Nov. 12, 1733.
32. Ibid., Nov. 19, 1733.
33. Ibid., Apr. 29, 1734.

Governor William Cosby's arrival gradually encouraged a transformation in political rhetoric. Because George II had appointed Cosby, he could not be directly vilified as a Stuart supporter. But he could be and was vilified for abuse of power when he joined with James and Stephen Delancey, Adolph Philipse, and others against the Morrisites. Only then did Morris, James Alexander, and others turn to libertarian rhetoric to justify their actions. The Morrisites denounced institutional placemen and celebrated agrarian life, a viewpoint Morris, a major landholder, developed in some of his writings. That much of what Morris drew on was actually written by high tories (supporters of a strong royal prerogative) has largely been ignored by subsequent generations.[34]

Even as the rhetoric shifted, both factions began to manipulate royal celebrations in order to identify themselves with the Hanoverian dynasty and gain popular support. The imperial rites remained superficially normal in the port city through 1734. But by October 1735, the hostile factions staged discreet imperial celebrations to garner support. On October 9, 1735, two days before the anniversary of George II's coronation, Governor Cosby dined with and was toasted by "the Principle Merchants, and other Gentlemen of this City" upon his return from Albany. The overt reason for the celebration was the governor's renewal of a treaty with the Iroquois, but it might also have been an effort to preempt the Morrisite-dominated coronation celebrations planned for the eleventh. The latter celebration was held; "the elected Magistrates with a considerable Number of Merchants and Gentlemen, not Dependent on [Governor Cosby] made a very handsome Entertainment in Honour of the Day." Morris's ally Rip Van Dam, "President of His Majesty's Council, Matthew Norris, Esq. [Morris's son-in-law], Commander of His Majesty's Ship Tartar, and Capt. Compton Commander of His Majesty's ship Seahorse, [were] at the House of Mr. John De Honeur in this City . . . while the great Guns of his Majesty's ship Tartar were Firing."[35]

Toasts during the celebration allowed the Morrisites to express their loyalty to the idea of Protestant monarchy and thus to implicate Cosby's actions as unconstitutional. The New-York Journal reported, "They drank the following Healths, the King, the Queen, the Prince, Duke and royal Family, the Prince and Princess of Orange, the Glorious and immortal Memory of King William the third; suc-

34. Bonomi, A Factious People, 107. The best study of Bolingbroke himself is still Isaac Kramnick, Bolingbroke and His Circle: The Politics of Nostalgia in the Age of Walpole (Cambridge, Mass., 1968). There are, of course, numerous studies of Country thought in the period.

35. New-York Gazette, Oct. 6–13, 1735; New-York Journal, Oct. 20, 1735; Sheridan, Lewis Morris, 144.

cess to Coll. Morris, in His Undertakings [referring to Morris's impending journey to London to get Cosby removed], to a speedy Election of a new Assembly." The special attention paid to William III during the toasts suggested the Morrisite attachment to the Glorious Revolution's settlement as Morris understood it and expressed their opposition to arbitrary rule, without ever accusing Cosby directly of Jacobite sympathies. Rather, Cosby was now being portrayed as corrupted by power, as a political personality type rather than as a partisan in the dynastic struggle.[36]

The royal holidays continued to be manipulated to partisan ends into 1736. The Prince of Wales's birthday celebration became a battleground in January 1736, as the Morrisite and Cosby factions set up rival events. The Morrisites celebrated the day "at the Black Horse [Tavern — their social stronghold] in a most . . . genteel Manner." There was "a most magnificent Appearance of Gentlemen and Ladies . . . the Company proceeded to Country Dances . . . the first of which was called The Prince of Wales, and the second, the Princess of Saxe-Gotha, in Honour of the Day." There was "a most sumptuous Entertainment afterward," at which "the Honourable Rip Van Dam Esq., President of His Majesty's Council began with the Royal Healths." The next day, the Cosby faction, aware that the celebrations shaped perception, held a rival event at Fort George. Cosby, already terminally ill, could not attend the ball, but his gentlemen supporters toasted the king and illuminated their homes.[37]

By the time Morris returned from his futile embassy to London in early October 1736, the colony seemed primed for some kind of civil war. Only the arrival of imperial documents proclaiming George Clarke, a member of the now-deceased Cosby's faction, council president, lieutenant governor, and provincial commander-in-chief brought a tenuous social peace.

Clarke immediately seized the initiative by asserting his control over the imperial ritual calendar. On November 1, 1736, a New York newspaper reported "His Majesty's Birth-Day, the same was observed here, with the usual Solemnity." The city's leading men "waited upon the Honourable GEORGE CLARKE, Esq., Lieutenant-Governor of this Province . . . to pay him the usual Compliments of the Day." The "royal Healths" were drunk "under the discharge of Cannon from the Fort." It was, finally, reported that "this happy Turn of Affairs diffused a general Joy throughout the City, to see a Period so effectually put to the Disorders

36. *New-York Journal*, Oct. 20, 1735.

37. Stokes, *Iconography of Manhattan Island*, IV, 544; *New-York Gazette*, Jan. 20–Feb. 3, 1736; Esther Singleton, *Social New York under the Georges, 1714–1776* (New York, 1902), 305–306.

that threatened us." The crisis began to subside with the King's Birthday celebration. The Morrisite faction realized that they could not challenge a magistrate who had just received George II's approval, and Clarke realized that that approval, publicly owned in a ritual of imperial power, was his strongest political weapon.[38]

Tensions persisted in the colony until the one thing that could truly resolve them, the creation of new institutional structures, was accomplished. In 1737, imperial authorities separated New Jersey from New York at the executive level and made it an independent colony. Its first governor, father to the polity, was Lewis Morris, and one of his appointments to the colony's council was James Alexander, who went on to become a multiple office holder. Lewis Morris's son, Robert Hunter Morris, became a judge of the colony's supreme court and eventually Pennsylvania's lieutenant governor. Other Morris supporters completed the new government. Their honor was thus served.[39]

Considered as a social and political conflict as well as an ideological one, it is evident that monarchical political culture shaped the Zenger affair. Language derived from imperial debates was used to define the factions. The contending parties usurped royalist political holidays for partisan goals. That they manipulated political language and holidays is hardly surprising, given the importance of celebrations and print culture in linking imperial subjects. And at the root of it all was a struggle for place in an empire that did not have enough of it to go around.

To accept the power patriarchy, monarchy, empire, honor, and place had to shape behavior in colonial America is to subtly rethink much of what we know and to retell American stories with a uniquely British accent. So it was with the Zenger Crisis and with many of the other stories that comprise the earliest parts of our national history.

. . .

American Stories Retold

A persistent theme emerges from events in the provincial period that have been generally considered in light of the liberal society that developed at the eighteenth century's end. Incidents interpreted in light of classical liberalism, Country ideology, or as manifestations of a budding American localism often began

38. *Collections of the New-York Historical Society for the Year 1826*, IV (New York, 1826), 30–31.

39. Sheridan, *Lewis Morris*, 173, 179–180. Morris had been sporadically interested in securing the governorship of New Jersey since at least 1701, when Queen Anne royalized its government (48, 80, 85).

as struggles for place on the town, county, or colony level. It was true in the witchcraft conflict in Salem village, in the Great Awakening, and in the land rioting in New Jersey, New York, North Carolina, and elsewhere. For certain, these events are complex, and explanations for them must be subtle and multilayered. But institutional creation in the provincial period, which we have equated with American voluntarism and democratization, was driven by the desire for institutional place and control.

Salem village experienced severe internal tensions over institutional control between 1650 and 1692. Friction between the Putnam and the Porter families erupted repeatedly in that period. By 1692, the interior's substantial landholders, led by the Putnam family, had long been shut out of town politics by the port's elite and their Porter allies in Salem village. After a struggle, the villagers in the interior were allowed to establish their own church, and they eventually invited in a strong figure to minister to them. But in 1690, the town leaders curtly rebuffed yeomen's efforts to create a new polity by splitting village lands from the town. Such a polity would have, in these dissident villagers' minds, reunited the social and political structures in their community. Their request was denied, which must have been especially galling for some of these villagers, particularly members of the once-powerful Putnam family, who knew their fathers and grandfathers had played prominent roles in Salem's governance. This rejection was in all likelihood linked to the deadly events that followed.[40]

The religious upsurge we call the Great Awakening has generally been understood in libertarian, antiauthoritarian terms. There is much to recommend this view, as untold numbers proclaimed the primacy of a personal relationship with God, often in defiance of well-established ministers. The power of that message and its chronological relationship to the Revolution have shaped our understanding of the entire period. The creation of new institutional structures in the Awakening's aftermath has been noted, but usually as evidence of a growing American voluntarism. The new churches, new synods, new colleges, and ultimately new Christian cults that appeared might have been voluntary in membership. However, they also were institutions that offered honor and authority to those who served in them.

As paradoxical as it may seem, on a certain level the Awakening might have been driven by the desire of men in an expanding society to realize institutional

---

40. Paul Boyer and Stephen Nissenbaum, *Salem Possessed: The Social Origins of Witchcraft* (Cambridge, Mass., 1974), 40–45, 51–52. Although many studies have since been done of the episode, this classic study of village life remains a valuable tool for understanding the community and family dynamics in late-seventeenth-century New England.

control and public patriarchy. This would explain the rapid institutionalization of a supposedly individualist rebellion against institutionalized authority and the rapid return to patriarchal structuring. And it helps explain the appearance of patriarchal religious cults in the 1760s and 1770s, some of whose leaders proclaimed themselves Old World prophets or even demigods, a trend that would continue into the 1830s.[41]

The revival's preachers tapped into the political culture's prevalent anti-Catholic themes. Christ and Antichrist were at war for the soul of Protestant people everywhere. The earthly enemy was Catholics and the Catholic powers, the king was a key figure in protecting the empire from them, and those who failed to acknowledge this threatened the realm. As early as 1739, George Whitefield, writing in his widely read *Journal of a Voyage from Gibraltar to Georgia*, declared that "there needs no other argument against popery, than to see the Pageantry, Superstition, and Idolatry of their Worship." The revivalist ministers were aware of the danger of popery and sought regeneration in part because those in a weakened spiritual state might succumb to its temptations inadvertently. In time, some of these evangelically inclined ministers, like Boston's Thomas Prince, would assign the struggle against Catholics, generally, and Catholic France, in particular, millennial meaning.[42]

This same trend toward patriarchal reorganization emerged in another unlikely place: among the agrarian dissidents who first emerged in New Jersey in the mid-1740s and then appeared in backcountry or frontier locales in New York, Pennsylvania, and the Carolinas. These yeomen dissidents quickly developed committees to govern their actions. In New Jersey, farmers opposed to the colony's proprietors initially created a committee structure, manned by the best established among them, that mimicked town councils and a central committee

41. The literature on awakenings is vast. Stephen A. Marini, *Radical Sects of Revolutionary New England* (Cambridge, Mass., 1989), addresses the initial appearance of these sects. See also Nathan O. Hatch, *The Democratization of American Christianity* (New Haven, Conn., 1989). The appearance of several female-dominated sects, particularly the Universal Friends and the Shakers, have obscured this much larger turn toward rigid patriarchal forms.

42. George Whitefield, *A Journal of a Voyage from Gibraltar to Georgia* . . . (Philadelphia, 1739), 17; Thomas Prince, *A Sermon Delivered at the South Church in Boston* (Boston, 1746). Thomas Kidd has begun to explore the role of anti-Catholicism in the Great Awakening. Nathan Hatch has developed aspects of the latter theme in Hatch, "The Origins of Civil Millennialism in America: New England Clergymen, War with France, and the Revolution," in Stanley Katz and John Murrin, eds., *Colonial America*, 3d ed. (New York, 1983), 617–638.

that resembled their assembly. This structure soon gave way to a more hierarchical one headed by an agrarian strongman named Amos Roberts, who proclaimed his followers "all his children and one family."[43]

Similar institutions and leaders appeared in the New York borderlands, in Pennsylvania's Wyoming Valley, in North and South Carolina, and in other areas of the interior where an expanding population was moving beyond the social-political structures of the coast and the tidewater. When the North Carolina Assembly sought to alleviate the tensions that led to a decade of agrarian violence in the 1760s, they created four new counties in the newly populated interior. Indeed, the entire violent upheaval known as the South Carolina Regulation was driven by the desire of those living in the interior to create new royal institutions in the face of opposition from the coastal elite, who controlled all institutional structures. Simply calling such episodes "localist" fails to capture the complexity of the participants' expectations and outlooks.[44]

The Salem incident, the religious revival, and the agrarian conflicts were, of course, tremendously complex. Such emotional changes cannot simply be reduced to any one cause or even set of causes. As revealing as their public actions were, to speculate on the inner motives of those who participated, and particularly to try to discern the relationship of these motives to changes in the broader political culture, is to do just that, speculate.

If any type of history can comfortably be said to be out of vogue, it is institutional history. Its study seems to create a dead language, leaving its practitioners unable to speak to those around them. However, if we imagine institutions as an expression of conditioned human behavior, as a site where honor and place were asserted rather than simply as buildings or records, then new possibilities emerge for using institutional change to understand the provincial period. The artificial boundaries between institution and political ritual blur; the intricate relationships between governing structure, historical perception, and aesthetic taste become visible. Print culture and institution become, if not one, then arms of the same creature.

The empire and the British peace would have endured if conflict in the society had remained restricted to elites struggling for patronage positions in the em-

43. *NJA*, VII, 180. I have discussed this issue at length in *These Daring Disturbers of the Public Peace*, 51, 137–156, 186–196.

44. Kars, *Breaking Loose Together*, 190. Fear of criminal gangs and frontier violence drove the South Carolina Regulators to push for institutions. That said, elite resistance and the general course of events very strongly suggest a much more complex mindset on the part of all parties. See Brown, *The South Carolina Regulators*, for a discussion.

pire. But the tensions caused by the confluence of population growth, the establishment of the imperial cult of monarchy, and stagnation in the creation of new
institutions led to more widespread disorder. As the society divided in new ways
and the British peace broke down, the parties to the resulting discord began to
invoke the king to their own ends. British America became a society of many
monarchs, each proclaiming a different vision of local and imperial order.

6

IN THE NAME OF THE FATHER

THE END OF THE BRITISH PEACE

In early 1754, with the European empires half-consciously preparing to plunge into all-out war, the movement of a few hundred troops would seem unimportant. But the three hundred men dispatched to the ironically named Lunenberg (ironic because it was the name of the Hanoverian dynasty's home region in Germany), "a place about 15 leagues West from Halifax [in Nova Scotia]," were sent to quell a disturbance that, although minor in scope, was pregnant with political implications for the first British empire. "A small Insurrection of the German Settlers" had broken out when a local man told his fellow Germans "that they were ill used, and that the King of England not only allowed them three Years Provisions, but Cloths also, and that they were deprived of many Privileges pertinent to British Subjects," which he "could make appear by Letters from England." Though quickly crushed, this unrest on a raw frontier spoke to the empire's central motif of authority, the king in imperial imagination, and revealed the separation of that king from the British state by those seeking property and power on the empire's fringes.[1]

Imperial institutions could not control the changes that began in eighteenth-century America. Population growth encouraged a massive migration to the northern frontier, the southern piedmont, and other interior areas. Imperial wars against the French, Spanish, and Native Americans led to vigorous economic growth funded by an unstable paper money supply. Print production increased dramatically and pamphlets and broadsides spread along the new trade routes.

The cult of monarchy, designed to link subjects harmoniously to the empire, often intensified rather than alleviated the stresses caused by these transformations. An institutionally unfixed king could be all things to all people, maintainer and destroyer of the imperial order, benevolent as well as restrictive, the source

1. *Pennsylvania Gazette* (Philadelphia), Feb. 19, 1754.

of hope as well as fear. In the empire's opening seams, on the millions of acres whose ownership was uncertain and where yeomen and gentlemen battled for control, on half-frozen and forgotten frontiers, and in the plantation fields where slave confronted master, the king lent moral support to his beloved children as they clashed with his authority. The fragmentation of order reached into the family as vigilante gangs struggled to define the limits of patriarchal authority in communities up and down the eastern seaboard. A world in disorder found it had a king with many faces.

· · ·

In the Name of the Father

The diffused struggle for the control of the American countryside that began in New Jersey in the 1740s and did not end until the Homestead Act of 1862 is one of our history's great, unknown epics. Like the blindfolded child that touches the elephant, we have seen and described parts of it without being able to describe the whole. The initial portion of this struggle pitted those who would build an estate-based landscape against an independent yeomanry. These conflicts became violent early on and would flare up into disorder again and again after 1740.

Strangely, the yeomen's ally in their struggle against this would-be aristocracy and the royal officials who supported them was Great Britain's imagined kings. The imposition of the cult of monarchy in the four decades before the outbreak of agrarian unrest had introduced a language of benevolent kingship to wide portions of the colonial population. The perception of a loving bond between king and subject existed in all regions of the colonies and manifested itself in the disputes over ownership of millions of acres in the interior. Supported by their kings, the yeomanry confronted royal officials. Violence erupted, first in northern New Jersey in the 1740s and 1750s, then in the eastern Hudson Valley after 1755; again in the Wyoming Valley and along the frontier in Pennsylvania that same decade; and in the Carolina interior as well as what became Vermont during the 1760s. Hundreds, sometimes thousands, of farmers and their families engaged in collective violence against the royal governments and local gentry in a battle for both actual property and the processes that controlled property acquisition. At stake was the character of community life in the countryside.

The tendency of these farmers to invoke nonroyal titles or titles derived from their charters to the contested lands was pronounced. Yet this only damaged their tie to the king's institutional authority, not to the loving imperial overlord himself. The benevolent Protestant father relentlessly described and discussed in the mass-print culture became a subversive against his own officials in the fields and forests on the edges of royal dominion. The yeomanry's love for the king threatened the imperial order even as it bound it together.[2]

How this happened, the actual progression that painted the king's face on the porcelain of protest and rebellion, is partly hidden, though the broader interplay of structure and language is evident. Expanded trade and communications carried accounts of the king into new areas. New roads allowed yeomen to travel to population centers for trade and to see the spectacles of royal authority performed. Goods bearing the royal likeness traveled the same roads as settlers who had participated in or seen royal rites.

However, the inner mechanics that created a benevolent king divorced from his own institutions in British America are difficult to discern. There was an English tradition of a benevolent king divorced from his evil ministers that stretched back to at least the Peasants' Revolt of 1381. Parliament had taken up arms in 1642 against Charles I in purported defense of a justly used royal prerogative. The constitutional principle that the king could do no wrong also created a fundamental distinction between ruler and state. For us, the problem is that, by the time subversive monarchy emerged in New Jersey in the 1740s, a well-formed perception of a benevolent monarch already existed.[3]

It is difficult, though, not to think that yeomen's attitudes were shaped by royal rites and a print culture that constantly invoked a loving Protestant ruler. Diaries and written accounts hint at how this happened, as visitors from the countryside noted seeing royal rites in larger towns. James Mackey, visiting Philadelphia from the Delaware countryside, heard George II proclaimed king in 1727 and returned home to spread the good news to friends. Aaron Leaming of isolated Cape May County, New Jersey, recalled being in New York during the celebration of George II's coronation day in October 1750, and there must have been tens of thousands who had similar experiences between 1689 and 1776. Rites and reading about a loving king allowed provincials an emotional tie to the monarchy apart from institutions. When the yeomanry came into open conflict with their superiors in the imperial government, they found no difficulty in aligning themselves with the king to resist his authority.[4]

2. The two recent studies of the prerevolutionary unrest are Brendan McConville, *These Daring Disturbers of the Public Peace: The Struggle for Property and Power in Early New Jersey* (Ithaca, N.Y., 1999), and Marjoleine Kars, *Breaking Loose Together: The Regulator Rebellion in Pre-Revolutionary North Carolina* (Chapel Hill, N.C., 2002). See also Richard Maxwell Brown, *The South Carolina Regulators* (Cambridge, Mass., 1963).

3. John Neville Figgis, *The Divine Right of Kings*, 2d ed. (Cambridge, 1914), 223–224.

4. Harold B. Hancock, ed., "'Fare Weather and Good Helth': The Journal of Caesar

Although the exact mechanics of this separation remain hidden, the chronology of its appearance is more apparent. As early as the Zenger Crisis, opposing political groups professing loyalty to differing visions of George II and the British constitution had appropriated royal ceremonies. That division, though, occurred at the top of the social structure. The parties to it had vested interest in the existing institutions and were in fact fighting for control of them.

But when New Jersey exploded into violence in the 1740s over ownership of more than 600,000 acres, angry yeomen quickly invoked a benevolent king to explain their illegal behavior. The conflict pitted a diverse spectrum of yeomen against members of the Board of Proprietors of the Eastern Division of New Jersey, many of whom held high positions in the royal government. Despite this, crowds of farmers attacking royal jails to free imprisoned friends repeatedly cheered for George II as royal officials read the king's proclamations against riots. One of their spokesmen asked God's blessing for the king: "Preserve him in Health and Strength, to vanquish and overcome all his [and presumably their] Enemies." The yeomen's leaders insisted that "We are . . . loyal Subjects of His Majesty King George" throughout a decade and a half of violence. Ultimately, these yeomen would send an "ambassador to the King" to deliver a petition begging deliverance from those who would deny them the king's justice.[5]

Such emotional attachment to the king by those who would oppose his formal authority was not confined to New Jersey. Sympathizers to Pennsylvania's Paxton Boys declared them "FREEMEN and the KING'S SUBJECTS" who took their murderous actions against Native Americans to deal with the "Enemies to his MAJESTY, his Government, and Subjects." During the violent upheaval known as the North Carolina Regulation, a group of Regulators proclaimed themselves "his Majesties most loyal subjects" in a communication with the royal government.[6]

It would be easy to assume that these declarations of loyalty were intended simply to avoid treason charges. Perhaps, but they continued long after treason charges had been filed in New Jersey and outrage had been leveled by all quarters against the Paxton Boys. A better question is, To whom and to what did they believe they were declaring their loyalty and affection? In the minds of Jersey

---

Rodeney, 1727–1729," *Delaware History*, X (1962), 51; Aaron Leaming diary, Oct. 11, 1750, HSP.

5. *NJA*, XV, *Journal of the Governor and Council*, III, 587–588, VI, 282, 296, VII, 179; *Calendar of the Stevens Family Papers*, I, *1664–1750*, New Jersey Historical Records Survey Project, WPA (Newark, 1940), note from Dec. 29, 1750, doc. 8062, 190.

6. *The Conduct of the Paxton-Men, Impartially Represented: With Some Remarks on the Narrative* (Philadelphia, 1764), 12; Kars, *Breaking Loose Together*, 197.

yeomen, the idea of a benevolent Protestant king current in the broader political culture became somehow linked to the long tradition of crowds' claiming to defend the British constitution. So completely did one central New Jersey rioter believe this that he could imagine the king taking up their cause. "When the King," this man proclaimed, realized his "Subjects in the Jerseys are turned Mob. . . . He will say, or think, what's the Matter with my Subjects? Surely they are wronged or oppressed, or else they would never rebell against my Laws . . . [and] . . . he will order us to have our Land." It was part of the king's natural role to defend their "liberties and properties!"[7]

The same sort of perceptions existed in other areas rife with social conflict. Orange County, North Carolina, farmers protested when Governor William Tryon planned to build an anglicized mansion house for himself in 1768. These yeomen declared, "The King requires no Money from His Subjects but what they are made sensible what use it's for." A year later, yeomen Regulators demanded that the colony's assembly notify the king of the cruel measures used by local officials to deny them their share of lands and "His Majesties liberality and Bounty." In this version of the British polity, all goodness flowed from a king divorced from the local state apparatus.[8]

At the core of this faith in the monarch was love. In 1752, Dutch-speaking yeomen in a central New Jersey county, while attacking a royal jail in order to free their leader, declared that they "Loved King George better than he or Any body" as they beat senseless a royal sheriff who invoked the king's name against their actions. The North Carolina Regulators used this emotional language in an address to Governor Tryon, to whom they declared their "unfeigned Love to Our dread Sovereigne Lord and Royal Master King Geo 3rd . . . and will when Occasion requires fight for and defend him to the last drop of Blood." These Regulators "highly venerate the British Constitution." Another pro-Regulator pamphlet, published in 1771, echoed these powerful royalist sentiments. Hermon Husband, author of *A Fan for Fanning, and a Touch-Stone to Tryon*, declared "how unfortunate is that Prince [George III], who is sorely wounded thro' the side of base designing wretches, who prostitute all things sacred and civil to deceive their King."[9]

7. *NJA*, VII, 422–423.

8. Kars, *Breaking Loose Together*, 137, 172–173.

9. *NJA*, XX, *Newspaper Extracts*, IV, 512–513, XVI, *Journal of the Governor and Council*, IV, 376; Regulators to William Tryon, [July–August? 1768], in William S. Powell, ed., *The Correspondence of William Tryon and Other Selected Papers*, II, *1768–1818* (Raleigh, N.C., 1981), 141; [Hermon Husband], *A Fan for Fanning, and a Touch-Stone to Tryon: Contain-*

The passions that held the empire together were what we would call socially unfixed, meaning they might well act as a solvent of as well as a binder of the provincial order. Love, it would seem, was a dangerous thing in the American provinces, perhaps more than we can possibly imagine. One special dissident group that expressed its faith in a benevolent king by rebelling made it clear just how completely the faith in the monarchy had become detached from the established order. For, as we reread the story of royal America, it becomes apparent that more than one defiant slave rebelled at the monarch's behest.

. . .

In Pharaoh's Name

Royalism's subversive potential is nowhere more evident than in the account of a South Carolina slave preacher's words in the 1770s. He told his followers that George II had "rec[eive]d a Book from our Lord by which he was to Alter the World [free the slaves]." Having failed to do so, that monarch was "now gone to Hell." Though this had been a major disappointment, the preacher assured his listeners that hope was still alive, as "the Young King [George III] . . . was about to alter the World and set the Negroes Free." This preacher expressed a view of Britain's monarchs that had, by 1775, become widely accepted in some slave populations: king above master; royal authority as subversion. As the eighteenth century progressed, more and more defiant slaves had come to believe that the king of Great Britain intended to free them. The development of this faith in the king occurred at the same time that royal rites spread and print culture expanded, and there is strong reason to believe there is a link between these changes. This royalization of slave resistance between the 1720s and 1776 seems to help explain the widespread phenomenon of slave loyalism during the Revolution.[10]

Royal celebrations were probably the primary means by which slaves learned of the king's benevolence. Accounts of royal celebrations, particularly Pope's Day, repeatedly mention an African-American presence. As slaves were present in all the major towns where rites were performed, it seems likely they saw these ceremonies and took away their own understanding of the king and royal benevolence.

As unlikely as it may seem, the same legal system that punished defiant slaves

---

ing an Impartial Account of the Rise and Progress of the So Much Talked of Regulation in North-Carolina (Boston, 1771), no. 1, rpt. in William K. Boyd, ed., *Some Eighteenth Century Tracts concerning North Carolina* (Raleigh, N.C., 1927), 344.

10. Robert A. Olwell, "'Domestick Enemies': Slavery and Political Independence in South Carolina, May 1775–March 1776," *Journal of Southern History*, LV (1989), 33–34.

might have been a conduit for subversive royal beliefs to spread to enslaved populations. Slaves attended court days, where the king's justice was invoked in elaborate rituals. It was also well known, at least in some areas, that the king had repeatedly asked his provincial governments to punish white men who murdered slaves or freemen. Somehow, the existing power structure came to educate enslaved peoples in the mainland colonies and the British West Indies about the benevolent nature of their monarchs, and they thus came to dream of a father-monarch that could deliver them from their mundane local pharaohs.[11]

Another unintentional conduit for this perception of a slave-loving monarch might have been the Church of England and the masters themselves. Some slaves attended services where prayers were said for the king, and, as important, heard the sermons that described the enslavement and freeing of the Israelites. This in part helps explain why masters often opposed Christianizing their slaves. Slave-owners in Charleston and along the Stono River in South Carolina complained bitterly when Church of England ministers tried to convert their slaves. "The extreme difficulty," one minister reported, was "to persuade their masters to have them taught the Christian religion, for which [the masters] give very frivolous reasons." The real reason, he believed, was the masters' fear that "after their slaves are Baptized they are no longer servants, Say they, but free." Although this issue came up repeatedly in the eighteenth century in regard to Dissenting sects and the Church of England, the latter's connection to the monarchy might have somehow convinced slaves that conversion under the auspices of the royally headed church would lead to free subjecthood.[12]

However they reached their understanding, over time, slaves in widely dispersed locations came to be convinced that the king intended to free them. When that freedom was not forthcoming, they revolted or conspired against slave masters who, they insisted, were denying the king's compassionate intentions. The nature of slavery makes it difficult to trace the development of this perception, as white accounts of organized slave resistance were subjective, to say the least. But, by culling eighteenth-century accounts, we can get an idea of how and at what rate enslaved populations adapted faith in the king to resistance to bondage.

11. *Boston Evening-Post*, Nov. 11, 1745. The *Pennsylvania Gazette*, Nov. 22, 1764, suggests the degree of African-American participation in the Pope's Day holiday in the years before the Stamp Act. The *Massachusetts Gazette and Boston News-Letter*, Nov. 7, 1765, recounts the whitening of Pope's Day during the Stamp Act Crisis.

12. William Dun to the Society for the Propagation of the Gospel in Foreign Parts (hereafter cited as SPG), Apr. 21, 1707, Charleston, SPG microfilm, reel 16; "Governor William Bull's Representation of the Colony, 1770," in H. Roy Merrens, ed., *The Colonial South Carolina Scene: Contemporary Views, 1697–1774* (Columbia, S.C., 1977), 260.

The emancipating king first appeared in slave conspiracies in the 1730s and was clearly tied to the imperialization of colonial life. We might take that decade as one that marks a shift in the character of organized slave resistance. Before the 1730s, slave resistance was centered on African ethnic and religious beliefs. Defiance shaped by African beliefs and identities continued, but after 1730, an increasingly American-born slave population began to adapt imperial political culture to their own ends. Widespread slave unrest that gripped Virginia in 1730 was apparently sparked when a sailor told slaves "that the King of England had ordered they should be all set free." This statement, which originated with a person who had a supposed wider knowledge of the world and which was apparently disseminated as a rumor, led to "Meetings and disorderly Cabals" among the slaves in "several Parts of the Country." At least one newspaper reported that a slave had himself smuggled on board a ship in order that he might go to England to parley with George II as "Embassador from the Negroes" in Virginia.[13]

Slaves believed the sailor in part because Virginia's governor, Alexander Spotswood, had recently returned to the colony from England and had prosecuted a white man for murdering a slave woman. Some among the conspirators apparently also believed that their baptism by Anglican ministers had led George II to order "all those slaves free that were christians," this despite the slaves' being assured by local ministers "that Baptism altered nothing as to their servitude." Local militia units strongly enforced local pass laws for slaves, but, nonetheless, "a considerable Body of them were got together, in Norfolk County, and had threatened the Lives of some Gentlemen." The conspirators were discovered and imprisoned. Officials hanged five of the rebels, and white vigilantes and Pasquotank Indian slave hunters hanged another twenty-five.[14]

A conspiracy in central New Jersey in 1734 suggests how divisions in the political elite encouraged the royalization of slave dissent. "I have," wrote a correspondent to the *American Weekly Mercury* early in that year, "been present at some of the Examinations of those Negroes [who rebelled]." The conspiracy was

13. *American Weekly Mercury* (Philadelphia), Nov. 12–19, 1730; *New York Gazette*, Nov. 30, 1730; Jill Lepore, *New York Burning: Liberty, Slavery, and Conspiracy in Eighteenth-Century Manhattan* (New York, 2005), 186.

14. Anthony S. Parent, Jr., *Foul Means: The Formation of a Slave Society in Virginia, 1660–1740* (Chapel Hill, N.C., 2003), 160, 161. Parent gives a detailed discussion of the conspiracy (159–162) and provides a detailed background (135–172). "All those slaves free": Sylvia R. Frey and Betty Wood, *Come Shouting to Zion: African American Protestantism in the American South and British Caribbean to 1830* (Chapel Hill, N.C., 1998), 70. Frey and Wood date this unrest to 1731, but newspaper accounts suggest the primary unrest occurred in 1730. "A considerable Body": *American Weekly Mercury*, Nov. 12–19, 1730.

apparently hatched by *"Thomas L——d"'s* [probably Thomas Leonard] slaves, who lived in quarters several miles from his home. Away from supervision, the slaves became "a pest to the Neigbourhood," stealing and encouraging disorder on other estates.[15]

In just such gatherings, slaves became aware of the Zenger Crisis. Whether a literate slave read the pamphlets and newspapers or slaves overheard whites arguing about the controversy is unclear. What is evident is that the perception of a paternal, loving king detached from his own authority legitimated a plot in which slaves turned to the empire's father for support.

The slave leaders apparently told their followers that George II had "sent to the governor of New York, to set them all free," an order the conspirators claimed he intended to follow out "but was prevented by his Council and Assembly." The slave leaders maintained that the order "was the Reason there subsisted now so great a difference between the governor and the People of both the Provinces." Only the claim of a drunken slave that "Englishmen were in generall a pack of Villians" and that "he was as good a Man" as a white man brought to light the conspirators' plan for a violent uprising and flight to the French and Indians. This account, whatever embellishments might have been added by white correspondents, shared a central characteristic with a number of slave rebellions and conspiracies in the period. In all of them, slaves invoked the British monarch to justify their actions.[16]

In some instances, slaves used their knowledge of royal rites and royal institutions to organize their resistance. Those conspiracies and rebellions suggest a connection, albeit conceptual, between servile unrest and the custom of slave elections and slave coronation common in the Afro-Puritan subculture in New England and perhaps portions of New York and New Jersey. Slave elections, taking place during colonial elections, set up slave kings and councils (in New Hampshire and sometimes the Bay Colony and Rhode Island) or governors (in Rhode Island and Connecticut) or kings and governors, and they have rightly been seen as an adjustment by those populations to their enslavement. Some of these elections concluded with treating and processions directly modeled on those conducted by white provincials. Slave elections and resistance that drew on royal institutions or rites were different aspects of a slave political culture that might have been far more complex than our present understanding allows. That subculture, if these conspiracies are an accurate indication, fused British political

15. *American Weekly Mercury*, Feb. 26–Mar. 5, 1733/4.
16. Ibid.

practices with African beliefs. A creole slave population had developed, at least in some places, a creole political subculture.[17]

The conspiracy that apparently occurred on Antigua in 1736 reveals how this fusion of African customs and imperial practices could be used to threaten white domination. The island's Ashanti population planned to seize control after a bloody uprising. In recruiting rituals adapted from African religion, the Ashanti plotters drew others into the conspiracy by giving them a glass of alcohol mixed with dirt from a grave. Several Ashanti religious leaders were involved, as was Court, the slave leader who had long been considered king by the island's Ashanti. He went as far as to perform the ikem, a traditional Ashanti dance done by a king when he decides to go to war, shortly before the uprising was to come off. The conspiracy called for the slaves to seize the capital, kill all the Europeans, and capture the shipping in the harbor.[18]

British political culture played as important a role as African in shaping the conspiracy. The plot was timed to go off on the King's Birthday, October 30. The crux of the plot was Court's plan to place a bomb underneath the banquet hall (stage?) where the island's whites gathered for the traditional holiday feast. This plan bears more than a superficial resemblance to Guy Fawkes's plot to blow up James I and Parliament, the foiling of which was celebrated on November 5,

---

17. Lorenzo Johnston Greene, *The Negro in Colonial New England, 1620–1776* (New York, 1968), discusses an incident at the opening of the Revolution that suggests this linkage. The slave of a captured British officer was made "governor" of Connecticut's African and African-American populations. There was a widespread fear that it was part of a broader plot to spark a pro-British, pro-monarch revolt (252–253). For another view, see Melvin Wade, "'Shining in Borrowed Plumage': Affirmation of Community in the Black Coronation Festivals of New England, ca. 1750–1850," in Robert Blair St. George, ed., *Material Life in America, 1600–1860* (Boston, 1988), 171–182; William Dillon Piersen, "Afro-American Culture in Eighteenth-Century New England: A Comparative Examination" (Ph.D. diss., Indiana University, 1975); Orville H. Platt, "Negro Governors," in *Papers of the New Haven Colony Historical Society*, VI (New Haven, Conn., 1900), 321, 325, 333–334. Lepore, *New York Burning*, 159, suggests a conceptual connection between the elections and slave unrest. Whether the practice of electing kings and governors together existed before the Revolution is unclear from Platt's piece, but it seems logical that this was so and that a vestige of the practice existed into the early nineteenth century. Again, the exact chronology of these parades is unclear.

18. David Barry Gaspar, *Bondmen and Rebels: A Study of Master-Slave Relations in Antigua with Implications for Colonial British America* (Durham, N.C., 1993), is the best general consideration of this conspiracy.

Pope's Day. Since the conspirators were aware of the royal holidays, it is entirely possible they drew some inspiration from that conspiracy.

These would-be rebels also used Christian religious rites to recruit followers. One hostile and probably embellished account maintained that slave leaders "had been taught the Christian Religion conformable to the frequent Admonition of our worthy Diocesan the Bishop of *London*." They had, according to this angry writer, sworn "the Multitude into their Scheme . . . administered the Sacrament to all such as professed themselves Christians according to the Rites of the Bishop's Church." Another account claimed that Court had adopted some British political rites; his followers, it was said, "crown'd him, under a Canopy erected for that purpose." The conspiracy was crushed before it could come off, however, and it was the subsequent trials and executions that exposed its political and cultural contours.[19]

A similarly structured conspiracy occurred on Saint Kitts in 1770. There, the slaves laid "a grand plan" to slaughter the white population, apparently drawing on British political institutions, celebratory practices, and Freemason rituals to shape their plan. "The chief ringleader was a negro named Archy [who] . . . was to be King — Mr. Phillips's negro man to be Governor, and to be called General Woodley [a British naval commander in the region]." Archy "had a suit of superfine blue cloth, turned up with scarlet, and trim'd with gold lace; Mr. Phillips negro a suit of superfine green, turn'd up with buff, and trim'd with gold." The rendezvous for this group was a place called "Monkey-Hill, and [they] called their assembly the Free Masons meeting." As with royal political celebrations, the slaves capped their meeting with toasting, which proved to be their undoing after a boy overheard them drinking to "success to their War and Liberty." Thus alerted, planters crushed the plot.[20]

The faith in a benevolent king probably helps explain the overwhelming tendency of conspirators and runaways in the Revolutionary era to favor the British. In 1768, persistent rumors gripped Boston that slaves assisted by a British officer or officers intended to rebel. One slave reportedly declared, "Now that the [British] soldiers are come the Negroes shall be free." In 1774, a group of Boston slaves apparently contacted Massachusetts governor Thomas Hutchinson with an offer to fight for the British in exchange for their freedom. In 1775, South Carolina officials hanged a well-known freeman named Jerry for supposedly plotting a slave uprising with the help of royal officials, who, he reportedly told his followers,

19. *Boston Weekly News-Letter*, Nov. 25–Dec. 2, 1736; *Virginia Gazette*, Dec. 17, 1736; *American Weekly Mercury*, Mar. 8–17, 1736/7.

20. *Massachusetts Gazette and Boston News-Letter*, May 3, 1770.

would "help the poor Negroes." Throughout 1775, North Carolina slaveowners heard rumors of planned royalist slave uprisings in four counties and the Tar River region.[21]

The success and limitations of Lord Dunmore's proclamation at the opening of the Revolution offering freedom to Virginia slaves who fought for the king should be understood in light of the royal political culture's influence on the African-American population. It was a slave delegation that initially approached Dunmore with the idea of fighting for the king to gain their freedom, and the subsequent flight of several thousands of slaves to British forces in 1775 and 1776 might have been as much a product of faith in a benevolent British king as it was a hope for personal liberty for slaves in a society as yet unwilling to grant it.[22]

Certainly, the slave encountered by Joseph Plumb Martin in Westchester County, New York, in 1776 had such faith. This slave, owned by Martin's host, "quickly began to upbraid me with my opposition to the British." George III, the slave insisted, "was a very powerful prince, he said — a very powerful prince; and it was a pity that the colonists had fallen out with him; but as we had, we must abide by the consequences." Martin, immersed in the prejudices of his time, believed that the slave could not have come to these thoughts himself and "concluded he had heard his betters say so. As the old cock crows, so crows the young one; and I thought, as the white cock crows, so crows the black one." This particular slave shortly thereafter "went to Long Island to assist King George." Similar respect for the monarch existed in the case of slaves who fought for the British army in Georgia in 1779. At the Revolution's end, they refused to surrender and fled to the interior, calling themselves soldiers of George III.[23]

Whether the conspirators drew on the idea of a benevolent, emancipating monarch to legitimate their actions or on British institutions or rites to form

21. Greene, *The Negro in Colonial New England*, 162; Robert M. Weir, *Colonial South Carolina: A History* (New York, 1983), 201–202; R. H. Taylor, "Slave Conspiracies in North Carolina," in *North Carolina Historical Review*, V (1928), 30; Jeffrey J. Crow, "Slave Rebelliousness and Social Conflict in North Carolina, 1775 to 1802," *WMQ*, 3d Ser., XXXVII (1980), 79–102. Ellen Gibson Wilson, *The Loyal Blacks* (New York, 1976), 7, quotes Abigail Adams concerning the supposed royalist slave conspiracy in Massachusetts in 1774.

22. Ira Berlin, *Many Thousands Gone: The First Two Centuries of Slavery in North America* (Cambridge, Mass., 1998), 257; Philip D. Morgan, *Slave Counterpoint: Black Culture in the Eighteenth-Century Chesapeake and Lowcountry* (Chapel Hill, N.C., 1998), 308–309, describes the extensive fears of a slave uprising in favor of the king's troops in the period.

23. James Kirby Martin, ed., *Ordinary Courage: The Revolutionary War Adventures of Joseph Plumb Martin* (St. James, N.Y., 1999), 34; Herbert Aptheker, *American Negro Slave Revolts* (New York, 1993), 201–208.

their conspiracies and control behavior within them, the influence of monarchical political culture is apparent. And that influence encouraged them to establish hierarchy within their conspiracies. The rebellions revolved around a free-unfree axis rather than represented an egalitarian rebellion against hierarchy itself.

At the same time, these distant rebels help to complicate our understanding of slave resistance. There was a clear shift from African-inspired revolts in the seventeenth and early eighteenth centuries to more republicanized or democratized ones in the late eighteenth and nineteenth centuries, but monarchical culture helped shape slave resistance in the seven decades after 1700. Slave belief in a sympathetic British monarch seems to have died hard. Apparently some slaves involved in Nat Turner's 1831 rebellion believed that the British would free them (perhaps having had word of British emancipation plans for the Caribbean). As late as 1840, slaves in Alabama claimed that British forces would free them during unrest in that state. Although these beliefs were obviously influenced by events after 1783, they may also represent an oral tradition among enslaved African-Americans of monarchical benevolence.[24]

Rebelling slaves who invoked the king expressed a change in the nature of authority in much the same way as the defiant yeomanry who so unsettled the countryside. In their ability to imagine a personal relationship with a paternal ruler existing apart from royal authorities, they revealed an internalization of authority that came, paradoxically, from the power structure itself. Their views and goals were egalitarian and hierarchical, liberating and confining, all in the same moment. The imposition of monarchical political culture into a demographically dynamic, ethnically diverse society had created multiple patriarchies, each with its own character and perception of order. Paralleling this political fragmentation was a growing disagreement over gender relations and the nature of patriarchy in the home.[25]

24. Aptheker, *American Negro Slave Revolts*, 83. The work of Eugene Genovese written in the 1970s is instructive in this regard. He postulated a shift from an African restorationist model of slave rebellions to a republican model of these rebellions. But the royalization of rebellion has been all but completely ignored.

25. Myra Jehlen, "J. Hector St. John Crèvecoeur: A Monarcho-Anarchist in Revolutionary America," *American Quarterly*, XXXI (1979), 204–222, suggests multiple patriarchies. She tries to wrestle with the paradoxical character of the revolutionary self that emerged by 1800. The theme is picked up by Paul Downes in *Democracy, Revolution, and Monarchism in Early American Literature* (Cambridge, 2002), 64–66.

. . .

The American Concert: Gender Roles, Power,
and the Fragmentation of Social Patriarchy

"We hear," reported the *New York Gazette; or, the Weekly Post-Boy* in 1752, "that an odd Sect of People have lately appeared" at Elizabethtown, New Jersey, "who go under the Denomination of *Regulars*." The group numbered "near a Dozen" who "dress themselves in Women's Cloaths, and painting their Faces, go in the Evening to the Houses of such as are reported to have beat their Wives." The group would grab the abuser, "strip him, turn up his Posteriors, and flog him with Rods most severely, crying out all the Time, *Wo to the Men that beat their Wives*." "It seems," continued the *Post Boy's* correspondent, "that several Persons in that Borough, (and tis said some very deservedly) have undergone the Discipline, to the no small Terror of others, who are any Way conscious of deserving the same."[26]

The Elizabethtown Regulars' behavior was an expression of Anglo-American customs known collectively as rough music. Community members performed rough music to police social and sexual norms. When these conventions were

---

26. *NJA*, XIX, *Newspaper Extracts*, III, 225–226. For a New England episode where men dressed like women in order to engage in extralegal action, see Laurel Thatcher Ulrich, *Good Wives: Image and Reality in the Lives of Women in Northern New England, 1650–1750* (New York, 1980), 195. Why men dressed as women is open to conjecture. The most prevalent explanation is that, because the common law treated violent women differently (and allowed for greater latitude, since they were "only women"), men assumed this identity when engaged in extralegal action. The question of cross-dressing in the early modern period is complex. See Vern L. Bullough and Bonnie Bullough, *Cross Dressing, Sex, and Gender* (Philadelphia, 1993); Kristina Straub, *Sexual Suspects: Eighteenth-Century Players and Sexual Ideology* (Princeton, N.J., 1992); and Peter Stallybrass, *The Politics and Poetics of Transgression* (London, 1986).

There is no detailed study of rough music in colonial America, perhaps because so many historians have accepted without question that the predominance of Calvinism in New England and the middle colonies inhibited the transfer of English plebeian culture to North America. By far the best study is Alfred F. Young's "English Plebeian Culture and Eighteenth-Century American Radicalism," in Margaret Jacob and James Jacob, eds., *The Origins of Anglo-American Radicalism* (London, 1984), 185–212. See also Richard Maxwell Brown's "Violence and the American Revolution," in Stephen G. Kurtz and James H. Hutson, eds., *Essays on the American Revolution* (Chapel Hill, N.C., 1973), 81–120; Pauline Maier, *From Resistance to Revolution: Colonial Radicals and the Development of American Opposition to Britain, 1765–1776* (New York, 1972), 3–26; and Peter Shaw, *American Patriots and the Rituals of Revolution* (Cambridge, Mass., 1981), 204–233. Also very useful is Bryan Palmer's "Discordant Music: Charivari and White Capping in North America," *Labour/Le Travail*, I (1978), 5–62.

violated, common people (often young men) used noise, processions, physical intimidation, and, in some cases, brutal violence to inform individuals or couples that their behavior was unacceptable.[27]

The use of these customary humiliations in British America suggests how European colonial society was. Yet rough-music customs transplanted to the provinces manifested themselves in fashions distinct in some respect from European norms, particularly the norms of England. In England, rough-music gangs focused on scolding women, cuckolds, and adulterous couples, although a variety of usages were known in the British Isles. In North America, violent and adulterous husbands as well as scolds and cuckolds were subjected to rough music, and men seem to have been the primary objects of these attacks.[28]

27. Recent studies of these customs in Britain reveal an array of extrainstitutional rituals intended to confine sexuality (particularly female) within marriage and uphold male dominance in the household. See David Underdown, *Revel, Riot, and Rebellion: Popular Politics and Culture in England, 1603–1660* (Oxford, 1985), 100–103, 106, 110–111, 216, 265, 279; Martin Ingram, "Ridings, Rough Music, and Mocking Rhymes in Early Modern England," in Barry Reay, ed., *Popular Culture in Seventeenth-Century England* (New York, 1985), 166–197; Underdown, "The Taming of the Scold: The Enforcement of Patriarchal Authority in Early Modern England," in Anthony Fletcher and John Stevenson, eds., *Order and Disorder in Early Modern England* (Cambridge, 1985), 116–136; E. P. Thompson, *Customs in Common* (New York, 1991), 467–538, esp. 482, 516–531. "Skimmington" seems to derive its name from a type of wooden ladle used to beat on pots during rough-music processions (Underdown, "The Taming of the Scold," 100–101, 116). In Devon, troublemakers witnessed bloody, ritualistic "stag hunts" that ended outside their own homes. In Wiltshire, "wooset-hunters" paraded night after night in noisy procession past the dwellings of adulterous couples. In some areas, young men beat wooden spoons on tins outside the bedchambers of newlyweds whose premarital relationships had a whiff of scandal. And, throughout England, scolds and cuckolds found themselves tied to poles and dragged through the streets while children hurled filth at them. Called "riding the stang" in the north of England, this custom was also known as "riding the wooden horse" and "riding skimmington." See S. D. Amussen, "Gender, Family and the Social Order, 1560–1725," in Fletcher and Stevenson, eds., *Order and Disorder in Early Modern England*, 196–217.

28. Alice Morse Earle, writing one hundred years ago, indicated that the ducking of scolds was common in the middle and southern colonies but not in New England; see Earle, *Curious Punishments of Bygone Days* (Chicago, 1896), 11–28. Earle goes on to maintain that New Englanders used cleft sticks and gags to punish scolds (101–105). But the majority of cases of rough music we know about seem to be directed against abusive men. The same shift occurred in Europe in the late eighteenth and the early nineteenth centuries. See Thompson, *Customs in Common*, 508–514, 522, 529–530, and Natalie Zemon

The broadening of targets in eighteenth-century America expressed, among other things, a growing subjectivity in understanding the father's authority in the home. While colonial "musicians" tried to uphold their idea of customary order, the nature of that normalcy was becoming more and more fragmented. Their behavior sometimes was interpreted as a challenge to community order and other times clearly reinforced it. Rough music's transformation from a social to a political phenomenon illuminates the shadowy but important process through which personal experience and social perceptions informed political attitudes.[29]

Rough music in America included a broad and seemingly contradictory spectrum of behaviors. On one boundary were those like the Elizabethtown Regulars who attacked violent men. This seems to have been the most common usage of these customs in the colonies. Shortly after the Elizabethtown incidents, another set of "Regulators," purported to have acted "in Imitation of those of Elizabeth-Town," took a Philadelphia man who had horsewhipped his wife after a quarrel, tied him up, "flagellated his Posterior with Birchin Rods, till the Blood trickled down to his Heels," and then ordered him "not to horse-whip or beat his Wife anymore." In the 1760s, newspapers reported rough music directed against violent and unfaithful husbands in New York City, Newark, New Jersey, near Providence, Rhode Island, and at Attleboro, Massachusetts. The *Boston Post-Boy and Advertiser* reported on November 5, 1764, that the Attleboro crowd used rough music in the form of a skimmington ride (strapping a transgressor to a wooden rail and running him or her through the streets) to discipline an adulterous husband.[30]

Davis, "Women on Top," in Davis, *Society and Culture in Early Modern France: Eight Essays* (Stanford, Calif., 1975), 150.

29. For the broadest discussion of the plebeian/patrician split, see Gordon S. Wood, *The Radicalism of the American Revolution* (New York, 1991). For a detailed discussion of the hostility between plebeians and patricians in one colony, see Edward Countryman, *A People in Revolution: The American Revolution and Political Society in New York, 1760–1790* (Baltimore, 1981), 5–98. E. P. Thompson, David Underdown, and Alfred Young have all demonstrated that, in certain contexts, rough music could be transformed from a means of maintaining a traditional social order into a tool of popular political protest (Thompson, *Customs in Common*, 516–526; Underdown, *Revel, Riot, and Rebellion*, 110–111; Young, "English Plebeian Culture," in Jacob and Jacob, *Origins of Anglo-American Radicalism*, 204–206).

30. See Young, "English Plebeian Culture," in Jacob and Jacob, *Origins of Anglo-American Radicalism*, 190; *New-York Gazette; or, the Weekly Post-Boy*, Feb. 12, 1753; Brown, "Violence and the American Revolution," in Kurtz and Hutson, eds., *Essays on the Ameri-*

Those who disciplined overtly assertive wives and women who violated sexual norms constituted the opposite behavioral pole. In September 1748, a wife perceived to be overly aggressive by her husband was rode skimmington near Philadelphia. Her husband "order'd a Man to take her on his shoulders, which he did, and there held her, while the Husband whipp'd her with Rods till the Blood run down her Heels." In the 1750s, New York City saw two incidents where women dressed as boys attacked a woman they called "whore" and "pocky whore." In the early 1760s, two Marblehead, Massachusetts, sailors seized a widow, ducked her from the deck of their ship, painted her face, and carted her ashore. Such incidents seem to have been less prevalent than the assaults against violent men, but extralegal assaults against women occurred up and down the eastern seaboard as well.[31]

In between these extremes, a number of customs related to rough music upheld local community norms by reinforcing marriage and social harmony. Consider, for example, the "throwing of the stocking" at the 1737 nuptials of a Baptist couple of New England descent in Monmouth County, New Jersey. "In the after part of the day," wrote Jonathan Holmes, "I went unto John Boords . . . it being wedding times there." A frolic followed the ceremony, at which "the young folks was a Showing tricks" in a colonial Puritan version of a French charivari, the custom of playfully (usually) harassing newlyweds. "The Groom and the Bride," wrote the amused Holmes, "Luckely Slipt into bed, and fastened the doore."[32]

But the new couple was far from safe. "Some notice," Holmes wrote, "was given of the matter before the groom was gott to bed, Some indeavoured to peep but the females hindred us with a Seeming desire to have all to themselves and that while the groom was undressing." The guests eventually broke into the chamber, and Holmes took to "throwing the Stocking of her Some threw I threw and hit the brides nose, which made a lafter . . . I saluted the bride and bid the

can Revolution, 120; Newport Mercury (Rhode Island), Nov. 9–12, 1764; Boston Post-Boy and Advertiser, Nov. 5, 1764.

31. Boston Weekly News-Letter, Oct. 20, 1748; Essex [Mass.] Sessions, 1761–1778, Mar. 30, July 13, and Dec. 28, 1762, microfilm, Massachusetts Archives, Boston. I would like to thank John Murrin for this citation. For the New York City incidents, see James Jackson, deposition, Mar. 1, 1754, New York City, and "The King agt Dorothy the Wife of William Tingue," Oct. 22, 1766, New York Supreme Court, in John Tambor Kempe Papers, Unsorted Lawsuits, NYHS. I would like to thank Tom Humphrey for this citation. See also Thomas J. Humphrey, "Crowd and Court: Rough Music and Popular Justice in Colonial New York," in William Pencak, Matthew Dennis, and Simon P. Newman, eds., Riot and Revelry in Early America (University Park, Pa., 2002), 109.

32. Jonathan Holmes diary, Apr. 25, 1737, in Holmes Family Papers, NJHS.

couple not to forget fulfilling the first commandment." The stocking throwers upheld the rule that sexual expression be confined to marriage.[33]

Did all the groups that engaged in these behaviors seek to uphold the same idea of patriarchy? The participants in rough music did not leave detailed, searching accounts of their inner motivations. But what they did during and after these incidents indicates that no consensus existed in late colonial society over the character of gender relations, the extent of male rule in the home, or the appropriate boundaries of sexual behavior. All agreed that men should dominate in the home and the society more generally, but the character of that rule was in question.

Competing patriarchal visions sometimes manifested themselves after rough-music incidents. Victims or community members offended by rough-music performances occasionally sought legal redress or revenge for the group's perceived excesses. The wife forced to ride skimmington near Philadelphia in 1748 had her husband arrested, "and carrying him before a Justice of the Peace, [he] was, after examination, sent to Prison, to which Place he was conducted thro' the Peltings, Hissings, and Blows of Two-thirds of the Women in the Town." Clearly, this man had asserted his authority too forcefully for many in the community. A Philadelphia man assaulted in 1753 for whipping his wife "applied to a Justice" afterward, and in the same year "Prudence Goodwife" reported to the New York newspapers that some in East Jersey wanted to see the "Regulators" in her town arrested for whipping a husband she described as a drunk and a hater of teacups. A writer commenting on Newark "Disciplinarians" who performed rough music against violent men in 1765 declared their actions "unlawful Enterprises" that should cease immediately. The Newark gang, this writer insisted, would cause "fatal Consequences" if they did not stop. He connected the incident to a similar one in Rhode Island where the intended victim of a skimmington killed one of his attackers and "dangerously wounded one or two more." In many communities, there was no consensus about the extent of male authority in the household.[34]

Even the seemingly benign rough-music performances conducted during weddings might bring forth a hostile response from those who held a different perception of order. When Yorkers George Kranchyt, David Williams, and James

---

33. Ibid. I believe that this is actually a reference to the saying, "Be fruitful and multiply." But this is just a guess. John D'Emilio and Estelle B. Freedman, *Intimate Matters: A History of Sexuality in America* (New York, 1988), 16–26, discusses the ways in which colonial society tried to confine sexuality to marriage.

34. *Boston Weekly News-Letter*, Oct. 20, 1748; *NJA*, XIX, *Newspaper Extracts*, III, 324–327, XXIV, *Newspaper Extracts*, V, 565–566.

Travis saluted a wedding at the house of Joseph Smith with music and antics in 1757, they found themselves attacked with "a Stout Cudgel Slung from Said House." Their actions, the three musicians explained to New York attorney general William Kempe, were "intended as a Compliment to them." When they "advanced towards the house to enquire the Reason of such treatment and Breach of manners," they were again attacked, and Smith had them indicted. The repeated efforts to criminalize rough music are suggestive of broad disagreements over the nature of patriarchy in families.[35]

This fragmentation grew in part from the provinces' diversity of cultures. Immigrants from all over Britain and western Europe were settling in North America by the 1740s, and each group brought the norms of its culture, region, and even village. In January 1736/7, Jerseyman Jonathan Holmes recorded a visit to a Scottish-dominated community in Monmouth County, where it was the "fashion that was in their parts to Whip the women." Some men "whipped their wives every day; others was not so apt to whip their wives although they did sometimes." In other social groups, and in other areas, such behavior was unacceptable, or at least would not be publicly acknowledged. Pennsylvania Quakers, Virginia tobacco planters, Carolina Scots-Irish settlers, each had their own vision of a normal household.[36]

In New England, seventeenth-century Puritan preachers consciously tried to alter traditional family relationships. In the ideal Puritan family, sober and level-headed men would have no need of violence to control their wives, and neither spouse would engage in adultery. Good wives would obey their husbands, and husbands would rule with love.[37]

Laws in the New England colonies embodied these changed beliefs. Women could and did go to court if their husbands beat or otherwise abused them. Spousal abuse or adultery might well be punished with fines, whippings, or even the dreaded scarlet letter. Women remained subordinate, and violence against

35. George Kranchyt, David Williams, and James Travis, Jr., to William Campe [Kempe], Feb. 8, 1757, Hanover, Kempe Papers, box 4, NYHS.

36. Jonathan Holmes diary, Jan. 28, 1736/7, Holmes Family Papers, NJHS.

37. Carol F. Karlsen, *The Devil in the Shape of a Woman: Witchcraft in Colonial New England* (New York, 1987), 160–166, gives a good, brief account of the transformations worked by Puritanism on gender roles; for the decline in legal protection for women, see C. Dallett Hemphill, "Women in Court: Sex-Role Differentiation in Salem, Massachusetts, 1636 to 1683," *WMQ*, XXXIX (1982), 164–175. English Puritans generally frowned on the excessive use of force by fathers in families. See Susan Amussen, "'Being Stirred to Much Unquietness': Violence and Domestic Violence in Early Modern England," *Journal of Women's History*, VI (1994), 72.

them sometimes gained official sanction, as in the sporadic witch trials of the seventeenth century. But, generally, the pulpit had begun to replace the rod as a legitimate tool of controlling women. Certainly women suffered domestic abuse, as the use of rough music in New England in the eighteenth century attests. However, in the New England subculture, violent husbands seemed to be seen as serious a threat to a godly society as scolds and were dealt with extralegally in the eighteenth century.[38]

Differences between towns and countryside also shaped the use of customary violence to maintain family order. Rough music directed against women seems to have been more common in the ports, whereas attacks against aggressive men occurred more frequently in the countryside. There are a variety of explanations for this — European norms' being more common in the ports, the prevalence of prostitution there — but the exact causes remain unclear.

At the same time that multiple understandings of the king became part of public life in provincial America, real questions had arisen over the extent of the fathers' rule over their families. That this development roughly paralleled the fragmentation in understanding of monarchy is, no doubt, in part an illusion of time, of the way print culture expanded at the time, and of scholarly wish fulfillment.

Yet there may indeed be a connection at the base of these developments. The notion of the man as king of his little commonwealth was widespread in provincial America. A Virginia woman could thus write she sought

> To gain my Prince, have scarce a thought of crowns;
> But hope to make the better wife, when I
> Obtain my princely Colonel by and by.

It was precisely this sort of perception that linked the broader political culture to the family structure, and it is this perception that gives political meaning, in a broad and loose sense, to rough music. The subsequent use of the customs against

38. Young, "English Plebeian Culture," in Jacob and Jacob, *Origins of Anglo-American Radicalism*, 191; Karlsen, *The Devil in the Shape of a Woman*, 190. Like abusive husbands, scolds were prosecuted in the courts of New England and elsewhere. On New England scolding, see Roger Thompson, *Sex in Middlesex: Popular Mores in a Massachusetts County, 1649–1699* (Amherst, Mass., 1986), 122, 125–126. For a discussion of gossip and defamation in Maryland, see Mary Beth Norton, "Gender and Defamation in Seventeenth-Century Maryland," *WMQ*, XLIV (1987), 3–39; for slander in Virginia, see Clara Ann Bowler, "Carted Whores and White Shrouded Apologies: Slander in the County Courts of Seventeenth-Century Virginia," *Virginia Magazine of History and Biography*, LXXXV (1977), 411–426.

royal officials and their supporters during the imperial crisis suggests this intersection of personal life with political culture.[39]

As with the political order, what was at stake at least superficially was not who should rule. The evidence concerning the fragmentation of social patriarchy as expressed in the various performances of rough music might be read as foreshadowing a liberalization of family authority. In fact, though, the situation was more complex: some asserted a stronger, more assertive male role in the family, whereas others thought the father should rule by love. It was not about patriarchy per se but rather how authority should be enacted and where that authority came from. And those same issues would erupt with force during the imperial crisis.

. . .

Of Dynasty and Dissent

Rebelling slaves, unruly yeomen, men dressed as women beating abusive husbands: it all makes eighteenth-century America seem like a politically correct dream come true. But to understand the empire's western marches after 1740 from our modern viewpoint, or simply as a product of scholarly free association, is to err. Those engaged in violent confrontation with the established order acted in the name of the father. They expressed faith in the king and in the justice of royal order. Patriarchy governed the way they thought about themselves.

Their behavior was subversive, though. Elements in the population could imagine royal relationships apart from institutional structures; they could also imagine different forms of patriarchal authority in the family. The lack of agreement over these relationships inhibited the normalization of the British peace in the American provinces. Overlapping and yet discrete idealized monarchs had come into being. Each was an expression of a distinctive vision of order that became instrumental in social and political conflicts involving the system of property that provided the society's material foundations.

Perhaps what was most dangerous about this development is that the use of the king's name and Protestant political culture in this fashion wasn't confined to just rebel slaves or agrarian rioters. It became part of every conflict, great and petty. In his near-epic account of the European settlement of the Carolina interior, Anglican minister Charles Woodmason wrote of how local Presbyterians put up a broadside "in order to disapoint me of a Congregation, and to laugh at the People." It stated "that the King having discovered the Popish Designs of Mr. Woodmason and other Romish Priests in disguise, to bring in Popery and

39. As in Mary Newton Stanard, *Colonial Virginia: Its People and Customs* (Philadelphia, 1917), 240.

Slavery . . . had sent over Orders to suspend them all, and to order them to be sent over to England." "This was," he continued, "believed by some of the Poor Ignorants, and kept them at home."[40]

The number of conflicts within British American society escalated as the eighteenth century progressed. The empire's incongruities became more and more apparent as the strain intensified. That led some to try to imagine the empire and the monarchy remade in an old new way. The things of God and the things of man would be put back together in the person of the king.

40. Richard J. Hooker, ed., *The Carolina Backcountry on the Eve of the Revolution: The Journal and Other Writings of Charles Woodmason, Anglican Itinerant* (Chapel Hill, N.C., 1953), 45.

7

NEOABSOLUTISM

. . . .
. .
. .
.

We live in an age whose rhetoric is relentlessly egalitarian and seems to become more so with each passing year. This egalitarianism infuses all that we do and say and has become part of our lives in ways both obvious and unseen. Its development in the eighteenth century is a fact of our national mythology, and perhaps that is why the questioning of it has gone on largely in restricted channels. As heirs to a revolution that helped create this profoundly democratic world, we are perhaps frightened to think that our history could be otherwise, that Americans were not always engaged in somehow becoming what we are. But to assume that is to rob the mid-eighteenth century's writers and thinkers of their voice.

In those decades, British Americans began to put God, king, and history back together again after their Humpty-Dumptylike fall in the seventeenth century. Some writers tried to make the Hanoverians' rule one with a British dynastic past cleansed of its violent disruptions. Others used language borrowed from absolutist and divine-right monarchies to describe George II, who, they began to insist, was one of "the *Lord's anointed*," the very "living *images* of the supreme and only potentate." It was all part of a disjointed effort to restore the spiritual and political relationships that existed before the English Civil Wars, to fix what had come apart.[1]

None who sought to repair the fabric of their world were absolutists or Jacobites in the sense that we understand those terms. All believed in what they called balanced monarchy and the Glorious Revolution's political legacy as they understood it. Nonetheless, across the eighteenth century's first six decades, the rhetoric of royalism in the provinces changed from one centered largely on contractual whig monarchy to a far more eclectic one in which language derived from divine-

1. Samuel Haven, *The Supreme Influence of the Son of God, in Appointing, Directing, and Terminating the Reign of Princes: A Sermon Occasioned by the Death of King George the Second* . . . (Portsmouth, N.H., 1761), 8–9.

right monarchies played a growing and important role. This transformation in provincial political language is essential to understanding the period before the imperial collapse in 1774. In the eighteenth century, the ideas of newness, of a rupture with the past and with God, troubled many, and they looked backward as much if not more than forward in search of a temporal and spiritual order that would resolve these tensions.

. . .

Time Amended: History, Aesthetics, and the Stuart Rehabilitation

In 1759, as the momentous struggle we call the Seven Years' War lurched toward its dramatic climax on the Plains of Abraham outside Quebec, the New York City newspapers ran an ad announcing the arrival of a new shipment of print portraits. The town's growing gentry population purchased such prints to decorate their homes in the fashion of London. Prominent among the prints to be sold were fine likenesses of "Charles Prince of Wales, James Duke of York, and Princess Mary, Children of Charles Ist," based on the famous Van Dyke painting of them. The seventeenth-century Stuart kings, the eighteenth-century British world's once and future bogeymen, had appeared on American shores, seemingly as suddenly as Bonnie Prince Charlie had landed on Scotland's coast to lead the '45 Jacobite uprising. The Stuarts' march in the American provinces is a far greater historical shock than Bonnie Prince Charlie's campaign, which led to the House of Stuart's final military defeat at the Battle of Culloden. Provincials denounced the Stuarts so regularly and with such passion that the sale of their likenesses in New York seems an anomaly of massive proportions.[2]

In fact, though, these portraits represented a strain of historical, political, and aesthetic thought that developed in the Anglo-American world after George I's death. This thinking came in response to the seventeenth-century calamities and accelerated in reaction to the unrest in the American countryside after 1740. Regicide and revolutions, Glorious and otherwise, had called into question the relationship of the political and spiritual worlds and especially their intersection in the royal person. It was against the break in historical and metaphysical logic that eighteenth-century writers began to remake the past. These historical reconstructionists were not Jacobites in any sense; all supported the Hanoverians and Protestant monarchy vocally. But the need for cosmic coherence between the human and divine orders, between history and Providence, encouraged some to invoke the Stuart monarchs even as all continued to denounce James II's exiled

2. Esther Singleton, *Social New York under the Georges, 1714–1776* (New York, 1902), 91.

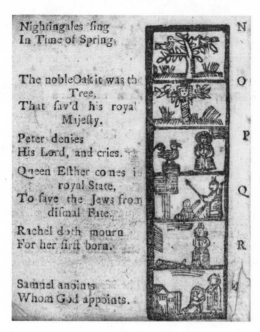

Nightingales sing
In Time of Spring,

The nobleOak it was the
Tree,
That fav'd his royal
Majesty.

Peter denies
His Lord, and cries.

Queen Esther comes in
royal State,
To save the Jews from
dismal Fate.

Rachel doth mourn
For her first born.

Samuel anoints
Whom God appoints.

PLATE 8. *"O Is for the Noble Oak."*
1750. From the New England
Primer. *"O" did not stand for just
any oak. Rather, the description
and crude drawing celebrated the
famed oak that hid the young
Charles II after he was defeated by
Cromwell at the end of the third
civil war. The image connected
seventeenth-century Stuart rule to
the Hanoverian dynasty. Courtesy,
American Antiquarian Society*

descendants, who refused to lay down their claim to the British throne. The aim was to present the Hanoverian dynasty as the culmination of an unbroken line of kings that stretched back to feudal England.

The Stuart revival began in the almanacs' time lines that provided many colonists with their historical education. The historian viewing these almanacs feels something like the Sovietologists of the 1950s and 1960s who examined May Day photos to determine who was in favor in a distant regime. The Stuarts had enjoyed a brief reign in the colonies' popular print culture in the late seventeenth century. In the early 1680s, with James II's looming ascension, colonials included some of the royal calendar's red-letter days in New England's almanacs. William Brattle's *Ephemeris of Coelestial Motions*, printed in 1682, marks the dates of James I's and Charles I's reigns, as well as the date when *"K. Charles 2 born 1630."* S. D. Philomath's *New England Almanack for the Year of Our Lord. 1686* recalled "1685, Apr. 12 KING JAMES II. Proclaimed in Boston."[3]

Such was the price of empire until Providence, in the form of William and Mary, allowed New England leaders to once again take a hand in controlling

3. W[illiam] Brattle, *An Ephemeris of Coelestial Motions: Aspects, Eclipses, etc. for the Year of the Christian Aera 1682* . . . (Boston, 1682), pages headed "March hath 31 days"; "May hath 31 days"; S. D. Philomath [Samuel Danforth], *The New England Almanack for the Year of Our Lord 1686* (Cambridge, 1685), April 12.

the culture. After 1689, imperial demands assured that things would never be as they had been in the decades of the first generation (1630–1660). But the Puritan leaders did reassert their power and, among other things, purged the Stuart rulers from the almanacs. Thus, on the morning of August 18, 1708, we find Samuel Sewall in his role as a councillor, censoring the almanacs of certain red-letter days. He recalled, with restrained amusement, that someone else had already "lined out, before I Saw it," January 30, the day of Charles I's execution, a day of mourning in some imperial circles during Queen Anne's reign. Sewall obviously approved of this particular pen-and-ink regicide just as he vehemently denied his participation in it. Certainly, few of Sewall's contemporaries would have complained. Even as the last Protestant Stuart monarch, Anne, continued to reign, Bostonians began dragging the Stuart Pretender's effigy through the tiny port's crooked streets on Pope's Day.[4]

Public hostility toward anything associated with the Stuart family intensified in the eighteenth century's first decades. A letter to the Boston News-Letter in 1724 denounced James I as a "weak Prince" who left "one as weak [Charles I] behind him. . . . Once destin'd to the Priesthood," Charles was "a Bigot, by Nature as well as Education." This hated prince brought popery and arbitrary power to the Protestant kingdom, assisted "by [Archbishop William] Laud," who issued injunctions that transformed the Church of England into a more Catholic church. "As Priestcraft and Tyranny are ever inseparable," the king soon placed new taxes on the people without Parliament's approval. This Boston writer went on to denounce Charles II for his "Leagues with France" as well as "his unjust Wars with the united Provinces [the Anglo-Dutch wars of the 1660s–1670s]." In 1735, New Yorker Vincent Matthews declared during a speech to the colony's assembly that Charles I relentlessly asserted arbitrary royal power at the expense of "English liberties," just as Governor Cosby was doing during the Zenger Crisis. In so doing, Matthews and those like him voiced imperial orthodoxy even as they bent it to their own use.[5]

But just as hostile rhetoric concerning the Stuart dynasty reached a crescendo in the early 1740s, a seemingly contradictory tendency to rehabilitate the seven-

4. The Diary of Samuel Sewall, II, 1699–1714, MHS, Collections, 5th Ser., VI (Boston, 1889), 229–230.

5. Boston News-Letter, Mar. 5–12, 1724; "Speech of Vincent Matthews Read before the General Assembly of the Province of New York on October 21, 1735," in The Letters and Papers of Cadwallader Colden, VIII, Additional Letters and Papers, 1715–1748, NYHS, Collections, LXVII (New York, 1937), 236–237. Matthews was attempting to protect a client's property rights from encroachment by Cosby.

teenth-century Stuarts emerged in colonial writings. As strange as it may seem, the hatred of the Stuarts and the historical embrace of them were linked at their base.

The Hanoverians and the royal bureaucracy itself encouraged this remarkable rehabilitation. Considerable doubt about the Hanoverians' legitimacy existed in the home islands and would not go away. The Hanoverians feared the kind of whispers one North Carolina Anglican attributed to visiting Quaker preachers, that "till the P of Wales is proved a bastard [James II's son was claimed by some to be a Catholic bastard child smuggled into the royal chambers in 1688 as part of the Popish Plot against the throne] the Queen [Anne] can have no pretensions to the Crown of England." As the Hanoverians' hereditary claim was significantly weaker than Queen Anne's, their anxieties were significantly higher. Conscious of their own Germanness, aware that the genealogical connection that brought them to the British throne ran through the Stuart family (a younger daughter of James I) and was inferior to that of many other European monarchs, and eager to loosen the sometimes stifling limits on monarchical power set by Parliament, the retainers of George II began a selective cultural restoration of the Stuart kings even as they vilified that family's exiled heirs.[6] By rendering their connection to past dynasties as natural, historical, and unbroken, writers who supported the Georges sought to strengthen the Hanoverians' position.[7]

Those who began to reorder the time line sought to portray the House of Hanover as British kings in an unbroken line reaching back to Alfred the Great. To do so would perhaps regain for them some of the power held by their seventeenth-century predecessors: the power conveyed by the mysteries of timelessness and hereditary legitimacy.

The Stuarts' historical rehabilitation initially turned on a few words in colonial America's burgeoning print culture. In the late 1730s and early 1740s, some almanac writers began to treat the House of Stuart in a less hostile manner than was common in the period. A few words changed, a few phrases dropped or

6. James Adams to the Society for the Propagation of the Gospel in Foreign Parts (hereafter cited as SPG), Sept. 18, 1708, North Carolina, SPG microfilm, reel 15. For discussion of the Hanoverians' political power as compared to other monarchs, see Linda Colley, *Britons: Forging the Nation, 1707–1837* (New Haven, Conn., 1992), 196; for aspects of their cultural imperatives, see 198–207. For tendencies toward divine-right thinking in the home islands, see the body of work produced by J. C. D. Clarke.

7. Colin Nicolson, *The "Infamas Govener" Francis Bernard and the Origins of the American Revolution* (Boston, 2001), 71; John Brewer, *Party Ideology and Popular Politics at the Accession of George III* (Cambridge, 1976), 42–46.

added, and it is apparent from the vantage point of 250 years later that the Stuart kings were somehow being rehabilitated. The *Virginia Almanac* of 1741 remembered January 30 as the day Charles I was "Mart.," martyred, rather than executed or removed. The same almanac writer remembered "King Charles II returned in Peace," suggesting national unity during the Restoration.[8]

It is possible to believe that this revival had a regional bias, as the southern colonies of historical mythology have had the reputation of being pro-Cavalier. In the eighteenth century, some southern gentlemen indeed professed this identity. William Byrd of Westover denounced Oliver Cromwell in correspondence to an English friend in 1739, and several decades later, Virginia's Arthur Lee proudly recalled that "this colony . . . is said to have been the first which threw off the yoke [of Cromwell], and proclaimed King Charles II." Eighteenth-century Chesapeake planters frequently referenced a monarchical past that included the Stuarts.[9]

But the Stuart revival in provincial print culture was actually quite widespread. Bostonian Nathaniel Whittemore's almanac, *Whittemore Revived*, like the *Virginia Almanac*, presented a dynastic chronology that stretched back to the "Saxon Line." Whittemore acknowledged various royal houses in the English past, but there is no mention that Charles I was executed, no mention of Cromwell, no mention of James II's being deposed, and no mention that William III was Dutch. The relationship between the seventeenth- and eighteenth-century dynasties is portrayed as an undisturbed line.[10]

Boston printer Nathaniel Ames tried a different tack to the same end. In 1747, the frontpiece of Ames's *Astronomical Diary; or, An Almanack for the Year of Our Lord Christ* contained the following couplets:

> Strange Things indeed has the last Century seen,
> King *Charles* dethron'd, surprizing *Cromwell* Reign,
> A Second *Charles* the regal Scepter gain,
> *Hanover's* House establish'd on the Throne.[11]

8. *The Virginia Almanac for the Year of Our Lord God . . . 1741* (Williamsburg, Va., 1741).

9. Marion Tinling, ed., *The Correspondence of the Three William Byrds of Westover, Virginia, 1684–1776* (Charlottesville, Va., 1977), 535; [Arthur Lee], *An Essay in Vindication of the Continental Colonies of America, from a Censure of Mr Adam Smith, in His Theory of Moral Sentiments, with Some Reflections on Slavery in General* (London, 1764), 21.

10. N[athaniel] Whittemore, *Whittemore Revived: An Almanack for the Year of Our Lord . . .* (Boston, 1738).

11. Nathaniel Ames, *An Astronomical Diary; or, An Almanack for the Year of Our Lord Christ, 1747* (Boston, [1746]), frontpiece.

PLATE 9.
*Silver communion spoon.
C. 1727–1760. The bowl
of this spoon is shaped
from a coin bearing the
likeness and arms of
George II, and the smaller
coin bears the image of
James II. Although this
linkage between the two
kings might have been
incidental, it seems rather
to reflect the desire to
connect the Hanoverians
to the Stuarts visually and
through religious ritual.
© Collection of the New-
York Historical Society*

Although Cromwell's existence is acknowledged, his political meaning was left ambiguous. The poet downplayed the seventeenth-century dynastic struggles and made no mention of James II's final flight or the contested circumstances surrounding George I's ascension to the throne in 1714. In 1755, Job Shepherd's *Poor Job* almanac for Newport, Rhode Island, stopped listing the "execution" of Charles I and instead noted his martyrdom. At the same time, youngsters in New England and the midatlantic were taught to rhyme "King Charles the Good / No Man of Blood" to learn their letter K. A new dynasty placed the historic Stuarts back on their throne to meet the needs of a new century, decades after that last Stuart queen had died.[12]

Visual representations of British monarchs in the halls of power reflected this Stuart revival. Sometime in the eighteenth century, the imperial government began to ship official portraits of historic British monarchs, including Charles I, Charles II, and James II, to the provinces with orders that they be displayed in council chambers. They continued to hang in these chambers for decades, and only the imperial crisis highlighted their presence. In Massachusetts Bay, the habitually unlucky Thomas Hutchinson found himself unsuccessfully resisting the removal of the portraits of two "tyrants" — Charles I and James II — from the Bay Colony's council chambers. Hutchinson insisted that they should be retained because they were part of the long line of English kings. In the 1760s, John Adams commented on the display of gold-framed, full-length portraits of Charles II and James II in Massachusetts's courthouses, displayed for the "imitation of all men."[13]

In insisting on maintaining these visual representations that linked the deposed Stuarts to the Hanoverians, Hutchinson only followed what had become official policy. In 1764, George III had two of his sons painted seated beneath the Van Dyke portrait of Charles I's children. The young king became a collector of Stuart portraits and attempted to restore Charles I's dispersed art collection.[14]

The Episcopal clergy's efforts to establish Charles I's execution day as a provincial day of remembrance was perhaps the most controversial part of this Stuart revival. They did so, not out of any Jacobite sympathies, but rather because the

12. Job Shepherd, *Poor Job, 1755* (Newport, R.I., [1754]); Gillian Brown, *The Consent of the Governed: The Lockean Legacy in Early American Culture* (Cambridge, Mass., 2001), 57.

13. Bernard Bailyn, *The Ordeal of Thomas Hutchinson* (Cambridge, Mass., 1974), 138; Gordon S. Wood, *The Radicalism of the American Revolution* (New York, 1991), 17; Charles Francis Adams, ed., *The Works of John Adams* (Boston, 1850–1856), X, 233, 244–245. See *Boston Weekly News-Letter*, Oct. 8, 1730, for a description of a royal portrait.

14. Colley, *Britons*, 207.

day represented an emerging imperial orthodoxy. Anglican congregations and Anglican-dominated areas were remembering this day by the 1730s and 1740s. A newspaper report from Williamsburg, Virginia, on a fire that broke out there on January 30, 1747, noted that it was the anniversary of "the fatal and ever memorable Day of the Martrydom of King Charles."[15] When the Church of England rebuilt King's Chapel in Boston in 1753, the congregation suspended its remembrance of "Thanksgiveing, The Fifth of November and Thirthieth of January" until "the Chappel be Rebuilt."[16]

This particular development provoked deep anxieties in some quarters. It brought forth the midcentury responses from Jonathan Mayhew and William Livingston, joined by the anonymous English writer "An Independent," whose tract was reprinted in Boston in 1750. Their writings, which in part ended up restoring the historical reputation of Oliver Cromwell, came in direct response to Charles I's political-historic rebirth and have been seized upon by later generations to demonstrate a trajectory toward republicanism.[17]

Did British Americans accept this Stuart restoration, or were Mayhew and Livingston representative? And what does it mean to "internalize," a term our psychologically saturated era has accepted without question? Although the supposed pro-Stuart feelings in the Chesapeake are well known, New England was not without those who sympathized with the Stuart kings as historic figures. The Boston diarist John Rowe could be called an "internalizer" when he recorded "King Charles Martyrdom" in his diary on January 30, 1769. So would the Mas-

15. *New-York Evening-Post*, Apr. 6, 1747.

16. Minute Book of Wardens, Vestry, and Meetings, 1753–1773, Oct. 31, 1753, King's Chapel Archives, MHS.

17. Carl Bridenbaugh, *Mitre and Sceptre: Transatlantic Faiths, Ideas, Personalities, and Politics, 1689–1775* (New York, 1962), 101; Jonathan Mayhew, *A Discourse concerning Unlimited Submission and Non-Resistance to the Higher Powers: With Some Reflections on the Resistance Made to King Charles I* . . . (Boston, 1750). Neo-whig scholarship has interpreted publications like the Mayhew sermon and Livingston's *Independent Reflector* as evidence of the penetration of Country ideology in America that eventually encouraged a revolutionary republic to emerge. There is much to recommend this view, based as it is on the extraordinarily sound ideas that events happen for a reason and that things that are similar are often related. But perhaps we have been too quick to accept these easy inferences. As difficult as it is to accept, the writings of Livingston, Mayhew, and "An Independent" were hardly typical for the period, even for the educated elite, nor were they consistent. Mayhew would, a year later, be writing of the divine origins of royal authority in *A Sermon Preached at Boston in New-England, May 26, 1751, Occasioned by the Much-Lamented Death of His Royal Highness, Frederick, Prince of Wales* (Boston, 1751).

sachusetts minister Samuel Chandler, a reader of Ames's almanac, who drew up his own time line in an undated entry in his diary sometime after 1764. He denounced England's ancient Catholic rulers, and yet he proclaimed James I a good king for producing a readable English Bible and blamed Charles I's problems on "his popish Queen." In fact, the only Stuart he denounced was James II, whom he (correctly) accused of popery. At Nantucket Falls in Rhode Island, the itinerant diarist Dr. Alexander Hamilton noted that a man named Angell had posted on the walls of his inn "the 12 Golden Rules taken from King Charles I's study, of blessed memory (as he is very judiciously stiled)." These men had accepted a version of imperial history that had appeared in their lifetimes, unaware or unconcerned that it problematized the relationship of past and present in provincial America.[18]

After 1730, political debate began to reflect this internalization as writers both defended and invoked the Stuarts during public controversies. This tendency manifested itself in Pennsylvania during the so-called "Z" debate, which erupted during the Zenger Crisis. When Z (probably John Webbe), a writer in the *Pennsylvania Gazette*, attacked the Stuart family and asserted that sovereignty resided in the people, a number of writers rebuked him for his continued hostility to "that *royal Race*." "Must he be told," one writer asked, "over and over again, that it borders on disloyalty to treat the Memory of our present gracious Sovereign's Ancestors, with so much Spite?" Were not such performances designed "to advance new Seditious Doctrines, and revive old ones, to the lessening of the Prerogative of the Crown, under pretence of maintaining the Rights and Liberties of the People?" The Stuarts "were in many things misled by *corrupt Ministers . . .* into errors and irregularities in their civil Administration." But he insisted that they were not all Papists and commended James I and Charles I for their loyalty and piety.[19]

Other middle colonies' scribes rushed to defend the Stuart family and, in so doing, redefined provincial liberties in terms that accommodated the extension of royal prerogative. A writer to the *American Weekly Mercury* declared on June 10, 1736, "I am astonished, my Dear, that You who profess your self a Patriot, should have endeavoured to stigmatize . . . the STUARTS." If Charles I "were guilty of Mistakes, in extending his Prerogative too far, You, a *Pennsylvanian*, ought not to have . . . cast a Veil over them." Although the Glorious Revolution

---

18. John Rowe diary, Jan. 30, 1769, MS, MHS; Samuel Chandler diaries, 1746–1772, microfilm, MHS; Carl Bridenbaugh, *Gentleman's Progress: The Itinerarium of Dr. Alexander Hamilton, 1744* (Chapel Hill, N.C., 1948), 149.

19. *American Weekly Mercury* (Philadelphia), May 27–June 3, 1736.

was necessary, it was, he insisted, "an extraordinary Case; the whole Frame of the Constitution being threatened, by the Administration of an unhappy Prince, misled by evil Counsellors." Only such a situation could justify removing a king. In any event, "such *Liliputians* as you and me" should not be questioning a prince's action. Another writer to the same issue denounced Z for being "so free with the illustrious Family of the Stuarts."[20]

Writers engaged in the Z debate also defended the January 30 remembrance. "Z affirms in the same paper," one of his critics spat, "that the Thirtieth of January is now little regarded in England, except by Tories and Jacobites. . . . Then the Three estates of the Realm, King, Lords and Commons must either come under that Denomination . . . For as the Statute which appoints that Day is still in its full force, 'tis well known these three Branches of the Legislature have Sermons preached annually before them, and join in the publick Offices adapted to that Occassion." In other words, the day became a formal part of the imperial calendar.[21]

A letter to the Boston papers in 1750 went a step further and rehabilitated Archbishop William Laud, believed by many to have been determined to enslave the English people in Charles I's reign. The writer defended the reputation of "the Royal Martyr King CHARLES the First, and the most Reverend WILLIAM LAUD, Arch Bishop of *Canterbury*, and Vindicating the most execrable Parricide committed on the 30th of *January 1648*." The author described Laud, perhaps the most vilified figure from the English Civil War period, as "a Man of Exemplary Virtues, an excellent Preacher, and a Scholar of the Most sublime Parts." Laud, the writer continued, died a martyr while being abused by his bloody-minded "Murderers."[22]

The seventeenth-century ordeals had set the society at war with its own past. Legitimacy of authority and the social order depended on a time line that melded cleanly with the supernatural, and Anglo-American history did not meet this criterion. The ruptures, the refoundings, the repeated defiances of constituted authority, the appearance of radical religious groups — these remained disturbing in the mid-eighteenth century. To temper these breaks, some American writers drew on words and images that had been rejected by the political society decades before.

20. Ibid., June 10–17, 1736.
21. Ibid.
22. *Boston Weekly News-Letter*, Mar. 1, 1750.

A Newtonian Sun King

Pennsylvanian Benjamin Rush arrived in Scotland in 1766 to begin his medical training very much the product of royal political culture. Imperial imperatives had encouraged provincial writers and speakers to raise the Hanoverian Georges above the commonality of men. Rush recalled that, throughout his brief life, he had "been taught to consider [kings] nearly as essential to political order as the Sun is to the order of our Solar System." Most eighteenth-century provincials shared these sentiments. In British America, the Georges, those distant Germans who inspired such apathy in the English, indeed seemed celestial monarchs, though in a different way from the French Sun King, Louis XIV.[23]

Rush's use of a solar metaphor to describe Britain's kings was no aberration. By the time he wrote, the use of such terms to describe the Hanoverians had become commonplace. The revival of solar imagery and other absolutist metaphors occurred as part of the same search for human-cosmic order as the time line's alteration in popular literature did. This imagery drawn from the absolutist past reflected the imperial constitutional structure as represented to colonials in royal rituals and proclamations. At the center of everything stood the monarch, who was bound to every British subject wherever he or she lived. Unlike in popish France, though, chains did not bind Britons to their sun king. Rather, love and affection, the human form of Newton's gravity, drew British subjects everywhere into the Hanoverians' orbit. Those who used this absolutist-tinged imagery in no way advocated an unchecked despotism, Jacobitism, or anything but restrained monarchy. They sought to portray the Hanoverians as kings whose political behaviors and attitudes reflected the laws of the natural world as revealed by Newton and other British geniuses. Newtonian sun kings for a new era of British liberty—this was the message of colonial writers who would use the royal language of the past in a new era.

In the late seventeenth century, the furthest thing from most British minds was ascribing absolutist attributes to their Protestant monarchs. The Glorious Revolution had supposedly stamped out absolutist metaphors that had been introduced into English political discourse in James I's reign and that had become associated with Stuart tyranny. James II's tight grip had so frightened colonials, particularly the provinces' ruling oligarchies, that they enthusiastically acknowledged Parliament as the empire's sovereign body and declared their allegiance to

23. Alan Houston, *Algernon Sidney and the Republican Heritage in England and America* (Princeton, N.J., 1991), 225–226.

whig monarchy. A New England writer visiting London in 1690 celebrated the fact that the "Body of the *English Nation* Assembled in Parliament have declared the Invasion made upon our Charters, to be illegal and a grievance." The writer reported that the Bill for the Restoration of Charters passed the House of Commons, which he understood as the supreme authority in political matters. That perception, of course, continued in London, and Parliament gradually asserted itself in the British Isles at the expense of Scottish independence, the Irish Parliament, and the monarchy.[24]

In America, though, the social peace between 1690 and 1740 hid a critical transformation in political perception about the monarchy's place in the British constitution. The most intriguing aspect of this development was the rapid separation of king from Parliament in constitutional perception. In America, the Assemblies came to be seen as a repository of the peoples' alienated sovereignty, the House of Commons was rarely invoked in political rites or political debates, and the king came to be seen as an autonomous location of imperial sovereignty.

Many colonials understood that the monarch alone bound the empire together and acted as imperial arbitrator. This understanding had its institutional and constitutional origins in the assertion of the primacy of the royally issued colonial charters. As early as the eighteenth century's first decades, some writers, officials, and observers claimed royal supremacy in the colonies via the charters. New York attorney general William Atwood stated, "I do not say Petitioning the King is a Crime, but it may be to petition the House of Commons in the Plantations, where the King governs by his Prerogative," during Nicholas Bayard's contentious trial for treason.[25]

The royal rites that celebrated the king and the royal family apart from Parliament reinforced and spread this perception. Those rites focused on the monarch's reign and life cycle in a manner that made the ruler the empire's symbolic center.

This developing understanding of constitutional structure intersected with change in the empire's intellectual fabric. Newton's discovery of a hidden force holding the physical world together intrigued a political community that feared the centrifugal forces created by an unbalanced constitution and a far-flung empire just beginning to take shape. Knowledge of the solar system's structure pro-

24. David Hackett Fischer, *Albion's Seed: Four British Folkways in America* (New York, 1989), 386–387; S. E., *Further Quaeries upon the Present State of the New-English Affairs* (Boston, 1690), in W. H. Whitmore, ed., *The Andros Tracts*, II (Boston, 1869), 5. Colley, *Britons*, discusses this transformation.

25. *An Account of the Commitment, Arraignment, Tryal, and Condemnation of Nicholas Bayard Esq; for High Treason* . . . (New York, 1703), 16.

vided a new metaphor for political writers that suggested a more benign, more natural form of political organization held together by love, the human form of gravity, rather than by fear, as was the case in Catholic-ruled realms. That Newton publicly supported the Glorious Revolution only encouraged pro-Hanoverian writers in these tendencies.[26]

It was in this context that the use of solar metaphors to describe the Hanoverian kings began. Sun imagery began to appear with increasing frequency early in George II's reign. A Boston writer trumpeting the arrival of Governor William Burnet could celebrate "Immortal WILLIAM [III]" for saving Protestant Britain from "Groaning in Romish Chains" and praised Burnet's father, "Blest *Phospher!*" for ushering in "the GEORGIAN Sun, / The happiest Light that e'er on *Britain* Shone!" It was a light that "can ne'er Expire, / Whilst his Fam'd Son, Rap't with Prophetick Fire," remained alive. A funeral sermon for George I described that ruler as one who "was as the *Light of the Morning*, when the Sun riseth." It was, of course, a fatherly image, but one associated with an earlier, more absolute perception of monarchy.[27]

The same solar imagery infiltrated formal imperial publications and decrees. The New Hampshire ruling elite declared, on the death of George I, that "the Beams of his Royal Goodness, like those of the Sun," had reached even "these distant Regions, where we dwell." It was the light of a king who had secured their liberties, who allowed commerce to grow, a type of solar monarch unique to the British nation. As educated a man as William Blackstone referred to a ruler as the focal point to which "all the rays of his people are united." These Newtonian sun kings—Protestant, restrained, rational, and more liberty-loving than their French counterparts—were at the center of the British universe, and colonials revolved in their orbit.[28]

Even with the British constitution's restraining power, by the death of George II, the British monarch was being described in language more appro-

---

26. Samuel Davies, *A Sermon Delivered at Nassau-Hall, January 14, 1761, on the Death of His Late Majesty, King George IId*, 2d ed. (New York, 1761), 4.

27. "A Gratulatory POEM Received from a Friend the Day after the Arrival of His Excellency Governour BURNET," in *Boston Weekly News-Letter*, July 18–25, 1728; Thomas Foxcroft, *God the Judge, Putting Down One, and Setting up Another: A Sermon upon Occasion of the Death of Our Late Sovereign Lord King George, and the Accession of His Present Majesty, King George II, to the British Throne* (Boston, 1727), 17.

28. *Weekly News-Letter* (Boston), May 23–30, 1728; Jerrilyn Greene Marston, *King and Congress: The Transfer of Political Legitimacy, 1774–1776* (Princeton, N.J., 1987), 335 n. 57; William Blackstone, *Commentaries on the Laws of England*, 4 vols. (Oxford, 1765), I, 252.

priate for Louis XIV than a guardian of international Protestant liberties. "The glorious Sun," wrote one Pennsylvanian, "*Britannia's* King,

> Withdraws his golden light,
> His setting Ray
> Glides swift away,
> And yields to conqu'ring Night.

Samuel Davies mourned the loss of "GEORGE, the Mighty, the Just, the Gentle, and the Wise, the Father of *Britian* and her Colonies, the Guardian of Laws and Liberty, the Protector of the oppressed, the Arbiter of *Europe*, the Terror of Tyrants and *France*; GEORGE, the Friend of Man, the Benefactor of Millions, IS No MORE!" The loss of this man who had reigned as the epitome of monarchical perfection in provincial hearts for thirty-three years marked more than a regime change. A throne, Davies continued, "is the shining Period, the golden Termination, of the worldly Man's Prospect. His Passions affect, his Understanding conceives, nothing beyond it, or the Favours it can bestow." The king on his throne, he insisted, eclipsed "the Sun, the Expanse of Heaven, or what lies higher." A mere man, a subject, Davies knew, "when . . . his Monarch dies, . . . is left in Darkness: *His* Sun is set: It is the Night of Ambition with him: Which naturally damps him into Reflection; and fills that Reflection with awful Thoughts." Happily, as more than one writer noted, another George was available, "Gay Youth and Glory beam around his Throne," thus preserving the dynastic line and the political universe.[29]

The empire's commercial expansion only intensified this perception. Not only did goods carry royal arms, initials, and likenesses to encourage loyalty to the empire. By late in George II's reign, some of these manufactures had adopted the sun motif as well, like the Staffordshire delftware manufacturer who produced dishes carrying the initials "GR2" bordered by sunrays during George II's reign.[30]

The practice of equating the king's person with the entire imperial dominion also grew from absolutism. When the New England militia won its spectacu-

---

29. *An Exercise, Containing a Dialogue and Ode Sacred to the Memory of His Late Gracious Majesty, George II* (Philadelphia, 1761), 6–8; Davies, *A Sermon Delivered at Nassau-Hall*, 1, 5, 7.

30. Leslie B. Grigsby, *The Longridge Collection of English Slipware and Delftware* (London, 2000), 64, Staffordshire dish, cream colored: "Waist-length portraits of the king [George II] are found on at least two other relief dish models. One is inscribed 'GR2' and the other 'GR II'; both include sunray borders."

PLATE 10. *Stoneware jug. C. 1720–1760. The king's initials ("George* REX*") sit at the center of a sun, marking his place as the center of the political solar system and a warming, benevolent light for Britons everywhere. Courtesy, Winterthur Museum*

lar victory at Louisbourg in 1745, a broadside declared, "We hold it to this very day for the Honour of George our King." In 1760, the minister Samuel Dunbar attributed the entire Seven Years' War to "envious . . . enemies [who] made encroachments upon our king's territories." The empire was made synonymous with the king. The appearance of this particular absolutist-tainted practice in the war years after 1745 was no accident. The rhetorical union of imperial dominions in the monarch's person was designed to rally the populace to defend the realm in wartime.[31]

Such views of the king and the realm permeated the print culture and provincial thinking. This is suggested in a number of affidavits and petitions taken by New York attorney general William Kempe in the 1750s. One man imprisoned for assaulting his wife pleaded to be released because his sons, his only support, had been pressed into the military at the Seven Years' War's outbreak. They continued "in his majesties service as true and loyal subjects would do in defense of his majesties Rites and privileges . . . Ready to venture life and health for Britains glory and the ooner [honor] of his Majesty." Another Yorker writing to Kempe in regard to a legal matter described himself as a subject who had served "King and Country" for more than fifty years in various roles. "Empire" and "king" were interchangeable in provincial minds by the 1750s.[32]

All the factors that kept the empire together—imperial pride, a shared economy, fear of external and internal enemies, language affinity, imperial political rites, and love of the king—alleviated but did not resolve the empire's fundamental paradox. Any perception that human authority was somehow not of or reflective of the divinely intended order disturbed all Anglo-Americans and contained the seeds of subversion. Human action had placed these Protestant Germans on Britain's throne, and contracts could be broken and broken and broken again. The cult of constitution had yet to appoint its high priests. The permeation of contract theory was a problem, not yet the ultimate solution.

An awareness of this existed at all levels of the empire, and, over time, Anglo-American writers began claiming the special sanction of God for the House of Hanover. In America, the pulpit's importance as a means of communication and the dominance of a state-controlled press strengthened this movement. Over

---

31. L. G., [A Brief] Journal of the Taking of Cape-Breton, Put in Metre . . . ([Boston], 1745), broadside 34, no. 43, Library of Congress Broadsides; Samuel Dunbar, The Presence of God with His People, Their Only Safety and Happiness: A Discourse Delivered at Boston, in the Presence of His Excellency the Governour, Thomas Pownall, Esq. . . (Boston, 1760), 2.

32. Joseph Gale to William Kempe, June 21, 1756, Poughkeepsie-Dutchess County, and letter from Samuel Garretson, [1754?], both in John Tambor Kempe Papers, box 4, NYHS.

time, this resacralization of monarchy came to be accepted by all groups in the society.

. . .

Divine Right Reborn

The execution of Charles I, the great wound in Anglo-American society before the American Revolution, remained gaping and open in British America in the eighteenth century. It was not so much the man, who was obviously misguided at best and a crypto-Catholic despot in the making at worst. Nor was it the temptations presented by his deposed heirs; the colonists were only too happy to have them gone. But the severing of the special tie between God and political man as embodied in the king, that was a different matter, infinitely more painful and unresolved. This rupture would have seemed especially troubling to British Americans because, for them, loyalty to the king was loyalty to Protestantism and reformation. And so their preacher and politicians began what is, to us, one of the most unexpected intellectual developments in eighteenth-century America. Over time, they adapted language derived from divine right to describe the Hanoverian kings and legitimate their rule. By the 1740s, Americans understood the Hanoverian monarchy to rule by a kind of benevolent divine right. Such assertions of the Hanoverians' legitimacy spoke to the efforts to reconcile the political order and the supernatural, the essential fabric that had come undone in the seventeenth century.

This seemingly antiteleological development grew logically from the empire's epistemological foundations. The pulpit's primary role as a source of knowledge in colonial society is well known, but no one has probed its full effect on imperial political understanding in the eighteenth century. Because ministers saw God as the wellspring of all things and tended to frame every worldly thing in relationship to the deity, they came to portray these virtuous Protestant monarchs as God's viceroys on earth and equated loyalty to the Hanoverians with loyalty to God. Thus Boston minister Benjamin Colman could preach, "Our faithful zeal for and adherence to the Protestant Succession in the House of Hannover, is our fidelity to CHRIST and his holy Religion." The Hanoverian monarchs stood at the nation's ritual center, the guarantors of Protestants' rights in the British Empire and ultimately of Protestantism itself across Europe. Surely only God could place such a burden on a royal house, and just as surely only a prince raised above the rest of mankind could bear it.[33]

33. Benjamin Colman, *Fidelity to Christ and to the Protestant Succession in the Illustrious House of Hannover* . . . (Boston, 1727), 1.

The theological key to understanding divine right's initial rebirth in the post-1688 empire was the idea of Providence. Belief in Providence, in a God active in this world as well as the next, remained strong in Anglo-American society and especially strong in the Calvinist-dominated colonies despite the Calvinist belief in a sealed covenant. Major events were explained as signs of God's Providences before, during, and after the Glorious Revolution. God's Protestant intentions for the English nation were made apparent with the shift of winds that brought William and Mary to English shores on November 5, 1688, Pope's Day (and William's birthday). The writers of the English Bill of Rights of 1689 declared that it "hath pleased Almighty God, in his marvellous providence, and merciful goodness to this nation, to provide and preserve their said majesties royal persons most happily to reign over us."[34] One London pamphleteer summed up providential intervention in the nation's politics in 1688 and 1689 in verse:

Tis done; the weighty Business of the State,
That has so Long been in Profound Debate
Is to Perfection brought:
Not by a Mortal thought,
For Heaven Inspir'd 'em with a greater Sence.[35]

Providential intervention remained a powerful trope in the British nation throughout the eighteenth century. The Hanoverian succession crisis in 1714 and 1715 brought forth another flood of tracts on both sides of the Atlantic applauding divine intervention in the English nation's destiny. The threat of a French-backed Stuart insurrection helped sustain the idea, current throughout the eighteenth century, that Providence had settled the British succession. When George I died in 1727, Boston preacher Thomas Prince compared the accession of George

34. David D. Hall, *Worlds of Wonder, Days of Judgment: Popular Religious Belief in Early New England* (New York, 1989), 77–78, 91–94, offers the best brief discussion for seventeenth-century America. Bill of Rights: W. A. Speck, *Stability and Strife, England, 1714–1760* (Cambridge, Mass., 1977), 87.

35. [R. Baldwin], *Britain Reviv'd: In a Panegyrick to Their Most August Majesties, William and Mary* (London, 1689). During Anne's reign, there was a revival of an older strain of divine-right discourse divorced from the idea of providential intervention. Lord Cornbury referred to "her most sacred majesty" during political debates with the New Jersey Assembly; see "His Excellency's Answer to the Said Remonstrance Given to the Said Assembly at Burlington, on Monday the 12th Day of Said May, 1707," in SPG microfilm, reel 12, 4; "A Remonstrance of the Assembly of Nova Caesaria or New Jersey, to His Excellency the Lord Viscount Cornbury . . . ," ibid.

I and his succession by George II to the biblical story of David and Solomon. "Thus did," he wrote, "the most high GOD provide himself a *King* among the Sons of *Jesse*." It was, Prince continued, "a wonderful Train of various Providential Changes did he carry and advance him to the Throne."[36]

By the time of George I's death, some provincial thinkers had fused contract theory and hereditary right to a kind of divine-right theory in order to legitimate the Hanoverian dynasty. Thomas Prince described George I as "descended of a Race of Ancient Princes, both in *Germany* and *Britain*. . . . His immediate Mother, was in the latter part of her Life, the nearest of any Protestant Royal Blood, to the Crown of *Great Britain*." He was, in short, part of that specially anointed royal tribe whose family lines ran back into the mists of time. But Prince would also describe him as having been "ordain'd and prepar'd by Heaven, for the raising *Great Britain* to that high Rank and Dignity." Thomas Foxcroft fused hereditary and divine right by declaring that "the Favour of GOD to this *Protestant Royal Family*" had led George I to the British throne. God favored George specifically because his family had suffered for Protestantism while rulers of Bohemia. "KINGS are subject to GOD; appointed by Him and dependent on Him . . . [they] rise to the Height that He hath decreed."[37]

Early in 1728, the *Boston Weekly News-Letter* printed a verse that captured this same fusion of hereditary right, divine right, and monarchical election when Queen Caroline provided another heir to the newly crowned George II:

> The Queen, the Gracious Consort, humbly Great,
> With Piety ennobles Regal State,
> Hail fruitful *Carolina*, hail! in thee
> Heav'n has approv'd our Senate's wise Decree,
> Has blest thy Womb with a fair num'rous Line,
> The lovely Pledges of Assent Divine,

36. Kathleen Wilson, *The Sense of the People: Politics, Culture, and Imperialism in England, 1715–1785* (New York, 1995), 89; Thomas Prince, *A Sermon on the Sorrowful Occasion of the Death of His Late Majesty King George of Blessed Memory, and the Happy Accession of His Present Majesty King George II to the Throne* (Boston, 1727), 8. As late as 1761, New Hampshire minister Samuel Haven would preach on God's providential justice in taking "the kingdom of our *British* Israel from the unhappy family of the *Stewards*, and (having a favour for our nation) placed it in the family of *Brunswick* and said, *let George be King*." Indeed, Haven began his sermon quoting from "PROV. VIII. 15, 16. By Me Kings reign, and Princes decree Justice" (*The Supreme Influence of the Son of God*, 17).

37. Prince, *A Sermon on the Sorrowful Occasion of the Death of His Late Majesty*, 17, 18; Foxcroft, *God the Judge*, 18.

Doubtful Succession, settled now by Fate,
Shall vex the Land no more with Civil Hate.[38]

By giving sacred meaning to the Hanoverian settlement, this writer sought to stabilize that family on the throne and to give the idea of contract sacred sanction.

Eventually, colonial writers began the British monarchy's resacralization in
earnest. Contract theory continued to be invoked, the idea of a legally restrained
monarch remained important, but over time writers elevated the king over other
men and made him semidivine. As early as 1716, Benjamin Wadsworth preached
that "rulers should know God, and acknowledge Him to be the Author of their
Power, and Him to whom they're accountable"; and, in 1722, Boston minister
John Hancock declared in his sermon *Rulers Should Be Benefactors* that "THE
Power that *Sovereign Princes* are Invested with, it is a Power of *Lordship* and Dominion." God "is the Sovereign LORD; but the Princes and Kings of the Earth
are his Lieutenants, his Deputies and Vicegerents." Hancock was claiming direct
divine sanction for the monarchy.[39]

George I's death led to a flood of sermons and pamphlets on the monarch's
character that intensified the trend toward elevating the royal person. After invoking 13 Romans concerning the civil powers and God, the minister of Boston's
New South Church, the Harvard-educated Samuel Checkley, laid the building
blocks of this neodivine right. He acknowledged the three basic forms of government common to early modern political theory—democracy, aristocracy, and
monarchy—and the right of a nation to contract for a particular type of government. In this respect, he followed the imperial political orthodoxy created between 1688 and 1715 to legitimate the Protestant succession. But Checkley recon-
structed British monarchs as a "Superiour order of Men . . . they bear the title and
character of Gods." Even monarchs would "as others return to Dust again," but
it was also clearly "God, who sets up Kings." Old South Church's Thomas Prince
said, "Kings are as *Gods* on Earth," as he paid tribute to the deceased monarch.
An article in the *Boston Weekly News-Letter* described George I as gone "to the
Tribunal of the Almighty King . . . to render an exact Account of his Vicegerency
on Earth."[40]

38. *Boston Weekly News-Letter*, Jan. 25–Feb. 1, 1728.

39. B[enjamin] Wadsworth, *Rulers Feeding and Guiding Their People with Integrity and
Skilfulness* (Boston, 1716), 27; John Hancock, *Rulers Should Be Benefactors, as It Was Consider'd in a Sermon Preach'd before His Excellency Samuel Shute, Esq.* (Boston, 1722), 3.

40. Samuel Checkley, *The Duty of a People, to Lay to Heart and Lament the Death of
a Good King . . .* (Boston, [1727]), 5, 7, 10; Prince, *A Sermon on the Sorrowful Occasion of
the Death of His Late Majesty*, 23; *Boston Weekly News-Letter*, Aug. 17–24, 1727.

The idea of divine sanction for the royal person permeated colonial society between the deaths of George I and George II. During the Zenger Crisis, one newspaper, assuming the persona of Sir Walter Raleigh, informed "Prince Henry" that "Your Father is the Vicegerent of Heaven . . . shall Man have Authority from the Fountain of Good to do Evil?" When George II's consort Queen Caroline died in 1737, Roger Price preached to a Boston audience that the "Power and Protection of Princes" derived directly from the supreme deity, as "GOD hath cloathed [them] with a Portion of his Authority." In the same year, the *Virginia Gazette* reprinted an English song that encouraged Britons to "give to Godlike GEORGE his Due." By 1751, even a supposed rationalist like Jonathan Mayhew could write of monarchs that "an inferior and subordinate trust may be fitly placed in those who are called gods in this world," while he continued to insist (as any Anglo-American would have agreed) that "the God of heaven . . . ought to be our first and last resort." The British king had been situated within a sacred language that fused the imperial political order with national Protestantism and a form of divine right mediated by that Protestantism. That this motif derived ultimately from Catholic realms did nothing to inhibit its use.[41]

By the time of George II's death, the king as a kind of semidivinity or God's earthly viceroy had been normalized. This under-studied and perhaps misunderstood monarch reigned for more than thirty years. When his heart failed in late October 1760, more than half of British North America's population had known no other ruler. Protestant political culture as well as victory in the cosmically infused struggle against the French had swelled public affections for George II.

This patriotic love helped raise George II to rhetorical demigod at the hour of his death. "PRINCES," wrote Samuel Cooper, "are represented in the divine Oracles, as a Kind of subordinate Deities." Monarchs "bear a faint Image of the Power and Authority of the Lord of all: And when they resemble Him also in Wisdom and Goodness; when they make the divine Government the Model of their own. . . . Such Monarchs merit and command the Reverence and Gratitude of their Subjects." Cooper was not calling for unchecked despotism. Since only God could be trusted completely, "it must then be highly unreasonable to place an

41. *New-York Weekly Journal*, Jan. 14, 1733; Roger Price, *A Sermon Preach'd at the King's Chappel in Boston, New England* . . . (Boston, 1738), 8; *Virginia Gazette* (Williamsburg), Mar. 25–Apr. 1, 1737; Mayhew, *A Sermon Preached at Boston in New-England*, 8. For an insightful account of Mayhew's commitment to a static and hierarchical order in relation to consumption, see T. H. Breen, "The Meanings of Things: Interpreting the Consumer Economy in the Eighteenth Century," in John Brewer and Roy Porter, eds., *Consumption and the World of Goods* (New York, 1993), 255.

absolute Trust even in the . . . most exalted of Princes." But he privileged the monarch and asserted divine origins for his authority. College of New Jersey president Samuel Davies cried rhetorical tears over George II's "sacred Dust" in his funeral sermon for the departed king. Even "those Gods of Earth" eventually died like other men, he warned his readers, but they were a different breed of men, "those Demi-gods enthron'd," as a Philadelphia contemporary of Davies's called them.[42]

Others wrote in the same vein. When a Boston writer described the king's actual death, he proudly declared "the same Providence which blessed his latter Years attended him to his last Moments . . . his Death sudden and free from Pain." Far from crying out and dropping his hot chocolate all over his bedchambers as his aorta burst, which was apparently the case, George had been "raised above the rest of Mankind . . . at the last almost exempted from the common Infirmities incident to them."[43]

Samuel Haven of Portsmouth, New Hampshire, preached that the spirit of the genuine Protestant religion had elevated George II. Haven asked, "Can any of our race lie under stronger engagements, or be urged with more powerful motives, than rulers to revere the supreme Deity"? For kings received their place from "the Son of God," who gave them "their power and eminence above their fellow-mortals." Haven knew it was useless to pretend "that this power is derived *immediately*" from God; "yet since it is *mediately* according to the different constitutions of empires, kingdoms and states, it comes to the same thing." Kings had to use their power as the Lord intended, within the agreed limits of the polity, but were still accurately called "the *Lord's anointed*," the very *"living images* of the supreme and only potentate." Seventy years after the Glorious Revolution, rhetoric derived from divine-right monarchy that ascribed some kind of elevated spiritual character to the king was playing an important role in provincial political culture.[44]

Monarchy's sacralization advanced rapidly through official proclamations and decrees as well as sermons and pamphlets. As early as 1733, the *American Weekly Mercury* printed Lord Howe's address to the Council of Barbados. Howe reassured the councillors, "Tho' you are at so great a Distance from His MAJESTY's Sacred Person . . . [you are] not out of his Thoughts, nor out of his tender Care. His gracious Love extends to all his Subjects." The idea of the king's

42. Samuel Cooper, *A Sermon upon Occasion of the Death of Our Late Sovereign, George the Second, Preach'd before His Excellency Francis Bernard, Esq.* (Boston, 1761), 8–10; Davies, *A Sermon Delivered at Nassau-Hall*, 3.

43. *Boston Weekly News-Letter*, Jan. 1, 1761.

44. Haven, *The Supreme Influence of the Son of God*, 7–9.

sacred person, common to many formal proclamations, became tropes in colonial petitions and addresses to the king as well. In 1766, the Virginia Burgesses pledged their "Attachment to his [George III's] sacred Person, Crown and dignity" after the Stamp Act's repeal. The Virginia Council outdid them, professing their "inviolable fidelity" to "your Majesty's sacred Person and Government." This usage continued through the time of the First Continental Congress and the Olive Branch Petition, suggesting the degree of acceptance these practices had achieved.[45]

Although the period's students have ignored the salutation "Sacred Majesty," it encouraged the broader semideification of the monarchy. As skeptical a whig as the Baptist preacher Isaac Skillman acknowledged this during the imperial crisis. Among provincial New Englanders, "the character of a *Prince* is very exalted, majestic, and superlative among men. Some say it is sacred: Hence you have that phrase, his SACRED MAJESTY." It was a perception Skillman tried to destroy; he tried to convince listeners that the king's authority came from the people and not God. But he knew that, for many, the king was, if less than a god, still somehow more than a man.[46]

The loyalist James Murray revealed how such language had shaped expectations in the late provincial world. "The stories," he wrote, "which they [exiled loyalists] read in news-papers concerning his *sacred Majesty*, their *Highnesses the Princes of the blood*, — and the *honourable Secretaries of State*, make them expect to see something very extraordinary" when they actually met their leaders. Loyal provincials had taken to heart what they had read and heard, allowing them to imagine a distinction between royalty and the rest of mankind.[47]

Efforts to use neodivine right for what we would call social control occurred repeatedly before 1776 in response to agrarian unrest. The president of the Board of Proprietors of the Eastern Division of New Jersey, one of the protagonists in a violent conflict in the 1740s and 1750s, fused the idea of royal divinity to a genealogical claim to the throne during an attack on land rioters who denied the proprietors' property rights. These people, he declared of his yeomen opponents,

45. *American Weekly Mercury* (Philadelphia), June 7–14, 1733; George Reese, ed., *The Official Papers of Francis Fauquier, Lieutenant Governor of Virginia, 1758–1768*, III, *1764–1768* (Charlottesville, Va., 1983), 1412n, 1413.

46. [Isaac Skillman], *An Oration on the Beauties of Liberty, or the Essential Rights of the Americans, Delivered at the Second Baptist-Church in Boston*, 4th ed. (Boston, 1773), 45.

47. [James Murray], *The Travels of the Imagination: A True Journey from Newcastle to London* (Philadelphia, 1778), 95; Susan Lindsey Lively, "Going Home: Americans in Britain, 1740–1776" (Ph.D. diss., Harvard University, 1996), 34.

denied the right of "His most Sacred Majesty" and his "Noble Progenitors, Kings and Queens of England" to ownership of the entire empire and had treated the king's clemency with contempt. At another point, New Jersey governor Jonathan Belcher described the rioters as men who had withdrawn "their Duty from His Most Sacred Majesty."[48]

A more extensive use of divine-right-tinged theology to try to quell social disorder occurred in 1768 during the agrarian upheaval known as the Regulation. The Reverend Dr. George Micklejohn, Church of England minister in Orange County, preached a sermon to Governor Tryon and the troops raised to suppress the violence in the countryside. After citing 13 Romans on the sacred origins of civil authority, Micklejohn told the assembled militia, "Upon these *guardians* of the public and general welfare [monarchs], God has been pleased to confer a divine authority, to render their persons, as well as ordinances, the more sacred."[49] It was God by whom "kings reign, and princes decree justice; by him princes rule, and nobles, even all the judges of the earth." Micklejohn went further still, citing the Bible: "*They that resist, shall receive to themselves* DAMNATION." The words sanctified the actions necessary to subdue unnatural rebellion.[50]

Other North Carolinians echoed these sentiments. Moravian ministers approached Governor Tryon during the King's Birthday celebration after the Battle of Alamance (1771), which saw the government triumph over the Regulators, to again pledge their loyalty to monarch and empire. Congratulating him on his victory, they asked God to pour down blessings on "the sacred person of our souverian King George III, and all his Royal family." These Moravians went on to express their thanks that the disorders in the province had finally been ended.[51]

In sacralizing the monarch, colonial writers unintentionally helped confuse the question of the location of sovereignty in the empire as a whole. When George III ascended to the throne, the New York Council issued a proclamation "beseeching God, by whom Kings and Queens do reign," to bless the young ruler. The power monarchs derived from God remained limited, bounded in the man-

48. *NJA*, XVI, *Journal of the Governor and Council*, IV, 17, 18, 132.

49. George Micklejohn, *On the Important Duty of Subjection to the Civil Powers: A Sermon Preached before His Excellency William Tryon, Esquire. . . .* (New Bern, N.C., 1768), rpt. as "Dr. George Micklejohn's Sermon to Tryon's Militia," in William K. Boyd, ed., "Some North Carolina Tracts of the 18th Century: X," in *North Carolina Historical Review*, III (1926), 457–474, esp. 462, 465.

50. Ibid., 467.

51. "Bethabara Diary, 1771," in William Powell et al., eds., *The Regulators in North Carolina: A Documentary History, 1759–1776* (Raleigh, N.C., 1971), 317.

ner appropriate for a Protestant prince. But it indicated a fragmented perception of sovereignty in the empire, one that challenged the unitary perception inherited in the settlement of the Glorious Revolution. Parliament received its authority from the people, the king from God.[52]

For monarchy to work, rulers had to seem somehow apart from their subjects. As trenchant an observer as Blackstone declared that the monarch must be considered "of a great and transcendent nature; by which the people are led to consider him in the light of a superior being." When commoners were "taught to consider their prince as a man of no greater perfection than themselves," they were "apt to grow insolent and refractory."[53]

The king's gradual redeification is difficult to measure in full, but the revolutionary generation's declarations that royalty and royal officials had "no more claim than another to be, *jure divino*, or of divine right" strongly indicates that divine-right thinking in some form had taken root among the population at large. Further outburst against "the doctrine of *passive obedience and non-resistance*, so zealously preached up by some artful and designing men, who act as creatures of the state," is clearly linked to the monarchy's earlier resanctification.[54]

This development, or the time line's alteration, or the use of solar imagery in no way amounted to an embrace of arbitrary government. Thinking of the period's political development as a teleological rise of liberty or enlightenment, or as the republicanization of monarchy, or even simply as colonials identifying as British is to distort that time to serve our own. The emergent political order was not unlike that in some East Asian states today, with a nepotistic bureaucracy headed symbolically by a semidivine figure celebrated in ritual and in print, presiding over a demographically expanding and commercially vibrant society. Such an imperial order does not neatly fit into our political theories or our history, because its strange mixture of concepts, some that we associate with tyranny and others with freedom or liberty, seem so contradictory to our modern eyes. For British Americans, though, to understand their Protestant prince as elevated above the rest of mankind, and to imagine themselves blessed with liberty, was no contradiction.

52. "Proclamation of Accession of George III by New York Council and Leading Citizens," in *The Letters and Papers of Cadwallader Colden*, VI, *1761–1764*, NYHS, *Collections*, LV (New York, 1923), 7.

53. Marston, *King and Congress*, 26; Blackstone, *Commentaries*, I, 241.

54. Samuel Sherwood, *A Sermon, Containing, Scriptural Instructions to Civil Rulers, and All Free-Born Subjects* . . . (New Haven, [1774]), 12, 29.

Time, the solar system, and even God: all were enlisted in the great enterprise to legitimate the Protestant monarchy. It was not a coherent movement but rather an expression of an overriding imperative of an era and a place, British North America. Protestant populations fearful of popish enslavement embraced the rites and beliefs of imperial Protestant monarchy and fused them to local customs. In so doing, they unwittingly created the logic for the resanctification and semideification of the British monarchy by Protestant ministers, royal officials, and newspaper writers, who all came to describe the king as a sacred figure in one way or another.

These intellectual changes intersected with the conflicts in the land tenure system. The entire time line question was connected, at least indirectly, to the issue of property rights that led to endemic violence in the countryside after 1745. The gentry based their claims to large swaths of the interior on grants made by Charles I, Charles II, and James II to their retainers. Portions of the gentry might well have invested themselves in a more historically legitimate House of Stuart precisely because it was in their interest to do so. The related claims of the gentry and the royal government to quitrents were also dependent on the Stuart grants and have been called alternatively part of a neofeudal or neoabsolutist tendency in the society. Ironically, those who resisted them invoked the king as well as John Locke in their cause, claiming that both their labor on the land and royal benevolence established their just right. Tremendous pressures developed in the countryside along this fault line, whether property rights in British America derived from the Stuart kings' massive seventeenth-century land grants or from the labor of yeomen on the land.[55]

The vision of a gentry-controlled land tenure system expressed a desire for a provincial order remade along the lines of Britain. Church of England officials hoped that the quitrents generated from these estates would be used to fund a

55. John Murrin coined the term "neofeudalism" in his important article "Feudalism, Communalism, and the Yeoman Freeholders: The American Revolution Considered as a Social Accident." I have used the term "neoabsolutist" to describe the same process, placing the emphasis on the origins of the dues in the Stuart land grants and the seventeenth-century context more broadly. Beverely W. Bond, Jr.'s discussion of quitrents remains the definitive study (Bond, *The Quit-Rent System in the American Colonies* [New Haven, Conn., 1919]). For a discussion of the importance of quitrents in one colony and the Crown's plans for them, see John Rutherford to William Tryon, Jan. 19, 1769, in William S. Powell, ed., *The Correspondence of William Tryon and Other Selected Papers*, II, *1768–1818* (Raleigh, N.C., 1981), esp. 294–296.

church establishment in the colonies. Royal officials saw the quitrents as a potential source of revenue that would fund governors and judges "altogether dependent for their tenure and salary on the mere will of the crown," as one Yorker declared shortly after the war. Had it occurred, it would have rendered "him [Britain's kings] more absolute here than he was in the realm of England." It was for this reason that royal officials repeatedly demanded to know "why so little improvement has been made in His Majestys Revenue of Quit Rents, notwithstanding the Rapid progress of Settlement," as one official put it to Governor Tryon in 1769 during the Regulation. There was an imperative on the part of royal officials and their clients to make the Stuart grants active, legitimate legally, and thus seen to be congruent with the realm's fundamental law.[56]

The gentry's legal effort in the countryside, and colonial writers' alteration of the time line and resanctification of the king, were part of a powerful but uncoordinated search for order in the American provinces. It expressed unease at seventeenth-century developments locally and in the home islands. And it expressed a desire to make the empire more coherent, more uniform. Some, though, realized that the changes that drove conflict in the society—the population growth, the expansion of trade it sparked, the imperial wars—all of it began to convince Britons that the empire needed to be remade, restructured, rethought. A host of dreamers in America and the home islands began to pen plans for a new polity, one that would comfortably straddle the Atlantic, assure imperial control over the king's restless American subjects, repel his foreign enemies, and bring lasting order to a diverse empire. Their dreams pointed to a different but quite possible future, a path not taken to a durable imperial America.

56. "A Brief Account of the State of the Church of England in the British Colonies in America," SPG microfilm, reel 10, 33–34; for a broader consideration of imperial land policy, see D. H. Murdoch, "Land Policy in the Eighteenth-Century British Empire: The Sale of Crown Lands in the Ceded Islands, 1763–1783," *Historical Journal*, XXVII (1984), 573–574; Edward P. Alexander, *A Revolutionary Conservative: James Duane of New York* (New York, 1938), 167; Benjamin Heron to William Tryon, Jan. 25, 1769, in William S. Powell, ed., *The Correspondence of William Tryon and Other Selected Papers*, II, *1768–1818* (Raleigh, N.C., 1981), 295.

8

DREAMS OF A NEW EMPIRE

A WORLD REMADE, AN EMPIRE
REIMAGINED

. . . . .
. . .
.

As the empire expanded and its bureaucracy grew to meet the demands created by the protracted wars against France, a new type of man appeared: the bureaucratic adventurer. He was a man on the make, but in a way only possible in the first and second British empires. The prototype for this new man was Thomas Pownall, the Cambridge-educated younger brother of the secretary to the Lords Commissioners of Trade and Plantations. In 1753, Pownall traveled to New York as an aide to its newly appointed royal governor, Sir Danvers Osborne. Pownall endured the governor's suicide shortly after their arrival, anointed himself a kind of roving official for the Board of Trade, attended the Albany Congress in 1754, and eventually became an imperial governor.[1]

Experience finally caught up to his inflated claims to imperial expertise, and in 1764, that year suspended between war and revolution, he stepped back and saw a new empire emerging. "It is now," he declared in his *Administration of the Colonies*, "the duty of those who govern us, to carry forward this state of things . . . that our kingdom may be no more considered as the mere kingdom of this isle, with many appendages of provinces, colonies, settlements, and other extraneous parts." Rather, it had become "a grand marine dominion" that demanded a new polity "consisting of our possessions in the Atlantic and in America united into a one interest, in a one center where the seat of government is." Perceiving the

---

1. Charles A. W. Pownall, *Thomas Pownall: M.P., F.R.S., Governor of Massachusetts Bay, Author of The Letters of Junius* (London, 1908), 1–2. For an older treatment of Albany, see George Louis Beer, *British Colonial Policy, 1754–1765* (New York, 1933), 16–30. Pownall was briefly appointed governor of New Jersey and then the Bay Colony. For a brief examination of his views on state and empire, see Peter N. Miller, *Defining the Common Good: Empire, Religion, and Philosophy in Eighteenth-Century Britain* (Cambridge, 1994), 195–213.

potential danger in the planned Stamp Act, he charged the London government with the critical task of "taking leading measures towards the forming all these Atlantic and American possessions into a one dominion," of which "Great Britain should be the commercial center." Commerce would form an "enlarged Communion," a broader transatlantic community held together by the unseen forces, not unlike Newton's gravity, created by trade. Pownall envisioned a greater Britain whose true physical center would be the Atlantic waterways themselves. It could contain the ambitions and passions that had overtaken the British Atlantic since the Glorious Revolution. This new empire would provide all free subjects with a uniform legal framework, a common perception of the location of sovereignty, and shared liberties.[2]

Pownall was one in a long line of would-be imperial reformers that began to write immediately after the Glorious Revolution and continued to plan imperial reform years after American independence. These thirty or more thinkers, like their contemporaries the first Anglo-American novelists, were no longer moored to the world that existed before them. The seventeenth century's political traumas, the North American settlements' nascent character, the encounters with other cultures, and the period's startling economic growth combined to encourage profound intellectual inquiry in the empire. Some of this energy came to be focused on the colonies and the imperial constitution, leading to a series of reform plans.

These musings over the empire's structure underwent a visible shift in emphasis between 1690 and 1774. Before the 1740s, defense issues motivated the would-be reformers. Some suggested using absolutist France and its North American colony as a model for remaking colonial institutions, whereas others sought to use Ireland or Scotland as a reforming template. At midcentury, though, writers began to address new concerns created by demographic and economic growth in the British Atlantic. A spate of proposals appeared that called for a new im-

---

2. [Thomas Pownall], *The Administration of the Colonies* (London, 1764), 6; G. H. Guttridge, "Thomas Pownall's *The Administration of the Colonies*: The Six Editions," *WMQ*, 3d Ser., XXVI (1969), 31–32. Pownall, writing in the 1750s, declared he thought society should be an enlarged communion. He was heavily influenced by Newton and felt society should have a principle like gravity that held it together. Pownall actually wrote to William Pitt at the end of the Seven Years' War asking to be allowed to shape the government of Canada. He was outspoken in his opposition to the use of troops in the colonies during the imperial crisis. See Clarence Edwin Carter, ed., *The Correspondence of General Thomas Gage, with the Secretaries of State, and with the War Office and the Treasury, 1763–1775*, II (New Haven, Conn., 1933), 116n.

perial constitution and institutional structure to permanently link not only the colonists but also Native Americans to the empire.

The timing of this shift in thinking suggests a connection to the American Revolution. But the link is not linear. Most of the plans for reform were not republicanizing or egalitarian. Those theorists imagined a more ordered polity where the distance between core and periphery, nation and state, language and institutions would narrow and ultimately close. A spectrum of possible imperiums emerged from their imaginations, stretching from neoabsolutist designs to Pownall's federated, economically liberal empire with London as its hub. Had any of them succeeded, the Atlantic might have become a British sea for centuries. They failed, though, to capture the imagination of those with the power to initiate real change, an oversight with momentous implications for the world.

. . .

Designs Shaped by Defense

From its beginnings in the 1680s, Quaker Pennsylvania stood out among British polities. Philadelphia was one of the Western world's first planned cities. The colony's legal codes reflected a changed view of human nature and the human soul. Religious toleration became the norm in a world that had been ripped apart by religious schisms for more than a century. Yet, if there is one thing that somehow leaps out to the modern mind about these innovations, it is the Quakers' commitment to peace. We can hardly mention Pennsylvania or its founder, William Penn, without thinking of their pacifist leanings.

Thus it comes as some surprise to find that one of Penn's earliest writings in America concerned creating a vigorous and hierarchical defense structure for the American colonies. Penn's "Briefe and Plaine Scheam," written in 1696 amid King William's War, contained the germ of many of the imperial reforms that would become stock-in-trade in such plans. He called on each colony to send two representatives "once a year, and oftner if need be, dureing the Warr, and at least once in two yeares in times of Peace" to maintain security in North America. The meetings would occur in New York City, with New York's royal governor acting as "Kings high Comr during the Session." This assembly would set defense quotas for money and men, settle some intercolonial disputes (particularly in regard to finance), and allow for coordination in case of emergency.[3]

3. "Draft of *A Briefe and Plaine Scheam*," in Richard S. Dunn, Mary Maples Dunn, et al., eds., *The Papers of William Penn*, III, *1685–1700* (Philadelphia, 1986), 482–483. There had apparently been a similar plan proposed by Governor Benjamin Fletcher of New York, but most of the colonies failed to respond (483).

That early America's best-known pacifist sketched a plan for intercolonial defense seems ironic, but Penn had already helped create a new colony, a new penal code, and a new city. Rethinking imperial institutional structures extended a process already at work in his mind. Dozens of others would follow his example, each reimagining the empire's institutional architecture. Before the 1740s, most writers recommended highly centralized governing bodies that could respond to the military threat posed by the French and Indians. These thinkers suggested that institutional changes should occur primarily or solely in America rather than in the empire as a whole. There would be a consolidation of authority into the hands of a royally appointed official, and some new, intercolonial assembly drawing members from each colony would be formed to raise war funds.

The outbreak of King William's War in 1689 encouraged the first post-1688 plans for institutional reforms. These plans contained the same sort of call for centralization of colonial defenses as "A Briefe and Plaine Scheam." *Discourses on the Publick Revenues, and on the Trade of England*, probably written by Charles Davenant, called for a colonial superassembly to meet at New York City and "adjust all Matters of Complaint . . . between Province and Province. . . . To consider of Ways and Means to support the Union and Safety of these Provinces, against their Common Enemies." New York's royal governor would be the king's high commissioner and commander in chief, with the power to set defense quotas on the colonies during times of war. An actual movement toward this structure began when Lord Bellomont became royal governor of Massachusetts and New York and was also given command of the northern colonies' defense. Throughout the period, high-level rumors circulated that a North American captain general would be appointed to coordinate colonial defense.[4]

In the 1730s and 1740s, this drive to centralize authority to coordinate defense led some writers to use absolutist France as a model for reform. There could be no greater irony than these efforts to save British liberties by making British colonies over on the model provided by the hated French and their New France colony. Changes in the writings of MP and Board of Trade member Martin Bladen over a twenty-year period illustrate this shift toward a hierarchical, absolutist structure in the plans for imperial design.

In the 1720s, Bladen put forth several plans that called for colonial defense

4. [Charles Davenant?], *Discourses on the Publick Revenues, and on the Trade of England* (London, 1698), part 2, 260–261. See John Miller, *New York Considered and Improved, 1695*, ed. Victor Hugo Paltsits (New York, 1970), 78–79, for another such call to unify the northern colonies for reasons of control and defense. He further advocated that a bishop be appointed for America and "be made Governour of New Yorke."

structures with a captain general appointed by the London government and some type of yearly meeting to raise defense funds. For certain, these were centralizing, but only in tightly defined matters of defense. In 1739, however, at the outbreak of the War of Jenkins's Ear against Spain, Bladen had become tightly focused on reforming all provincial institutional structures so that they might be consistent with one another and reflect the unity of sovereignty that was the Glorious Revolution's constitutional legacy in England. Bladen's *Reasons for Appointing a Captain General for the Continent of North America* focused on creating a unified imperial framework for the colonies. As long as "they shall continue in the State they are in, divided into so many different Provinces," constantly squabbling over "Trade and Boundarys," they would remain vulnerable to Spanish and French predation.[5]

Bladen in particular indicted the charter governments, which he saw as unruly and atypical with the empire's institutions. Rhode Island and Connecticut inflated their currencies, ignored royal orders, and circumvented the Acts of Trade. "It were," Bladen wrote, "therefore much to be desired, that they might all be reduced under his Majesty's immediate Directions" on the model of the other royal governments in America. Such standardization would allow for ease of military control and make more readily apparent the King-in-Parliament's ultimate sovereignty, something Bladen felt was somehow threatened in theory and reality by institutional heterogeneity.[6]

Bladen suggested New France as a model for the British colonies' reorganization because its structure seemed to provide important advantages in matters of defense. Despite massive numerical inferiority, the Gallic foe "had the advantage of Us in their Dispositions" from "being under One Uniform Government." He called for a parallel centralization in British America at the executive and legislative levels. The planned government would be led by a powerful executive captain general who would be based in New York and act as the royal governor of that colony as well as of the New England provinces in the manner that Lord Bellomont had in the 1690s. The intercolonial assembly would be structured to give the royal colonies greater representation than the charter colonies. Assemblymen would be in frequent contact with the captain general, who would get constant reports of "the Conducts of his several Governours, and of the Dispositions of the People."[7]

5. Jack P. Greene, "Martin Bladen's Blueprint for a Colonial Union," *WMQ*, 3d Ser., XVII (1960), 516–530, esp. 523.

6. Ibid., 524.

7. Ibid., 528–530. Bellomont had been named governor of New York, Massachusetts,

Georgia leader James Oglethorpe put forth a similar proposal. Fearful that Georgia and the other colonies would soon be under assault by the Papist powers, Oglethorpe called for a combined British and colonial military force that would be "put under Some Single persons command." Oglethorpe's belief that provincial governors would squabble if left to their own devices was based on a sound reading of imperial politics, and he called for creation of an "Inspector Genl." This officer would have control over all colonial forces in times of war.[8]

Henry McCulloh also developed a plan for imperial reform in part modeled on absolutist France and its North American colony. McCulloh, a Scotsman who served as an imperial official in the Carolinas, declared repeatedly that "without an Union of the Colonies we cannot prosecute a War" against French Canada with any hope of victory. New France's structure imparted unity of purpose, which explained "the Advantages they have gained over us" despite being heavily outnumbered by British settlers.[9] Gallic institutions, McCulloh declared, circumvented corrupt bureaucratic practices by easing communication between imperial officials and their ruler. Under the French model, the "said Council of State is the high Watch-Tower, from which the King may survey all his Dominions and sometimes all the Dominions of the World, in order to consult the Honour, Defence, Profit and Peace of his Subjects." Such a structure was appropriate, he continued, because "the King may be properly said to be in his Kingdom, what the Soul is in the natural Body, which, according to the proper Direction of its Powers, brings either Happiness or Misery." Such absolutist and divine-right-tinged musing reflected that same tendency that had emerged in other parts of the print culture.[10]

This centralizing tendency in the reform plans intensified in the 1750s and 1760s. McCulloh's *Wisdom and Policy of the French in the Construction of Their Great Offices* and *Proposals for Uniting the English Colonies on the Continent of America* called for central control over the British colonies in order to facilitate defense movements and attacks on Canada. Various revenue acts, including a stamp tax, would be imposed, with the caveat that the funds thus raised would be

---

and New Hampshire during King William's War in the 1690s. The arrangement did not work well and was not repeated.

8. Robert G. McPherson, ed., *The Journal of the Earl of Egmont: Abstract of the Trustees Proceedings for Establishing the Colony of Georgia, 1732–1738* (Athens, Ga., 1962), 232–233.

9. [Henry McCulloh], *Proposals for Uniting the English Colonies on the Continent of America . . .* (London, 1757), 30, 37.

10. [Henry McCulloh], *The Wisdom and Policy of the French in the Construction of Their Great Offices . . .* (London, 1755), 32–33, 36.

used only for defense. In short, he advocated extending the British fiscal-military state structure to the colonies, which would have firmly established the King-in-Parliament's constitutional supremacy over the colonial governments. Political commentators believed that Lord Halifax intended to put forward a plan centralizing imperial control in matters of colonial defense at the outbreak of the Seven Years' War.[11]

Wilmot Vaughan, Earl of Lisburne, penned the most extreme plan for an anglicized, hierarchical state structure in British America. Recognizing that "compulsive obedience is ever productive of bad consequence," Vaughan nonetheless declared that government was "founded upon . . . power." Inequality, Vaughan insisted, "of rank and fortune" was critical to society's very existence. All colonial governing institutions should be uniform, "all charter and propriatary shall be annulled," and all "American Governors shall be appointed by the Crown and removable at pleasure." In this plan, America would be constituted into a separate kingdom ruled by its own governor general. The new polity would be allowed its own parliament, which would be elected every *nine* years. He went on to advocate the appointment of Anglican bishops for America, who would sit in the upper house. He also supported the establishment of "the same mode of Worship [the Church of England]." The Church would be "approved of in general, and many who are now violent adversaries, will not only become reconciled to it, but be glad to have their children or friends partakers." This blueprint for a new royal America, its hierarchy reinforced by centralized institutions, would once and for all settle the relationship of church and state in the colonies and the empire as a whole.[12]

A London pamphlet writer inspired by the controversy over the Quebec Act (which preserved much of the French institutional and religious structure in Canada) in 1774 echoed these sentiments. While maintaining that the French Canadians would see the sort of assembly and trial by jury common in the older British colonies as a form of ethnic aggression, the writer declared that representative assemblies were not suitable for colonies as a whole. Such places were "ill suited" to representative government, being peopled by "chiefly planters and traders" who would act out of self-interest rather than the common good. Indeed, Britain's unruly colonies "would have experienced a much greater degree of felicity, had their government consisted only of a governor and council, with

11. *The Letters and Papers of Cadwallader Colden*, V, *1755–1760*, NYHS, *Collections*, LIV (New York, 1923), 16, 25–26.

12. Wilmot Vaughan, "A Plan for the Better Government of British America, 1769," NYHS MSS, 8–12, 14, 22–25, 27–28.

a board of trade . . . instead of their assemblies." Popular assemblies, he insisted, threatened the health of local polities as well as the empire. He urged the London authorities to essentially adopt whole cloth New France's pre-1763 absolutist governing structures.[13]

The appeal of such reforms to imperial officials was obvious: control. But, after 1750, even the staunchest advocate of imperial consolidation came to realize that the problems of defending the colonies were linked to changes in British North America and the larger Atlantic world driven by the provinces' explosive population growth. As they groped for a new imperial template, the majority turned, not to New France's autocratic model, but rather to the British Empire's other subordinate polities, until the pressure of change brought forth more comprehensive proposals for imperial reform that would have altered the British state's entire structure.

. . .

America as Ireland?

In 1770, the *Pennsylvania Gazette* reported one among the many rumors that flew during the imperial crisis. "We hear," wrote the paper's correspondent, "that there is to be a total Change in the Government of America." Britain's new world would be governed by a "Vice-roy . . . similar to the Lord Lieutenant of Ireland." This new government would be "modelled in such a Manner, as to put an End to the present alarming Disputes between Great-Britain and the Colonies." As this passage suggests, the self-appointed advocates for a new imperial order in North America often turned to existing imperial polities, particularly Ireland, for inspiration. The Irish model's initial appeal for reformers grew from its utility for organizing colonial defenses. However, a reform on the Irish model left unresolved the questions of constitutional structure and the location of sovereignty. These questions became significant in the reform plans written after 1740 as the situation in the empire changed. Existing imperial models, though still invoked after midcentury, began to lose force as writers suggested entirely new imperial arrangements that might contain the passions unleashed by population growth, commerce, and imperial warfare.[14]

We take it for granted that new polities will be created from time to time, but in the early modern period, such creation was known but not acknowledged. History was still perceived dynastically, and thus political change was perceived

---

13. *Thoughts on the Act for Making More Effectual Provision for the Government of the Province of Quebec* (London, 1774), 12–13.

14. *Pennsylvania Gazette* (Philadelphia), Mar. 22, 1770.

in terms of ruling families. Most of the polities that came into being in the seventeenth century — the various colonial governments, the Commonwealth, the Protectorate, the Convention Parliament, and the government of English Ireland — were largely the result of adaptation to circumstance rather than philosophic contemplation or well-planned designs.

Nonetheless, imperial planners culled inspirations from these haphazard developments, particularly from the English government in Ireland. That Ireland's government had been formed in part to answer the needs of defense (though, in that case, it was protection from the local Catholic peasantry) recommended it to imperial reformers concerned with military issues before and after 1750. The powerful American lord lieutenant that appeared in a number of plans was modeled on that of Ireland and presumably designed to appeal to a London government that wanted the level of control in America that it already had in the British Isles. As late as 1766, Lord Shelburne wrote to Thomas Gage recommending that the royal quitrents due in the provinces be used to form "an American Fund to support the Exigencies of Government . . . as is done in Ireland." Such a fund would "encrease rather than diminish the Powers of Government in so distant a Country." A captain general or other such figure could then organize provincial responses to enemy attacks, thus easing the burdens of imperial defense.[15]

The empire's central institutional problem was its vast size and cultural diversity, and this helps explain the Irish model's appeal. Ireland, like America, was geographically distinct; eighteenth-century political thought linked nation and national institutions to defined geographic areas as well as religion, language, and history. Many reformers, hoping to make all the empire's composite polities alike, would have agreed with Wilmot Vaughan that America needed "a Lord Lieutenant or Governor General . . . with the same rank, authority and power as the Lord Lieutenant of Ireland . . . That a Chancellor and other proper Officers of State shall be appointed for North America and the Isles, the same or nearly the same as in Ireland." Granville Sharp wrote in 1774 that the Irish Parliament offered a *"true constitutional mode of connecting British Dominions that are otherwise separated by nature."* The dilemma created by institutional incongruities, space, and authority lay at the core of many of the later reform plans.[16]

15. Earl of Shelburne to Thomas Gage, Dec. 11, 1766, in Carter, ed., *Correspondence of General Gage*, II, 49–50.

16. Vaughan, "A Plan for the Better Government of British America, 1769," NYHS MSS, 24; Granville Sharp, *A Declaration of the People's Natural Right to a Share in the Legislature* . . . (London, 1774), ii. Sharp realized that the constitutional issues raised by his

How would reform of the subordinate polities on the Irish or other models be related to a constitutional reconceptualization of the Anglo-American polities that had come to ring the Atlantic basin by the mid-eighteenth century? Reformers became keenly aware that a new imperial institutional structure would somehow entail a new constitution. But their perception of where the ultimate sovereignty would lie changed over time. Broadly put, the change was from a general acceptance of parliamentary supremacy over a reformed empire, thus preserving the Glorious Revolution's settlement, as understood in London, to a more wide-ranging consideration of constitutional structure.

The earliest plans for imperial reform preserved the London government's constitutional supremacy. Since defense needs drove the reform plans and defense demanded centralization, acceptance of the King-in-Parliament seemed logical; sovereignty was seen as unified and absolutely vested. Davenant's *Discourse on the Publick Revenues, and on the Trade of England*, written in 1698, called for a yearly assembly in the colonies that would then lay any actions or initiatives "before the Parliament only" for approval. This plan was resurrected in part by an unknown writer who contacted Benjamin Franklin around 1750. This writer called Davenant's plan the most "reasonable" of all he had heard and went on to recommend a defense structure based in New York, complete with a twenty-six-person assembly and a king's high commissioner "after the manner of Scotland. (Formerly)." He accepted that any laws or actions of this body would be "laid before the Parlament only" for approval.[17]

Reformers who harkened to an Irish or Scottish model as a template accepted the idea of parliamentary sovereignty. The attraction of such plans from the metropolitan perspective was that, in theory, the Irish Parliament was subordinate to the British. Its powers were limited and proscribed by the senior body. It thus seemed to provide a suitable model for reformers interested in changing America's place in the empire without threatening the Glorious Revolution's settlement.[18]

---

statements on Ireland had become embroiled in the question of constitutional location of sovereignty. The best general discussion remains Charles Howard McIlwain, *The American Revolution: A Constitutional Interpretation* (New York, 1923), chaps. 1–5.

17. [Davenant?], *Discourses on the Publick Revenues*; Leonard W. Labaree et al., eds., *The Papers of Benjamin Franklin*, V (New Haven, Conn., 1962), 464–466.

18. The issue of the Irish Parliament came up repeatedly during the imperial crisis and the Revolution. William Smith, Jr., discussed his own and others' involvement with a plan based on the Irish model in August 1775, itself based in part on the earlier Albany plan. Smith acknowledged parliamentary supremacy and yet was sympathetic to the American cause. His ambiguous loyalism during the Revolution expressed his torn allegiance

Even under the Irish model, the empire's constitutional issues would not have gone away. In fact, in the 1760s and 1770s, with the colonists demanding actual instead of virtual representation, members of the Irish Parliament began to question the English Parliament's supremacy over *them*. Like some colonists, they claimed that their relationship was to the king apart from Parliament. During the American Revolution, an unknown provincial still hoping to save the empire commented that the danger of having a supreme American parliament modeled on that of Ireland was "that the American Parliament having only to transact with the King and His Council . . . they will grow like the Irish Parliament to dispute, deny, and reject the Authority of the British Parliament altogether." Americans would thus again imagine themselves a "separate Dominion governed by the same King." It was a problem not easily resolved in theory, and never in practice.[19]

This central constitutional issue was taken up by some of the reformers. They had come to realize that institutional changes merely in America would be insufficient to solve imperial problems. The military situation, the colonies' startling population growth, the explosion in the Atlantic trading networks, and a spreading cosmopolitan awareness of the empire's diversity called for an entirely new imperial structure.[20]

For some writers, the dreams of a new empire had become tied to the hopes for a new imperial constitution. Like many innovators, they acted to preserve what was and, in so doing, suggested something new: not an American republic, but a monarchical America firmly situated in a new constitution. It can be said to have begun as early as the 1754 Albany Congress, when a group of colonists, including Benjamin Franklin and Thomas Hutchinson, took the opportunity to call for substantial imperial changes that would have forced constitutional reform. This trend accelerated in the 1760s and 1770s under the pressures of warfare and then the imperial crisis. It was then that Thomas Pownall put forward his design for an Atlantic-based empire in *The Administration of the Colonies*.[21]

(Smith, *Historical Memoirs from 16 March 1763 to 9 July 1776*, ed. William H. W. Sabine, I [New York, 1956], 235); J. Russell Snapp, "An Enlightened Empire: Scottish and Irish Imperial Reformers in the Age of the American Revolution," *Albion*, XXXIII (2001), 388–403.

19. Plan for the Government of America, 1780, unsigned MS, HSP. Franklin raised the issues of the empire's component polities, particularly Ireland, and their relationship to the Crown. See J. C. D. Clark, *The Language of Liberty, 1660–1832* (Cambridge, 1994), 103–104.

20. Snapp discusses a similar sensibility in the Scottish and Irish placemen who were increasingly running the empire in the 1750s and 1760s, some of whom ended up in American postings ("An Enlightened Empire," *Albion*, XXXIII [2001], 390–391).

21. For an excellent discussion of Franklin's role at Albany, see Timothy J. Shannon,

The plans for constitutional change ran along a spectrum that had two distinct poles. The writers at one pole imagined a universal polity in which all subjects would enjoy the same rights and be governed by the same institutions. At the other end of the spectrum, imperial theorists imagined a federated empire with a number of polities or kingdoms united in the royal person. A Massachusetts writer aptly summed up the former position and its effect on the dilemmas of institutional architecture when he called for "a wise established *Representation* of all *considerable Parts* of the British Dominions in Europe and America in One Central Parliament." Such a body guarding commonly held rights and liberties "would give Stability, Unity, and Concord" to the entire empire. Granville Sharp also believed that "all British subjects, whether in Great Britain, Ireland, or the Colonies, are *equally free* by the law of *Nature*" and had the right to *"a share in the legislation."* It was also a natural right that could not "be withdrawn from any part of the British Empire *by any worldly authority."* That said, Sharp suggested that the best way to preserve these rights was to have discrete kingdoms based on the same British constitution "firmly united by the circle of the British Diadem so as to form *one vast Empire*, which will never be divided." Vaughan advocated a federated empire, but his hierarchical plan called for subordinate polities on the imperial fringe united to the empire through the king's person.[22]

These reformers were all keenly aware that the empire's population was in-

---

Indians and Colonists at the Crossroads of Empire: The Albany Congress of 1754 (Ithaca, N.Y., 2000), 52–56. Shannon understands that the link between the pre–1764 reform plans and the Revolution is a creation of postrevolutionary society and, more generally, the whig tradition. But contemporaries noted that the Albany Congress marked a shift as well. According to William Pulteney, Esq., *Thoughts on the Present State of Affairs with America, and the Means of Conciliation* (London, 1778), 78, Franklin asserted, in relationship to the Albany Plan of Union, that the colonists should not be taxed by Parliament because "the Colonies have no Representatives in Parliament. . . . That it would be treating them as a conquered people, and not as true British subjects." For these reasons, he insisted a lower house be added to the Albany Plan's grand council. Pulteney was among the first to read back the Revolution onto the plan (though hardly the last), a tendency which has mercifully been corrected by Shannon. However, Pulteney is correct in seeing Franklin as raising the intertwined issues of sovereignty and institutional architecture.

22. *Boston Weekly News-Letter*, Jan. 19, 1769; Sharp, *A Declaration of the People's Natural Right*, 2–3, 27. David Ogden, a provincial jurist born in New Jersey and loyal to the Crown during the Revolution, also suggested a federated empire. His little-known plan, reproduced in Lorenzo Sabine's *Biographical Sketches of Loyalists of the American Revolution, with An Historical Essay*, suggests an American polity united to Britain by the king (Sabine, *Biographical Sketches of Loyalists*, II [1864; Port Washington, 1966], 124–125).

creasing dramatically, and their plans re-created the polity's philosophic and institutional foundations in order to keep up with these changes. As the population continued to expand and interest in securing orderly control of the western lands sharpened, confronting the threat posed by the French and Native Americans became critical to all Britons. The Native Americans' importance to this struggle for the interior drove some would-be reformers to consider expanding the empire beyond the frontier and beyond its Eurocentric population base.

. . .

An India for Indians?

In November 1753, a Cherokee delegation visited Williamsburg, Virginia, on a diplomatic mission. With war looming between Britain and France, colonial officials placed great significance on the visit of "the Emperor of the Cherokee Nation" and his empress "to renew the Treaty of Friendship with the Government." Greeted by the governor and council as friends and allies, the Cherokees were given numerous presents and taken to the theater, where they saw "the Play, (the Tragedy of Othello) and a Pantomime Performance, which gave them great Surprize . . . the fighting with naked Swords on the Stage, which occassioned the Empress to order some about her to go and prevent their killing one another." They next attended the King's Birthday celebrations, at which "the whole City was illuminated"; the emperor, empress, and their young prince attended "a very elegant Entertainment, at the Palace," where they joined "a brilliant Appearance of Ladies and Gentlemen" to dance and view the "beautiful Fireworks."[23]

This description expresses the hope of a polity remade in the nature of its relationship to the Native Americans on its farthest borders. Could there have been an India for Indians, the tribes royalized and treated as real polities subordinated within the empire? The planners who redesigned the empire on paper from time to time considered the Native American's situation within their newly imagined polity. Although early reformers seemed hardly aware of Native American issues, the conflict with France in the 1750s brought native-white relations to the fore. Two competing visions of native-European relations arose: one of imperial integration, with the Native American nations brought into the empire as subordinate polities; the other of physical separation by some sort of defensive barrier that would have allowed the western tribes to continue on in their traditional way of life.

From the time of the first contact with Powhatan in Virginia, and certainly since the visit of the four Indian "Kings" to London during Queen Anne's reign,

23. *Pennsylvania Gazette*, Jan. 16, 1753.

PLATE 11. *George II pewter Indian peace medal. 1757. By Edward Duffield. This medal commemorates the building of strong ties between George II and Native Americans.* Courtesy, Massachusetts Historical Society

there had been a tendency among officials and writers to rhetorically anglicize and Europeanize the Indian tribes' political structures. Again and again, royal officials described the tribes as subjects to the monarchy and anglicized their identities. "Headmen" became "princes" to Europeans, when, in fact, Indian power relations were radically different from those in contemporary European societies. As early as 1673, George Fox would describe the headman of Native Americans he encountered in Maryland as "Emperor." That the natives had very different power structures seems to have been entirely lost on many observers.[24]

Increased diplomatic contact between the native powers and the king's agents led repeatedly to the Indians' rhetorical and symbolic subjugation by imperial officials. British authorities believed that the Indians within New York who owned the Covenant Chain were somehow subjects within the empire. During a conflict with the French in upstate New York in 1687, Governor Thomas Dongan wrote Louis XIV's governor in Canada that the Indians were "his Matys of Great Britain's subjects and that he must not molest them." He further "sent the arms of his Royal Highness now his Majesty to bee put up in each [Indian] castle as far as Oneigra" in order to display his authority in the northern wilderness. For Europeans, the exchange of symbolic gifts, particularly gifts from the royal family, made visible the hierarchical imperial order.[25]

24. Clayton Colman Hall, ed., *Narratives of Early Maryland, 1633–1684* (New York, 1910), 404–405. For a modern consideration of these Indian "Kings," see Eric Hinderaker, "The 'Four Indian Kings' and the Imaginative Construction of the First British Empire," *WMQ*, 3d Ser., LVI (1996), 487–526.

25. See Milton W. Hamilton, *Sir William Johnson, Colonial American, 1715–1763* (Port

The natives apparently did not understand these exchanges this way and did not see themselves as subjects in the word's European sense. The Native Amercian habit of referring to the king as a parent sometimes confused the issue. Umpachenee, a Stockbridge Indian headman, once stated that "the King of England had declared himself to the Indians as their Father" during a meeting with colonists. But Native Americans understood patriarchal motifs quite differently than Britons, coming as they did from matrilineal societies where maternal uncles played as much a role as fathers in raising male children. The tribes did not generally perceive that recognizing the king in this way made them subjects, which in part explains why the Covenant Chain eventually ruptured. In 1761, with the Covenant partially resurrected, the leaders of the Five Nations told the famed Indian agent Sir William Johnson that "the death of the Great King George must be a very severe loss to his people," "his people" apparently not including them.[26]

Other Britons living in that same moment of crisis during the Seven Years' War began thinking about the Native Americans' place in the imperial order. Henry McCulloh understood their importance to the French position in North America, and, in *Proposals for Uniting the English Colonies*, he called for an integration of the tribes into the empire. "At least," he wrote, "Twelve Thousand Pounds Sterling *per Annum*" needed to be committed to the Five Nations, Creek, Cherokee, and other major tribes to assure their loyalty in wartime. He realized their allegiance was the key to the struggle for the North American interior.[27]

The war, followed closely by Pontiac's Rebellion, encouraged more reform writers to address the issue. Although a wide variety of possibilities appeared apart from the existing structure of trade and diplomacy as the tools of empire, they essentially flowed in two channels: those who would separate the colonists from the natives and those who would integrate them into the empire and create an India for them.

Several writers suggested full separation or barrier plans. In 1754–1755, a Briton

---

Washington, N.Y., 1976), 46; "Gov. Dongan's Report on the Province of New-York," Feb. 22, 1687, Journal of George Fox, in E. B. O'Callaghan, ed., *The Documentary History of the State of New-York*, 4 vols. (Albany, 1850), I, 93–118.

26. Shekomeko diary, Apr. 29, 1745, Records of the Moravian Mission to the Indians of North America, box 111, folder 1, Moravian Archives, Bethlehem, Pa.; Shannon, *Indians and Colonists at the Crossroads of Empire*, esp. 1–50; Fred Anderson, *Crucible of War: The Seven Years' War and the Fate of Empire in British North America, 1754–1766* (New York, 2000), 11–76, 453–471; Milton W. Hamilton, ed., *The Papers of Sir William Johnson*, X (Albany, N.Y., 1951), 218–219.

27. [McCulloh], *Proposals for Uniting the English Colonies*, 29.

named Josiah Tucker apparently advocated a one-mile-wide no-man's-land, extended along the colonies' western border. His intent was to keep the Indians from the colonists, but the effect would have been a preserve for Native Americans and a physical limitation on European settlement. These natives would be nominally subjects to the king but, in fact, left in benevolent isolation.[28]

The Reverend Mr. Hartwick, a New Yorker and contemporary of the famed royal Indian agent Sir William Johnson, presented a more detailed but equally impractical version of this border-barrier model. He recommended that "a Circling Line might be improved and at convenient Places and Distances Forts and Towns erected" along with "a Borroagh Grave or Guard a limit settled at Camp Johnson, at Oswego, at Lake Erie and at Ohio." These new entities would be "immediates that is independents of the Respective Governments but only depending on his Majesty's Orders, and only accountable to him." This type of militarized, royalized frontier, Hartwick continued, "is the Method, by which the German Emperors have preserved their Extensive Territories against the Incursions of the Barbarians . . . it doth not signify, to claim and even conquer large territories, if you can not keep them, and you cannot keep them except you can settle them." Again, the cause was fear of the natives and the French, but the effect would have been a native preserve in the west. Indian agent John Stuart apparently considered a similar, but smaller, preserve in the early 1770s in reaction to further white colonization west of the Appalachians.[29]

Although the idea of a native preserve never received much backing, the Proclamation Line declared after the Seven Years' War was a paper version of these plans. The proclamation, based on a plan drawn early in 1763, created no civil government for whites in the newly conquered western territories, leaving military authorities in charge. The natives, though nominally British subjects, would be left to their own devices. Indeed, British officials continually assured the natives that "the English have no intention to make Settlements in your Hunting Country beyond the Allegheny hills."[30] But the white settlers kept coming, and

28. Labaree et al., eds., *Papers of Benjamin Franklin*, V, 411n.

29. "Reverend Mr. Hartwick to Sir. William Johnson . . . Staatsborough the 18th Janury 1756," in O'Callaghan, ed., *Documentary History of the State of New-York*, IV, 294–295; Snapp, "An Enlightened Empire," *Albion*, XXXIII (2001), 399n; Jack M. Sosin, *Whitehall and the Wilderness: The Middle West in British Colonial Policy, 1760–1775* (Lincoln, Neb., 1961), 188–189.

30. John Richard Alden, *John Stuart and the Southern Colonial Frontier* (Ann Arbor, 1944), 241, 241n; Verner Crane, ed., "Hints relative to the Division and Government of the Conquered and Newly Acquired Countries in America," *Mississippi Valley Histori-*

the Indians repeatedly asked the imperial agents to enforce the Line. It was designed, as the Mohawk Tyorhansere and the Oneida Canaghaguieson explained through Sir William Johnson, "to ascertain and establish our Limitts and prevent those intrusions and encroachments of which we had so long and loudly complained." This boundary never worked properly, leading the two Six Nations representatives and numerous other natives to note "that the line may not be strictly observed" by the provinces' land-hungry white population. The Proclamation Line represented one end of the range of imagined imperial relationships with the Native Americans.[31]

The other option explored was the native tribes' formal political integration into the empire. McCulloh hinted about such an imperial arrangement in the 1750s; it was suggested in the Plan of 1764, presented in the declining moments of Pontiac's Rebellion, and eventually advocated by several key Indian agents. In fact, the Plan of 1764 called for a "beloved man" to be elected by the natives to guard imperial interests. Oaths of allegiance to the Crown and a British-modeled legal system would be established. In other words, the plan laid the foundation for a multiracial imperium modeled on the multicultural one that had come into existence in the seventeenth and eighteenth centuries.[32] Indian testimony would be allowed in all cases, Indian property rights in the interior would be confirmed on an English model, and contact between the tribes and the empire would be normalized under "one general System."[33]

Wilmot Vaughan's "Plan for the Better Government of British America, 1769," provided a political sketch for just such an empire. That plan called for "an Indian council" that would sit at the same time as the American parliament that Vaughan envisioned. The "Indians of every Nation" would send "deputies" to

------

cal Review, VIII (1922), 367–373; Daniel Richter, "Another 'Uneasy Connection': Native Americans, the Plan of 1764, and the British Empire That Never Was," 4 (unpublished paper supplied by the author); [Samuel Hazard, ed.], *Minutes of the Provincial Council of Pennsylvania, from the Organization to the Termination of the Proprietary Government* (Harrisburg, Pa., 1838–1852), VIII, 269.

31. "Deed Executed at Fort Stanwix November 5, 1768, Convened by Sir William Johnson and the Sachems and Chiefs of the Six Confederate Nations," in O'Callaghan, ed., *Documentary History of the State of New-York*, I, 587–588; Daniel Richter, "Another 'Uneasy Connection.'"

32. Richter, "Another 'Uneasy Connection'"; see also Alden, *John Stuart and the Southern Colonial Frontier*, 242–243; "Plan for Indian Affairs," in George Reese, ed., *The Official Papers of Francis Fauquier, Lieutenant Governor of Virginia, 1758–1768*, III, *1764–1768*, 1113.

33. "Plan for Indian Affairs," "Board of Trade to William Johnson," July 10, 1764, both in Reese, ed., *The Official Papers of Francis Fauquier*, III, *1764–1768*, 1110–1118.

this assembly, where they would "be maintained by the crown" for a week as they settled disputes and consulted with America's parliament. Vaughan, an aristocrat, was aware of the powerful role royal rituals played in establishing imperial authority. "As the native Americans," he astutely declared, "who have never been in England can have no notion of the magnificence and grandeur of . . . the British Court, it should seem requisite to display as much as possible of both on so important an Occassion." Like the officials in Virginia who brought their Cherokee visitors to the King's Birthday celebration in 1753, Vaughan understood the power of ritual to bind the participant to the empire.[34]

The dream of this political union of colonists and Native American tribes under the king was hardly confined to the plans. With the natives' assistance crucial to the prosecution of the war against the French in Canada in the late 1750s, the *New-York Gazette; or, the Weekly Post-Boy* began running a new print on its masthead. The print showed a colonist and a Native American holding an imperial crown over their heads, with a shield with arms situated between them. This represented the empire as some imagined it, as a union of native and newcomer under a benevolent king.[35]

Others imagined even more intimate relations binding the natives into the empire. As early as 1721, a report from the Board of Trade urged the king to encourage intermarriage between native populations and British subjects as a way of gaining military advantages over the French in Canada. Later, North Carolina governor Arthur Dobbs toyed with the idea of encouraging British women to marry Native Americans, literally using kinship to extend imperial power over the tribes. Perhaps he was aware of the level of intermarriage in New France that had helped expand French power in the American interior. If such a plan had been adopted, a very different empire might have emerged, and a common subject of Victorian novels might have been the tortured Anglo-Cherokee at Oxbridge trying to come to terms with his origins and identity as he struggled for acceptance in English high society.[36]

Might some form of integration have worked? The natives seem to have had a powerful faith in the monarch and monarchical power. From the time of Charles II's reign onward, they "desired that all Differences between the Indians and Your

34. Vaughan, "A Plan for the Better Government of British America, 1769," NYHS MSS, 33–35.

35. *New-York Gazette; or, the Weekly Post-Boy*, Dec. 5, 1757.

36. Robert V. Wells, *The Population of the British Colonies in America before 1776* (Princeton, N.J., 1975), 27; O'Callaghan, ed., *Documentary History of the State of New-York*, IV, 591–630; Snapp, "An Enlightened Empire," *Albion*, XXXIII (2001), 398.

Majesty's Subjects might be referred to Your Majesty's Royal Determination," as the Delaware Teedyuscung told Benjamin Franklin in the late 1750s. There was a history of appeals to royal authority by natives that stretched back to the Restoration period. Perhaps such an integrated polity might have thrived and avoided the abuses that defined Indian-white relations in nineteenth-century America.[37]

As it actually came to be, the Cherokee empress's reaction to *Othello* serves as a powerful metaphor for the experience of Native Americans with the empire. The empire's motifs, rituals, and institutions were haphazardly presented to them, to be embraced and loved. But what was real in this offering and what was an illusion was unclear. Could such a diverse but stable empire united in a common identity under one great monarch have come into being in North America and endured? Could a durable footing have been created for such a polity?

• • •

Counterfactual Speculations

By February 1789, all that was left for Benjamin Franklin was contemplation and remembrance. The astonishing achievements of a long and celebrated life — the rise from humble beginnings, early literary triumphs, international scientific fame, imperial influence, revolutionary leadership, diplomatic intimacy with Europe's crowned heads, a career capped by the role of elder statesman in the Constitutional Convention — were already becoming distant memories. He had begun to remember friends living and dead, experiments that ended with a jolt, a son found and lost, and he had begun to speculate over a road not taken long ago, when he was an ambitious subject in the first British empire.

"On Reflection," he said, "it now seems probable, that if the foregoing Plan [the Albany Plan of Union of 1754] or some thing like it, had been adopted and carried into Execution, the subsequent Separation of the Colonies from the Mother Country might not so soon have happened." Indeed, "the Mischiefs suffered on both sides" might have been put off until a later century. The united colonies, he speculated, would have been "sufficient to their own Defence," and thus an "Army from Britain, for that purpose would have been unnecessary." The extension of the British state's financial structure to the colonies as embodied in the Stamp Act would "not have existed, nor the other Projects for drawing a Revenue from America to Britain by Acts of Parliament, which were the cause of . . . such terrible Expence of Blood and Treasure." As Franklin knew, the 1754

37. Petition of Benjamin Franklin, n.d., in O'Callaghan, ed., *Documentary History of the State of New-York*, II, 447–448.

plan had failed. "It was," he remembered, "unanimously agreed to" by the Congress, but it died in the imperial political bureaucracy. "The Crown disapprov'd it" for having "too much Weight in the democratic Part of the Constitution; and every Assembly as having allow'd too much to Prerogative." And with it went a dream of a new, restructured empire. More than two hundred years later, we are left with the questions that grew from Franklin's lost dream.[38]

Why was the empire never reformed? Institutional incongruities alone would seem to have demanded it. Royal colonies, charter colonies, proprietary colonies, the absorbed kingdom of Scotland, the kingdom of Ireland, and England itself each had its own political and governmental order, creating myriad problems of imperial control. Why had a new empire able to contain the passions not appeared? Perhaps the failings were intellectual as well as political. Britain had as fine a group of political thinkers and institutional mechanics as any society. But their ability to deal with change and particularly what we call political economy was constrained by custom, history, transitory political issues, and a failure of philosophy.

The fatal flaw might have been that the plans for imperial reform centered on change in the empire's political structure rather than its political economy and financial structure. The demographic and commercial expansions were tied to a fantastic transformation in the Anglo-American world's financial structures. The demands of international warfare encouraged the creation of decentralized public and private credit markets in America. The ability to mortgage landed property at county loan offices created hundreds, if not thousands, of secondary micromarkets for that world-transforming invention, investment capital in the form of paper money. These new credit venues undermined the status of the elites who loaned hard money and who often had close ties to London. An inflated money supply thus indirectly threatened imperial institutional control.

Remarkably, while the assemblies and the governors quarreled and quarreled over paper money from 1690 forward, imperial officials failed to address the underlying problems in their empire's financial markets. Viewed from London, the empire had a sophisticated financial structure, one centered on the Bank of England's hard currency and the deficit spending system that allowed Britain to contain and ultimately best its far larger continental enemies, particularly France, in the imperial wars. The paper money emissions in America seemed a nuisance best dealt with by the imperial restrictions against colonial money supported by the London merchant community and enforced with vigor at the end of the

38. Labaree et al., eds., *Papers of Benjamin Franklin*, V, 417.

Seven Years' War. Throughout the eighteenth century, London authorities acted oblivious to the economic devastation wreaked on the provinces by fiscal policies that repeatedly inflated and then deflated colonial economies.

Beginning in the 1750s, some reformers tried to come to grips with this problem and imagine the empire on a new financial footing. But even they had no adequate plan to deal with the matter of political economy. Henry McCulloh understood that the colonies needed to be put on a sounder fiscal footing. He knew the cycle of paper money inflations and deflations had created chaos in the provinces, and he knew that the Currency Acts would create more unrest. However, he never offered more than a half-solution.[39] He recognized the need for an imperial currency but called for one whose use by provincials would be restricted to "the Payment of provincial Taxes, in the Payment of the Quit-rents to the Crown, and of the Customs, and . . . Payment of . . . provincial Troops." McCulloh and others knew that the colonial trade enriched the empire, but he consistently sought to link it to a modified mercantilist system within a more centralized polity. Even this sort of limited reform, bounded by McCulloh's neo-absolutist imperial vision, never gained support.[40]

Only the empire's most penetrating observers understood the broadest implications of the changes that were occurring, and only its sharpest minds offered solutions to the problems these changes caused. Late in 1765, Thomas Pownall and Benjamin Franklin, one a former imperial governor, the other the colonies' most famous public figure, together advocated a more workable resolution to the empire's smoldering crisis of political economy. On December 3, 1765, Pownall wrote to Thomas Hutchinson that "Ben Franklin and I are going this Morning to Lord Rockingham's on the subject of a Paper we have jointly given." It concerned "the procuring a general Paper currency for the Colonies by Authority of Government here and connected with the Bank of England." In essence, the plan called for a tax on money as a way of raising revenue and circumventing direct internal taxes like the Stamp Act. Initially, this plan got no visible support from the power structure. Eventually, however, Parliament took up a similar idea.[41]

39. Jack P. Greene, "'A Dress of Horror': Henry McCulloh's Objections to the Stamp Act," *The Huntington Library Quarterly*, XXVI (1963), 253–262. The piece contains a transcription of McCulloh's "General Thoughts".

40. [McCulloh], *Proposals for Uniting the English Colonies*, 23.

41. Pownall to Thomas Hutchinson, Dec. 3, 1765, Thomas Hutchinson Letterbook, I, 115, microfilm, MHS. For discussion, see Edmund S. Morgan, *The Challenge of the American Revolution* (New York, 1976), 38n; V. W. Crane, "Benjamin Franklin and the Stamp

For one moment, those close to the wellsprings of power discussed the issue of imperial financial reform. In May 1767, William Strahan reported to Philadelphian David Hall that debate in Parliament over raising a colonial revenue had taken an unexpected, and welcome, turn. "The Chancellor of the Exchequer," he noted, "made a long speech" declaring the need for revenue from America, "yet such as should be as little as possible burdensome to them, or be attended with some advantage." The MPs debated modifying the Navigation Acts, but Prime Minister George Grenville slighted the duties that would be collected "as Trifles." He made a radical suggestion instead "and proposed emitting a Paper Currency for America by Act of Parliament to be issued on Loan, the Interest to be disposed of by Parliament." For that moment, it seemed that this solution might gain support and create imperial revenue from the provinces in a manner less volatile than by direct taxation. But Parliament became sidetracked by other questions, and the moment was lost.[42]

A year later, a Hartford, Connecticut, writer expressed much the same idea about the provinces' economic growth and political economy. The king, he informed his readers, was in "no way offended at the Economy of the Americans, —is much pleased that they should provide for themselves, and that no Part of his Subjects should be oppressed by other Parts." He noted that there had been "strange Confusion about Paper Currency, some have petition'd for, others against it" for some time. He assured his readers that they were to have "a Bank as they have in Ireland and Scotland." "Cosmopolite," author of *A Plan for Conciliating the Jarring Political Interests of Great Britain and Her North American Colonies*, also made vague calls for currency reform. Another planner during the imperial crisis declared that it was impossible to restrict Americans from having a foreign trade. He had no plan for currency reform, but he did call on imperial officials to embrace provincial economic growth and all that came with it. The reform, of course, never came to pass. The empire's financial structure remained as fragmented in 1774 as it had been fifty years earlier.[43]

Could the empire have survived with a centralized financial structure that al-

---

Act," Colonial Society of Massachusetts, *Publications*, XXXII, *Transactions, 1933–1937* (Boston, 1937), 56–77.

42. William Strahan to David Hall, May 16, 1767, William Strahan Letters, HSP.

43. *Massachusetts Gazette and Boston News-Letter*, May 5, 1768; [Cosmopolite], *A Plan for Conciliating the Jarring Political Interests of Great Britain and Her North American Colonies . . .* (London, 1775); *A Plan to Reconcile Great Britain and Her Colonies and Preserve the Dependency of America* (London, 1774), 3, 11.

lowed for economic expansion and the creation of microcapital markets? Could the divisive questions of sovereignty and institutional structure have been somehow alleviated by a controlled but expansionist fiscal policy with a central bank and a gold-backed paper currency? Could the demographic expansion onto which historians have pinned so much in terms of understanding economic growth and political change in the period been somehow harnessed by the empire to its own ends?

The answer is a firm "perhaps." If a massive, centralized currency could have been funneled through the treasury to the assemblies and the interest or taxes split between the assemblies and the imperial bureaucracy, a financial bond and a political-financial link would have been created and circumvented much of the tension over finances and sovereignty. The assemblies would have become an extension of the treasury department whose power flowed from London rather than acted as a bulwark against it. The disputes between the provinces and London would have diminished, since the colonies' economic expansion would have benefited the imperial state as well as its economy. A centralized paper currency might well have also created a different footing for war funding and debt retirement, thus avoiding the crushing debt that led to the Stamp Act. The societal divisions that became linked to the provinces' financial boom-bust cycle might never have arisen.

Financial reform itself, no matter how comprehensive, would not have saved the empire without marriage to real political change, and there, again, was the rub. Even those aware of the enormous positive potential of the colonies' explosive growth called for hierarchical political structures. McCulloh was the first of such thinkers, but others emerged during the imperial crisis. Cosmopolite demanded free trade for the colonists even as he advocated new assembly structures in which half of the members would be royally appointed. It was a plan more in line with McCulloh's neoabsolutism than the federated structure that came to be associated with free and inflated economies. Whether such an Anglo-American polity might have endured was never tested, although polities of similar character have emerged in East Asia in the twentieth century. Only Thomas Pownall, it seems, had the vision to imagine a political order truly divorced from mercantilism, one that used the provincials' commercial and demographic expansion as a binder of a newly imagined Atlantic British imperial polity. The speed of change in the empire confounded the reformers' plans.[44]

44. [Cosmopolite], *A Plan for Conciliating*. The plan encouraged economic growth that would have helped consolidate imperial political control.

Other factors explain the reformers' failures. The plans floated to change the empire's institutional structure originated primarily with individuals acting on their own rather than within the state's bureaucratic structures. These people were often connected to or part of those structures, but they were trying to drive reform from below or outside, without official endorsement. The ideas for provincial reorganization introduced by Franklin and Hutchinson at the Albany Congress, in fact, far exceeded its imperial-derived directive to coordinate a policy toward Native Americans and restore the Covenant Chain. This helps to explain why London rejected it and the colonial assemblies ignored it. Only twice — in the early 1750s, with war with France looming, and in the mid-1760s, when the aftermath of that war unhinged the empire — was there any real consideration of the plans by those in power. In both cases, events and entrenched interests conspired against change.[45]

Those with the power to actually implement such change — the London bureaucrats and their supporters in Parliament — had little to gain overall by any of these plans. All these designs consolidated governmental authority in a manner that would have either curtailed the metropolis's patronage opportunities or created a legislative body that would have institutionalized the fragmentation of sovereignty. Most of the plans essentially called for a cadet parliament in America whose ties would be directly, or at least in part, to the king and whose members would have expected a say, if not control, in the distribution of patronage positions in the provinces. Moreover, none of the plans addressed the problem of multiple officeholding in the colonies. Had that practice been curtailed, the imperial state's reach would have automatically been greatly extended, and more families would have been vested in the empire for acknowledgment of their place and honor. Together with real financial reform, it might well have been enough to hold the empire together. But it never came to pass.

Whatever speculations we may offer, they pale beside the spectacular flights of imagination of 250 years ago, the plans written by the men who dreamed of a new empire. Among them were the first Anglo-Americans to think of actively participating in remaking the fundamental law and institutions, revolutionaries and counterrevolutionaries in the same breath. But their hope for revolution was a British one, not the American and republican upheaval that ultimately engulfed them all.

45. Shannon, *Indians and Colonists at the Crossroads of Empire*, 205–233, esp. 218–219.

Dinner in Marseilles: Dreams, Realities, and the Fate of Empires

For British officials, 1784 was the year of bitter realization. The empire in America was half gone. The frozen north and the sweltering islands remained, but the portion filled with Britons and most like the home islands in flora and fauna had slipped away. In the wake of this crushing blow, two former imperial governors and would-be reformers, Thomas Pownall and Henry Ellis, found themselves at dinner together in the south of France. It was one of those meetings into which much can be read about what had occurred and what would follow.[46]

For our purposes, it is sufficient to see both men as representatives of opposing ideas of imperial reform in the 1750s and 1760s, either of which, if enacted, might have saved the empire and avoided the American Revolution. Pownall repre-sented a neoliberal empire, one of commerce and equality. This was the empire that might have harnessed the colonies' growth to the common good. Ellis, a Scotsman and the onetime governor of Georgia (1757–1760), held neoabsolutist views about colonial government. If his plans had been put into action, the ma-chinery, political or military, might have been in place to force taxation on the colonies. Ellis had urged a crackdown the year before Lexington and Concord; it was already too late then, but a real show of force in 1765 might have yielded a different result. Both sorts of plans had existed as possibilities, but the London government lacked both the foresight and the will to follow either path.[47]

All of those politically active in the period, writer-reformers, preachers main-taining royal divinity, rioter, and slave sought to assert or establish their vision of royal order. Viewed together, their actions made visible the problem at the core of Britain's American empire. King and constitution were subjectively under-stood, not only within the empire as a whole but even within individual polities and communities. With awareness of this came danger to the polity as a whole. That threat came not in the form of republicanism, democracy, or even economic liberalization per se. The threat was the king himself, the monarch of American imaginations, demigod and friend, constitutional broker and well of sovereignty, symbol through which values intersected. A new structure on either the model of Pownall or Ellis might have contained the confusion and channeled the energy in a manner that strengthened the empire. But it was not to be.

---

46. This account is entirely based on John Shy's superb piece, "The Spectrum of Im-perial Possibilities: Henry Ellis and Thomas Pownall, 1763–1775," in Shy, *A People Numer-ous and Armed: Reflections on the Military Struggle for American Independence*, rev. ed. (Ann Arbor, 1990), 43–80.

47. Ibid., 51.

A few sentences in a commonplace book kept by a young Virginian in the 1760s and early 1770s aptly summarized the empire's problems. "It is," he wrote, "as dangerous and almost as criminal with Princes, to have the Power to [do] good, as to have the Will to do Evil." In the American provinces, the danger was perhaps as much what it was imagined that the monarch could do as what he was actually doing. But the idea was the same; an empire of love was a dangerous thing. In another spot, the same writer declared that "The King's and the People's rights never agree better than by not being spoken of." James Madison wrote these words that revealed what had already occurred and what was to come. The Founder was, as a boy, also a scribe and a prophet.[48]

48. William T. Hutchinson and William M. E. Rachal, eds., *The Papers of James Madison*, I (Chicago, 1962), 8.

PART THREE
A FUNERAL FIT FOR A KING

．　．　．　．
　．　．　．
　．　．
　．

The fragmentation of patriarchy and the problems of imperial control that manifested themselves in the 1740s led to a crisis in the 1760s. The aftermath of the Seven Years' War saw the London government attempt to extend the central state's tax and financial structure to the imperial fringe, to British America. The resulting resistance revealed that multiple perceptions of the king and constitution existed within both the empire and the provinces.

The initial consequence of this subjective understanding was a rhetorical flight to the king by the beleaguered colonists. They demanded that the imperial father of their imagination restrain a tyrannical Parliament. The king's failure to do so led to a collapse of royal institutional legitimacy in 1773 and 1774.

An iconoclasm followed this collapse. The practices and symbols that maintained the imperial order were thrown down and trampled. Those who would support the old order were attacked and humiliated by crowds controlled by committees and congresses that invoked the authority of the people to legitimate their actions. Symbolic regicides conducted in numerous communities announced the end of royal America and the first British empire to a startled world.

9

HISTORY FULFILLED,

HISTORY BETRAYED ·

.   .   .   .

.   .

.

Dream as they might, the empire's Cassandras could gain no formal backing to reform the sprawling institutional framework that in 1763 stretched from Scotland to the West Indies to the frozen Canadian tundra. Their failures foretold a constitutional disaster, though it did not become evident until 1776 that they had been prophets worthy of a Greek tragedy. It was not simply that the empire was institutionally unwieldy or unable to absorb the Native American tribes or control population movement and economic expansion. The problem was deeper. Though Americans emotionally pledged allegiance to king and country, they understood the monarch's nature, the British constitution, imperial history, and the state subjectively. There was not simply a colonial view; ethnicity, region, religion, status, and economic circumstances had fragmented understanding of the imperial state's structure.

With the Stamp Act Crisis, the incongruence between royal political culture as experienced in the colonies and the imperial state's structure as understood in London became apparent. Parliament's persistent efforts to tax the colonists caused the empire to fall into disorder over the questions of the British state's actual structure and the monarch's role in it. Ironically, from our perspective, it was the monarch on whom colonials pinned their hopes of evading a rupture they never desired. The logic imparted by royal political culture convinced many provincials that the monarch existed constitutionally apart from Parliament and was a location of sovereignty in his own right.

Faith in the Protestant prince, and a related fear that the crisis amounted to some kind of popish or Jacobite plot, explain much of the imperial crisis's chronology. The continuing tensions over taxation and authority led colonists to proclaim the monarch to be the empire's central link and the chief defender against a grand conspiracy to somehow establish popish government on both sides of the Atlantic. As the crisis continued, though, manipulation of imperial history and symbols became more pronounced, creating doubt about the meaning of the empire itself and the relationship of imperial concepts and components. By 1773, all that remained was faith in the king. When the weight of events—the Boston Port Bill, the Quebec Act, the widespread introduction of troops—implicated George III, the political and emotional apparatus that maintained the empire began to collapse in a rolling cascade that ended in sacrilege and iconoclasm.

Seen this way, the imperial crisis seems more British, not only in the sense that it threatened the empire as a whole or that the colonists claimed the rights of Englishmen. Placing a kind of benevolent royalism and antipopery among the ideological constructs that can be used to explain behavior among large numbers of colonists who ended up rebelling makes the upheaval that began in 1764 much more like earlier British upheavals stretching back to the Civil Wars in its internal ideological and emotional dynamic. In all cases, an aroused Protestant population sought to defend its political rights and spiritual inherence from popish corruption that threatened the realm and ultimately infiltrated the ruling dynasty.

· · ·

Love, Patriarchy, and the Imperial Constitution

During the Stamp Act Crisis, "C. P.," a New York broadside writer, asked George III to allow "an unworthy, but loyal subject to approach your Majesty's throne in this manner, as your ministers will not let me do it in any other." He forcefully declared that he was ready to "lose my life in . . . defence of your royal person and family and also of my country." He asserted, as did many others, the right of American assemblies to tax the various provinces. He also made a series of declarations that, although typical to the period, are almost completely unexplored in terms of their constitutional ramifications. America's sovereign was "your Majesty," of course, and "the pretence of your parliament of Great-Britain to tax your American subjects, is an absolute insult upon your Majesty's understanding, and a robbery of your sole right to govern them."[1]

The idea that C. P. expressed, mainly that the king was a location of imperial sovereignty, had developed in the decades between 1690 and 1760. That fact is the key to understanding the imperial crisis's contours between 1764 and 1774. Clearly, some among the colonists had come to perceive the empire as a federated body of states united by and in the king. Provincials understood the king as the imperial constitution's upholder, much as the Supreme Court upholds our own constitution today. Provincials' royal political culture and confusion over the meaning of British constitutional thought concerning mixed government

1. C. P., *A Letter to His Most Excellent Majesty, George the Third, King of Great-Britain . . .* ([New York, 1765]), broadside 102, no. 40b, Library of Congress Broadsides.

had gradually fractured the Glorious Revolution's conceptual settlement in the colonies. The Stamp Act opened what had been invisible fissures in constitutional understanding. Forced to adapt intellectually by the continuing pressures over taxation and sovereignty, provincials quickly abandoned any pretense of parliamentary supremacy in the empire and began voicing faith that the king they loved could somehow save America from legislative tyranny. Their charters, they came to insist, derived from the king's absolute right to the lands of the empire and embodied the values of the Protestant political culture. In certain ways, the imperial crisis between 1764 and 1774 can be understood as a flight to the king's love and justice.[2]

The journey to the monarch began in the immediate aftermath of the victory in the great war against the French that had swelled British patriotism on both sides of the Atlantic. In 1763, the empire seemed to be on firmer ground than ever. The London authorities, however, knew that war debt threatened to overwhelm the state's finances. They turned to the idea of taxing the American provinces to raise revenue, albeit with taxes that, by English standards, were slight.

The provincials' violent responses to the ministerial initiatives reveal deeply held values and perceptions. The deepest of these was an intense attachment to George III that grew from the complex intersection of historical and constitutional thinking with the provincial cult of monarchy. This attachment took on momentous meaning as colonists turned to their king for political salvation. As counterintuitive as it may seem, the love of the king and country reached its zenith at the split second before imperial collapse. As the imperial crisis progressed, the yawning gulf between the imperial passions and state institutions broadened still more until the entire structure came down.

In 1765, many in the provincial elite accepted the King-in-Parliament's supremacy. James Otis, the most prominent early leader of resistance to the stamp tax, did not question Parliament's right to rule the colonies but rather maintained that the House of Commons had breached the national constitution in this

2. Jerrilyn Greene Marston, *King and Congress: The Transfer of Political Legitimacy, 1774–1776* (Princeton, N.J., 1987), 36, hints at this flight to the king. The literature on the empire and its constitution is, of course, massive, and yet I believe it still quite incomplete. The standard works in America include Gordon S. Wood's *Creation of the American Republic, 1776–1787* (Chapel Hill, N.C., 1969), and Willi Paul Adams's *First American Constitutions: Republican Ideology and the Making of the State Constitutions in the Revolutionary Era* (Lanham, Md., 2001). Both focus on bicameral legislatures for the seemingly logical reason that such structures predominated eventually in the republic and in the individual states. However, a close examination of the period before 1776 and the revolutionary period suggests the unicameralist's significance.

particular case. Virginian Richard Bland, writing in *An Inquiry into the Rights of the British Colonies*, said he would "not dispute the Authority of the Parliament, which is without Doubt supreme within the Body of the Kingdom, and cannot be abridged by any other Power." He went further still, declaring that Parliament, as the empire's location of sovereignty, could "by a full Exertion of their Power . . . deprive the Colonists of the Freedom and other Benefits of the *British* Constitution." Such an extreme notion went well beyond even contemporary assertions of parliamentary power.[3]

Pennsylvanian John Dickinson tempered his words, but he acknowledged in *Letters from a Farmer in Pennsylvania* that "we are but parts of a *whole*; and therefore there must exist a power somewhere, to preside, and preserve the connection in due order." The South Carolina assemblymen declared they would "submit most dutifully at all times to acts of Parliament" even as they prayed that the same body would not tax them without representation. Maryland assemblymen petitioning against the Stamp Act reaffirmed that "their Subordination to the Parliament was universally acknowledged." This was the constitutional orthodoxy as understood in London and in the House of Commons.[4]

The imperial crisis's continuation revealed that acceptance of parliamentary supremacy had been socially limited and that other perceptions of king and constitution had arisen during the British peace. By 1767, a fierce debate over representation had erupted that provided future generations of Americans with a slogan, "No taxation without representation," through which they could comprehend the Revolution's origins. With its emphasis on localism and the assemblies, that debate has fitted neatly into American history. The pressure of the imperial

---

3. James Otis, *The Rights of the British Colonies Asserted and Proved* (Boston, 1764). For a useful discussion of Otis's contradictory views, see H. Trevor Colbourn, *The Lamp of Experience: Whig History and the Intellectual Origins of the American Revolution* (Chapel Hill, N.C., 1965), 70–73; Richard Bland, *An Inquiry into the Rights of the British Colonies . . .* (Williamsburg, Va., 1766), 21, 26.

4. [John Dickinson], *Letters from a Farmer in Pennsylvania, to the Inhabitants of the British Colonies* (Philadelphia, 1768), 7. For another example, see Robert A. Rutland, ed., *The Papers of George Mason, 1725–1792*, I, *1749–1778* (Chapel Hill, N.C., 1970), 67. Mason declared in 1766, "We do not deny the supreme Authority of Great Britain over her Colonys, but it is a Power which a wise Legislature will exercise with extreme Tenderness and Caution." South Carolina assemblymen: "The First Remonstrance from South Carolina against the Stamp Act to Charles Garth, Esq. . . ," Sept. 4, 1764, MSS of Christopher Gadsden, South Carolina Historical Society Archive Online. Maryland assemblymen: "London, 26th of Febry 1766, Stamp Act Papers," *Maryland Historical Magazine*, VI (1911), 286.

crisis, though, also led to other constitutional innovations now ignored but at the time central to the defense of colonials' liberties and properties. Contemporaries turned to the king in that moment, with a mixture of hope, affection, and fear, to try to solve the crisis. In so doing, they completely abandoned the perception that strong kings tended to threaten liberty.

The Protestant king apart from Parliament and acting as the British constitution's sovereign broker had been evident in the print culture before the imperial crisis. A writer to the *Gentleman's Magazine* in 1757 described the king's prerogative as "a Fulness of Power to cause all Laws to be put in Force. He is the natural Judge of all Differences arising between Man and Man, and the Courts of Justice are his Courts. . . . And the power he has is good and natural, as without it we should be striving for Power among ourselves." Three years later, Massachusetts governor Francis Bernard said to his charges, "Our gracious Sovereign is not more illustrious in protecting the Persons and Estates of His Subjects against the common Enemy, than in vindicating their Rights and Liberties against civil Encroachments."[5]

The love of the king inculcated during the long British peace as a means of binding a dispersed empire together became, in the new context that emerged after 1763, a danger to London's power. Provincials raised in the imperial Protestant political culture saw the king as a sovereign apart from the rest of the constitutional structure, with the ability to correct its deficiencies and rein in those who exceeded their authority. As early as 1764, the New York Assembly proclaimed its confidence that George III would protect its rights. The Hanoverians, as Protestant monarchs, had "long been the guardians of British liberty." The king, the assemblymen were convinced, would continue to "protect our rights, as to prevent our falling into the abject state of being forever hereafter incapable of doing what can merit, either his distinction, or approbation." Writings carried in the *Pennsylvania Gazette* in August 1769 described this perception of the monarch. "Kings are," it was announced, "in all free Countries, the Executors of the Laws, the great Guardians of the Liberties of the People, and the Administrators of Justice. This, amongst us, is made part of the *Coronation Oath*. Our Kings swear . . . to do Justice to their People. . . . For this Reason is He invested with Authority." It is a perception that belies the historical reasoning that had portrayed overreaching monarchs as the primary threat to liberty.[6]

The same benevolent king that drove slave conspiracies and agrarian unrest

5. *Boston News-Letter*, Dec. 29, 1757–Jan. 5, 1758, Aug. 14, 1760.

6. *South-Carolina Gazette* (Charleston), Nov. 26, 1764; *Pennsylvania Gazette* (Philadelphia), Aug. 10, 1769.

now took on a critical importance in colonial political imagination. The New England Baptist Isaac Skillman sketched these sentiments. "For the brightest gem," he declared, "which the King of *England* wears in the *British* Crown, is that majesty, trust, and confidence, which the *Americans* invest him with, as the King and Guardian of their Rights and Liberties." This understanding spread widely even as colonial agents in London tried to explain the metropole's constitutional settlement to beleaguered provincials. Maryland's agent wrote to his constituents, "The Crown was but a Part of the supreme Power of the Realm . . . by no Construction cou'd be deem'd to have granted that which he had no Power to grant, that which belonged to the supreme legislative power." This writer correctly relayed the historical and constitutional precedents that established parliamentary supremacy, but he transmitted them to a different political culture, one that had been oriented in a decidedly royalist way.[7]

The danger of this monarchical love became apparent in 1766. In that year, Massachusetts's Governor Bernard, only too eager to represent the empire in the person of a loving king six years before, now reported with alarm that Bay Colonists had declared the sole imperial authority they answered to was "the King, and him only in the Person of the Governor." In the same year, South Carolinian Christopher Gadsden lamented that the Stamp Act Congress had "desired to lay the matter before Parliament" since "we neither hold our rights from them or the Lords." He wished instead that "we had stopt at the Declarations and Petition to the King," for that was the central imperial tie. In 1768, Boston Congregational minister Andrew Croswell, in a bitter attack on the Church of England specifically and imperial policies generally, asked, "Who can tell but our Assembly's address, so loyal . . . may touch the heart of the King? *Save Lord, let the King hear us when we call.*"[8]

In 1769, the Virginia burgesses voiced the same perception of the monarch's role in the constitutional structure. Assuring the king of their "firm attachment to your Majesty and your royal ancestours," they proclaimed themselves "ready

7. [Isaac Skillman], *An Oration on the Beauties of Liberty; or, The Essential Rights of the Americans. . .* (Boston, 1773), 60; "March 5th, 1766, Stamp Act Papers," *Maryland Historical Magazine*, VI (1911), 295, 296.

8. Edmund S. Morgan, *The Challenge of the American Revolution* (New York, 1976), 9 n. 10; The Papers of Sir Francis Bernard, IV, Letter Book, 203, Harvard University, Cambridge, Mass.; "Christopher Gadsden to Charles Garth, Agent of the Colony, Charles Town, So. Carolina, Dec. 2nd, 1765," in R. W. Gibbes, ed., *Documentary History of the American Revolution . . . 1764–1776* (New York, 1855), 9; Andrew Croswell, *Observations on Several Passages in a Sermon Preached by William Warburton, Lord Bishop of Gloucester . . .* (Boston, 1768), 21.

at any time, to sacrifice our lives and fortunes in defense of your Majesty's sacred person and government." Their loyalty declared, they called on George III to intervene against the Parliament's "dangerous invasions of dearest privileges." They beseeched their "King and Father, to avert from your faithful . . . subjects of America those miseries which must necessarily be the consequence of such measures." Although the views expressed colonial Protestant political culture's logic, in terms of the empire as a whole, they suggested a constitutional innovation based emotionally, at least, on a form of benevolent royalism.[9]

The constitutional meaning of the affectionate tie to the monarch soon became clear: king above Parliament, king as father, king as honest broker. As late as 1774, a New Haven, Connecticut, writer declared, "*This* is a dispute between the parliament of Great Britain, and the Colonies. We have no controversy with the king; nor in the least, dispute his regal authority over us." The real point in contention was "whether his majesty's legislative body in Great Britain has a right to exercise sovereign authority over his majesty's legislative Assemblies in the Colonies." They believed Parliament's actions constituted an assault on the Glorious Revolution's settlement as understood in the colonies, where the empire was now perceived as a federated body of states united in the king and a shared commitment to Protestant political culture.[10]

What is perhaps most interesting about these developments in political thought is how far they were behind the popular curve. The constitutional logic of imperial political rites seems to have been obvious to a broad swath of the population from the crisis's beginning. When the people of Middleboro, Massachusetts, petitioned their representative concerning the Stamp Act in 1765, they declared themselves "True and Loyal Subjects to our King"; of Parliament, all they would say was that they held it in the "highest esteem." Bay Colonist Harbottle Dorr, having read Governor Bernard's comment in the Boston newspapers that "in an Empire, extended and diversified as that of *Great-Britain*, there must be a supreme Legislature, to which all other Powers must be subordinate," responded in the margin, "Now the wolf shews himself notwithstanding his sheeps cloathing." When Buckingham County, Virginia, freeholders sought to explain their actions in 1776, they declared that, in 1765, "we felt our hearts warmly attached to the King of *Great Britain* and the Royal family" but looked upon Parliament and the imperial bureaucracy as "fountains from which the bitter waters flowed." King apart from Parliament, an institutionally unfixed patriarchy — a

9. *South Carolina and American General Gazette* (Charleston), July 17–20, 1769.

10. Samuel Sherwood, *A Sermon, Containing, Scriptural Instructions to Civil Rulers, and All Free-Born Subjects* . . . (New Haven, Conn., [1774]), 30n.

central result of the colonies' royalization—became a vehicle that drove the imperial crisis on a constitutional level between 1764 and 1773–1774.[11]

The royal political culture's role in creating this mindset seems obvious. For some seventy-odd years, authority had been represented in the royal person alone, without reference to Parliament, in the rites and the rituals of power that maintained the imperial order in America. The linkage between the ritual practice in the imperial political culture and the provincial separation of king from Parliament in the defense of the colonists' rights is suggested in the protest banner carried by several hundred little boys in Boston during the Stamp Act Crisis, "on which was [written] King, Pitt and Liberty." That banner expressed the lesson of their political culture, recognized by Francis Bernard when he took up the Bay Colony's governorship. George III "is acknowledged to be the Maintainer of the Privileges of His Subjects, and the People are become the Supporters of the Prerogative of the Crown."[12]

This assertion of the king's role in the imperial constitution came to be linked to the claim that the colonial charters embodied the fundamental law of the empire, each a little Magna Charta in its own right. These charters had, with the exception of Georgia's, been issued either before the Glorious Revolution or in its aftermath and came directly from the monarchy. The absolutist-derived practice of relating the king's person to the entire physical empire became the foundation of this defense of the meaning of their charter rights. The colonists insisted that, as Arthur Lee put it, "all territory taken possession of in any manner whatsoever, by the king's subjects, rests absolutely in him." Thomas Hutchinson cogently observed such a perception existed only in "absolute Monarchies."[13]

Pennsylvania jurist James Wilson seconded that the charters derived solely from the monarchy based on possession by discovery and conquest. The assumption beneath this was absolutist: all lands in the empire were vested in the king.

11. Thomas Weston, *History of the Town of Middleboro, Massachusetts* (Boston, 1906), 107; Harbottle Dorr Collections of Annotated Massachusetts Newspapers, 1765–1776, reel 1, 1765–1767, 95, MHS; "The Address and Instructions of the Freeholders of the Said County [Buckingham County, Virginia]," in Pauline Maier, *American Scripture: Making the Declaration of Independence* (New York, 1997), app. B, 226–229.

12. Peter Shaw, *American Patriots and the Rituals of Revolution* (Cambridge, Mass., 1981), 10, 85.

13. J. C. D. Clark, *The Language of Liberty, 1660–1832* (Cambridge, 1994), 107. Clark's probing along these lines of inquiry are among the most useful writings on the imperial crisis in recent years. Late in the imperial crisis, Jefferson would use the idea of a feudal contract that predated the Norman invasion. See [Thomas Jefferson], *A Summary View of the Rights of British America* (Williamsburg, Va., 1774), and Clark, 107–108.

Colonists, Wilson declared, "held the lands under *his* grants, and paid *him* the rents reserved upon them: They established governments under the sanction of *his* prerogative, or by virtue of his charters. No application for those purposes was made to the Parliament." Richard Bland hinted at this innovation against the Glorious Revolution's settlement in an afterthought to his declaration of parliamentary supremacy. He described the colonists' political rights as having "been secured to them by our Kings." He was referencing the royal charters that underlay the legal foundations of authority in most of the colonies. As one Pennsylvania writer put it, "When the emigrants from *Great-Britain* crossed the *Atlantic* . . . they brought with them the spirit of the *English* government . . . the formula of their government once settled in some measure to their satisfaction, with the concurrence of those officers appointed by the Crown."[14]

Some colonials saw an even more fundamental tie to the king. William Henry Drayton, indicting the behavior of South Carolina's last royal governor, Lord William Campbell, declared that Campbell's actions amounted to an effort to break "the original contract between king and people." In Drayton's conceptualization, that contract was divorced even from the monarch's direct representative in the provinces. These perceptions informed the debate over virtual and actual representation and were refined as the imperial crisis continued. And yet they also spoke to an understanding of the king and sovereignty that have been masked.[15]

Statements declaring the king a location of autonomous sovereignty appeared with increasing frequency after 1765. A Pennsylvania writer declared that, in removing to America, provincials "totally disclaim all *subordination* to . . . the two inferior estates of their mother country," thus not only locating sovereignty in the king but elevating its value in the imperial constitution. Another Pennsylvania writer wrote in the same vein. "Never," he asserted, "were a people more in love with their King, and the constitution by which he has solemnly engaged to govern them." Americans readily acknowledged "their dependance on the crown as they always have, and hope forever will." Now, however, it seemed as though they were being forced into an innovation, to "swear allegiance to the British parlia-

14. [James Wilson], *Considerations on the Nature and the Extent of the Legislative Authority of the British Parliament* (Philadelphia, 1774), 29; Bland, *An Inquiry into the Rights of the British Colonies*, 26; *Pennsylvania Journal; and the Weekly Advertiser* (Philadelphia), Feb. 11, 1768. An example was published in the *Massachusetts Gazette and Boston News-Letter*, Mar. 31, 1768.

15. "Mr. President Rutledge to Mr. Chief Justice Drayton. . . . The Charge to the Grand Jury, May 2d, 1776," in Gibbes, ed., *Documentary History of the American Revolution*, 281.

ment, and recognize their unlimited right both of legislation and taxation." This motion "indeed seems new to Americans." In other words, they believed sovereignty was divided between the three estates rather than unified in the King-in-Parliament.[16]

The idea of a united sovereignty, the key imperial orthodoxy in London, broke down in the American provinces. This perception became as important, perhaps, as the parallel debate over virtual versus actual representation, since it addressed the question of constitutional structure. The idea of checks and balances was now openly reinterpreted as a division of sovereignty within the constitutional structure.

Many, perhaps most, provincials understood the king's power as autonomous, but they could not agree among themselves about the origins of his sovereignty. There was an entire spectrum of belief about where the king's sovereignty, and indeed all sovereignty, came from. Some saw God as the wellspring of the king's power—the modified divine right. Those at the Stamp Act Congress were only too anxious to express their "affection to your Majesty's sacred person and government." A Pennsylvania writer thought that "all power or government is derived from God through the instrumentality of Kings or the People," a clear expression of divided sovereignty, tinged in this case with divine-right thinking. In 1773, the Reverend Charles Turner of Duxbury, Massachusetts, told his congregation and anyone who would read his published sermon that "civil rulers, in this world, are in the number of His ministers, or servants." They are, Turner continued, "*constituted* by *Him. There is no power* (says the Apostle) *but of God: the powers that be, are ordained of God.*" Turner was a whig, like many others who held these views, and he went on to try to reconcile the idea of contractual monarchy and constitutional thinking with government's divine origins.[17] Divine-right strains in colonial thought remained strong until 1774 and 1775. The possibility of ambiguous meanings of this divine right, particularly in regard to

16. *Pennsylvania Journal; and the Weekly Advertiser,* Sept. 24, 1767, Feb. 11, 1768.

17. *Authentic Account of the Proceedings of the Congress Held at New-York in MDCCLXV, on the Subject of the American Stamp Act* (London, 1767), 10; Charles Turner, *A Sermon Preached before His Excellency Thomas Hutchinson, Esq., Governor* . . . (Boston, 1773), 6. Turner's project seems to have been to reconcile the modified divine right that had developed in the eighteenth century with elected monarchy, contract theory, and the reality of elected officials and representative government. God, Turner wrote, "never designed, mediately or immediately, to appoint rulers over the people, in state or church, so as to debar *them* from the privilege of choosing their own officers." In summary, "magistrates, that are lawful, are appointed of God, to be his ministers; but for what purpose? . . . He appoints them to be his ministers, *for good to the publick*" (7–8).

the absolutist-tainted doctrines of passive obedience and nonresistance traditionally associated with divine-right government, led to a wave of denunciations
of the king's sacred character in 1774 that continued through 1776 and beyond.[18]

Others saw royal authority as deriving from natural law. The Massachusetts
representatives who wrote to London in 1768 implied that the "foundation" of
the king's authority and their own rights was the same, "in the immutable laws of
nature." Such thoughts were logical to those who believed all human authority
grew from nature and its obscured laws.[19]

The constitutional flight to the king was not simply a theoretical abstraction
or a rhetorical device. The actions of people in the streets and in their homes
reflected it. As counterintuitive as it may seem, participation in the royal political celebrations might have increased between 1764 and 1773. When the Stamp
Act was repealed in 1766, the "pyramid" erected by Boston's sons of liberty was
dominated by huge "Figures of their Majesties" for all to see. In June 1766, Philadelphian Jacob Hiltzheimer recorded dining "on the Banks of the Schuylkill in
Company with about 380 Persons Several Healths drank," it being "the Kings
Birthday." That same year, the men of Savannah, Georgia, staged an elaborate
celebration of the King's Birthday "in token of our loyalty and gratitude to our
beloved Monarch." Three hundred and forty leading subjects attended a private
entertainment while the general population was treated with roast meats and ale.
In 1772, large crowds attended royal celebrations in both Savannah and Augusta.
In 1775, South Carolina planters, fearful of change, declared that they "still bear
the warmest attachment to our present sovereign George the Third. . . . We sin-
cerely deplore those slanderous informations . . . by which he has been mislead"

18. *Pennsylvania Packet; or, The General Advertiser*, Oct. 31, Nov. 14, 1774. The prevalence of discussion of and denunciation of passive obedience, nonresistance, and divine
right is shocking to the scholar educated in the tradition of the Country/republican tradition. Clearly a form of divine-right thought was widespread in the colonies, probably
being used by those opposed to independence as well as, obviously, those that ultimately
came to support it. Moreover, the latent divine-right and neoabsolutist thinking that had
crept into the provincial political culture was also commented on at length. See "Against
IDOLATRY and BLASPHEMY," in *Royal American Magazine or Repository of Instruction
and Amusement (Boston)* (January 1774), 11: "It has long been matter of astonishment that
Protestant Christians, should practice *idolatry* and *blasphemy*—which I think they have
often done, even in the British nation, in their addresses to their Kings and Queens. Such
epithets as these, *Most Gracious Sovereign*—*Most excellent Majesty*—can justly be applied
to none but GOD; and therefore, applying them to men, is idolatry, for it is paying divine
honour to mortals."

19. *Massachusetts Gazette and Boston News-Letter*, Mar. 31, 1768.

about their behavior. These committeemen said prayers for the king on his birthday before conducting business.[20]

The same pattern appeared in Massachusetts. In 1765, Boston celebrated the birthday of the Prince of Wales "with the greatest demonstrations of joy, and with marks of unfeigned loyalty" to the heir to the throne. "Every Apartment in town," this account continued, "rung with the pious and loyal ejaculations — 'God bless our true British King' — 'Long live their Majesties' — 'Heaven preserve the Prince of Wales, and all the Royal Family' — 'Pitt and Liberty for ever.'" Bostonian John Rowe reported on June 4, 1773, that the King's Birthday rites drew "such a Quantity or Rather multitude of People as spectators I never saw before — they behaved very well."[21]

People flocked to the celebrations in the midatlantic as well. When Thomas Penn arrived to take up the Pennsylvanian governorship, "there was a greater concourse of People than has been seen on a similar Occassion." Certainly, he was a proprietary governor, but his entrance ceremonies mimicked those in royal colonies, and his authority was referenced to the king. As late as 1775, the Reverend John Witherspoon could write that "far greater insults were offered to the sovereign, within the city of London . . . than were ever thought of, or would have been permitted" by crowds in America, and members of the Rhode Island militia who rushed to Boston after Lexington and Concord did so "In His Majesty's Service."[22]

King as constitutional broker, king above Parliament, king as salvation anointed by God, man, and nature — provincial America's political culture encouraged such thoughts; indeed, they were its end product. Only in this light can we understand the First Continental Congress's petition to the king who "glories in the name of Briton," asking for "his Clemency for Protection." These senti-

20. William Tudor, ed., *Deacon Tudor's Diary* (Boston, 1896), 22; Jacob Hiltzheimer diaries, I, Apr. 14, 1766, APS; *Georgia Gazette* (Savannah), Aug. 23, 1766; Harold E. Davis, *The Fledgling Province: Social and Cultural Life in Colonial Georgia, 1733–1776* (Chapel Hill, N.C., 1976), 167; "The Provincial Congress to Lieutenant-Governor Bull," in "Miscellaneous Papers of the General Committee, Secret Committee and Provincial Congress, 1775," *South Carolina Historical and Genealogical Magazine*, IX (1908), 182–183; "Transactions of the Provincial Congress for June 4, 1775," ibid., VII (1907), 142.

21. *Pennsylvania Gazette*, Sept. 5, 1765; John Rowe diary, June 4, 1773, MS, MHS.

22. James Allen diary, Aug. 3, 1773, HSP; Andrew Jackson O'Shaughnessy, "'If Others Will Not Be Active, I Must Drive': George III and the American Revolution," *Early American Studies*, II, no. 1 (Spring 2004), 17; John Witherspoon, *The Works of the Rev. John Witherspoon*, III (Philadelphia, 1800), 48–50. For the Rhode Island militia, see Richard M. Ketchum, *Decisive Day: The Battle for Bunker Hill* (New York, 1974), 60.

ments were voiced by men "yielding to no British Subjects in affectionate At-tachment to your Majesty's person, Family, and government." The colonists still sought at that late moment, not a "diminution of the Prerogative," but rather its extension in order to guard them from ministerial conspiracy and parliamentary tyranny. Even Thomas Jefferson in essence called for an extension of preroga-tive in his famous "Summary View" essay by pleading with George III to use the royal negative on parliamentary legislation, a veto power not deployed by a Brit-ish monarch since Queen Anne's reign (1702–1714).[23]

Indeed, some feared that the conspiracy afoot was not directed at them but rather the king specifically and Protestant monarchy more generally. In their warnings of a Jacobite, Catholic conspiracy against the monarchy, provincials re-vealed the depth of their fears.

· · ·

Dynastic Conflict, Anti-Catholicism, and the Contours of Conspiracy Theory

The cosmic significance provincials placed on the British political order led many among them to speculate on the Stamp Act's hidden meaning. To a people im-mersed in a political culture that fused the spiritual and secular, it seemed likely that the forces of Antichrist would try to subvert the constitution with the ulti-mate goal of bringing on the reign of Rome. Boston minister Joseph Emerson described precisely how this would occur in his sermon celebrating the Stamp Act's repeal. The Act had led the "true lover of Zion" to "tremble *for the ark of God.*" With Parliament threatening their liberties, Protestant colonists "feared the breaking in upon the act of *toleration,*" the taking away of the right of congre-gations to select their own ministers, "then imposing whom they pleased upon us for spiritual guides," and finally, after Anglican bishops were imposed, "making us tributary to the See of Rome." Since politics and religion were intertwined, the subversion of the political order directly threatened the empire's soul.[24]

23. *South-Carolina Gazette*, Feb. 24, 1775; [Thomas Jefferson], "A Summary View of the Rights of British America," in Paul Leicester Ford, ed., *The Writings of Thomas Jeffer-son* (New York, 1892), I, 440–446; O'Shaughnessy, "'If Others Will Not Be Active,'" *Early American Studies*, II, no. 1 (Spring 2004), 17 n. 30.

24. Joseph Emerson, *A Thanksgiving-Sermon Preach'd at Pepperrell, July 24th 1766 . . .* (Boston, 1766), 12. Some of the most eminent American historians have addressed the role of conspiracy theory in early American politics. Products of a secularizing century, these scholars treated the colonists' persistent fears about the grand designs that informed the Stamp Act in a secular fashion. Some saw conspiratorial thinking as evidence of paranoia, others as a manifestation of a prescientific means of explaining events and occurrences. Bernard Bailyn, *The Ideological Origins of the American Revolution* (Cambridge, Mass.,

Emerson's sermon suggests the imperial considerations that informed provincial understanding of parliamentary actions. Some Americans believed the conspiracy against their liberties originated in the dynastic struggles between Catholic Stuarts and Protestant Hanoverians. It was thus related to the struggle between Christ and Antichrist. Seen this way, their fears of conspiracy seem a good deal less secular than they have been portrayed and a good deal more rational politically. This understanding of the conspiracy suggests that the idea of a secular political culture at all as we would experience it is anachronistic.

It took the colonists more than ten years to blame George III for the plot many insisted was afoot. Before that, they blamed a series of evil ministers for the conflict in the empire. But what motivated the evil ministers? To answer that question, we must try to think like an Anglo-American in 1765. The answer suggests that the colonists had rational reasons to fear a conspiracy based on the reality of their world and their mode of reasoning. Because they tended to think historically and cosmically, some provincials situated the Stamp Act Crisis in relation to the empire's recent history. Born sometime before 1750, they watched, and quite possibly participated in some way, in the imperial wars that stretched between 1739 and 1763. The enemy was Catholic France and Catholic Spain, and, it would seem, Catholics in general.

Protestant Britons, of course, particularly hated the Catholic House of Stuart. The Stuart Pretenders launched invasions and plots to regain the British throne throughout the eighteenth century. The major efforts, the '15 and the '45, are well known to historians now and to the population then. However, there were other conspiracies, scares, or minor landings in 1708, 1717, 1719, 1721, 1743–1744, and 1759. Charles Carroll sent a detailed letter to his father in Maryland about the

---

1992), 144–160, argues that conspiracy theory was part of the period's political culture. Although this is undoubtedly true, his description is relentlessly secularizing, ignoring the political culture's intense anti-Catholic, antipopish character and its relation to England's seventeenth-century history. This tendency is evident in his choice of quotes, and those that reference antipopery are misread. Note, for example, the quote on 146 that mentions "the end of Charles II's reign," the period of the Popish Plot, the Exclusion Crisis, widespread fears of the Catholic Duke of York and his designs for toleration, and the tendency of both brothers to ignore Parliament and act arbitrarily. All of this goes uncommented on. Gordon S. Wood, "Conspiracy and the Paranoid Style: Causality and Deceit in the Eighteenth Century," *WMQ*, 3d Ser., XXXIX (1982), 401–441, casts conspiracy theory as part of the explanatory apparatus available to people in this period before scientific and social scientific theory as we understand them were available. Like Bailyn, Wood situates conspiracy in terms of secular intellectual mechanics.

1759 scare. It was impossible to tell whom the Stuarts had corrupted with the promise of place or money. Eighteenth-century Anglo-Americans lived in a time of actual, sustained plots against the Hanoverian dynasty that led to two minor civil wars in the home islands. They thus had good reason to fear conspiracy.[25]

In the 1750s, fears of Jacobite conspiracies became intertwined with increasing ethnic tensions within the empire between the English and the Scots. The rapid influx of Scottish officials into the empire's institutions in the 1750s and 1760s fueled an anti-Scottish prejudice within England. Scotland, lacking natural resources but rich in universities, spilled out college graduates eager to take up positions in the London bureaucracy and, indeed, throughout the empire. The reaction against them was predicated on the idea that somehow the Scots were injecting Jacobite or absolutist political ideas into the government. In November 1774, New Englander Josiah Quincy could report from London, "I have been every day more and more astonish'd to find the extravagant hatred there is prevailing among the multitudes of this Kingdom against the Scotch nation." The fear of a closet assault on liberty was situated in part within the broader ethnic tensions in a culturally diverse empire.[26]

Many colonials shared this fear of the Scottish nation. Throughout the 1760s and 1770s, South Carolina planters feared that the ever-increasing number of Scottish officials in their colony would act arbitrarily. In 1775, Robert Alexander, a Maryland delegate to the Continental Congress, declared that Lord North's conciliatory act reflected a "further step in that system of Tyranny, hitherto pursued by —— who under the influence of a Scotch Junto now disgraces the British Throne." The powerful Virginia planter Landon Carter repeatedly expressed anti-Scottish sentiments and anti-Stuart feelings during the crisis. In 1774, he noticed that "the Gent of the Scotch Nation . . . seem active in endeavoring to Persuade a Submission to this Arbitrary taxation." These men, most of whom were tobacco factors for Scottish merchant houses, "were strangers to Liberty themselves and wanted the rest of Mankind to live under the same slavish [Jacobite] notions, that they had ever done, that is from a tendency to be arbitrary themselves." Two years later, Carter would write approvingly of a "Mr. Bruce" who

25. Linda Colley, *Britons: Forging the Nation, 1707–1837* (New Haven, Conn., 1992), 24; "Charles Carroll, May the 16th, 1760, Extracts from the Carroll Papers," *Maryland Historical Magazine*, X (1915), 322–323.

26. Josiah Quincy diary, Nov. 24, 1774, MHS. The influx of officials was related to the extension of the university system in Scotland and, more generally, to the Scottish Enlightenment.

proved himself a strong supporter of the American cause "although a Scotch-man; I have had much conversation with him detesting the behaviour of his countryman." In 1775, Carter declared that "some Highlanders" had joined run-away slaves in fleeing to Virginia's last royal governor, Lord Dunmore, thus join-ing Carter's ethnic hatreds to his racial fears.[27]

These intertwined apprehensions about Stuarts, Catholics, and Scots shaped American understanding of the conspiracy in 1764 and 1765. As eager as they might have been to legitimate dead Stuart kings, provincials feared live Stuart heirs. Supposed budding rationalist Jonathan Mayhew voiced the fear that the "evil-minded individuals" who were at the root of the Stamp Act served in the interests "of the Houses of Bourbon and the [Stuart] Pretender, whose cause they meant to serve, by bringing about an open rupture between Great Brit-ain and her colonies!" James Otis labeled his opponent Martin Howard and his friends "Jacobites." A New York broadside warned George III "of a plot which Lord Bute," George III's much-hated Scottish adviser, "laid, on his dismission from his office," which was "that the Pretender was to be brought in, and you dethroned. . . . What is the reason of the nation being divided, and the one half at war with the other?" A New Hampshire paper carried a satirical "Advertise-ment Extraordinary" in April 1766 denouncing the "infernal, atheistical, Popish and Jacobite Crew, on BOTH sides of the Atlantic; who by the kind Providence of Almighty GOD are totally, and tis to be hoped EVERLASTINGLY frustrated in their DIABOLICAL Purposes towards Great Britain and her Colonies."[28]

People did not just write about the conspiracy against George III; they dis-cussed it in all sorts of settings. In part, it reflected extremely powerful, long-held anti-Stuart values, inculcated by royal rites and imperial history. In 1767, Bos-ton's Irish Protestants, celebrating Saint Patrick's Day, toasted their Hanoverian ruler and added, "May we never want a Williamite to kick the A——e of a Jaco-bite." In 1768, it was rumored in Boston that radical John Wilkes had prevented "Ld Bute and 8 Noblemen" from murdering George III. In 1770, fear of a Stuart conspiracy was apparently so strong in South Carolina that the population pro-

27. John Richard Alden, *John Stuart and the Southern Colonial Frontier* (Ann Arbor, 1944), 169–170; "A Maryland Loyalist," *Maryland Historical Magazine*, I (1906), 319; Jack P. Greene, ed., *The Diary of Colonel Landon Carter of Sabine Hall, 1752–1778*, II (Charlottes-ville, Va., 1965), 821, 1053, 1054.

28. Jonathan Mayhew, *[The Snare Broken], a Thanksgiving-Discourse Preached at the Desire of the West Church in Boston* . . . (Boston, 1766), 9; Shaw, *American Patriots and the Rituals of Revolution*, 97; C. P., *A Letter to His Most Excellent Majesty*, broadside 102, no. 40b, Library of Congress Broadsides; *New Hampshire Gazette*, Apr. 25, 1766.

fessed itself ready to rebel should a Stuart somehow gain the throne. According to one Pennsylvanian, some believed that the Quebec Act (1774) was designed "to prepare the way for the Pretender's coming to the throne." It seemed a logical conclusion because the bill allowed toleration for Catholics in Quebec. As late as the fall of 1774, a New Hampshire crowd in confrontation with Governor John Wentworth referenced the issues of dynastic struggle, history, and religion when they declared themselves "Subjects of King George and not King James [II]."[29]

All this suggests that, in the decade of imperial tension between 1764 and 1774, many British Americans saw themselves as the bulwark against Jacobite conspiracy. George Mason, enraged by the Stamp Act, revealed the relationship between love of the monarch's sacred person and resistance to the apparent Stuart conspiracy. Mason proclaimed in one outburst that he was "an Englishman in his principles, a Zealous Asserter of the Act of Settlement, firmly attached to the present of the royal family . . . unalienably affected to his Majesty's sacred Person and Government . . . who looks upon Jacobitism as the most absurd infatuation, the wildest chimera that ever entered into the Head of Man." In a few lines, Mason summed up much about the empire, the love of monarchy and the Protestant succession that held it together, the fear of a conspiracy that threatened to destroy it, and the contempt of Jacobites that made the Hanoverians' position seem all the more unassailable.[30]

The same sort of sentiments permeated British North America until 1774. A "Freeholder of South Carolina" stated in 1769 that there never "was an American Jacobite, the very air of America is death to such monsters . . . and if any are transported, or import themselves, loss of speech always attends them." Americans' loyalty to their king "hath not only been ever untainted, it hath never been as much as suspected." A Massachusetts writer said, "Sh'd Hosts rebellious, shake our Brunswick's Throne, / And as they dar'd thy Parent, dare the Son, / To this Asylum stretch thine happy Wing, / And we'll contend, who best shall love our KING." Such was the strength of this dynastic-centered worldview that, incredibly, in the summer of 1775, one New York Anglican, later to be a loyalist, declared that the budding revolutionaries were Jacobites. The "Whiggs as they are called"

29. *Massachusetts Gazette and Boston News-Letter*, Mar. 19, 1767; Jeremy Belknap, diary in *Bickerstaff's Boston Almanac . . .* (Boston, 1768), MHS; *Massachusetts Gazette and Boston News-Letter*, Apr. 12, 1770; *Pennsylvania Packet; or, The General Advertiser*, Oct. 31, 1774; Paul W. Wilderson, *Governor John Wentworth and the American Revolution: The English Connection* (Hanover, N.H., 1994), 249.

30. Robert A. Rutland, ed., *The Papers of George Mason, 1725–1792*, I, *1749–1778* (Chapel Hill, N.C., 1970), 71.

were behaving the way they were "to make themselves strong to Bring the Pretender to the throne." It was the loyalty born in love, a love that intensified until the weight of events overtook it in 1774 and 1775.[31]

That George III ultimately came to be seen as the instigator of the grand conspiracy and was bitterly denounced as such in the Declaration is perhaps the Revolution's greatest irony. In understanding the imperial crisis as part of a conspiracy, provincials expressed neither paranoia nor a premodern theory of politics but rather a heightened, Protestant understanding of dynastic and religious conflict as lived by their immediate ancestors. In fact, the appearance of conspiracy theory was part of broader application of the past's lessons to the crisis at hand.

· · ·

History Fulfilled, History Betrayed

In 1776, with the empire in cardiac arrest, Samuel Sherwood sought to explain what had occurred in the years after the Seven Years' War. A "popish mysterious leaven of iniquity and absurdity" that went well beyond "the territory of the Pope's usurped authority and jurisdiction" had once again seduced imperial leaders. It was a heady intellectual brew designed to "spread in a greater or less degree, among almost all the nations of the earth; especially amongst the chief rulers, the princes," because it offered them the prospect of tyrannical power. This had occurred once before, during "the reign of the STUART family," when "three or four of our kings successively" were "seduced . . . by the . . . bewitching inchantments of the old whore of Babylon . . . to the entire destruction of two of them." As during the imperial crisis, "jesuitical emissaries" had worked covertly throughout the seventeenth century to spread the "darling doctrines of arbitrary *power, passive obedience and non-resistance*" in order to prepare the way for the British people's popish enslavement. The same "corrupt system of tyranny and oppression" was, he believed, now afoot in America, having "late been fabricated . . . by the ministry and parliament of Great Britain" in order to prepare the way for despotic government.[32]

31. *Georgia Gazette*, June 28, July 5, 1769, cited in *An Humble Enquiry . . . by a Freeholder of South Carolina; Massachusetts Gazette and Boston News-Letter*, May 22, 1766; Philip Ranlet, *The New York Loyalists* (Knoxville, Tenn., 1986), 142. [Benjamin Franklin], *The Causes of the Present Distractions in America Explained: In Two Letters to a Merchant in London* ([New York?], 1774), 15, voices similar sentiments.

32. Samuel Sherwood, *The Church's Flight into the Wilderness: An Address on the Times . . .* (New York, 1776), 10–11, 15, 16, 30.

The fears of Jacobite and Scottish conspiracies expressed a general tendency to situate the imperial crisis in historical frameworks familiar to eighteenth-century Anglo-Americans. This tendency to historical reasoning lay at the provincial society's epistemological core. From the moment the crisis erupted to the final imperial collapse in 1776, colonists like Samuel Sherwood drew on historical precedent to illustrate, compare, and ultimately comprehend. Their central historical focus was England's calamitous seventeenth-century history. The idea that late provincial writers predominately referenced antiquity is a modern one, read back through the revolutionaries' desperate search for a workable republican order after 1775. In fact, before then, they primarily fixated on England's seventeenth-century struggles to make sense of the spreading imperial conflict.

The use of this past went through loosely bounded stages. Initially, Parliament's actions were made synonymous with those supposed arbitrary actions of Charles I in the period of Personal Rule and the Civil Wars. As the empire began to stumble, there were increased references to an impending civil war somehow like that of the seventeenth century. At the moment of collapse, new historical time lines were asserted to legitimate republican government.

The Stamp Act Crisis led a host of provincial writers to turn to England's tumultuous seventeenth century to explain colonial defiance. Typical in this vein was a piece published in January 1765 in the *Pennsylvania Journal; and the Weekly Advertiser*. "The RIGHTS of COLONIES Examined" probed the origins and location of political sovereignty. That writer declared of the origins of society, "Mankind have by no means been agreed about it: some have found it's origin in the divine appointment: others have thought it took it's rise from power: enthusiasts have dreamed that dominion was founded in grace." These views, the writer believed, were difficult to reconcile, and he recommended "leaving these points to be settled by the descendants of *Filmer* [author of the seventeenth-century absolutist tract *Patriarcha; or, The Natural Power of Kings*], *Cromwell*, and *Venner* [the head of the Fifth Monarchists]." The seventeenth-century upheavals clearly remained current with eighteenth-century Anglo-Americans as they struggled with a new crisis.[33]

The calamities of the English Civil Wars quickly became a tool that allowed polemicists to explain the imperial crisis to their readers. A 1766 writer to the *Boston Gazette* invoked the Book of Sport (issued in the reign of Charles I, it enumerated recreational activities the Church of England allowed on the Sabbath) and Archbishop Laud (associated with the popish activities of Charles's reign) to explain to his readers the moral and spiritual standards of those who would

33. *Pennsylvania Journal; and the Weekly Advertiser*, Jan. 17, 1765.

impose the Stamp Act. Assuming Charles I's voice, the writer instructed *"Canterbury* see [meaning Laud]" that "our Royal Declaration concerning Recreations, Sports and Pastimes, on the Lord's Day . . . be printed." This "was drawn by the Arch Butcher Laud, at about the same time was a gracious, pious Proclamation, prohibiting the carrying any Food to the Presbyterians in New England." He recommended to "[George Grenville] and [Charles Townshend], and the Rest, in their next Speeches [in Parliament] against North America, to bear in Mind this and a thousand such-like Instances of parental, tender Love and Care of these Colonies in their infancy."[34]

Between 1765 and 1775, writers frequently invoked Charles I's efforts to tax without parliamentary consent during the period of Personal Rule in the 1630s to explain why parliamentary taxation was illegal. In 1768, a writer to the *Georgia Gazette* excerpted Dickinson's *Letters from a Farmer in Pennsylvania* concerning the Ship Money controversy of the 1630s to establish precedent for colonial resistance. "When Mr. *Hampden's* ship money cause . . . was tried," he informed his readers, "all the people of *England*, with anxious expectation, interested themselves in the important decision." James Otis used "Hampden" as a pseudonym during the Stamp Act Crisis, and in 1774, "Freeman," a South Carolina writer (probably William Henry Drayton), wrote a letter to the First Continental Congress, whose resistance to parliamentary taxes he compared to the actions of the English Parliament in 1628, when the realm was "oppressed by illegal taxes, violation of property, billeting soldiers and martial law." Massachusetts minister Andrew Croswell denounced the Bishop of Gloucester for advocating an American bishop in the very language that "Archbishop *Laud* [used] to [describe] the puritans."[35]

Historical understanding based on the Civil Wars was not exclusive to the provincial elite. In 1766, Marblehead, Massachusetts, sailmaker Ashley Bowen recorded in his diary that a mob "assembled to the Number of several Hundreds"

34. Albert Matthews, "Joyce Junior Once More," Colonial Society of Massachusetts, *Publications*, XI (1907), 291–292; *Boston Gazette*, January 1766.

35. *Georgia Gazette*, Jan. 27, 1768; Colin Nicolson, *The "Infamas Govener" Francis Bernard and the Origins of the American Revolution* (Boston, 2001), 18; "A Letter from Freeman," in Gibbes, ed., *Documentary History of the American Revolution*, 11; Croswell, *Observations on Several Passages*, 21. For an example of the applications of this historical understanding to local debate, see Peter S. Onuf, ed., *Maryland and the Empire, 1773: The Antilon-First Citizen Letters* (Baltimore, 1974), which republished this debate between Charles Carroll and Daniel Dulany, Jr., over an issue of fees. In particular, the issue of Ship Money is repeatedly invoked as historical precedent.

and burned a number of their parliamentary tormentors in effigy on January 30, the anniversary of Charles I's execution in 1649 at the end of the English Civil Wars. They then expressed their "Loyalty to the King, and Love to their Country," and followed that with a celebration of the ancient constitution.[36]

The paralleling of Charles I with Parliament in the 1760s might seem strange, given the antagonism between the Stuart kings and the House of Commons. However, provincials understood both as having violated the British constitution in their respective quests for arbitrary power. As James Wilson pointed out in 1774, even parliaments could be corrupted, and "Long Parliaments have always been prejudicial to the Prince." Wilson declared that "Kings are not the only tyrants . . . Kings are not the severest tyrants." The comparison carried an indictment of a Parliament that was continuing on an illegal, arbitrary path.[37]

By 1769, the representation of the conflict as a budding civil war within the empire had become commonplace. Predating Abraham Lincoln's thinking on the question of civil war by some eighty years, South Carolina pamphleteer John Joachim Zubly headed his *Humble Enquiry into the Nature of the Dependency of the American Colonies upon the Parliament of Great-Britain* with the banner phrase "A House divided against itself cannot stand." Deriving his thoughts in large part from the *History of the Long Rebellion*, Zubly explained how Ship Money and other taxes imposed by unjust ministers had led to the unnatural civil war that nearly destroyed England.[38]

In the same period, the Reverend John Graves, Anglican minister in Providence, Rhode Island, used the Civil Wars to highlight the gravity of the imperial crisis. Graves wrote to a friend, "The face of public affairs here is melancholy. Altar against altar in the Church, and such open, bold attacks upon the State, as, I believe, the English annals do not furnish us with the like since the reign of King Charles I." Massachusetts minister John Lathrop believed a "*long* civil war" would be a calamity for the empire. So powerful was the identification of the imperial struggle with the past that, when the fighting at Lexington and Concord broke out, Massachusetts diarist Ebenezer Bridge declared "Civil Warr began."[39]

---

36. Philip Chadwick Foster Smith, ed., *The Journals of Ashley Bowen (1728–1813) of Marblehead*, I, Colonial Society of Massachusetts, *Publications*, XLIV (Boston, 1973), 141.

37. [James Wilson], *Considerations on the Nature and the Extent of the Legislative Authority of the British Parliament* (Philadelphia, 1774), 4, 9, 10.

38. [John Joachim Zubly], *An Humble Enquiry into the Nature of the Dependency of the American Colonies upon the Parliament of Great-Britain . . .* ([Charleston, S.C.], 1769).

39. Lorenzo Sabine, *Biographical Sketches of Loyalists of the American Revolution, with*

With a "civil war" looming, historical understanding was again consciously redefined to legitimate violent resistance to imperial authority. Specifically, Oliver Cromwell and then the regicides as a whole came to be understood as politically just actors. Cromwell's rehabilitation in the period before 1765 had been specific to the issues of foreign policy and the Church of England's growth in the colonies. Now, as this new crisis opened the joints in the imperial structure, writers again invoked the lord protector.

Initially, Cromwell's hostility to Parliament fueled this reinterpretation. Cromwell's famous speech that described Parliament as a "factious crew ... [a] ... pack of mercenary wretches" that acted like "sordid prostitutes" in their search for venal advancement was repeatedly cited by colonists aroused by parliamentary taxation. Cromwell was the avenging angel who had cleansed the institutional Augean stable a century before by repeatedly purging the House of Commons. In 1765, young protesters in a mock lament beseeched "thee, O Cromwell, to hear ... us" as they complained about the conspiracy against liberty and property then afoot. During the debates over the Virginia Resolves, Patrick Henry would remark, "Caesar found a Brutus, Our Charles met with a Cromwell; And who knows but in this our day some Cromwell may arise and procure Us justice." These words signaled a seismic shift in provincial historical perception driven by the crisis.[40]

This rehabilitation continued throughout the 1760s. The Boston Sons of Liberty, according to a hostile observer, believed that "Oliver Cromwell was a glorious fellow," and they wished they had another like him to do battle with a corrupt ministry. The accuracy of that particular account may be in doubt, but the invoking of Cromwell by the whig movement did become more common. In 1773, during the tea crisis, handbills signed by "O. C." threatening importers appeared in the Boston area. The following year, the pamphlet *The American Chronicle of the Times* invoked Cromwell repeatedly in an effort to spark resistance to British troops and portrayed the lord protector in his battle armor. A Connecticut preacher declared that England was never happier than when "the head of the

an Historical Essay, I ([1864]; rpt. Port Washington, N.Y., 1966), 487; John Lathrop, *A Discourse Preached, December 15th 1774, Being the Day Recommended by the Provintial Congress* (Boston, 1774), 38; Ebenezer Bridge diary, Apr. 19, 1775, Houghton Library MSS, Harvard University, Cambridge, Mass.

40. *Georgia Gazette*, June 29, 1768; Shaw, *American Patriots and the Rituals of Revolution*, 178; Edmund Pendelton to James Madison, Apr. 21, 1790, in Edmund S. Morgan, ed., "Edmund Pendleton on the Virginia Resolves," *Maryland Historical Magazine*, XLVI (1951), 75.

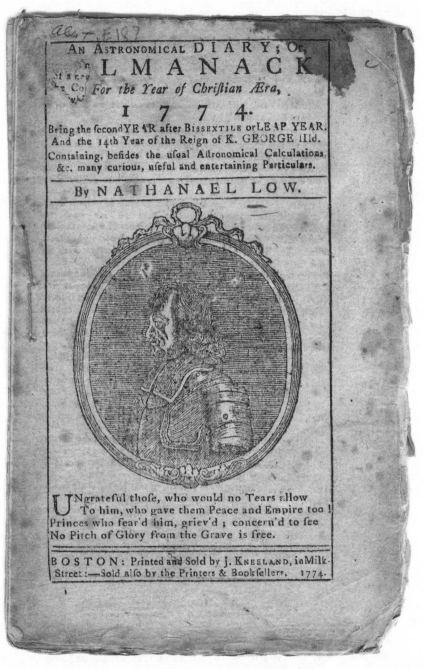

An ASTRONOMICAL DIARY; Or,
LMANACK
For the Year of Christian Æra,

1 7 7 4.

Being the second YEAR after BISSEXTILE or LEAP YEAR,
And the 14th Year of the Reign of K. GEORGE IIId.
Containing, besides the usual Astronomical Calculations,
&c. many curious, useful and entertaining Particulars.

By NATHANAEL LOW.

UNgrateful those, who would no Tears allow
 To him, who gave them Peace and Empire too!
Princes who fear'd him, griev'd; concern'd to see
No Pitch of Glory from the Grave is free.

BOSTON: Printed and Sold by J. KNEELAND, in Milk-
Street:—Sold also by the Printers & Booksellers. 1774.

PLATE 12. *Cover of Nathanael Low,* An Astronomical Diary. . . . *1774.*
*Cromwell, enjoying an eighteenth-century rehabilitation in many quarters, is featured
in full battle armor, ready to defend the colonists from tyrannical ministers.*
Courtesy, Massachusetts Historical Society

first Stuart was severed from his body, and while it was under the protection of Oliver Cromwell." These references are evidence of alternative political models and political histories that existed within the Hanoverian regime and came ultimately to be used against it.[41]

Other radicals and those perceived as antiparliamentarians from the English Civil Wars also enlisted in the provincial cause. The *Virginia Gazette* of December 11, 1766, contained a letter signed "Elizabeth Barebones," the rhetorical wife of Praisegod Barebones, the seventeenth-century English radical whose name adorned the purged Parliament in the early 1650s. The writer declared, "I am not content with half freedom, half inquiry, half honesty or any other thing done by halves. . . . I have at heart the good of my children . . . I shall not wonder to find myself opposed by a *strong anti-barebonian party*." In 1769, a Boston writer gave an account of "Lt. General Whaley and Maj. General Goffe," the regicide judges who had fled to New England at the Restoration. They went into hiding in the countryside near Hadley, Massachusetts, until disaster threatened New England in the form of King Philip's War, a desperate struggle between the Puritan New Englanders and a Native American coalition. Hadley was attacked and seemed doomed until a strangely dressed elderly man rallied the townspeople and saved the community. When the Native American attackers "were repulsed," the writer continued, "the deliverer of Hadley disappeared instantly. . . . This was General Goffe," who had lived in hiding nearby. The obvious parallels—colonists again, as they had been in 1675, in grave danger—were stressed by writers.[42]

Political protestors expressed this historical understanding in the streets during the riots and unrest that defined the period between 1764 and 1776. "Joyce, Junior," a figure dressed like Coronet Joyce, who had arrested Charles I before his execution, became part of Pope's Day processions and in fact continued to appear in Boston in crowd actions after independence. The figure bespoke both the society's historical reference point and its potentially subversive dangers.[43]

41. Sparks Collection, III, fol. 10, no. 18, Houghton Library, Harvard University, Cambridge, Mass.; Alfred F. Young, "English Plebeian Culture and Eighteenth-Century American Radicalism," in Margaret Jacob and James Jacob, eds., *The Origins of Anglo-American Radicalism* (London, 1984), 185–212, esp. 186; *The American Chronicle of the Times*, book 1 (Philadelphia, 1774); Young, "English Plebeian Culture and Eighteenth-Century American Radicalism," in Jacob and Jacob, eds., *Origins of Anglo-American Radicalism*, 196.

42. *Virginia Gazette*, Dec. 11, 1766; *Boston Gazette and Country Journal*, Nov. 20, 1769.

43. Matthews, "Joyce Junior Once More," Colonial Society of Massachusetts, *Publications*, XI, 294n: "A person [Mr. Lamberton] wrote to Matthews about his paper [on Joyce Junior], and recalled 'Captain Joyce' seems to me like a once familiar nickname, which I

PLATE 13. *Oliver Cromwell miniature, watercolor on ivory. C. 1656. By Samuel Cooper. This image was owned by and probably carried by Thomas Jefferson during the imperial crisis and the Revolution. Courtesy, Massachusetts Historical Society*

Not everyone in the colonies accepted this rehabilitation, and some retained the traditional hostility to Cromwell and other regicides. When Georgia governor Sir James Wright tried to explain the pattern of resistance to imperial authority in Georgia, he focused on several settlements of New Englanders in the colony. They were, he complained to the Earl of Dartmouth, "of the Puritan Independent sect," with a "strong tincture of Republican or Oliverian principles."[44]

Because they thought historically, provincials turned to other aspects of English and British history to bolster their political positions. Driven by that mindset to seek parallels in the past, they turned to the event that had established the very sovereignty they now challenged. Without any sense of the inherent constitutional contradictions in their position, some writers turned to the Glorious Revolution to challenge parliamentary supremacy. They tended to see its settlement as part of a periodic restatement of the rights of Englishmen that had begun with Magna Charta. In 1768, Isaac Bickerstaff's *Boston Almanack* celebrated the monarchs "then called and known by the name and stile of William and Mary" and the "DECLARATION of RIGHT or new Magna Charta" they had

---

had not heard since childhood. You observe I say 'Captain Joyce,' which is the form lodged in my memory."

44. Orville A. Park, "The Puritan in Georgia," in *Georgia Historical Quarterly*, XIII (1929), 351–352.

helped secure for the English people. What readers took away from this is impossible to know, but it was something. In 1774, Samuel Sherwood wrote, "I am sensible that the present controversy . . . stands upon a different footing" than that between James II and his subjects "at the revolution," because the present contest pitted Parliament against the provinces, and the earlier one had been between king and people. Nonetheless, "altho' therefore our present controversy with *Great-Britain* is on quite another footing than the contest of the nation in the days of king *James*; yet revolution-principles in their general nature, will fully justify the present constitutional opposition." Colonists' own inability to see the irony of their defiance of Parliament via the Glorious Revolution's settlement reveals just how fragmented understanding of that contract was.[45]

By 1774, certainly, provincials began to turn to classical history, to Sparta and Athens and Rome, for legitimization. The print culture, oration, and casual conversation became studded with classical allusions. But it would be an error to attribute too much enlightened universalism to provincials even in that moment of collapse. British history between 1640 and 1660, and more generally British history as a whole, remained current in the society until 1776 and indeed probably long after independence. It remained so current that, when Benedict Arnold opened his correspondence with the British that would lead to his betrayal of the American cause, he signed his letters "Monk" and "Monck" in reference to General George Monck, whose march on London precipitated the Stuart Restoration in 1660. Imperial symbols and the lessons of Britain's past retained their emotional power until at least 1774. Nowhere is this more evident than in the treatment of Shakespeare during the imperial crisis.[46]

· · ·

Shakespeare, Satire, and Subversion in the Imperial Crisis

In October 1774, the *Pennsylvania Journal; and the Weekly Advertiser* carried another piece in the endless torrent of political writings about the imperial crisis. Like so many in that time of confusion, the writer turned to his monarch and addressed his piece "To the King." Relaying a broader sense of growing despera-

45. *Bickerstaff's Boston Almanack* . . . (Boston, 1768); Samuel Sherwood, *A Sermon, Containing, Scriptural Instructions to Civil Rulers*, 30n; Fred Shelley, ed., "Ebenezer Hazard's Travels through Maryland in 1777," in *Maryland Historical Magazine*, XLVI (1951), 49.

46. Thomas Fleming, "Unlikely Victory: Thirteen Ways the Americans Could Have Lost the Revolution," in Robert Crowley, ed., *What If? The World's Foremost Military Historians Imagine What Might Have Been* (New York, 1999), 174.

tion over a peaceful solution to the crisis, this writer added, "'HEAR ME! For I WILL speak'—SHAKESPEAR" to the title page.[47]

There is little surprise that this writer should turn to the Bard of Stratford-upon-Avon to bolster a political declaration to the monarch. Like a host of other provincials, the contributor to the *Pennsylvania Journal* sought to use Shakespeare to protest imperial policy. The potency of this manipulation grew from Shakespeare's importance as a British national symbol and the historicist reasoning common in colonial society. Initially, these provincial commentators understood Shakespeare as, if not exactly a historian, then as a kind of historical chronicler/philosopher and sought parallels in Shakespeare to explain the Stamp Act Crisis and the subsequent turmoil. Over time, however, writers turned from using Shakespeare for historical reasoning to using his plays to create satires that mocked the London authorities and their American supporters. In so doing, they revealed how the intellectual system that maintained imperial cohesion had eroded.

Of the intellectual demigods believed to have shaped Britain's national history, and there were several, Shakespeare was the most ambiguous in his meaning. Perhaps this explains why colonial writers so aggressively manipulated his words. His symbolic compatriots, Isaac Newton and John Locke, supported the Glorious Revolution and its settlement. The former had resisted the efforts of James II to control Cambridge University and taken part in the Convention Parliament and was appointed Warden of the Mint by William III. Locke championed contractual monarchy; contemporaries understood him as an intellectual supporter of William and Mary.[48]

Shakespeare, however, was different. Simultaneously commodity, political symbol, national literature, and art form, the Bard's words bound the empire's peoples together in a common identity as certainly as any royal decree. His name

47. *Pennsylvania Journal; and the Weekly Advertiser*, Oct. 5, 1774; for one of the few considerations of the Bard's career in America, see Lawrence W. Levine, "William Shakespeare in America," chap. 1 in *Highbrow Lowbrow: The Emergence of Cultural Hierarchy in America* (Cambridge, Mass., 1988); see also Louis B. Wright, *The Cultural Life of the American Colonies, 1607–1763* (New York, 1957), 176–195.

48. *American Magazine* (January 1745). Locke's tacit support of the Glorious Revolution's settlement was still invoked by imperial observers as late as 1773, when a Boston writer reminded readers that "Mr. Locke's two Treatise on government . . . contributed more essentially to the establishing the Throne of our Great Deliverer King William, and consequently to securing the Protestant Succession" (*Massachusetts Gazette and Boston News-Letter*, Mar. 4, 1773).

was at least as well known as Locke's and Newton's in the provinces, perhaps more so, but its use suggests a far more flexible and thus elusive national symbol.

The lack of theater in provincial America initially made the Bard of Avon a literary experience only. By the 1740s, though, attendance at Shakespeare's plays had become tools of genteel display in many colonies. The port town populations south of New England put on productions of *Richard III, Othello, Merchant of Venice, Macbeth, King Lear, Julius Caesar*, and other classics. In 1762, Shakespeare gained a toehold in the Puritan colonies when *Othello* was performed at Newport. Across British America, gentlemen and their ladies prided themselves on seeing the plays performed.[49]

The plays' political importance is revealed in their use as diplomatic devices in formal negotiations. In 1753, with tensions between France and Britain rising and control of the continental interior at stake, Virginia's political elite used a performance of Shakespeare at Williamsburg to impress a visiting Cherokee delegation. Cherokee visitors to New York City in 1767 took in *Richard III*, and visiting Iroquois saw the same play a few months later. The Iroquois viewed the play with "Seriousness and Attention," but they knew insufficient English "to understand the Plot and Design" and expressed "Surprise and Curiosity, [rather] than any other Passions." Before 1765, writers tended to tap the Bard's symbolic power for such patriotic ends.[50]

49. Plays were being performed as early as 1737 in New York. See Esther Singleton, *Social New York under the Three Georges, 1714–1776* (New York, 1902), 272. As to the players, most seemed to be from England, some being British military officers who produced versions of the plays while on garrison duty (I. N. Phelps Stokes, *The Iconography of Manhattan Island, 1498–1909*, IV [New York, 1922], 618). March 5, 1750: "The theatre in Nassau St. Opens with a performance of 'Richard III'" (*New-York Gazette, Revived in the Weekly Post-Boy*, Feb. 26, 1750). Plays performed in colonial Charleston, S.C.: *Hamlet, Romeo and Juliet, The Merchant of Venice, Richard III, The Tempest, Henry IV, Othello, King Lear, Julius Caesar, Macbeth*, as well as *King John, The Mourning Bride, She Stoops to Conquer*, and *Beggar's Opera* (Edward McCrady, *The History of South Carolina under the Royal Government, 1719–1776* [New York, 1899]). In New England, plays and theaters were seen as ungodly, a view aptly summed up by Josiah Quincy during a visit to the London theater in 1774 (Josiah Quincy diary, Nov. 18, 1774, MHS). For Newport, see Lorenzo Johnston Greene, *The Negro in Colonial New England, 1620–1776* (New York, 1968), 245.

50. Alden, *John Stuart and the Southern Colonial Frontier*, 223; *Pennsylvania Gazette*, Jan. 16, 1753; *Massachusetts Gazette and Boston News-Letter*, Dec. 24, 1767. Both performances were presented as part of a diplomatic initiative to bring peace between the Cherokee and the Five Nations. Francis Goelet, a New York merchant visiting London, recorded his attendance at Shakespearean performances attended by "His Majesty and the Prince

However, like so many other experiences that shaped imperial perception in America, the plays were not understood in a uniform manner. Each reader, each viewer came away with his or her own understanding about Shakespeare's explorations of human nature, even royalty's nature. The exploration of the historic flaws of royals and nobility indeed played a central role in his writing. Because of this, they touched the deepest recesses of the thought processes that tied subject to ruler and nation in the sprawling maritime polity. As a literary phenomenon, this was insignificant; as a political phenomenon, it threatened the imperial order.[51]

A number of writers drew on Shakespeare to place the Stamp Act Crisis in the context of British history. A writer to the *Boston-Gazette and Country Journal,* "looking over Shakespear Henry VIII," felt a "singular Pleasure in reading one of the Scenes, which I thought peculiarly adapted to the present Circumstances of our most gracious Sovereign's American Subjects." The scene "is a part of the English History, and shows the Success of the People's Application for Relief from a burthensome tax . . . to a Monarch in all Respects much inferior to HIM, who now fills the British Throne." This Boston writer presented a dialogue involving Henry, his queen, and Cardinal Wolsey that expressed themes common to Anglo-American political culture. The monarch was represented as benevolent and his underlings' base. Henry's queen "solicited, not by a few, and those of true condition, that your subjects are in great grievance" because of an unjust tax. Henry had been deceived by the Catholic Wolsey, who continually "places himself under the King's Feet, on his Right side." It was this evil councillor in particular whom the population had denounced to the queen "most bitterly . . . almost . . . in loud rebellion." The king declared against these unknown measures and ultimately repealed the tax and punished the rogue cardinal.[52]

This particular polemicist understood Shakespeare's writings as essentially historical. He believed his own king wanted justice for his subjects and had fallen victim to an evil, absolutist-minded, Catholic-tainted councillor as good king Henry VIII had. The ability to show the past and the present as parallel addressed a belief in the consistency of human nature alien to our own era.

The eventual political satirization of Shakespeare after 1765 was related to the effectiveness of his words as a symbol. In the creation of British nationality after

and Princes of Wales and the royall famely" (Francis Goelet diary, Feb. 15–28, 1746/7, NYHS).

51. For its use in historical-political reasoning, see the *Boston-Gazette and Country Journal, Supplement,* Dec. 30, 1765.

52. Ibid.

1688, writers had borrowed freely from history, literature, science, secular and religious rites, as well as political theory to support the legitimacy of Protestant princes and to create a common identity for a diverse transatlantic empire. Shakespeare became known as a British genius, and provincial writers twisted his words precisely because they knew such manipulations would have an emotional impact. To use a modern term, twisting Shakespeare's words had shock value, and writers trying to mobilize the population to action after 1765 used that value with increasing abandon.[53]

Shakespeare's widespread satirization for political ends during the imperial crisis is difficult to date precisely, but it seems to have begun in 1768 and 1769 during the struggle over the Townshend duties. The need to keep the population mobilized encouraged writers to use new rhetorical devices as they sought to continually focus attentions on imperial concerns. Although drawing on all the plays, they focused on *Richard III, Henry V*, and especially *Hamlet*, whose most famous address was so pregnant with ambiguity. "To be or not to be"—it was perhaps the best-loved phrase in late colonial America, apart from "Liberty and property" and "No taxation without representation." The tortured possibilities of paths taken and ignored, the treatment of language, all these recommended themselves to a troubled imperial population. "A PARODY on Shakespear" written in Georgia asked, "Be taxt, or not be taxt, that is the question; / Whether 'tis nobler in our minds to suffer / The sleights and cunning of deceitful statesmen, / Or to petition against illegal taxes, / And by opposing end them." Such parodies became a regular part of provincial writing. The phrase even made its way, eventually, into the Second Continental Congress, from which a delegate wrote, "To be or not to be is now the Question" to a kin.[54]

The turn to parody allowed those opposed to radical measures to contest the whig movement's appropriation of Shakespeare. Portions of a conservative, entrenched gentry repeatedly sought to manipulate the national symbols themselves in order to blunt what they saw as the protest movement's growing radical tendencies. The conservative usages took two courses: an effort to recast Shakespeare's traditional nationalist meanings as a tool of imperial unity; and their own use of parody, in turn, to mock those they labeled radical.

53. There had been sporadic examples of such satires in periods of heightened political conflict in the 1750s. The bitter divisions that appeared over religion, paper money, land tenure, and consumption only furthered such usages.

54. *Georgia Gazette*, Mar. 1, 1769; Samuel Ward to Henry Ward, Nov. 11, 1775, in Edmund C. Burnett, ed., *Letters of Members of the Continental Congress* (Washington, D.C., 1921–1936), I, 252.

The movement to cast Shakespeare as a symbol of national greatness and imperial unity again can be dated roughly to the early 1770s. Typical of this usage
was a piece in the *Pennsylvania Packet; or, The General Advertiser* in 1772 that
reported "His MAJESTY and his amiable QUEEN" often spent their afternoons
reading favorite authors. The German-born queen demonstrated her growing
Britishness "by conceiving the greatest attachment to Shakespeare's most es-
teemed plays." Such statements reasserted Shakespeare as part of the formal symbolic system that maintained a fundamental imperial British identity.[55]

The use of Shakespeare to satirize radical impulses began in the same period.
Like their counterparts in the colonial protest movement, these writers tended
to parody a few specific plays, particularly (again) *Hamlet*. The Anglican minister Thomas Bradbury Chandler's *Friendly Address to All Reasonable Americans,
on the Subject of Our Political Confusions* drew on *Julius Caesar* and *Henry V*.
The thrust is a long plea against war with Britain, against what he calls, significantly, "civil war." It is an interesting paragraph because it seems to internalize
Shakespeare and uses it as an organizing device. The paragraph opens, *"Friends,
Countrymen and Fellow-Subjects!* let me entreat you to rouse up at last from your
slumber." Although this might not be a take on "Friends, Romans, Countrymen," certainly the sentence "HAVOC will be the cry; and the *dogs of war* will
be let loose to tear out your vitals" was. The answering pamphlet, *Strictures on
a Pamphlet Entitled, A Friendly Address to All Reasonable Americans, on the Subject of Our Political Confusions, Addressed to the People of America*, is masted with
a motto from Shakespeare, suggesting a tussle over control of the Bard's legacy
within the provinces' literate population.[56]

Such uses of Shakespeare were not confined to the written page. A North Carolina woman at dinner with whig militia leader Robert Howe in 1775 asked him to
read a passage from Shakespeare for the assembled diners. Such a reading was not
uncommon, as knowledge of the plays was considered part of a gentleperson's
education. Howe agreed to amuse his dining party, only to discover the passage
described Falstaff and his band of motley recruits.[57]

"Cato," a Pennsylvania writer opposed to ministerial excess but equally ap-

55. *Pennsylvania Packet; or, The General Advertiser*, May 18, 1772.

56. [Thomas Bradbury Chandler], *A Friendly Address to All Reasonable Americans, on
the Subject of Our Political Confusions* . . . ([Boston], 1774), 33; Charles Lee, *Strictures on a
Pamphlet Entitled, a "Friendly Address to All Reasonable Americans, on the Subject of Our
Political Confusions," Addressed to the People of America* . . . (Philadelphia, 1774).

57. Charles Royster, *A Revolutionary People at War: The Continental Army and American Character, 1775–1783* (Chapel Hill, N.C., 1979), 27.

palled by the idea of American independence, also turned to Shakespeare to question the turn of events. He asked, "To write, or not to write; that is the question— / Whether 'tis nobler in the mind to bear / Th' unlicens'd wrongs of furious party-zeal, / Or dip the pen into a nest of hornets" after several hostile responses to earlier writings. Was he ready to "bear the scoffing of the times, / The TORY's hated name. . . . Who would endure this Pain, / This foul discharge of wrath from Adam's sons / Marshall'd in dread array, both old and Young."[58]

Provincials' use of Shakespeare is indicative of his centrality to imperial British identity, and yet it also raises intriguing possibilities. Shakespeare's humanization of royalty, his illuminations of its bitter and all-too-human ambiguities, was unique among the writer/intellectual symbols in the eighteenth-century empire's pantheon of heroes. And thus it may be that Shakespeare was the original antiroyalist in the eighteenth-century empire. Although Locke and Newton criticized the Stuart dynasty, both essentially believed in monarchy, and both were successfully harnessed to Hanoverian needs after 1715. So had Shakespeare, but his exploration of a human nature shared even by kings somehow diminished royalty, though provincials had not read him this way until events forced them to. Shakespeare, like Cromwell, may be conceived crudely as one of America's first populist symbols.

The imperial crisis had transformed the Bard into a dissident. England's greatest plays had been harnessed to the protest against Parliament and to the collective denial of the Glorious Revolution's settlement as understood in London. To be or not to be: that had truly become the imperial question. As writers adapted Shakespeare to political ends, other appropriations occurred across British America that would provide an answer to that most hackneyed of questions. Provincials in the streets adapted the empire's political rituals to imperial protest and manipulated royal emblems and the royal person to rally support to their cause, until the empire collapsed in a final iconoclasm punctuated by a funeral fit for a king.

58. *Pennsylvania Gazette*, Mar. 27, 1776. The identity of "Cato" is unclear, but I suspect it to be either Wilson or Dickinson for a variety of reasons.

10

A FUNERAL FIT FOR A KING

. . . .
. . .
. .
.

"The most shocking cruelty," wrote New Englander Anne Hulton, "was exercised a few Nights ago." Boston patriots targeted "a Tidesman one Malcolm" because he continued to proclaim his loyalty to king and country. He was seized, "taken, and Tarrd, and featherd. Theres no Law that knows a punishment for the greatest Crimes beyond what this is, of cruel torture." Beaten, his arm dislocated, covered in tar and feathers, "he was dragd in a Cart with thousands attending, some beating him wth clubs and Knocking him out of the Cart, then in again," to be whipped in another part of town. It went on for five hours. "The unhappy wretch," Hulton continued, "behaved with the greatest . . . fortitude all the while. Before he was taken, defended himself a long time against Numbers, and afterwds when under Torture they demanded of him to curse his Masters the K: Govr etc which they could not make him do, but he still cried, Curse all Traitors." He was then dragged to the gallows with a rope around his neck and threatened with death before being dumped in the street, still half-alive. "This," she concluded, "is lookd upon more to intimidate the Judges" (the Massachusetts superior court judges were being offered spots on Britain's civil list that would have provided them with salaries from London). This terror, the use of carefully coordinated violence to affect political change, helped bring the empire down and make the Revolution.[1]

What began as an effort to preserve the nation, honor the constitution, and revere the king by collectively resisting Parliament ended in terror and imperial dissolution. The turning point came sometime in 1773 and 1774. Before, mobs raised in response to imperial legislation targeted those enforcing specific parliamentary acts. They proclaimed their love of the king and the empire as they understood it. The central motifs and assumptions of royal authority remained

---

1. Anne Hulton to [?], Jan. 31, 1774, *Letters of a Loyalist Lady: Being the Letters of Anne Hulton, Sister of Henry Hulton, Commissioner of Customs at Boston, 1767–1776* (Cambridge, Mass., 1927), 70–71.

unchallenged, at least directly. In 1773 and 1774, though, that changed as faith in the king and the British constitution visibly eroded. Provincials openly denied royal authority as mobs controlled by revolutionary committees attacked the people's real and supposed enemies.

The suffering of these individuals suggests the human cost of what many now describe as a paradigm shift. The idea that societies' traumatic structural transformations occur by way of impersonal, metahistorical forces is a comfortable one, but not sustainable. That world's numerous tortured Malcolms paid the price of what more than one historian has called the easy transformation to republicanism. Privacy disappeared; the Revolution now intruded into every aspect of life.

The falling estimation of the king began at the time of the assaults on the tea ships, intensified with the introduction of more troops and the passing of the Quebec Act, and culminated when the royal government hired Hessian mercenaries. Crowds attacked individuals and groups who remained loyal to the king in deed, word, or thought. In the final spasm of this deluge, violence came to be directed against preachers, particularly though not solely Church of England ministers, who continued to pray for the king. These sacrilegious acts marked the final collapse of civil society as it had existed in the empire.

This breakdown was not some abstraction for those who lived through it. Rather, it was the critical moment of their lives, the beginning of a long change that redefined who they were.[2]

• • •

Jonathan Saywood's Journey

On December 31, 1775, Jonathan Saywood of York, Maine, turned to the diary that had become his major solace in a radically changing world. He recorded his thoughts about the previous twelve months, a year of remarkable transformations. "I am," he wrote, "now arrived to the close of the year through the forebearance of God it hath been a year of Extraordinary trials." His wife had died;

2. Jerrilyn Greene Marston, *King and Congress: The Transfer of Political Legitimacy, 1774–1776* (Princeton, N.J., 1987), is the best general discussion of this period. Marston, influenced by John Murrin, was more aware of the centrality of the king to the provincial political order. Philip Lawson, *The Imperial Challenge: Quebec and Britain in the Age of the American Revolution* (Montreal, 1989), gives a useful account of the effects of the Quebec Act on the already deteriorating situation in the empire. Murrin has noted that it is perhaps remarkable that there was no anti-Catholic pogrom in America in 1774 and that there was one in London during the Gordon riots. Lawson's book fully confirms the irony of this situation.

his merchant business had suffered crushing losses, including the disappearance of a new sloop and "one or more Cargoes in the West Indies."[3]

Yet all these things, as bitter as they were, paled beside the ferocious attacks on Saywood's authority and social standing. He explicitly declared, "This is small compared with the harassment I have and still in on account of my political sentiments." He had supported the royal government and parliamentary supremacy. He was under a kind of house arrest, "often threatened . . . afraid to go abroad . . . continually on my guard." The year closed with "all my offices, as Judge of the probate, Judge of Court of Common Pleas, Justice of Quoram, Justice of the Peace" taken from him. He kept a secret fund of "£200 lawful in Gold and paper Currency" in case he was driven from his house, a move made after he had "been Examined before committees and obliged to lay open my letters from Governor [Thomas] Hutchinson," the last civilian royal governor of Massachusetts. Still, he stubbornly clung to the view that the colonists must remain loyal to the empire, insisting that "all the above I have suffered from principle." The principle was love of country — in his case, the first British empire.[4]

What would we think at the world's end? What would we mourn? What would we hold fast to when all that we knew was thrown into question and then leveled? A significant portion of provincials faced these questions when the imperial crisis began to spin out of control and the sustaining values of their society suddenly became defined as wrong. They were the terror's victims, those who suffered intimidation, mobbing, carting, and tarring. Jonathan Saywood, judge, merchant, landholder, one of York's leading men, recorded his path on this lonely journey to social obliteration and in so doing became, like Thomas Hutchinson, William Franklin, and a thousand others, one of our guides to this moment of change in America and the Western world.

That Saywood lived on the empire's physical margins only makes his account more important to our understanding. Saywood's tragic passage through humiliation and terror began in 1773. York was a small port town, in the Maine district of Massachusetts, just over the border from New Hampshire. By the time Saywood began to write in earnest, the colony's royal government had already been fatally undermined. Saywood sadly recounted seeing "6 letters said to be wrote by Governor Hutchinson, and a Secretary of one of the ministers of state printed in a Pamphlett." These letters sentenced Hutchinson to political death, and "in consequence . . . our House of Representatives have drawn a Resolve of Redress to the King to Remove from this government for ever." As he explained

3. Jonathan Saywood diary, Dec. 31, 1775, York, MS, AAS.
4. Ibid.

himself, "for my own part I confess I have looked over them carefully and I see no foundation for such a Resolution of the Court [the Massachusetts Assembly]." Hutchinson, he continued a week later, "hath been most injuriously treated by the court and I think the province will repent of this conduct." But they never did, and Saywood's world, the royal America created between 1689 and 1774, continued to slide away from him.[5]

It was another piece in the unfolding crisis that destroyed Saywood's life and transformed his politics. Like many of those who became loyalists, Saywood was a parliamentary whig. He accepted the unitary sovereignty of the King-in-Parliament and the actual dominance of the lower house over England and the empire as a whole. It was this crisis that turned Saywood and thousands of others into royalists of a decidedly absolutist tone. Before 1774, they referenced authority in the empire to the King-in-Parliament; thereafter, they became the "king's friends."[6]

At a certain moment, the imperial crisis became a crisis of local authority, a struggle for control of legal and political processes fought out in courthouses and town meetings across the countryside. At York, that moment came on January 20 and 21, 1774. For two days, Saywood and others with patronage connections to the Boston imperial elite fought tooth and nail against a proposed proclamation saluting Boston for destroying the East India Company's tea shipment. After "a most severe opposition made by Mr. Samuel Clark and my self," they got the "resolves so far moderated as to thank them only for what they had [substantially] done." Saywood feared that "this opposition to Parliament will undo us," which, in the sense of unraveling the empire, it did. Saywood's valiant but doomed efforts to swing the town meeting's resolution proved to be his last moment in authority. He now began a forced march from the pinnacle of local society to house arrest.[7]

The overthrow of the old York elite by committees and crowds began in May 1774 when the community, like others in the Bay Colony, held their elections for General Court representatives. "Capt. Daniel Bragdon," Saywood gloomily recalled, "was chosen by a Great Majority to Represent us at the Great and General

5. Ibid., June 22, July 1, 1773.

6. Colin Nicolson, *The "Infamas Govener" Francis Bernard and the Origins of the American Revolution* (Boston, 2001), 38, remarks accurately that Massachusetts governor Francis Bernard, often accused of tyrannical designs, was in fact an advocate of limited monarchy and the settlement of the Glorious Revolution as understood in Parliament. Although Bernard was a royal official rather than a loyalist, his position was shared by Hutchinson, William Franklin, and others.

7. Saywood diary, Jan. 20, 21, 1774, MS, AAS.

Court." Saywood himself had once held the position, and in his own defense he wrote, "I think it was not the prudent part of the town that choose him notwithstanding he had a Majority."[8]

Worse yet, Saywood found himself and his friends not only out of power but socially marginalized. Indeed, he had been rhetorically expelled from the polity as "after meeting the former selectmen and all the justices and . . . [others considered loyal to the royal government] . . . [are] . . . called Tories." *Tory*—it signified disloyalty not only to a ruler or an elite but also to the political body as a whole, for it had historical connotations of both Jacobitism and royal prerogative rather than representative authority. All that was left was his position as a justice and assurances of friendship from once-great men like Thomas Hutchinson, who sent him a note "replete with friendships to me and the Province" shortly before going into permanent exile in England.[9]

Saywood's continuing such politically dangerous correspondence seems irrational, yet he could not do otherwise. To do so would not only mean giving in to the pressure of a populace he came to disdain but also severing connections to the imperial reality that gave his life meaning. His correspondence with the Hutchinsons and other leading men in the imperial bureaucracy had become the most important ties to him. The letters gave a human face to the empire, a real connection to a real person with a real personality. Saywood couldn't make sense of his world without these ties to officials, and he indeed became disoriented as these tentacles that linked him to the imperial order withered.

In the mounting debris of empire, new institutions dominated by other political actors intruded more and more into Saywood's life. Committees and congresses meeting outside the sanction of royal authority assumed power across northern New England in the winter of 1774 and 1775. As the power of these extralegal institutions increased, the danger to Saywood became evident. On November 25, 1774, a friend informed him that he was to be "mobbed this day." He responded by writing to another gentleman, begging him to restrain the populace. The effectiveness of such traditional means of social control was already collapsing, but Saywood put his trust in Benjamin Chadborne of the nearby town of Bowich, and that particular mobbing never happened.[10]

For Saywood, the empire ended on January 5, 1775, when he presided over a tumultuous sessions court meeting. The court was held "with Great difficulties and some danger to the justices. The jurors were sworn after a Great dispute and

8. Ibid., May 7, 1774.
9. Ibid., May 7, Aug. 3, 1774.
10. Ibid., Nov. 25, 1774.

the Judges threatened to be pulled from their seats," all while "John Sullivan Esq. who was one of Continental Congress kept [frightening?] the people by Haranguing them on the loss of their [liberty?]." Sullivan told the assembled group that the justices' "not Inpaneling the jurors was accquessing in the acts of parliament and giving up our charter." The disgusted Saywood denounced Sullivan for inciting "the people to a Civil war." He held one more court meeting, the probate, but his authority was gone.[11]

The war that Saywood feared soon came and engulfed them all. On April 20, Saywood heard rumors about a battle, and the next day he watched incredulously as a number of his townspeople rushed forward to assist in besieging the British army in Boston. Events then accelerated. Governor Wentworth fled from New Hampshire, the Battle of Bunker Hill created hundreds of casualties, the British navy ravaged the Maine coast, and committeemen repeatedly called on Saywood to explain himself politically. On July 17, 1776, the onetime judge found himself beyond his depth and "lost in wonder" as "I this day saw the Declaration of the Continental Congress in which this Continent of the 13 United Collonies are Declared free and independent States." The world had come to an end; Saywood now realized that "a desperate war in North America" lay ahead, one that would pit his countrymen against his king, the standard bearer of his political existence in this new world and new identity. He knew himself now to be an outcast.[12]

The same journey, to the empire's death, came to all provincial Americans. The nascent revolutionaries appropriated the rites that established emotional ties to the king or simply stopped them from being performed. In this way, the king began to die in the hearts of his subjects, and once released from their ties of love and obedience, they turned first on those who would remain loyal to the empire and then on the things that represented imperial authority with a profound fury. Jonathan Saywood's journey was not an isolated story but rather part of an ever-growing transformation that touched everyone in the provinces.

· · ·

A Terror of Bodies, a Terror of Words

To precisely date the loss of confidence in the monarchy and the British constitution is impossible. In some areas, it had occurred as early as 1770, whereas other populations clung to their loyalty through 1776 and beyond. But in 1773 and 1774, a change came over the majority of provincials, and their public behavior reflected it. The Tea Party, the Boston Port Bill, the Quebec Act, and the introduc-

11. Ibid., Jan. 5, 1775.
12. Ibid., July 17, 1776, Feb. 23, 1777.

tion of more troops eroded confidence in the king. Attacks against specific royal officials gave way to a generalized assault on the language and physical symbols that maintained the king's authority and the king's peace. This terror expanded to engulf those private individuals and groups whose hostile words seemed to threaten the cause of American liberty. They became the targets of campaigns of violent intimidation carried out by well-organized crowds. It ended with sacrilege, as crowds assailed anyone, even clergy, loyal to the king and the Hanoverian dynasty. By 1776, liberty's supposed guardian had become its foe, and as that realization spread, the empire came down. From traditional mobbing to sacrilege—this transformation signaled the end of the first British empire.

Between 1765 and 1773, colonists frequently used mobbings, rough-music ridings, and other forms of intimidation against those perceived hostile to "the country," as provincials commonly called the British Empire. These actions against officials and their clients impeded the implementation of specific legislation or state policies. Typical was the action launched in late October 1769 against supposed Boston informer George Geiger, who had alerted imperial officials to the activities of smugglers in the port. A crowd seized him, "stripped [him] naked and sprayed him all over with Tarr and then covered him with Feathers." He was carted "thro all the Main Streets of the Town huzzaing." The message to others was not lost: "This matter occassioned much terror and in some fearfull People."[13]

There was an inherent revolutionary potential in some of these early actions. The leading provincial families had long colonized what existed of an imperial bureaucracy. They had solidified their control by naming relatives and friends to posts, then passing their positions on to their children. Both elected and appointed officials engaged in this sort of nepotism. Now the members of these kin groups sometimes found themselves assailed, often at the instigation of rival families of similar status. The most famous of such rivalries occurred in the Boston area, as the Otis family attacked the Hutchinson-Oliver clan that dominated Massachusetts. Otis's verbal abuse of Lieutenant Governor Thomas Hutchinson was followed by mob actions that repeatedly humiliated Hutchinson's family and clients. Such assaults occurred everywhere, against the Ingersolls in Connecticut, the Wentworths in New Hampshire, the Delanceys and others in New York, the Ogdens and the Coxes in New Jersey, Benjamin Franklin's client John Hughes in Pennsylvania, and Henry Laurens and others in South Carolina. Vilification and physical harassment threatened such families' well-established dignity by iden-

---

13. John Rowe diary, Oct. 28, 1769, MS, MHS. Similar incidents occurred up and down the seaboard.

tifying them with the hated imperial ministry and showing their vulnerability to the popular will.[14]

Undermining the authority of these leading families weakened the sociopolitical bonds that allowed the empire to function. But deep into the imperial crisis, such mobbings remained restricted to those who were most directly involved in implementing the Stamp Act, the Townshend duties, and similar affronts to British liberties.

A sudden change in the character and targets of these attacks began in 1773 and accelerated in 1774 as anyone assumed disloyal to the whig movement was a target for brutal reeducation. The Boston Tea Party, the Coercive Acts that closed the port of Boston in response, the Quebec Act that normalized Catholicism in Quebec in 1774, and the hiring of Hessian mercenaries in 1775—these actions turned suspicion on George III. For many, the Quebec Act and the presence of the Hessians dissolved what remained of their eroding confidence in the monarch and completed their journey to rebellion. Only a tyrant would establish the Catholic religion and hire foreign mercenaries to attack his own people.

The Quebec Act provided a particularly lurid example of what awaited the American colonists under the new, militarized tyranny. The 1774 act essentially preserved the French political and cultural structures already present in Canada, including the Catholic Church. As there had been no assembly or English legal processes in New France, the home government made little allowance for the creation of such things; trial by jury for criminal action was introduced, but civil juries remained absent.[15]

From London, this looked like sensitivity to local custom in an ethnically compound empire. To provincials, it looked like the establishment of popish government in full bloom right on their doorsteps. Products of militantly Protestant churches and a Protestant political culture in part built on virulent anti-Catholicism, provincials bitterly resented this 1774 act that allowed the Catholic religion to continue among the king's French subjects in Canada and preserved absolutist-tainted political traditions. As one ardently royalist provincial said of ministerial policy toward Canada as early as 1766, "It is surprising that they

14. John M. Murrin, "The Legal Transformation: The Bench and Bar of Eighteenth-Century Massachusetts," in Stanley N. Katz and John M. Murrin, eds., *Colonial America: Essays in Politics and Social Development*, 3d ed. (New York, 1983), 555–571; Ellen Elizabeth Brennan, "James Otis: Recreant and Patriot," *New England Quarterly*, XII (1939), 691–725.

15. "Mr. President Rutledge to Mr. Chief Justice Drayton—the Charge to the Grand Jury, May 2d, 1776," in R. W. Gibbes, ed., *Documentary History of the American Revolution*, I, *1764–1776* (New York, 1855), 281.

should not reflect upon the glaring reproach to a protestant Kingdom of admitting a Popish Bishop to gratify a part of the subjects of one small province."[16] A South Carolinian bitterly declared that the king had established in Quebec "the Roman Catholic religion, and an arbitrary government; instead of the Protestant religion, and a free Government." The Georgia Assembly, in a heartfelt petition to "our Common Father" the king, denounced the settling of popery in "a Country in America . . . of greater importance and Extent than several Kingdoms in Europe." The Catholic religion was "not only tolerated (which we conceive would have been but an act of justice) but an indulgence has been granted little short of a full establishment to a religion which is equally injurious to the rights of Sovereign and of Mankind." French and arbitrary laws "have by authority taken place of the just and mild British Constitution and all this has been done with the professed and avowed design to overawe Your Majesty's antient Protestant and loyal subjects some of whom had no small share in the Merit of that Conquest." The act was seen as an attack on Protestantism as it had been practiced in the colonies since the seventeenth century.[17]

Radicals shouted the same sort of charges against the king and the ministry in the colonies to the north. With New York City in turmoil after the news of Lexington and Concord arrived, a crowd turned out to sign the association against the British ministry heard Isaac Low denounce George III as a Catholic who had established the Catholic Church in Canada and intended to impose it on the rest of the colonies. New Englanders similarly expressed their horror. The Quebec Act was, Samuel Sherwood preached, "the flood of the dragon that has poured forth" to bring on "the establishment of popery" in the empire. Several writers noted that it effectively extended Catholicism not only to the area around Quebec but throughout the entire transappalachian west, which was joined to

16. Henry Caner to the Society for the Propagation of the Gospel in Foreign Parts (hereafter cited as SPG), Oct. 20, 1766, Boston, SPG microfilm, reel 12.

17. "Mr. President Rutledge to Mr. Chief Justice Drayton," in Gibbes, ed., *Documentary History of the American Revolution*, I, 279; "Petition to the King from the Assembly of Georgia," [1775?], Pennsylvania Misc. Coll., American Revolution vol., APS. From the House of Assembly, Georgia, January 1775: "Also, the act passed in the same session [of Parliament], for establishing the Roman Catholic Religion in the Province of Quebec, abolishing the equitable system of English laws, and erecting a tyranny there, to the great danger from so total a dissimilarity of religion, law and government to the neighboring British Colonies, by the assistance of whose blood and treasure the said country was conquered from France" (Allen D. Candler, comp., *The Revolutionary Records of the State of Georgia*, I [Atlanta, 1908], 53).

Quebec by the act. A widespread wave of pope burnings and denunciations of popery followed and further radicalized the population.[18]

The introduction of more and more troops in the same period further indicted the king. The use of the British military had aroused colonial suspicions about the monarchy as far back as the late 1760s, as the royal prerogative extended over "peace and war." That power, as the Massachusetts Assembly readily acknowledged in 1769, was "in the king's hands, and . . . it is an indisputable part of royal prerogative necessary for the preservation of the commonwealth." When troops arrived in Boston, the resulting unrest culminated in the Boston Massacre of March 1770. General unease intensified as the British military presence grew. In 1775, rumors (eventually confirmed) began circulating that the king intended to hire German mercenaries to suppress provincial unrest. By 1776, "the Army of the King of Great Britain," as Rhode Islander Theodore Foster called it, was seen as the tool of arbitrary government across North America.[19]

The king's position in provincial politics eroded visibly in the year that followed the Quebec Act. By July 1775, Pennsylvania's James Allen announced himself as some kind of international militant and his king as the enemy. "It is," he wrote of the ongoing struggle, "a great and glorious cause, the eyes of Europe are upon us." If the American cause failed, "liberty no longer continues an inhabitant of this Globe, for England is running fast to slavery." The king "is as despotic as any prince in Europe, the only difference is the mode and a venal parliament are as bad as a standing army." In Alexandria, Virginia, traveling Englishman Nicholas Cresswell complained resentfully that provincials cursed the king in the streets. A New Yorker summed up these feelings: "If the King gives his sanction to acts of Parliament, subversive of that grand charter by which he holds his crown, and endeavours to carry them into execution by force of arms, the people have the right to repel force by force." The king was now seen as violating the British constitution and the rights of his subjects.[20]

18. Thomas Jones, *History of New York during the Revolutionary War and of the Leading Events in the Other Colonies at That Period* (New York, 1879), 42–43; Samuel Sherwood, *The Church's Flight into the Wilderness: An Address to the Times . . .* (New York, 1776), 33, in Nathan O. Hatch, "The Origins of Civil Millennialism in America: New England Clergymen, War with France, and the Revolution," in Katz and Murrin, eds., *Colonial America*, 517; *Thoughts on the Act for Making More Effectual Provision for the Government of the Province of Quebec* (London, 1774), 12–13; Peter Shaw, *American Patriots and the Rituals of Revolution* (Cambridge, Mass., 1981), 199.

19. *South-Carolina and American General Gazette*, July 17–20, 1769; Theodore Foster diaries, Jan. 1, 1776, Rhode Island Historical Society, Providence.

20. James Allen diary, July 26, 1775, HSP; Nan Netherton et al., *Fairfax County, Vir-*

The emergent revolutionary committees coordinated the response to these developments and, in so doing, launched the American terror, an attack on the monarchical fabric of provincial society. The central authority's weakness and the lack of a prison and police structure gave this terror a diffuse and limited character, but it was no less real for those who, like the tidesman Malcolm or Jonathan Saywood, lived through it.

Authorized by the First Continental Congress to enforce the nonimportation association enacted by that body, the revolutionary committees professed to represent the people as a whole. Their purpose was to expose "all such foes [those who supported the British ministry or broke the nonimportation agreements]" in order that these enemies "to the rights of British America may be publicly known and universally condemned as the enemies of American liberty," as the Philadelphia committee put it. While seeking to restrain the destructive excesses of early crowd actions, the committee members outlined the legitimate ways of proceeding. The committees assaulted liberty of conscience as they had previously understood it, targeting individuals, groups, and even churches in the frenzy of revolutionary release. Intimidation by committee-sanctioned mobs became the chief means by which the revolutionaries negated the love of the king.[21]

The committee members increasingly maintained that the social contract was dissolved, and the transformation in extralegal behavior that ended with the collapse of imperial authority reflected this changing perception. It began with refusal, and those refusals in total marked the end of provincial deference. The practices that maintained the empire's culture of authority lost their force. The unseen fabric of assumptions and emotional attachments to practices and visual signs of imperial authority decayed and then disintegrated. Men like Jonathan Saywood who had received respect their entire lives based on their birth, wealth, and institutional participation suddenly found their authority derided.[22]

ginia: A History (Fairfax, Va., 1978), 110; Joseph S. Tiedemann, Reluctant Revolutionaries: New York City and the Road to Independence, 1763–1776 (Ithaca, N.Y., 1997), 244.

21. William Duane, ed., Extracts from the Diary of Christopher Marshall, 1774–1781 (New York, 1969), 12. Marston, King and Congress, 128–129, gives a very useful account of the committees' process. For the committees in New York, see Edward Countryman, A People in Revolution: The American Revolution and Political Society in New York, 1760–1790 (Baltimore, 1981), 125, 128–129, 137–139, 143–148; for Philadelphia, see Richard Alan Ryerson, The Revolution Is Now Begun: The Radical Committees of Philadelphia, 1765–1776 (Philadelphia, 1978); Dirk Hoerder, Crowd Action in Revolutionary Massachusetts, 1765–1780 (New York, 1977).

22. Neil R. Stout, The Perfect Crisis: The Beginning of the Revolutionary War (New York, 1976), 152–156, gives a brief but cogent overview.

As royal authority began to collapse, the committees launched a terror that focused on those who would utter a word or phrase in favor of the king or British government. "The Passions of jealousy, hatred and revenge," as one writer recalled, "were freely indulged." Speaking out, and even alleged incorrect thinking, became crimes in the new era of republican revolution as the committees of safety and correspondence established their right to police political and even social behavior. Rumor became fact and prompted action. A vague remark for king and empire could be construed as a speech crime as the revolutionaries acted to create a unitary, and politically limited, revolutionary public. Those who resisted these efforts were attacked and forced to flee to safety.[23]

As the revolutionaries struggled to create one political truth, they meted out public humiliations to their enemies. At Freetown, Massachusetts, the local committee threatened Colonel Thomas Gilbert after his appointment to the post of high sheriff. When he proved unbending in his desire to take the post, one hundred men surrounded his house, though he escaped injury. Crowd leaders later denounced him as "an inveterate enemy to his country, to reason, to justice, and the common rights of mankind" for his pro-British activities, and a mob plundered his home. In 1774, a mob attacked Bay Colonist Timothy Ruggles when the London government named him a mandamus councillor for Massachusetts. Angry revolutionaries assaulted Ruggles's home at night, painted and defaced his horse, and mutilated his livestock. He fled under duress toward Boston on August 10, finally reached British lines, and went into permanent exile. The same sort of attacks occurred in the Carolinas. When the local committee of safety in North Carolina suspected (rightly) that Thomas Brown retained his loyalties to the empire, they singed his feet, tarred and feathered him, and cut off his hair.[24]

Others acknowledged their political sins in public to avoid attack. In New York, pro-Crown newspaper editor James Rivington printed a confession about his activities and promised to "publish nothing more Agt: the American Proceedings" as armed mobs roamed the streets outside his door seeking out the disloyal after Lexington and Concord. Oliver Delancey and other prominent New Yorkers were forced to deny any activities against the American cause as another, more focused wave of organized violence began in the city. At Hillsborough, North Carolina, James Cotton and two other men were given the option of signing the Association of the Provisional Congress or being immediately hanged. Perhaps the most famous person to receive such an education was Philadelphian Joseph

23. Jeremy Belknap, *The History of New-Hampshire* (New York, 1970), 361.

24. Wilbur H. Siebert, *Loyalist Troops of New England* ([Boston], 1931) 3–6, esp. 4–5; A. W. Savary, ed., *Colonel David Fanning's Narrative* (Toronto, 1908), 9.

Galloway, a member of the First Continental Congress and an ardent advocate of imperial reconciliation. For his efforts, he received a halter, a noose, and a note telling him how they would be used if his politics did not change. Up and down the coast, a diffused terror took hold as the empire drifted to ruin.[25]

Even a casual remark against the emergent regime could lead to intimidation or torture. One unlucky Philadelphian admitted that, having made frequent use of "rash and imprudent expressions, with respect to the conduct of my worthy fellow citizens, who are now engaged in a noble and patriotic struggle against the arbitrary measures of the British Ministry," he deserved the population's anger. "I now confess," he continued, "that I have acted extremely wrong in so doing, for which I am exceedingly sorry, and humbly ask pardon and forgiveness of the public; and I do solemnly promise . . . I will conduct myself in such a manner as to avoid giving any offence." He closed by announcing himself now a friend to American liberty. No mention was made of who helped him to make this change or what punishments were threatened if he did not.[26]

As the empire deteriorated, the persecution of speech crimes intensified. After a meeting with the new authorities, Philadelphian Mordecai Levy, who had apparently spoken disrespectfully of the First Continental Congress, took the opportunity to publicly declare "that my conduct proceeded from the most contracted notions of the British constitution, and of the right of human nature." He was "ashamed of my folly," had experienced a political rebirth, and "now believe all Assemblies to be legal and constitutional, which are formed by the united suffrages of a free people; and am convinced that no soldiers are so respectable, as those citizens who take up arms in defence of liberty." As far as his once-loved monarch, he now asserted that "Kings are no longer to be feared or obeyed, than while they execute just laws; and that a corrupted British Ministry, with a venal Parliament at their heels, are now attempting to reduce the American colonies to the lowest degrees of slavery." He was only too eager to demonstrate his reformation. To give satisfaction for it, he publicly prayed that anyone "who behaves as I have formerly done, may not meet with the lenity I have experienced" but rather suffer the full consequences.[27]

25. William Smith, Jr., *Historical Memoirs from 16 March 1763 to 9 July 1776*, ed. William H. W. Sabine, I (New York, 1956), 222. By far the best discussion of this period in New York is Countryman, *A People in Revolution*; see also Carole Watterson Troxler, *The Loyalist Experience in North Carolina* (Raleigh, N.C., 1976), 4; Sheila L. Skemp, *William Franklin: Son of a Patriot, Servant of a King* (New York, 1990), 178.

26. *Pennsylvania Packet; or, The General Advertiser*, July 17, 1775.

27. Ibid., July 24, 1775.

Philadelphian John Bergum also had a change of heart brought on by intimidation. After a visit by committeemen, he confessed to having "made use of sundry expressions derogatory to the liberty of this country." Assisted by local whigs, Bergum came to realize that he was "very much to blame for my behaviour," and he promised in the future that he would "conduct myself as a true friend to America, and assist those of the inhabitants thereof who are now struggling against the encroachments of arbitrary power by every means I am capable of." This assault on private language became a key tool in a very public revolution.[28]

Numerous others in the Philadelphia environs received the same revolutionary education. The city's committees used a decree to formalize the process and legitimate the attacks. Responding to reports that "there is an intention formed by some of the inhabitants . . . of publicly exposing and punishing . . . certain persons supposed to be unfriendly to the cause of liberty," the committee denounced unsanctioned actions. But they also declared that, "in the opinion of the Committee, no person has the right to the protection of a community or society he wishes to destroy: And that if any inhabitant, by speeches and writings, evidences a disposition to aid and assist our enemies," they would be considered targets for revolutionary prosecution.[29]

The policing of private words and thought, this terror against the tongue and mind, was hardly confined to the City of Brotherly Love. Up and down the seaboard, violent crowds silenced the voices for empire. Delaware's Joseph Cord "had always been a King's subject," was willing to fight with the king's troops to "the last drop of his blood," and damned "Committees and Congresses." A subsequent meeting with the local committee allowed him the opportunity to recant. Cord became only too eager to express his regret at the "imprudent speeches abovementioned" and promised that in the "future I will pay a strict regard to the resolves of the American Continental Congress." A mob dragged John Sherlock of Accomack County, Virginia, to the local liberty pole in order that he might sign a statement denouncing his actions after Sherlock mentioned in private conversation that he thought local rebels should be hanged. Fellow Virginian John Armstrong of Norfolk confessed his own political sins of speaking against the local committee in private after a wave of attacks against those who would not denounce the king and ministry in his area. Cornelius Stowell of Worcester, Massachusetts, received a nocturnal visit from a mob that believed him to be loyal to the imperial government. A man named Clarke who uttered a few words in

28. *Pennsylvania Gazette* (Philadelphia), Aug. 16, 1775.
29. Ibid., Sept. 27, 1775.

the king's defense was made to ride skimmington by a Hartford, Connecticut, crowd that severely injured him. Such political reeducation made the Revolution all too real for those who opposed it.[30]

Ultimately, the belief that someone was thinking inappropriate thoughts came to be sufficient grounds for attacks on his person or property. When the counties that would become Vermont sent John Peters to the First Continental Congress, he detoured to his boyhood home of Hebron, Connecticut, to visit relatives. Peters was known in the Vermont marches as a friend of New York's royal government. He made no public pronunciations on his trip, but local radicals viewed Peters and his relatives with suspicion, and when he visited, "I was mobbed with my uncles, the Reverend Mr. Samuel Peters, Mr. Jonathan and Mr. Bemslee Peters, by Governor Trumball's Liberty Boys, because we were accused of Loyalty." The mob had a point, though, because Peters refused to take the Congress's secrecy oath. On the way home, Peters suffered more attacks "at Wetherfield, Hartford, and Springfield" in Connecticut and Massachusetts. He was assaulted again in April 1775: "Another Mobb seized me and threatened to execute me as an Enemy to Congress." Peters was dragged before a local committee and "soon after another Mobb seiz'd me, and Insisted I should sign their Covenant." But Peters refused and eventually became a loyalist and an officer in the king's army. In October of the same year, Nicholas Cresswell, the unhappy English traveler stuck in Alexandria, Virginia, confided to his diary that "I am suspected of being what they call a Tory—and am threatened with Tar and Feathers."[31]

Others suffered stonings. At Plymouth, Massachusetts, crowds repeatedly hurled rocks at women from families deemed hostile to the cause of liberty. Rhode Islander William Vassal and his wife received the same punishment at Bristol when they returned to their homes after visiting Boston. Though a known sympathizer with royal authority, he was called an unoffending man by Peter Oliver and apparently played no active role in supporting imperial officials.[32]

The final act in this forced transformation of political language and public be-

30. *Pennsylvania Packet; or, The General Advertiser*, Jan. 29, 1776; Lorenzo Sabine, *Biographical Sketches of Loyalists of the American Revolution with an Historical Essay*, 2 vols. ([1864]; rpt. Port Washington, N.Y., 1966), II, 296–297; Adele Hast, *Loyalism in Revolutionary Virginia: The Norfolk Area and the Eastern Shore* (Ann Arbor, 1982), 26, 337; Stout, *The Perfect Crisis*, 164.

31. John Peters, "A Narrative of John Peters Lieutenant Colonel of the Queens Loyal Rangers in Canada, Drawn by Himself to a Friend in London," bound vol., in Peters, NYHS MSS, 2; Netherton et al., *Fairfax County, Virginia*, 110.

32. Douglass Adair and John A. Schutz, eds., *Peter Oliver's Origin and Progress of the American Rebellion: A Tory View* (Stanford, Calif., 1961), 154, 156.

havior came with attacks against churches and ministers, a development sparked by preachers who continued to pray for the royal family or preached nonresistance. Custom and royal decree called for prayers for the royal family each Sunday. The attacks against the ministers—many of them Anglican—occurred in almost every colony. The assaults rent the empire's spiritual and political structure of God and king. A public, unified by force in its hostility to the king and his troops, was created at the expense of liberty of conscience as understood by Protestant provincials in the eighteenth century.[33]

This sacrilege began in 1774. Anglican cleric Samuel Peters of Hebron, Connecticut, fled to Boston after he preached nonresistance to his parish in September 1774. In the ensuing turmoil, local Sons of Liberty cursed the offending imperial institutions "the King and Lord North, General Gage, the Bishops and their cursed Curates and the Church of England," the interrelated face of tyranny, tarred and feathered several Anglicans, and proceeded to destroy Peters's "Windows and rent my Cloathes, even my Gown, etc Crying out down with the Church, the Rags of Popery etc." The Lord, he wearily continued, "deliver us from Anarchy." Like seventeenth-century Puritans, this mob had linked the Church of England with the Catholic Church. The Anglican reverend Jeremiah Leaming, of Newport, Rhode Island, looked on helplessly as local whigs took his portrait, defaced it, and nailed it upside-down on a signpost, apparently because he would not stop praying for the royal family. The Newburyport, Massachusetts, revolutionary committee forced Anglican minister Edward Bass to read committee proclamations from the pulpit, culminating in a reading of the Declaration of Independence. He did as he was told to "preserve the church from destruction." In February 1775, a mob attacked and humiliated a clerk of the Church of England chapel in East Haddam, Connecticut. When his nephew complained and denounced the local committee, a mob vandalized his home, tarred and feathered him, then forced him to eat hog dung.[34]

Similar violence broke out across the South. In Georgia, the Anglican cleric

33. See *The Letters and Papers of Cadwallader Colden*, V, *1755–1760*, NYHS *Collections*, LIV (New York, 1923), 406–408, for an example of the decrees that established the form of these prayers; see also Allen D. Candler, comp., *The Colonial Records of the State of Georgia*, VIII, *Journal of the Proceedings of the Governor and Council*, Mar. 8, 1759–Dec. 31, 1762 (Atlanta, 1907), 486–488.

34. Henry Wilder Foote, *Annals of King's Chapel from the Puritan Age of New England to the Present Day*, II (Boston, 1896), 303; Sabine, *Biographical Sketches of Loyalists*, II, 7; Edward Bass, *A Brief Account of the Treatment Which Mr. Bass . . .* (London, 1786), 6; Adair and Schutz, eds., *Peter Oliver's Origins and Progress of the American Rebellion*, 157.

Haddon Smith, well known for his loyalist sympathies, was told to stop preaching after he ignored an order from Georgia's provincial congress to hold a day of fasting for the colonies. His coreligionist the Reverend John Rennie refused to stop saying prayers for the king; he and the other Anglican clerics ultimately fled the colony.[35]

Clerics who continued to preach loyalty in Anglican-dominated Virginia experienced intimidation and torture. A mob organized by the committee of safety in Nansemond silenced the Reverend John Agnew when he refused to stop preaching passive obedience. In a famous incident, local whigs threatened the Reverend Jonathan Boucher of Saint Mary's Parish in Caroline County with death if he continued to preach submission to the powers that be. At the next service, Boucher appeared in the pulpit armed with two pistols. Boucher, a friend of Washington, complained bitterly to him about the treatment: "You cannot say that I deserve to be run down, vilified, and injured in the manner you know has fallen to my lot." Yet the persecutions continued, even after Boucher removed to Maryland. There he was stoned, his church doors were shut against him, and public officials shunned him. Eventually, armed men seized his pulpit, and he was forced to take one of them hostage at gunpoint to escape.[36]

Boucher continued to preach, though, and intensified his efforts to spread modified divine-right theories and passive obedience. Rebellion was an affront to God. "Kings and princes," he insisted, "the evil as well as the good, reign by God's ordinance and subjects are bound to obey them. . . . It were a perilous thing to commit unto subjects to judge which prince is wise." In other writings, he stated that "a non-resisting spirit never made any man a bad subject."[37]

The Anglican liturgy, particularly prayers for the king, became an explosive issue in the supposedly more religiously tolerant midatlantic as fighting spread and the push toward independence accelerated. Pennsylvania Anglican the Reverend Samuel Tingley, reporting to the Society for the Propagation of the Gospel in Foreign Parts from New York in 1782 after seven years of broken communications, told them that he had "amidst threats, and ill treatment persevered" in doing his duty and keeping his churches open. After the Declaration, he could not

35. Harold E. Davis, *The Fledgling Province: Social and Cultural Life in Colonial Georgia, 1733–1776* (Chapel Hill, N.C., 1976), 230.

36. John S. Pancake, *1777: The Year of the Hangman* (University, Ala., 1977), 106; Marshall Wingfield, *A History of Caroline County Virginia* (Richmond, Va., 1924), 13–14, 23, esp. 14.

37. James E. Pate, "Jonathan Boucher, an American Loyalist," in *Maryland Historical Magazine*, XXV (1930), 318.

"with safety, either to myself, family, or hearers, be explicit in the prayers for the King (whom God preserve and crown with success)." Thrown back on his own devices and heaven's guidance, he "was directed to adopt the following words in prayer.... Instead therefore of saying ... O Lord save the King, I said, O Lord save those whom thou hast made it our especial duty to pray for. We were surrounded by armed men, who had thrown out severe threats." He further altered the litany, dropping direct mention of "thy servant George our most Gracious King and Governour" and replacing it with "those whom Thou has left in authority over us." He walked this rhetorical fine line for more than six years, ministering to the needs of Pennsylvania Anglicans in the interior while avoiding the tar, feathers, and arrest that the new republic commonly meted out to its internal enemies.[38]

His fellow Pennsylvania minister Thomas Barton was not so lucky. Forced to shut up his churches in the Lancaster area "to avoid the Fury of the Populace, who would not suffer the Liturgy [praying for the royal family] to be us'd," Barton found himself ejected from the countryside. "My Life and Property," he continued, "have been threaten'd upon mere suspicion of being unfriendly to, what is call'd, the American Cause." Of the other Church of England clergymen in his area, he reported that "some of them have been drag'd from their Horses ... Assaulted with stones and dirt — ducked in Water — obliged to flee for their Lives ... laid under Arrests, and imprison'd," most for their refusal to omit the offending prayers.[39]

New Jersey and New York also saw sacrilegious attacks. Committeemen forced Abraham Beach, the Anglican cleric at New Brunswick and Piscataway, New Jersey, to stop praying for the king, and he suspended services altogether in July 1776. The Reverend John Stuart, Anglican minister to the Mohawks in New York, continued to pray for the king in 1776 despite the political upheaval. In response, a crowd ransacked his home and church, then later placed a barrel of rum in his pulpit to mock him. Sacrilegious attacks against the older spiritual-political plausibility structure helped define the new nation at its birth.[40]

Anglicans bore the brunt of the iconoclasm, but all Protestant churches conducted prayers for the king in one fashion or another and were exposed to mob actions. Revolutionary committees coordinated attacks on Congregational, Baptist, and Presbyterian ministers who continued to pray for the royal family in 1774

38. Samuel Tingley to the SPG, Mar. 5, 1782, New York, SPG microfilm, records, letters–series B, 1701–1786, APS.

39. Thomas Barton to the SPG, Nov. 25, 1776, Lancaster, in Extracts from the Journals of the SPG, HSP.

40. Sabine, *Biographical Sketches of Loyalists*, I, 218, II, 339.

and 1775. In March 1775, for example, the Massachusetts Congregational minister Samuel Dana preached on the theme of nonresistance. His congregation turned on him, and some shot bullets into his home. In Amherst, Massachusetts, the Congregational minister Daniel Parsons was forced to say "God save the Commonwealth of Massachusetts" early in the war, but then added, "but I say, God Save the king." One of his listeners shouted back, "And I say, Sir, that you're a rogue." This self-authorized critic initiated years of harassment against Parsons by local townspeople.[41]

After independence, the new states outlawed prayers for the king and certain aspects of the Anglican liturgy. Maryland's revolutionary legislators suspended "every prayer and petition for the King's Majesty in the book of Common Prayer and administration of the sacraments" in late May 1776. "His Britannic Majesty, King George," officials explained, "still prosecutes a cruel and unjust war against the British Colonies in America." Heavily Anglican Virginia issued a similar proclamation, and Rhode Island criminalized prayers for the king. Under this banner of legality, sporadic attacks against pulpits deemed hostile to the American cause continued throughout the war and after.[42]

Even as provincials accepted the inevitability of a rupture, a kind of nostalgia for the royal past held on. William Henry Drayton, in his May 2, 1776, charge to a South Carolina grand jury that was eventually widely circulated, noted that their ancestors had gladly accepted George I's charter (presumably meaning the government's royalization in 1719), that "the virtues of the second George are still revered among us—he was the father of his people," and that, at the time of George III's ascension, "he possessed of the hearts of his subjects." Only tyrannical abuse "under color of law" by the king and Parliament had severed those affections.[43]

Others had already begun to suffer from the same longing for the past, for the empire, and for the hierarchical certainty of monarchy. Landon Carter stated in June that "I rather chose to be compelled to Independency, rather than to ever have it out of choice, because as a constitution of government none was so good as the British." Writing from Philadelphia in October 1775, John Adams heard "whispered about in Coffee Houses" in the City of Brotherly Love that America

41. Ibid., I, 357; Leonard L. Richards, *Shays's Rebellion* (Philadelphia, 2002), 94.

42. *Continental Journal, and Weekly Advertiser* (Boston), June 27, Aug. 2, 1776; *Pennsylvania Packet; or, The General Advertiser*, Aug. 5, 1776; Sabine, *Biographical Sketches of Loyalists*, II, 361.

43. "Mr. President Rutledge to Mr. Chief Justice Drayton," in Gibbes, ed., *Documentary History of the American Revolution*, I, 278.

needed "a North American Monarchy" that "may appoint a Governor for every province, as his Brittannic Majesty used to do." His sarcastic description of this new royal government expressed his own views, yet "there are [those] who wish it." In the end, independence engulfed all of them, and the nostalgia and affection for the past was suppressed to make way for love of a new set of values and symbols.[44]

The terror of abused bodies as well as words raises the stubborn question of the Revolution's realness, whether it was a struggle over who would rule in America as well as an anti-imperial revolt. The attacks against imperial bureaucrats and their clients that began in 1765 and culminated in the loyalist expulsions at the war's end amounted to simultaneously a social, political, and anticolonial revolution. How could it be otherwise in a world where social and political hierarchies were conceived as interlocked, spiritually empowered, and conceptually linked to one another?

The terror and the intimidation, the collapse of imperial structures, the expulsions and the subsequent seizures of property bespeak an upheaval very clearly. What has confused the issue is the existence of localized social hierarchies essentially apart from the imperial state that were either able to weather the attacks upon the imperial structures or encouraged those attacks out of sincere patriotism, ambition, or simple malice fueled by political rivalry. Whatever their motivation, those who rebelled ended up engaging in a symbolic regicide that ended in iconoclasm.

. . .

Denying the King

In late 1774, Josiah Quincy of Massachusetts found himself in a uniquely uncomfortable situation. Visiting London, he repeatedly rubbed elbows with the imperial elite. For many provincials, it would have been the thrill of a lifetime, a crowning social achievement. Quincy, though, had lived through ten years of debate over sovereignty. He had seen British troops occupy Boston and watched the waves of violence wash over his native New England. Throughout it all, he, like many others, had remained loyal to his king, but the cumulative effect of what had occurred between 1764 and 1774 became apparent during his London visit. At the opening of the House of Lords, he "saw the grand procession of the

44. Jack P. Greene, ed., *The Diary of Colonel Landon Carter of Sabine Hall, 1752–1778*, II (Charlottesville, Va., 1965), 1050; John Adams to James Warren, October 1775, in Worthington Chauncey Ford, ed., *Warren-Adams Letters: Being Chiefly a Correspondence among John Adams, Samuel Adams, and James Warren*, I, *1743–1777* (Boston, 1917), 167–168.

PLATE 14. *"Boston Affairs—the North End" (detail). By Pierre Eugène Du Simitière.*
In 1767, the North End cart carried a large British flag and celebrated the British dissident
John Wilkes, who was seen as an ally to the colonists in their struggle against arbitrary
taxation. The Library Company of Philadelphia

King—His reception of the New House of Commons in his robes and Diadem, surrounded with his Nobles and great officers." It should have been a highlight of the trip, but instead, "I was not awe-struck with the pomp. . . . The gigling and [————] of his Majesty impress. The trappings of a monarchy will set up a Commonwealth." And so they did, in a place far from the throne.[45]

Quincy was not alone in his growing contempt for royal ceremony and symbols. By 1774, the imperial rites that helped establish the loving bond between subject and ruler began to collapse. In those final moments of royal America, provincial crowds that had appropriated imperial rites early in the imperial crisis now began to refuse to mark the annual holidays or allow others to. It was the beginning of the monarch's death.

Between 1764 and 1774, protestors against arbitrary taxation repeatedly used imperial rites, most notably Pope's Day, to organize resistance to parliamentary

45. Josiah Quincy diary, Nov. 29, Dec. 1, 1774, MHS. Two days later, invited to a High Church service, he sourly recorded hearing the "Bishop of Litchfield and Coventry read prayers—as most bishops do, without grace in heart, or expression."

tyranny. At Savannah, Georgia, sailors paraded a mock stamp collector through the streets with a rope around his neck, shouting, "No stamps, no riot act, gentlemen, etc." At Boston, November 5, 1765, the North and South End Pope's Day confraternities joined forces to carry signs and effigies protesting the Act. In 1774, the Rev. Ezra Stiles reported from Newport, Rhode Island, that "three popes etc. paraded thro' the streets, and . . . they were consumed in a Bonfire—among others were Ld. North, Gov. Hutchinson, and Gen. Gage." On the same day in Charleston, South Carolina, "the effigies . . . included Lord North and Thomas Hutchinson," demonstrating that the holiday had become a vehicle of intercolonial unity and whig politicization. These protests endangered imperial control, but at their core, they continued to express the values of the first British empire, albeit in opposition to London's authority. But in 1774, the character of protest began to change and express a fundamental distrust of king and empire.[46]

Refusal began the push toward eradicating the monarch from provincial life. In September 1774, Boston jury foreman Ebenezer Hancock declined to be sworn in; the other jurymen joined him. "They one and all refused" to be sworn by judges who served at the king's pleasure rather than at good behavior. They based their refusal on their rights as Englishmen and the ancient constitution but established these through their genealogical and historical connection to the seventeenth-century Bay Colonists. "Our acting," they wrote, "in concert with a Court so constituted . . . would be so far betraying the . . . sacred rights of our native land, which were . . . purchased solely with the toil, the blood and trea-

46. Kenneth Coleman, *The American Revolution in Georgia, 1763–1789* (Athens, Ga., 1958), 19; Henry W. Cunningham, ed., "Diary of the Rev. Samuel Checkley, 1735," Colonial Society of Massachusetts, *Publications*, XII, *Transactions* (Cambridge, 1909), 290; *South-Carolina Gazette* (Charleston), Nov. 21, 1774; Charles Tilly, "Collective Action in England and America, 1765–1775," in Richard Maxwell Brown and Don E. Fehrenbacher, eds., *Tradition, Conflict, and Modernization: Perspectives on the American Revolution* (New York, 1977), 69; Gary B. Nash, *The Urban Crucible: The Northern Seaports and the Origins of the American Revolution* (Cambridge, Mass., 1979), 164–165; Paul A. Gilje, *The Road to Mobocracy: Popular Disorder in New York City, 1763–1834* (Chapel Hill, N.C., 1987), 17, 25–30; Dirk Hoerder, *People and Mobs: Crowd Action in Massachusetts during the American Revolution, 1765–1780* (Berlin, 1971); Simon Newman, *Parades and the Politics of the Street: Festive Culture in the Early American Republic* (Philadelphia, 1997), 21; Francis D. Cogliano, *No King, No Popery: Anti-Catholicism in Revolutionary New England* (Westport, Conn., 1995), 30. Alfred Young's unpublished paper, "The Crowd and the Coming of the American Revolution: From Ritual to Rebellion in Boston," presented at the Shelby Cullom Davis Center for Historical Studies, Princeton University, 1976, first articulated many of the views held by these scholars.

sure of our worthy and revered ancestors, and which we look upon ourselves under the most . . . inviolable obligations to maintain." Other New England towns joined in this refusal. In the same year, the town meeting at Ashburnham, Massachusetts, assembled for the first time without invoking the king's name. At Amherst, townsmen refused to acknowledge Justice of the Peace Josiah Chauncey's authority unless he burned his royal commission. In New Hampshire, "town committees had a discretionary, but undefined power" to annul the "former authority."[47]

In the South, appropriation and refusal fused. In Virginia, writers and some burgesses began calling the assembly a "Parliament." One, adopting the historically loaded alias "Hampden" (the leader of the resistance to Charles I's efforts to collect Ship Money in the mid-1630s), stated, "Names have an influence upon things. It is by hearing often of the *attributes* of Kings that we forget that they are men. . . . It is because our supreme legislative bodies in America have been called Assemblies . . . that they have been treated as inferior to the legislative body in Britain." In 1776, a man held for stealing his brother's ox refused Landon Carter's request to reply to testimony given against him "in behalf of the King." Such refusals signaled the growing dissolution of British power in the American provinces. And as one power dissolved, loyalty was reallocated to the congresses and committees that were seen as defenders of liberty and property.[48]

In New York, a gradual deterioration in respect for royal authority and motifs accelerated sharply with the news of Lexington and Concord. Crowds seized weapons, the mayor declared that "the Magistratic Authority was gone," and "little business was done" in the days after news of the battle arrived. Committee members proposed enlarging the "Powers of the Committee of Observation." The royal institutional framework remained in place, but the emotional attachments that maintained it now began to disappear.[49]

As this alienation took hold, provincials began to parody the empire's edicts. David Ramsay, writing two decades later in his famous *History of the American Revolution*, recalled how "burlesquing royal proclamations, by parodies and doggerel poetry, had great effects on the minds of the people." The forms that had conditioned behavior and created a provincial American mindset tuned to

47. *Pennsylvania Gazette*, Sept. 14, 1774; Ezra S. Stearns, *History of Ashburnham, Massachusetts* . . . (Ashburnham, Mass., 1887), 128; *The History of the Town of Amherst, Massachusetts* (Amherest, Mass., 1896), 82; Belknap, *History of New-Hampshire*, 361.

48. *Pennsylvania Packet; or the General Advertiser*, Oct. 25, 1773; Greene, ed., *Diary of Colonel Landon Carter*, II, 973.

49. Smith, *Historical Memoirs from 16 March 1763 to 9 July 1776*, ed. Sabine, I, 221–222.

the British monarchy were turned into weapons against the monarchical order as "royal proclamations and other productions . . . were, by the help of a warm imagination, arrayed in such dresses as rendered them truly ridiculous" to the broader populations. What had been routine became, in the context of a revolutionary society, politically humorous and thus explosively subversive.[50]

The imperial collapse accelerated with the forced withering of royal rites. The monarchical celebrations that did occur in 1774 and 1775 were in sharp contrast to those earlier in the crisis, when the rites remained popular even as the whig movement appropriated them in places. In 1774, Christopher Marshall of Philadelphia recorded that "scarcely, if any, notice was taken" of the King's Birthday in the City of Brotherly Love. "Not one of our bells suffered to ring, and but very few colors were shown by the shipping in the harbor; no, nor not one bonfire kindled." The king was dying, symbolically and politically.[51]

This same sort of corrosion became visible in South Carolina when Lord William Campbell, the unlucky new royal governor, arrived in June 1775. The committee of safety allowed the militia to receive him but prohibited cheering. Fewer than fifteen civilians appeared to escort him to his residence. In the same year, the King's Birthday celebration in New York City evidenced the collapse of royal prestige that had occurred in the port town. The warship *Asia* fired the traditional remembrance cannonade, and the crew "gave three cheers." A few inhabitants answered, but there were "no illuminations in the city" except in one home, whose owners apparently had more loyalty than sense. A crowd demanded they extinguish the lights, which they promptly did. A newspaper account continued, "Not that the people [meaning the mob] had the least disaffection to his Majesty's family, or person . . . they . . . are friends to monarchical government — But take every opportunity to shew their abhorrence of the public measures . . . the permission of which is [now] imputed to him." Even in a port dependent on imperial trade, the population refused to publicly own their allegiance to the British monarch in the manner that had been customary throughout their lives.[52]

As fighting raged in Massachusetts, the New York committees began to alter imperial rites to legitimate the emerging political order. On May 6, the New York gentry conducted what amounted to an "imperial" entrance procession for the

50. David Ramsay, *The History of the American Revolution* (Dublin, 1793), 321–322.

51. Duane, ed., *Extracts from the Diary of Christopher Marshall*, 6.

52. Edward McCrady, *The History of South Carolina in the Revolution*, I, *1775–1780* (New York, 1901), 6 ("The whole of his escort did not exceed fifteen persons" [7]); *New-York Journal*, June 8, 1775; I. N. Phelps Stokes, *The Iconography of Manhattan Island, 1498–1909*, IV (New York, 1922), 890.

New England delegates to the Continental Congress. "They were," reported the *New-York Mercury* on May 8, "met . . . by a great Number of the principal Gentlemen of the Place." They were escorted into "the City by near a Thousand Men under Arms; the Roads were lined with greater Numbers of People than were ever known on any Occasion before." In the subsequent weeks, the townspeople continued to use processions to assert their new political identity and nullify imperial authority. An officer on a British warship reported that "the spirit of . . . parading still continues to rage High in Town." It all came to a surreal termination on June 25, 1775, when both George Washington and New York's last imperial governor, William Tryon, entered the town.[53]

The townspeople became excited by the impending drama as the men approached the city. What magistrate William Smith called a "pompous attendance" greeted Washington, including "the Provincial Congress, those of the city committee, the parsons of the dissenting meeting-houses." "All the leaders . . . [of] . . . rebellion . . . waited upon the beach to receive them upon their landing . . . and conducted them up to [Leonard] Lispenard's" house. Accompanied by militia units, they "made a Procession to Hulls Tavern" and "in the Evening they patrolled the Battery followed by a gazing Multitude." In other words, the procession impressed the beholders with the new official's authority and dignity, just as the royal rites once had.[54]

Even while this evening parade proceeded toward the waterfront, a royal processional event developed around William Tryon, then arriving in the city. Upon landing, Tryon was attended "by the members of his Majesty's Council, the Judges of the Supreme Court, the Attorney General, the Speaker and Members of the General Assembly then in town, the Clergymen of the Church of England, the Mayor, Recorder and Aldermen of the City, the Governors of King's College, of the Hospital, the Members of the Chamber of Commerce, and Marine Society, with a numerous train of his Majesty's loyal and well affected subjects." What remained of the existing power structure now turned out to convince the population that British authority remained in effect. According to one account, "Much shouting [occurred] in the Procession—A Proof that the Populace esteem the Man, tho' they at this Instant hate his Commission." The procession concluded with Tryon safely at his temporary home.[55]

53. *New-York Mercury*, May 8, 1775; Stokes, *Iconography of Manhattan Island*, IV, 885, 890.

54. *William Smith's Diary*, IV, in Stokes, *Iconography of Manhattan Island*, IV, 894–896; Jones, *History of New York during the Revolutionary War*.

55. Ibid., esp. 895.

Contemporaries long remembered the bizarre day's strangest aspect. According to one observer, many of the same people who greeted Washington later "joined in the Governor's train, and with the loudest acclamations, attended him to his lodgings, where, with the utmost seeming sincerity, they shook him by the hand." The transition in authority had created a kind of duality in New Yorkers' minds and in minds throughout the colonies.[56]

It could not continue this way. The need for certainty and direction, for a resolution, built to a dramatic conclusion. Once released from their traditional restraints, the passions of empire could not be rechained, and the result was iconoclasm and symbolic regicide.

. . .

The Iconoclasm

At the end of empire, Americans engaged in an orgy of iconoclastic violence in the streets: attacking churches, ripping down tavern signs, beheading royal statues, searching for any imperial symbol to destroy. In towns and counties named for the House of Hanover and William of Orange, this final crisis saw the swelling love for the monarch become mistrust and then uncontrollable hatred expressed in the destruction of royal arms, portraits, emblems, and, most visibly, royal statues and effigies. In some areas, the populace went so far as to bury the monarch's effigy. A funeral fit for a king-turned-tyrant—this was how the first British empire came to termination. This emotional ending stands as testament to the powerful grip the monarchy had on provincial imagination and emotions for the seventy-five years before 1764.

The iconoclasm began in 1774, in isolated incidents that foretold the political nation's symbolic cleansing by an emergent citizenry whose unrequited monarchical love had turned to loathing. Middleboro, Massachusetts, militia officer Daniel Dunbar found himself surrounded by a mob that demanded he surrender his unit's flag. The offending pennant carried the insignia of the British Crown, and its tyranny over Middleboro could apparently no longer be tolerated. When Dunbar resisted, local whigs tore him from his home, tarred and feathered him, made the unwise militiaman ride the wooden horse, then held him until he collapsed. A flag also became the herald of change in Charleston, South Carolina. In September 1775, the first flag not bearing a royal insignia was hoisted over the capital, apparently causing a wave of anxiety for those still loyal to the king. The

56. Ibid, 894–895.

PLATE 15. *Tavern sign with bullet hole, Medford, Mass. At the outbreak of fighting, royal symbols began to be desecrated and attacked. This sign, one of a number in the Boston area with royal arms or symbols, was reputedly shot by troops returning from the fighting of April 19, 1775. Courtesy, Isaac Royall House*

blue field and the rising moon hoisted that autumn had no connection to the House of Hanover.[57]

With the Declaration's public readings in July 1776, the royal father truly came crashing down in a torrent of acts designed to delegitimate royal rule. Many of the mobs drew on the funeral motif that had been part of imperial protest since liberty's repeated burial during the Stamp Act Crisis. In Boston, a ceremony "absolving the United Colonies from their allegiance to the British Crown" drew a large crowd, which milled in the street until some decided to destroy all signs of the now-hated king. "On the same evening," it was reported, "the King's arms, and every sign with any resemblence of it, whether lion and crown, pestle and mortar and crown, heart and crown, etc together with every sign that belonged to a tory was taken down, and the latter made a general conflagration of in King street." How many more people privately closeted or destroyed personal belongings bearing the royal likeness can only be imagined.[58]

57. Thomas Weston, *History of the Town of Middleboro, Massachusetts* (Boston, 1906), 146; McCrady, *History of South Carolina in the Revolution*, I, 69.

58. See Shaw, *American Patriots and the Rituals of Revolution*, for a discussion of these

Baltimore's symbolic regicide was more graphic and involved mock execution. After the Declaration was read there, in a punishment typical for a condemned man, "the Effigy of our late King was carted through the town," then committed to the flames before several hundred spectators, "the just reward of a Tyrant," as one writer described it. At Huntington on Long Island, a crowd fashioned the liberty pole into a royal effigy that they then marched and finally blew up before the town's residents. Late in July, Providence, Rhode Island, crowds burned the king's emblems and arms after parading them through the town's streets.[59]

In the midatlantic, the situation developed more gradually. Hot whigs, mild whigs, tories of various stripes, and a considerable body of Quaker and Pietist neutrals whose religious views precluded participation in any violent conflicts jostled for control of Pennsylvania. James Allen recorded on May 15, 1776, that, when the congressional resolves ordering new governments to be formed were read in public in Philadelphia, "only one man Huzzead, in general it was ill received; we stared at each other." On July 1, however, attendees at a trial in Philadelphia demanded the "King's Arms in [the] Court Room should be taken down. The same . . . was done." Even with such a signal of general resolve, doubt and dissent remained. Charles Thomson, the congressional recorder, reported that "the boldness of the measure," meaning the Declaration, "frightened, and appalled, even its wellwishers." When it was read, "the citizens mostly kept aloof— the crowd that assembled at the state house was not great and those among them who joined in the acclamation were not of the highest order, or the most sober and reflecting." Yet according to Thomson, "Its decisive character soon firmly united its supporters," and in the wave of defiance that followed, the king's arms in the city courts were taken down, paraded, and publicly burned at nightfall in front of a large crowd. On the eighth, patriots removed the king's arms from another courtroom and the statehouse. In Dover, Delaware, a leader of the committee of safety hurled the king's portrait into the flames.[60]

---

motifs. On the Boston ceremony, see *Pennsylvania Packet; or, The General Advertiser*, Aug. 5, 1776.

59. Ibid., Aug. 5, 1776; David Waldstreicher, *In the Midst of Perpetual Fetes: The Making of American Nationalism, 1776–1820* (Chapel Hill, N.C., 1997), 30–31; *Providence Gazette*, July 27, 1776. This iconoclasm continued sporadically into the Revolutionary War itself. When the British evacuated Newport, Rhode Island, in 1779, whigs destroyed the altarpiece emblazoned with the royal crests at Trinity Anglican Church.

60. James Allen diary, May 15, 1776, HSP; Duane, ed., *Extracts from the Diary of Christopher Marshall*, 80, 83; Charles Thomson's opinion of the Declaration of Indepen-

New York's royalist culture came to an end with the legendary toppling of George III's equestrian statue on the city's bowling green on July 9. By then, the statue had become more than an irritant to those determined to break the imperial tie. The lead monarch signaled their intended enslavement by a tyrant made more powerful by the impending arrival of thirty thousand British and German troops in New York harbor. American troops brought up to defend the city had "long had an inclination" to remove the statue, and the Declaration's reading pushed them over the edge. On July 9, Continental troops, joined by a crowd of New Yorkers, attacked the four-thousand-pound likeness of George III dressed as Marcus Aurelius and knocked it from its pedestal. In an action that strongly suggests the intersection of English history, particularly that of the Civil Wars, with provincial political consciousness, the crowd decapitated it (eventually denosing it as well) in emulation of the regicide of Charles I. The Americans melted down the statue for 42,088 bullets, thus referencing both the outbreak of the English Civil Wars in 1642 and the Glorious Revolution of 1688. A daring British officer saved the rhinochallenged head, however, and it was subsequently shipped to London, where the exiled Massachusetts royal governor Thomas Hutchinson remarked, "It retains a striking likeness" to the king.[61]

In the days and weeks that followed this famous event, iconoclastic incidents multiplied in the once firmly Hanoverian city. Small crowds ripped the wrought-iron crowns from the fence surrounding the equestrian statue. At the courthouse, the king's coat of arms was "tore to Pieces and burnt in the Presence of the Spectators" after the Declaration was published. The violence spread, and religious violation again became part of the equation of parricide. Committeemen ordered Anglican clerics to take down the royal insignia in their churches. "It was proposed," recalled Ensign Caleb Clap, "that the Bodies of Church shoud, have the Honour of taking down their [royal] coat of Arms in their Respective Churches themselves, and if not the People are allowd to proceed in the like manner as this day herd" and destroy them by mob action. Even Trinity Church's Reverend Charles Inglis complied, realizing it might cost his life if he did not. "All the king's arms," reported Inglis, even "those on signs of taverns," were demolished in the

dence, Logan Family Papers, HSP; Thompson Westcott and J. Thomas Scharf, *A History of Philadelphia, 1609–1884* (Philadelphia, 1886), II, 458; Andrew Jackson O'Shaughnessy, "'If Others Will Not Be Active, I Must Drive: George III and the American Revolution,'" *Early American Studies*, II, no. 1 (Spring 2004), 19.

61. Stokes, *Iconography of Manhattan Island*, IV, 992, 993; O'Shaughnessy, "'If Others Will Not Be Active,'" *Early American Studies*, II, no. 1 (Spring 2004), 21.

PLATE 16. *Fragments of the statue of George III. In New York City, the reading of the Declaration of Independence led a mob of soldiers and civilians to attack the large lead statue of George III that stood on the city's bowling green. In one of the Revolution's most famous events, the statue was toppled, and most of it was sent to be melted into bullets. These are among its few remains. © Collection of the New-York Historical Society*

city. Revolutionaries eliminated scraps of paper, tokens, anything signaling royal authority.[62]

For those New Yorkers who remained silently bound to their king, salvation would soon come. The British army eventually occupied the city and seized the homes of all avowed whigs, painting "GR" — George REX — on their doors, thus reclaiming them for the king. But rescue must have seemed a world away as the

62. *New-York Mercury*, July 22, 1776; Susan Burgess Shenstone, *So Obstinately Loyal: James Moody, 1744–1809* (Montreal, 2000), 96; Stokes, *Iconography of Manhattan Island*, IV, 995; E. B. O'Callaghan, ed., *The Documentary History of the State of New-York*, 4 vols. (Albany, 1850), III, 642; Charles Inglis, "State of the Anglo-American Church in 1776," ibid., 1058, CD-ROM (Abilene, Tex., 1994).

mobs that cruised the city streets engaged in symbolic regicide in that summer of revolution.

The iconoclasm spread through the small colonies as well. In New Hampshire, "portraits of any branches of the royal family, were pulled down or defaced." Crowds attacked tavern signs with the king's arms or crowns on them. The landscape's political meaning was retold as streets and counties named for monarchs were remade anew. Even coins bearing the king's likeness were refused or devalued as the empire gave way. On August 10, the Declaration was publicly read in Savannah, Georgia, and the king's effigy was then buried before the courthouse.[63]

In a span of a few short years, really from 1773 to 1776, a unique provincial monarchical worldview collapsed, suddenly and violently. Two authorities, one based on popular acclaim and an outgrowth of the patriot king and the other based on institutional power and the King-in-Parliament, were at war in the general population in those years. The new symbols and personages of authority survived and grew. The emotional intensity of the actions that collectively amounted to symbolic regicide demonstrate the power the monarch had once held over provincial imagination as well as the imperial crisis's tortured character.

In the decades that followed, those freed by revolution fought to remake their world, to find meaning in republicanism and a republic, and to channel their emotional energy into its symbols, institutions, and forms. This chaotic effort continued for five decades, until Martin Van Buren and Andrew Jackson (along with a thousand local politicians and a thousand evangelical Protestant preachers) created a new system that again united man and God in a working political-spiritual order, albeit a very different one. Until that time in an unknowable future, Americans struggled with their unbound passions. They tried on new faiths, new institutions, new symbolic systems and political identities, until the death of an old generation and the birth and maturity of a new one allowed them to find political peace and accept a new order. That the march to the democratic millennium was so slow is hardly surprising. The past they were so keen to forget and to minimize, an act we have too eagerly joined in, retained some hold on them. For, although they could execute the tyrant's symbols in their towns and villages, ending the monarchy within each of them proved more difficult.

63. Belknap, *History of New-Hampshire*, 368; Elizabeth Forbes Morison and Elting E. Morison, *New Hampshire* (Nashville, Tenn., 1976), 76; Coleman, *American Revolution in Georgia*, 79.

EPILOGUE

OF PRINCES AND THE PEOPLE

.   .   .   .
.   .   .
.   .
.

So ended the first British empire, finally destroyed by an alarmed population that used terror and iconoclasm to sever the bonds of loyalty to king and country. The monarch's symbolic death came amid an emotional release that defined the period around the Declaration of Independence. The passions reigned, uncontrolled by custom or convention. The imperial contract, the annual cycle of political celebrations, a historical identity that stretched back to the Anglo-Saxons, and an emotional structure that focused on a benevolent, restrained, Protestant demigod-king, all disappeared in a matter of months. Nearly a century of habit and emotional conditioning now sought new channels of expression.

The focus of our national story in the decades that followed the outbreak of fighting has been on the practical side of this abstract struggle, the effort to create a working constitutional order and the development of a capitalist economy. It is a compelling, if disjointed, story of the rise of American nationalism and continental expansion in the fifty or so years after the last British transport left New York harbor in 1783. There seems to be little reason to discuss king, empire, or monarchical political culture in relation to this later period except perhaps to examine the fate of the loyalists and the creation of Canada.

The Revolution's success shaped this perception. But it also grows from faith in a nascent Americanization that long predated the Stamp Act Crisis and a corresponding misunderstanding of the degree to which imperial political culture shaped life in the provinces. When we start to think of the provincial past as a profoundly royalist one, then our understanding of what followed also changes. What, if anything, survived from the imperial past in the new America that emerged after 1783? The iconography of empire vanished without a trace, but did deeper patterns of thought and emotion and perception remain? Faith in exceptionalism has helped to keep these questions from being asked, for the very asking of them endangers that exceptionalist worldview.

If we accept that not all ties to that unwanted past were broken, myriad complexities emerge in the Early National Period that change our understanding of democracy and capitalism as historical destinations. It is more than the supplanting of George III by Washington as the nation's patriarchal figure in popular imagination and iconography—though that was a real phenomenon—and more than the strange career of Charles I's head in the 1790s, where it appeared repeatedly in American prints to warn (mostly Federalist) politicians of the price of tyranny. There was a continual referencing of English and British history, and popular songs, sung well into the 1790s, mourned the death of Wolfe on the Plains of Abraham outside Quebec in 1759. A host of newspaper and pamphlet writers continued to use the same history (histories) to instruct and explain the world to the new nation. But there was, I think, more to it than even these developments suggest.[1]

Much of the empire's epistemological and behavioral norms remained, shorn of their ritualistic expressions and iconography. Acceptance of this survival requires a peculiar but sustainable reading of what occurred between 1776 and the Jacksonian period. The struggle between the unicameralists and bicameralists in the 1770s and 1780s for control of institutional architecture pitted adherents to two very different republican worldviews against one another. The unicameralists, those who viewed the world anew, tabula rasa, and believed human nature plastic, moldable and remakeable, battled against historicists trying to remake the governing institutions they had known in the past in a new form. The bicameralists' triumph suggests the power of a historicist worldview over the revolutionaries' collective consciousness.

The later appearance of Jacksonian democracy has been interpreted as a decisive break with the past. Yet the patronage system that appeared resembled nothing if not an eighteenth-century patronage network, formalized and made available to the two emergent parties who espoused an egalitarian language in a world where the son of a president had already been elected to that same office and the distribution of wealth was more inequitable than it had ever been before 1776. Indeed, the history of the early republic might have been a very different one had the Virginia oligarchy that initially dominated the presidency been as virile in the home as they were in public life. Unlike Adams, who lived to see

1. Richard Brookhiser, *Gentleman Revolutionary: Governeur Morris, the Rake Who Wrote the Constitution* (New York, 2004), 98. Gordon Wood has written an unpublished paper that explores the question of Washington's relationship to the deposed monarch. I would like to thank him for his permission to cite this paper here. I would also like to note that crowds sang odes to Washington to the tune of "God Save the King" as he journeyed northward to take up the presidency at the beginning of his first term. It is a fitting metaphor for the process I am trying to explore here, the continuation of the form, linked to a changed content.

his son president, Washington, Jefferson, Madison, and Monroe all lacked direct male heirs, and we might wonder at the world that would have emerged if it had been otherwise.[2]

Similarly, the period's religious history can be reread as a restatement of the past. The Methodists' rise to predominance in the religious culture by the 1830s is indicative of those ties to the colonial period. A Church of England offshoot, the Methodist Church preserved Anglican hierarchical structure and married it to an evangelical language that empowered the uneducated to preach and the listeners to save themselves. And although much has been made of the democratic or American character of the Second Great Awakening's radical new sects, many, if not most, of these tended toward extreme forms of patriarchy in their organization. Even the turn toward experimentation in family and gender relations in the form of polygamy (most famously by the Mormons, but hardly restricted to them) can be understood as an effort to reconstitute the extended kinship network dominated by a patronage-distributing patriarch common to the eighteenth century in the highly mobile society of nineteenth-century America. Even the female-headed sects tended to conform to the past; Jemima Wilkinson, the leader of the Universalist Friends, a sect that initially appeared in Rhode Island at the opening of the war, often imagined herself a kind of monarch engaged in a battle against the Antichrist. It was an image that fused Christianity with a perception of order drawn from the colonial period.[3]

We could go on and on. The aping of the fashion of European aristocracy, the obsessions with European architectural forms, and the reporting of every movement of distant royalty and parliamentary debate began in that time and continue into our own. They speak to a craving for distinction in a society that professes to disdain it. Yet these behaviors also reveal a desperate need for ties to a past — sometimes it seems any past — in a society that has constantly reinvented itself since 1783.

The American democracy that emerged in the 1820s was a fusion of past and present and future, bolted together in a seemingly haphazard fashion. It is those now-unseen unions that have given it its fantastic appeal, its durability and its malleability, growing into not only a political ideology or a form of institutional architecture but a civic religion whose only reference is itself. American democracy's power to drown out other voices, even those from its own past, has become

2. I would like to thank Professor John Murrin for this observation.

3. Susan Juster, *Doomsayers: Anglo-American Prophecy in the Age of Revolution* (Philadelphia, Pa., 2002), 200–221.

as absolute in its own way as the power of any divine-right prince. It is thus we have come both to understand our past as a prologue to our present and to deny a historically recoverable America profoundly different than we have been willing to acknowledge. That lost past has its own soul and its own messages to us, worth hearing even now.

INDEX

Sewall's objections to, 50–52. *See also*
Holidays
Pontiac's Rebellion, 234
Pope Joan, 61
Pope's Day: in Boston, 1–2, 56–59, 61, 79, 195,
272; as imperial rite, 56–63; and neighborhood rivalries, 62; in Georgia, 75, 76;
as historical event, 85, 91–92; and slave
unrest on Antigua, 179–180; and revolutionary crisis, 272–273, 301–302; sketch of,
301
Popish Plot, 34
Population: increase of, as threat to imperial
order, 152–159
Portraits: of royalty, 128–137; of Princess
Sophia, 129; and royal ceremonies, 130;
mass production of, 131–133; miniatures,
133–134, 273; satire and inversion of, 134–
135; of Stuart kings, 199; destruction of,
306–311. *See also* Consumption
Pownall, Thomas, 109, 220–221; and imperial
reform, 230, 242, 244
Proclamation Line (1763), 235–236

Quakers, 51, 82, 93, 108, 151; invasions of,
during 1650s–1660s, 39; and Ranters,
100–102; and plans for imperial reform,
222–223
Quebec Act (1774), 226; and revolutionary
crisis, 282, 286, 288–290
Queen Anne's War (1702–1713), 52
Quitrents, 31–32, 218–219

Randolph, Edward, 33
Ranters, 100–102
Regicides, 17, 30; as symbols in American
Revolution, 271–273
Revolutionary committees, 291; and torture,
281–282; and terror, 286–300
Rhode Island, 26
Rioting, 9; and Dutch populations, 46; and
patriarchal organization, 167–168; and
popular royalism, 171–175
Rodney, Thomas, 81
Rough music, 183–184; historiography

of, 183n; and conflict over patriarchy,
183–190; in New Jersey, 183, 185–187; in
England, 184n; against violent men, 185;
in Pennsylvania, 185; in New York City,
186; against assertive women, 186
Rowe, John, 1, 77, 200
Rump Parliament, 93
Rush, Benjamin: and English Civil Wars,
103; and solar imagery, 203

Sacrilege: during revolutionary crisis, 296–
300
Saint Andrew's Day, 72; in Georgia, 75
Saint Bartholomew's Day massacre, 34, 85,
91, 113
Saint David's Day, 71, 72; in Georgia, 76
Saint George's Day, 71–73; in Georgia, 74–76
Saint Patrick's Day, 70–72
Salem village, 166
Saywood, Jonathan, 282–286
Scots: fear of, during imperial crisis, 263–264
Seven Years' War, 69, 111, 221n, 234, 235
Sewall, Samuel, 29, 32n, 73, 83, 102; versus
royal political culture, 34, 50–56
Shakespeare, William: and satire, 274–280
Shaw, Peter, 4n
Ship Money: and American Revolution, 268
Shrovetide, 29. *See also* Holidays
Slave election: and slave rebellion, 178–180
Slave rebellion: in New York, 91; as expres-
sion of royalism, 175–182
Slipware: political meaning of, 126–127
Smith, William, 91
Solar imagery: and Hanoverian dynasty,
203–209
South Carolina: and Yamassee War, 47; and
royalization, 66; and Queen Caroline's
birthday, 68; political turmoil in, 94–95;
and royal portraits, 130; and wax figures,
136; and slave royalism, 175; and imperial
collapse, 304, 306
Spanish Armada, 85, 99, 113
Speech crimes, 293–295
Spotswood, Alexander, 177
Stamp Act, 249, 267

Stephens, William, 73–76

Stoning: of suspected loyalists, 295

Stuart dynasty, 8, 15, 16, 29–30, 31, 113; and land policies, 31–32; and disorder, 37; portraits of, for sale in New York, 193; historical rehabilitation of, 193–202; and land grants, 218–219. *See also* Almanacs; Catholicism; Portraits; Stuart Pretender; *individual monarchs*

Stuart Pretender: in Pope's Day processions, 58–59; fear of, 112, 161, 262–263

Subcultures: defined and delineated, 22–29

Sydney, Algernon, 19

Tavern sign: vandalism of, *307*

Terror of 1775–1776, 288–300

Tooth decay: and imperial politics, 119

Tryon, William: and patronage, 158; and North Carolina Regulation, 174; entrance of, as imperial governor, 305–306

Van Dam, Rip, 159–165

Vaughn, Wilmot, 226

Virginia: First Families of, 40; and imperial contract, 47; Alexander Spotswood as governor of, 67; spread of royal rights in, 67; and Saint Andrew's Day, 72; and imperial diplomacy, 232; and imperial crisis, 255, 303

Wale, Edward, 102

War of Jenkins's Ear, 74, 76, 109

Washington, George: and hand kissing, 111–112; entrance of, into New York, 304–306; as symbol, 314

Wax figures: of royalty, 128, 136–137

Wentworth, John, 157, 286

West New Jersey, 28

Whitefield, George, 88, 167

William III and Mary II, 16, 22, 41, 42, 64, 85, 86, 107, 113; remembrance of, 54, 55, 72, 90, 163, 205. *See also* College of William and Mary

Wilson, James, 256–257

Wise, John: and imperial contract, 42–46; and English Civil Wars, 93; and love, 106

Yamassee, 114

Zenger Crisis, 203; and patriarchy, 159–165; and slave unrest in New Jersey, 178–179